THE JACOBITE CAMPAIGNS:
THE BRITISH STATE AT WAR

Warfare, Society and Culture

Series Editors: *Paul E. J. Hammer*
Louis Sicking
Frank Tallett
David J. B. Trim

Titles in this Series

1 Military Economics, Culture and Logistics in the Burma Campaign,
1942–1945
Graham Dunlop

2 Orde Wingate and the British Army, 1922–1944
Simon Anglim

Forthcoming Titles

Arming the Royal Navy, 1793–1815: The Office of Ordnance and the State
Gareth Cole

Militant Protestantism and British Identity, 1603–1642
Jason White

The 1641 Depositions and the Irish Rebellion
Eamon Darcy, Annaleigh Margey and Elaine Murphy (eds)

Citizen Soldiers and the British Empire, 1837–1902
Ian Beckett (ed.)

Military Manpower, Armies and Warfare in South Asia
Kaushik Roy

THE JACOBITE CAMPAIGNS:
THE BRITISH STATE AT WAR

BY

Jonathan D. Oates

Routledge
Taylor & Francis Group

LONDON AND NEW YORK

First published 2011 by Pickering & Chatto (Publishers) Limited

Published 2016 by Routledge
2 Park Square, Milton Park, Abingdon, Oxfordshire OX14 4RN
711 Third Avenue, New York, NY 10017, USA

First issued in paperback 2015

Routledge is an imprint of the Taylor & Francis Group, an informa business

BRITISH LIBRARY CATALOGUING IN PUBLICATION DATA

Oates, Jonathan (Jonathan D.)
The Jacobite campaigns : the British state at war. – (Warfare, society and culture)
1. Great Britain – History – George I, 1714–1727. 2. Great Britain – History – George II, 1727–1760. 3. Jacobite Rebellion, 1715 – Campaigns. 4. Jacobite Rebellion, 1719 – Campaigns. 5. Jacobite Rebellion, 1745–1746 – Campaigns. 6. Great Britain – History, Military – 18th century.
I. Title II. Series
941'.071-dc22

ISBN-13: 978-1-138-66441-8 (pbk)
ISBN-13: 978-1-8489-3093-3 (hbk)
Typeset by Pickering & Chatto (Publishers) Limited

CONTENTS

Acknowledgements   vi

Introduction   1
1 Raising the Men   7
2 The Army on Campaign   23
3 The Battle   67
4 The Siege   97
5 The Formation of the Militia and Posse   125
6 The Formation of the Loyalist Volunteer Forces   145
7 The Militia and Volunteer Forces in Action   161
Conclusion   195

Notes   199
Works Cited   235
Index   245

ACKNOWLEDGEMENTS

There are several people to whom I would like to offer my thanks to in the creation of this book. Firstly to Professor Speck, whose work I have known since my schooldays, who has read through the draft and offered invaluable comments. Jamie Boulton kindly gave the author transcripts of correspondence relating to Staffordshire in 1745. Professor Taylor assisted with access to material at Cambridge University Library. More anonymously, I would also like to thank all those archive and library staff, especially at the National Archives and the British Library, who have assisted with research inquiries and in the production of archives and books, without which this book could not have been produced. I also acknowledge the permission of Her Majesty Queen Elizabeth II to reproduce extracts from the Royal Archives (Cumberland Papers). WWM (Wentworth Woodworth) is reproduced with permission from the Milton (Peterborough) Estate CO and the Director of Culture, Sheffield City Council.

This book is dedicated to my father whose love of military history was passed onto me at an early age.

INTRODUCTION

Much has been written about the Jacobite campaigns of 1715 and 1745, especially the latter, for both the popular and academic markets. Bruce Lenman, one of the foremost historians of Jacobitism, wrote, 31 years ago, 'I have always respected the view that it is one of the misfortunes of Scottish history that far too much attention is focused on a limited number of personalities and episodes, such as Mary Queen of Scots and Jacobitism'.[1] This large output has certainly been variable in quality since the eighteenth century, but there has been much that has been very impressive in recent decades, by historians such as Speck, Reid, Szechi, Black, Duffy and McLynn.[2] All these concentrated on the campaign of 1745, with Duffy's volume being currently the standard work on the topic, and studies solely on the Fifteen have been limited to two volumes (and one forthcoming) in the past four decades.[3] Usually the Fifteen is relegated to a single chapter or two in a more general study of the Jacobite campaigns or as articles in specialist publications.[4]

The battles of the Forty-Five have been well covered, on the whole. There are seven books devoted to Culloden,[5] one to Falkirk[6] and another to Prestonpans,[7] as well as one concentrating on all three.[8] Those for 1715 and 1719 only appear in books on the campaigns as a whole, though a forthcoming study covers Preston.[9] Other aspects of the conflicts receive less attention. Siege warfare is given some coverage in one book, though it is limited to Scotland,[10] and studies of the Crown's other forces, the militia and volunteer forces are often dismissed or neglected, except in specialist publications.[11]

Moving slightly away from the Jacobite campaigns, there have also been a number of books about the British state in the eighteenth century.[12] These have tended to concentrate on the important financial sinews which are the very necessary adjunct of a great power. Recent studies of the eighteenth century British army, include those by Houlding, Guy, Hayter, Brumwell, Chandler and Reid[13] These support the view that the British Army was a capable force, one that was well officered, usually victorious and unlike the popular stereotype which portrays an army of amateur officers and downtrodden rank and file who went onto miserable failure against American Indians or patriotic rebels, as shown in films such as *The Last of the Mohicans* and *The Patriot*.

Coverage of the Jacobite campaigns has certainly been uneven, as Duffy has noted, 'far more has been written about the wanderings of the Prince after Culloden than about the perspectives of the London government and its forces during the whole episode of the '45'.[14] The situation is perhaps not so stark as all that. Oates, Speck and Reid each have much to say about the responses in 1745–6 of those loyal to the government, and the latter concentrates especially on the military factors, through a narrative approach.[15]

This book concentrates on a military analysis of the state's responses to the three Jacobite campaigns in the eighteenth century which took place on British soil (1715–16, 1719 and 1745–6), rather than as a narrative. It does not consider the strategy or tactics of the Jacobite army, except in passing, and where these had a direct effect on that of the British state. No apology is made for such an omission and anyone wanting more on the Jacobite perspective should consult the works of Duffy and Reid. Instead this study allows greater analysis of the difficulties facing the regulars and how successfully these were overcome. Comparison will be made with other conflicts of the seventeenth and eighteenth centuries prior to 1789.

Throughout this book I will refer to the state's professional forces as regulars, which was the term most commonly used by contemporaries who were not Jacobites. This will not please some purists, who will rightly state that there were regular French troops in Jacobite employ from November 1745 to April 1746 and Spanish in 1719. When these are referred to their nationality will be made explicit. Yet the term 'regular' seems least bad. To use the term 'English' would be incorrect, for many of the men were Scottish or Irish; to use the term beloved of Jacobite historians, namely 'Hanoverian', is also misleading as the Hanoverian forces proper were on the Continent in 1745–6. 'British' is also misleading for there were both Scots and English in the Jacobite army, too. However, as will be shown, there were other forces at the back of the state as well as the regulars.

Although the Jacobites ultimately failed, we should remember that this was not preordained, as Black notes, 'Military history is the most obvious field in which it is dangerous to adopt the perspective of hindsight ... War is not always won by the big battalions'.[16] It was not known in 1715 or 1745 that the Jacobite cause would fail ignominiously. Some scholars have argued that the Jacobites could have been victorious in 1745, especially if there had been a successful French landing and a Jacobite advance on London from Derby.[17] After all, there was to be a successful rebellion by irregular forces backed by the French and Spanish against the British Crown in 1775–81, albeit not in Britain. A victory for the Jacobites might well have been unlikely, but it was not impossible. To state that loyalist success was inevitable underplays both the Jacobite triumphs and the difficulties faced by those in support of the Hanoverian dynasty. As we shall see, the latter did have to overcome numerous problems, and not merely those caused by the Jacobites. Stating that their triumph was inevitable serves to undermine their achievement in overcoming the obstacles they faced.

Rebellion was an occasional fact of life for the early modern British state, with rebellions under the Tudors, the Great Rebellion of the 1640s, the Covenanters' rebellion of 1679, the two rebellions of 1685, the 1688 invasion, the rebellions of 1689–91, 1715, 1719 and 1745, and then the American War of 1775–81. Only three of these were successful in overturning the status quo, and of these, only one was so without major intervention from abroad. Generally speaking, the longer a conflict lasted, the greater possibility there was of success for the rebels, as they gained allies and their forces became increasingly well armed, professional and experienced.

However, most failed after a relatively short campaign of less than a year. After 1645 there was never a successful armed rebellion on the British mainland. This was partly because the state was so much stronger vis-à-vis its subjects, which was part of a long-term process initiated in the later fifteenth century and which rapidly accelerated after 1688. The executive grew in terms of both power and financial muscle, and this issue will now be briefly addressed.

The late seventeenth and early eighteenth century saw Britain become one of the major world powers, a significant change from being a regional power during most of the seventeenth century, except for the brief period of the Commonwealth. Historians have termed this new creation the 'fiscal-military state' and a successful foreign policy for much of the eighteenth century was its result.

State bureaucracy became increasingly professional and efficient in these years. Departments of state, such as Excise and Customs, grew in scope and manpower. It is estimated that from 1688 to 1714 the number of civilians employed by the central government trebled. Officials were increasingly given long tenures in office and a number of able senior officials fostered a new ethos of service to the state. These reforms led to higher taxation yields. In 1690, £0.9m was raised from the Excise; in 1720 this was £2.8m. Customs yielded £0.7m and £1.7m in the same years, and direct taxation rose from £1.4m to £1.6m. Overall, tax yields doubled to £6.1m in these three decades, and this was increasingly taken from indirect taxation. All these rises were in decades of stable prices.[18]

Furthermore, major financial reforms came about during the Nine Years War of 1688–97 and these enabled the state to borrow far more than ever before and so more troops could be employed (from 116,666 in 1689–97 to 167,476 in 1756–63). The formation of the Bank of England and the National Debt in the 1690s meant that the government could raise more money, and more cheaply, since the debt was guaranteed by Parliament. During the War of Spanish Succession of 1702–13, loans accounted for 40 per cent of government expenditure, which may have made the difference between victory and defeat. Debt rose from £16.7m in 1697 to £49.9m in 1719, but this could be managed as interest took an increasingly large percentage of peacetime public expenditure.[19]

Foreign policy was the major preoccupation of states in the eighteenth century. Therefore most expenditure was on the armed forces and on debt (which had mostly been incurred on war); for Britain in the war years of 1739–48, this was 65 per cent and 25 per cent respectively. This paid for a standing army far larger than achieved previously, and for an increasingly professional navy. Had Charles I possessed such resources as George II did a century later (or even those of Charles II), a successful rebellion would have been unlikely as it could have been strangled at the onset by professional soldiery (the insurgents of 1688 would have not dared rise without William III's forces arriving in Britain). The eighteenth century standing army, even in peacetime, was a fact of life, and was stronger than the limited numbers available to Charles II of 'guards and garrisons'.[20]

Finally, we should briefly turn to the military challenge posed by the Jacobites. Any rebellious movement has to create an army with which to overturn that of the status quo. There were four main sources of manpower for the Jacobites, both in Britain and abroad. Most apparent were the Scottish clansmen. It has been estimated that the number of fighting men in the Highlands was about 39,000. Yet the clans' political allegiances were divided, with many supporting the government, such as the Campbells, the Mackays and the Grants. Many were neutral or divided. Some were enthusiastic Jacobites, such as the Camerons, most of the MacDonalds and the Appin Stewarts. Support for rebellion was at best variable; the Act of Union of 1707 was deeply unpopular and acted as a recruiter for the best supported of all the Jacobite rebellions in 1715, but in 1745, despite initial success, overall support was lower. Clan chiefs were owed allegiance by their tenants and servants and so could draw men to fight with them. The Highland clansmen provided the backbone of the Jacobite armies as they were crack shock troops in melee, although less well suited to a firefight or siege, though sometimes proved successful in these, as at Preston in 1715. They were also more often than not armed with muskets rather than swords, and were organized and officered on regular lines, just as the American rebels in 1775–81 were.

Not all Jacobite Highlanders fought in clan units; the Atholl Brigade was made up of Highlanders in non-clan units. Another major source of manpower, though often overlooked, was from the Scottish Lowlands, including Roy Stuart's Edinburgh regiment in 1745. Then there were the English Jacobites, a force from which much was expected, but these hopes were never realized. Finally there was the expectation, during wartime, of regular troops from Britain's enemies. Professional regulars, such as the French in 1745–6, could rectify deficiencies otherwise evident from British support alone, especially in terms of cavalry and artillery. However in times of peace they would not be forthcoming and during war faced a perilous voyage at sea, as well as conflicting priorities.

The weaknesses of the Jacobite army were that they were not led by professional soldiers and their artillery and cavalry could not match those of their opponents. None of the senior Jacobite commanders, neither the Earl of Mar, Thomas Forster MP, Lord George Murray and the Duke of Perth, had any experience of military command at a senior level, and sometimes none at all. There were never many professional gunners; even in 1746, they were outclassed at Culloden, and there was no Jacobite artillery employed at Sheriffmuir, Prestonpans nor Falkirk. Their cavalry were outnumbered and unable to fight their opposite number. They could not match the regulars in exchanges of volley fire, nor did they have the financial and administrative support enjoyed by the regulars.

Yet, for all these deficiencies, in both 1715 and 1745 the Jacobites were able to form armies with which to confront the regular troops of the Crown. They were able to raise men, arm and supply them, and form them into units capable of battle. They were not the forces easily defeated in 1685 in Scotland and at Sedgemoor. In 1745 they were able to march into England and back, without falling apart. Their amateur generals were capable of great feats, especially Lord George Murray in 1745. It is a moot point whether victory was in their grasp, but they could not be dismissed as an idle threat that would inevitably be defeated by the forces of the modern state.

As John Home, who had opposed the Jacobites in 1745, wrote of that episode:

> The conclusion of this enterprise was such as most people at home and abroad expected; but the progress of the rebels was what nobody expected; for they defeated more than once the king's troops; they over-ran one of the united kingdoms, and marched so far into the other, that the capital trembled at their approach, and during the tide of fortune, which had its ebbs and flows, there were moments when nothing seemed impossible; and, to say the truth, it was not easy to forecast, or imagine anything more unlikely, than what had already happened.[21]

We shall now examine the land armed forces of the Crown, their strengths and weaknesses and how they dealt with the internal rebellions of the early eighteenth century. Chapter 1 examines how the regulars were raised and trained and surveys their peacetime roles. Chapter 2 studies their operations on campaign: strategy, numbers, supply, transport, marching, accommodation and generalship. In Chapter 3, the battles of the campaign are analysed, broken down between the effectiveness of the three arms of artillery, infantry and cavalry. It also looks at morale, the role of the general and the prelude and aftermath of the battle. Siege warfare is covered in Chapter 4. Apart from the construction and amendments to the fortresses, there will be an examination of their state at the onset of the danger, moving on to attempts to rectify any deficiencies and finally to how effective these fortifications were. The one siege carried out by the regulars will also be explored. The raising of the militia is examined in Chapter 5, and the formation of less regular loyalist armed bodies in Chapter 6. A consideration of the effectiveness of these civilian soldiers will then be made in Chapter 7, before an overall assessment on the Crown's domestic military performance will be made.

1 RAISING THE MEN

This chapter examines how Britain's regular army was raised in the eighteenth century, surveying both why and how officers and men came to be in its ranks. There will be details about their training, weapons and equipment, uniforms and conditions of service. Finally their peacetime employment will be explored.

The infantry of the British army was made up of regiments/battalions (the terms are interchangeable in this period). Each was comprised of thirteen companies, including a grenadier company, made up of the regiment's best men. The regiment was commanded by a colonel, then there would be a lieutenant colonel and a major. Each would also be the captain of one of the companies. The other companies would be led by a captain. Beneath the captain was a lieutenant and then an ensign (in a cavalry unit this most junior of officers was titled a cornet). Cavalry was divided into horse and dragoons (originally mounted infantry in the Civil Wars), but in practice there was little difference between the two arms. Regiments were formed into squadrons and troops. There were also the regiments of guards (both horse and foot), the monarch's household troops, often stationed in and about London, and the artillery corps, the most recently recognized branch of the army, formed officially as the Royal Regiment of Artillery in 1716.[1]

Officers and men were often viewed as belonging to two separate spheres, and while this was not always the reality, we shall deal with them separately, noting the fact that the seeming chasm was often crossed.

Army commissions up to the rank of lieutenant colonel could be purchased and usually were – from 1660 to 1871, about two-thirds in total. The ensigncy was least expensive and a colonelcy the most; with select regiments, such as the Guards, having higher tariffs. However, the market in commissions was regulated. The royal warrant of 1720 set a tariff (£200 for an ensigncy, £9,000 for a colonel of horse, but prices were often higher; in 1740 the price of an ensigncy was over double the amount set), and also stated that an officer could only sell to another with a rank immediately beneath his own. Finally, the Crown had the right to approve any purchase, and the Georges took their role in this process very seriously. Children were barred from being commissioned, as was not uncommon before 1711 and not wholly unknown thereafter, with Lord George Lomax becoming an ensign in 1751, aged thirteen, while James Wolfe (1727–59) was fourteen when he became a lieutenant in 1741. From the 1720s, it was stated that an ensign should be aged between sixteen and twenty-one, but in the case of older NCOs being promoted, the upper age limit was waived.[2]

The purchase system has often been criticized, but it did ensure that men with independent means dominated the officer corps, rather than mercenaries and professionals. The latter were thought to be politically dangerous, as the army had been under Cromwell. It also meant that officers were bound over for good behaviour, because to be cashiered for misconduct resulted in the loss of their commission and of their investment. Finally, on retirement, a man could sell his commission and so have a fund which he could then invest for a pension.[3] Henry Pelham, First Lord of the Treasury from 1743 to 1754, put it thus, 'our liberties can never be in danger so long as they are entrusted to men of family and fortune'.[4]

Once there was a vacancy among the regiment's officers, the officer below the rank of the vacancy would usually be offered first refusal, so if he had the funds available, he could buy it and then offer his now more junior commission to the next man on the ladder. Officers of the same rank were marked out in seniority by the length of time they had held their present commissions. So if there was a vacancy of major, the longest serving captain would be offered it first.[5]

Not all commissions had to be paid for. When an officer died or was cashiered, the officer immediately beneath this rank would be offered the vacancy for free. In wartime, when deaths in battle or on campaign were frequent, promotion was easier and more rapid. Sometimes deserving NCOs were put into these vacancies, and this was not uncommon in wartime. Feats of bravery sometimes led to promotion from the ranks. An example from our period is the case of Sergeant Terrence Molloy. In 1745, he was in command of Ruthven Barracks, which was threatened by a substantial Jacobite force. Refusing to surrender, the barracks held out and Molloy was made a lieutenant on Sir John Cope's recommendation.[6] In the period 1739–93, 598 NCOs were raised from the ranks to become officers, which was about 3 per cent of the total. Joshua Guest (1660–1747) enlisted in the ranks in 1685 and ended his career as a general.[7]

The other method was to enlist as a volunteer, as the fictional Tom Jones seems to have done. In this instance a young man accompanied the army at his own expense, but carried a musket and marched and fought in the ranks. He would, however, mess with the officers and would hope to pick up a free commission. In the 1800s, 4.5 per cent of commissions were taken by such gentlemen rankers, and perhaps the same figure is true of the eighteenth century.[8]

As important as money and seniority were for an officer wishing to ascend the career ladder, there was also the matter of 'interest', as there was in all aspects of life. In fact in order to be accepted as an officer in a regiment, a young man needed someone who could speak on his behalf to the regiment's colonel. Samuel Bagshawe obtained his first commission because his family were clients of the powerful Cavendish family. Often, though, it was a case of the young man's relations seeking help through a chain of individuals until locating one who could deal directly with the colonel in question. Or a commission broker could be negotiated with, though this was illegal.[9]

James Boswell sought help, though unsuccessfully, in obtaining a commission in the Guards in 1763. Lady Northumberland told him 'I shall certainly, Sir, recommend you to Lord Granby in the strongest manner; and as the Blues are his own regiment, I should think that they will not interfere but allow him to do what he pleases'.[10] John Kynaston, in 1704, was eager to become an officer and went to London, where new regiments were being raised. He recalled, 'I apply'd myself to my friends in order to get a commission. I was recommended by two members of Parliament to James Craggs [a senior politician and close to Marlborough] and he was pleased to use his interest to the Duke of Marlborough and got me colours in the regiment of Foot'.[11] The fictional elderly lieutenant in *Tom Jones* had his career hindered by 'having no Friends amongst the Men in Power' and also 'had the Misfortune to incur the Displeasure of his Colonel'.[12] Viscount Irwin (1691–1761), Lord Lieutenant of the East Riding of Yorkshire, wrote to the Duke of Newcastle (1693–1768), Secretary of State, in 1746 asking for him to assist one Storr with a possible military career, 'speak a good word for him to the Duke of Bedford', and asked him to assist his brother likewise. Irwin thought that he deserved a quid pro quo 'considering the great expense and trouble I have been for the support of the cause'. Irwin had raised volunteer forces against the Jacobites in 1745 as we shall later note.[13]

Although this gave the colonel great powers over the prospects for promotion of those under him, they were not absolute, except when he was seeking officers for a wholly new regiment, which occurred at the outbreak of wars and rebellions. In other times, he had to submit all recommendations to the monarch. Commissions, except those of ensigns, could be sold only to serving officers. Colonels were expected to adhere to the principle of seniority as outlined above, so the junior captain could not be given the rank of major ahead of the more senior captains, unless none of the latter could afford the price. Appointing relations or sons of friends to vacant ensigncies was another matter, however, and could be done at will. Monarchs alone could promote above the rank of colonel.[14]

The king's power over military patronage was not to be sniffed at, as Lord Hervey (1693–1743), a courtier, complained in 1736:

> There was a great number of commissions in the army vacant, which the King [George II], from a natural dilatoriness of his temper, joined to a particular backwardness in giving, had postponed filling up all this winter, notwithstanding the frequent and pressing instances made to him by Sir Robert Walpole [the leading minister], who never received any other answers on these occasions form his Majesty, than 'My God! It is time enough. I will fill them up at the end of the session.'

Hervey explained that the delays were because it was a case of the King 'loving nobody well enough to have any pleasure in preferring them'.[15]

There was no official training for officers (except in the artillery), nor any educational standards to be required until 1801 when the Royal Military College at Sandhurst was established, and that was designed for the staff. Training was deemed to be 'on the job'. But for the gunners, it was different. Technical knowledge was clearly crucial in this the most recently formed arm of the regulars. The Royal Military Academy at Woolwich was founded in 1741 to train officers of the artillery and engineers. Promotion in this instance was by seniority alone, commissions could not be purchased.[16] Having said that, there were a number of drill books and instruction books for soldiers, the most famous being Humphrey Bland's *Treatise on Discipline*. This was a manual explaining tactical drill, musketry fire and other essential aspects of the soldiers' trade.

Although most officers were men of means, they were from a variety of backgrounds. Unlike Continental armies of the period, the British army was not dominated by the scions of the aristocracy, partly because there were so few of them in Britain. In 1780 it has been estimated that 24 per cent of army officers were noblemen, and they were concentrated in the guards regiments. Other officers were from the gentry (16 per cent in 1780) or, increasingly, from the sons of clergymen and the professional classes who had some spare cash. Many, too, were the sons of soldiers, such as James Wolfe, whose father and grandfather served in the army. This tradition of 'army families' developed in the years 1715–30.[17] The officers in *Tom Jones* include 'one of whom had been bred under an Attorney, and the other was Son to the Wife of a Nobleman's Butler'.[18] Officers were from all parts of Britain. In the American War of Independence, 42 per cent of British army officers were English, 27 per cent Scottish and 31 per cent Irish, though of the rank and file, 60 per cent were English, 24 per cent Scottish and 16 per cent Irish.[19] There were also American and Huguenot officers among them, too.

We shall now turn to the rank and file of the army. Men joined the ranks as volunteers. There was no conscription in Britain until 1916. However, individual social and economic circumstances often bore heavily on a man's decision to take the King's shilling.

It has traditionally been often asserted that the army was filled with the desperate of Georgian society. It is certainly true that it was not uncommon for some men lounging in gaol to enlist. For example, in April 1704 it was noted that John Watson, imprisoned for debt in the Gatehouse prison in London, owing money to John Buckmaster, was to be discharged because he 'has enlisted in the regiment of Colonel Thomas Handaside'.[20] In 1696, Robert Dale was convicted, fined and ordered to stand in a pillory in Bloomsbury, then was to be gaoled for a month 'unless he shall, in the meantime, voluntarily list himself to serve His Majesty as a soldier'.[21] Another was John Quin, convicted before a Surrey Justice of the Peace (JP) in September 1777 of theft, of whom it was said, 'He is willing to serve as soldier. I have therefore committed him to the House of Correction in Guildford to await your [Lord Barrington, Secretary of State] orders'. In the following year, a Berkshire magistrate wrote that there were men awaiting the death sentence for theft but that they were 'Exceedingly proper Fellows either for the Land or the Sea service'.[22] Other recruits were men imprisoned in houses of correction for debt or for theft or awaiting trial who also enlisted. One Richard Wells, deemed a 'dangerous person' enlisted in 1705.[23] Bounties were offered to promote enlistment during war; in 1703, £2 per man was offered and in 1708 it was £5.[24]

Foreign prisoners could also be enlisted in the army, too.[25] Prisoners taken after the Jacobite rebellions also sometimes volunteered for military service, while facing transportation. Sir William Pepperell, governor of Massachusetts, finding his regiments lacking men, wrote to Newcastle on 24 June 1746: 'Could it not be thought expedient that 200 of the rebel prisoners, who may have been unwarily seduced, should be sent over for Mr Shirley's and my regiment, it might be a means of making good subjects of them, which I mention to Your Grace with all submission.'[26] In the following year, Henry Fox, Secretary at War, stated 'His majesty having had pleased to consent to the enlisting as many of The Rebels now at Carlisle as are fit for the service of the Independent Companys'.[27] It seems that about ninety-two Jacobite prisoners enlisted thus.[28]

One such was James Miller, once a private in the Jacobite Manchester Regiment. He and his fellows were incarcerated in Carlisle castle under grim conditions, and all pleaded guilty. Sentenced to death, they were reprieved. They remained there till the Duke of Newcastle sent over one of the King's Messengers and lieutenant general Corden to enlist as many as were fit and able: 'acquainting us that we were obliged to go to the East Indies upon a secret expedition against the French'. They marched to Portsmouth where major Mompesson 'then asked every man if he was willing to go. Those who answered in the negative being about 25 were closely confined'.[29] Under such conditions, prisoners such as Miller enlisted.

As well as recruiting Jacobite prisoners, the government also sought to recruit volunteers from the independent volunteer companies raised against the Jacobites in 1745. When the latter stood down in early 1746, efforts were made to enlist them into the regulars. Irwin stated that in the case of his East Riding companies, 'very few of them would enlist with ye marching regiments, tho' we offered ym a bounty of four guineas a man & took all ye pains we possibly could to make ym'. Only about seventeen out of 350 did so.[30]

Enlistment in the army was theoretically for life, though usually lasted until middle age. Temporary enlistment was also possible in times of emergency. Associations were formed in the autumn of 1745 to help to support the government's military strength by assisting in recruitment to the regulars. This occurred in counties which included Kent, Cambridgeshire, Surrey and Hertfordshire. They raised money from loyalists and used it to pay bounties to men enlisting into the army for the duration of the emergency. In Hertfordshire, recruits had to be a minimum of 5 feet 5 inches high and aged between seventeen and forty-five. They would serve for six months or until the emergency was over, would not serve overseas and would receive an enlistment bounty of four guineas each.[31]

Likewise, there were proclamations issuing forth similar methods. On 19 October and 16 December 1745 the following was issued:

> His Majesty's service requiring at this time a speedy augmentation of his forces it is this day ordered in council that Sir Dudley Ryder, His Majesty's Attorney General do forthwith prepare the draught of a proclamation for encouraging able bodied men to inlist into His Majesty's Land service and for that purpose to declare His Majesty's Royal pleasure that all such as shall inlist in His Majesty's service on or before the 25th of December next shall upon their request be discharged accordingly at the end of six months from the time of their inlisting in case the rebellion be extinguished within that time and if not then as soon as the rebellion shall be extinguished.

A bounty of £6 was paid for enlistment into the foot guards, and £4 for two years' enlistment in any other regiment.[32]

The government would also increase the number of regiments in the army during wartime. Noblemen and others would be given the King's commission to raise new regiments. At Stafford, this was because 'it was found impractical to make the militia useful as the law now stands'. Lord Gower (1694–1754) was given a commission, and of him it was said:

> that His Majesty had given him a commission to raise a regiment and had signed blank warrants to appoint officers, the officers and soldiers to be paid by the king as all others are paid, and the soldiers to be discharged as soon as the troubles were over and not to march out of great Britain, that they were rank as other officers, but not to have half pay after discharged, that they were to be cloathed by those of reckoning, though the arms were to be sent them by the king and as soon as the lord lieutenant should certify that half of the men was raised that the whole regiment was to receive whole pay.[33]

Men were also encouraged to enlist because a special fund was being raised to recompense their families. Gower wrote that 'I most highly approve the proposal for subsisting our soldiers wives during the absence of their husbands, and shall with great pleasure subscribe most bountifully to it'.[34]

These new regiments proved controversial and Horace Walpole (1717–97) wrote 'these most disinterested colonels have named none but their own relations and dependents for the officers', and so a political storm ensued. George II was furious. In reality, only a few were raised; one of the most effective being Kingston's light horse, which proved its worth at Culloden.[35]

One which was formed was Lord Gower's. On 4 October 1745, William Congreve was given a commission as lieutenant colonel to raise a battalion of infantry, with the royal instructions reading thus:

> appoint you to be lord lieutenant colonel of the regiment of foot; to be forthwith raised, for our service, to be commanded by our right trusty and wellbeloved councillor John, Lord Gower and likewise to be a captain of a company in the said regiment. You are therefore to take our said regiment as lieutenant colonel, and the said company as captain into your care and charge...you are to observe and follow such orders and directions from time to time as you shall receive from us, your colonel or any other superior officer, according to the rules and disciplines of war, in the pursuance of the trust we hereby repose in you.[36]

Civil magistrates were encouraged by the government to assist in the recruitment of soldiers. On 5 December 1706, a letter was sent by the lords of the council to the Duke of Bedford, 'recommending the vigorous execution of the Act for the better recruiting the army and marines' and he was asked to send their lordships a return of 'his proceedings in the matter, with the numbers and names of the recruits raised'.[37]

Certainly the civil power was to be rewarded for their efficiency in providing men for the army. In 1708, it was noted, 'The sum of 20s is to be paid to the parish officers for each person brought before the magistrates to be enlisted'.[38] In 1705, the justices of the peace were ordered 'to assist in the work of raising the recruits required for carrying on the war'.[39] There was certainly every incentive for men to enlist; in 1708, a bounty of £5 was to be offered, and each man was given the option of short service, being discharged after three years if he wished.[40]

Sometimes illegal methods were employed to enlist men. In 1695, the Middlesex sessions recorded that the provost marshal was ordered to release Richard Lumbley, forced by Captain Edward Taylor to take twelve pence for enlisting. The money was returned and 'The Court ... was of opinion that Lumbley having been oppressed, and not being qualified as a seaman, ought not to be impressed as a soldier'.[41] William Hall, junior, was apparently made drunk in 1704 by Lieutenant Sterry while the latter was recruiting in a tavern, then broke into Hall's house and seized him 'in a riotous manner ... under pretence of a warrant'.[42] In 1709 it was complained that seamen were enlisted in the army on the pretence that recruiters were taking men for the Navy.[43]

However, it is worth noting that on all the aforesaid occasions, such methods were only employed during wartime. The army could be quite selective in who it chose. In 1760, Colonel Bagshawe told his recruiting officers that they were only to enlist Protestants, the able bodied, men aged between sixteen and thirty-five, and none who could be described as 'strolers, vagabonds, tinkers, chimney sweeps, colliers and saylors'. Care was to be taken not to recruit men who had already deserted. Men should be at least 5 feet 5 inches high if aged sixteen to twenty and 5 feet 6 if between twenty and thirty-five.[44] Those who enlisted in Hertfordshire in 1745, were mostly labourers, twenty-six out of the sixty-eight, the remainder being of various other occupations, mostly craftsmen, and mostly aged between seventeen and thirty. One man later said, 'Most of us left good trades to go and fight'. Even though this was an emergency, some were turned down; one because he was an Irishman, another on account of his age.[45]

However, the most common method of recruiting was by the means of a 'beating order' given by the War Office. Each recruiting party would be given a different district in which to beat up in order to avoid competition with other parties. In 1708, the two regiments of foot guards were allocated Middlesex, Westminster and the City.[46] Others did so, too: William Todd's regiment sent out parties into numerous parts of England and Scotland in 1755.[47] Regiments were not based on counties as in the nineteenth century and beyond, though the Royal Fusiliers were linked with London and the Royal Scots recruited in Scotland.[48]

In this instance, men enlisted after being entranced by recruiting parties, consisting of an officer, two sergeants and a drummer, who set up their stall at markets and fairs (both traditional places for recruiting servants and labourers). Even in March 1746, men from Cumberland's army at Aberdeen were out recruiting; 101 sergeants, 68 drummers and 55 privates being detailed for such duty. The recruiters would speak extravagantly of the wonders of army life and would often take potential recruits to a tavern. Todd wrote that on 5 September 1752, 'Lieutenant Appleton was ordered a recruiting with Sergeant Barnsley, Corporal Todd and Drummer Jones ... [we] received orders to hire a drummer at Hull and to recruit every market day at each place [until 27 February 1753]'.[49] The fictional sergeant in a contemporary story, written in 1706 by a former soldier, gives the following pitch:

> If any gentlemen soldiers, or others, have a mind to serve her majesty, and pull down the French king; if any prentices have severe masters, any children have unnatural parents; if any servants have too little wages, or any husband too much wife; let them

repair to the noble Sergeant Kite, at the Sign of the Raven, in this good town of Shrewsbury, and they shall receive present relief and entertainment.[50]

A critical contemporary account notes that a soldier was 'commonly a Man, who for the sake of wearing a Sword and the Honour of being term'd a Gentleman, is coaxed from a Handicraft Trade'.[51]

Alcohol was an important part of the process. A sergeant noted:

> your last recourse was to get him [the recruit] drunk, and then slip a shilling into his pocket, get him home to your billet, and next morning swear he enlisted, bring all your party to prove it, get him persuaded to pass the doctor. Should he pass, you must use every means in your power to get him to drink, blow him up with a fine story, get him inveigled by the magistrates, in some shape or other, and get him attested, but by no means let him out of your hands.[52]

Captain Henry Conway (1719–95) told Horace Walpole, in 1742 that 'no one enlists in [the army] without being made drunk first'. Fellow captain, John Blackadder, wrote in 1703, 'I see the greatest rakes are the best recruiters'.[53]

Nevertheless, economic motives often played their part among those enlisting. Donald McBane, an apprentice to a tobacco spinner in Inverness, was certainly influenced by such. He later declared, 'my mistress began to lessen my Dish, which I could not endure, I being a raw young fellow who would have eaten two meats in one day. So I went and listed myself a soldier ...'[54] Daniel Defoe wrote in 1726, that there was 'a kind of Poverty and Distress necessary to bring a poor man to take Arms'.[55]

The desire to escape family responsibilities was another motive. In 1702, John Bland of Bishop's Stortford, Hertfordshire, deserted his wife and two children and enlisted in the army. Forty-five years later, it was noted, 'John Fisher, labourer, committed for want of sureties in respect of the bastard child of Ann Taylor is ordered by the consent of the inhabitants of the parish of Great Munden ... to be delivered to a file of His Majesty's soldiers, he having enlisted himself as a soldier'.[56]

However, there were other motives, too. Defoe added that these 'poorest of men may have Principles of Honour and Justice in them'.[57] The fictional Tom Jones agrees to enlist in the army in 1745 as a volunteer. Fielding tells the reader, 'Jones had some Heroic Ingredients in his Composition, and was a hearty Well-Wisher to the glorious Cause of Liberty, and of the Protestant Religion. It is no wonder, therefore, that in Circumstances which would have warranted a much more romantic and wild undertaking, it should occur to him to serve as a Volunteer in this Expedition'.[58] Jones later says, 'he was most zealously attached to the glorious cause for which they were going to fight and was very desirous of serving'.[59]

It is needless to say that women were barred from the army. Yet some women did enlist. Hannah Snell did so, in 1745, and went by the name of John Gray, and Mrs Davis had done so earlier in the century. But these figures were rare, and any women in uniform had to conceal their sex.[60]

Yet the lot of a recruiting officer was not always easy, as Tom Woodward found in 1755:

> the Captain has met with so little success, that he never intends to come a recruiting any more if he can help it; and indeed I think it no desirable employment, for it leads them into expense, which they can't very well bear unless they have great good luck … they are allowed £5 for every man, that is received by the regiment, when he is sent over; and out of this £5 they are to pay them perhaps one or two guineas for enlisting money, send them over with three good shirts, and subsist them at the rate of sixpence a day till they get to the regiment; these are hard terms, and not much to be got by the bargain; so that if they don't pass muster when they come there, the recruiting officer is all this money out of pocket[61]

Cavalrymen also had to help gather horses for their units, too. An order on 25 April 1733 read thus, requiring an officer, a sergeant and fifteen dragoons of His Majesty's own regiment from Wakefield to Warwick, and 'there to receive 30 recruit horses and then return'.[62]

Traditionally, army life has been described as horrific and so only the most desperate would join. Certainly pay was low and discipline was harsh, quite apart from the dangers of disease in the West Indies or death or wounds in battle. Yet life as a civilian was also hard and wages irregular. A soldier was guaranteed both pay and food. He was also entitled to engage in other employment while at home to supplement his army wages. The promise of adventure and, at times, a relatively easy life beckoned.[63] Life was certainly not all bad, as Todd wrote that whilst in Ireland in 1753, 'Here we live tolerably well as everything is moderate'. Todd increased his income by teaching at a local school and so, on the fees he earned, he 'liv'd well'.[64] It was not only the educated who did likewise. As a contemporary publication declared, of soldiers, 'Do we not see them at work every Harvest? Do they not follow their Trades in every market town where they are stationed?'[65]

Once a man had expressed an interest in joining, he would be given a shilling to seal the bargain. He then had to be approved by the officer in charge and passed as fit by a doctor. He was then shown to a magistrate and sworn in. The Articles of War would be read to him, and these outlined behaviour which was unacceptable and punishable. His bounty would be used to buy his kit.[66]

The said articles, in 1745, included the following phrase:

> I swear to be true to our sovereign Lord, King George, and serve him honestly and faithfully, in defence of his person, Crown and Dignity, against all his enemies and

opposers whatsoever, and to observe and obey His Majesty's orders and the orders of the generals and officers set over me by His Majesty, so help me God.[67]

When a man had enlisted, the next step was to turn him into a soldier. He was issued with his uniform, a red coat, unless he was an artilleryman, who wore blue, and his equipment. Then he had to be taught how to manoeuvre and how to load and fire his musket. Training mostly consisted of drill, though this was at a basic level because it was rare for a few companies to be together in one place at any one time. There were few barracks, so men were usually billeted at public houses. Training involved very little target practice, because in peacetime there was very little ammunition available, and so blanks were used. They would learn to volley fire in platoons. This meant that only a proportion of the men in the lines (three deep) fired at any one time, the remainder reloading. This meant that the rate of fire would be continuous. However, in actual combat, the system did not always function and massed fire by regiment occurred. Bayonet drill was rare, though sometimes sword drill was taught.[68] Those already enlisted would work with the new recruits. Todd once wrote after a recruiting session, 'We are very bussy [*sic*] in exercising the recruits who are coming in daily'.[69]

When entirely new regiments were raised from scratch in October 1745, there was an even more urgent need for the men to be trained. William Congreve, lieutenant colonel of Gower's foot, was told 'duly to exercise as well the officers as soldiers thereof in arms, and to use your best endeavours to keep them in good order and discipline'.[70] Yet it was not until the following month that there is a reference to NCOs from Bligh's regiment being rewarded 'to help you to discipline our men' and Lord Gower believed that his regiment was being 'sooner disciplined than any of our contemporary regiments, who at this crisis cannot get good serjeants and corporals for love or money'.[71]

Finally, we should remember that a significant proportion of the forces employed by the first three Georges, whether in the Jacobite rebellions, the Seven Years War or the American War of Independence were foreign born, especially Hessian and Dutch. Such was not uncommon in other armies of the time – over half of Frederick the Great's armies were composed of men who were not his own subjects, and French armies included German, Swiss, Irish and Scottish units.[72]

Having dealt with how the army was raised, we shall now examine its peacetime role. When soldiers were stationed at home they were often called upon by magistrates to deal with crime and public disorder. This should be no surprise. There were no police forces in Britain until the nineteenth century and parish constables were often too few in number to deal with serious disorder. Therefore the justices of the peace often called upon the trained and armed soldiery to bolster their authority. Between 1737 and 1743, 12 per cent of the infantry's activity was spent on combating smugglers and rioters; for the cavalry over the same period it was 11 per cent.[73]

Orders from the War Office were frequent on this subject. A Troop of Gore's dragoons stationed at Columpton in September 1733 was instructed thus:

> if you should have advice from the civil magistrates at Tiverton, that they appre-
> hended mischief from the weavers and other disorderly persons there, then to march
> the troop, if desired by them, there and be aiding and assisting them in suppressing
> the said disorders there ... not to repel force with force at Tiverton ... unless it shall be
> found absolutely necessary by the civil magistrates.[74]

Riot duty was a traditional role for soldiers. Samuel Pepys refers to soldiers being called upon to disperse crowds in London on several occasions in the 1660s and in 1688 they helped quell anti-Catholic rioters. This remained their lot in the following century, with the guards being summoned to deal with anti-dissent riots in London in 1710. This should be no surprise. Rioting was not an uncommon part of economic disputes or in making political or religious protest. Between 1740 and 1775, there were 159 major riots in England alone.[75]

If a crowd did not disperse after a magistrate had read the Riot Act, force could legitimately be deployed. Yet it was often the government, acting via a Secretary of State, who initiated military action. In 1715, Viscount Townshend (1674–1738), a Secretary of State, informed Ralph Aston, a Lancashire magistrate, that troops were to be sent to Manchester 'at Request of the Sheriff, J.P or other civil magistrate' to help 'extinguish this turbulent and outrageous spirit', which was 'insolent, illegal and treasonable ... destructive to all government and of so dangerous consequence to the peace and tranquillity of his good and loving subjects'.[76] Then the Secretary at War would issue the command to the soldiers most conveniently situated to deal with the situation.

A few examples will suffice. In December 1738, weavers in Melksham were rioting, 'but some soldiers being sent to the town, they have not returned'.[77] Two years later, there were grain riots in Newcastle and Norwich. After the magistrates failed to disperse the mobs, the latter ran wild. At Newcastle, 'in the evening three companies of Harrison's regiment entered the town and dispersed the rioters, 40 of which were gaoled'. In Norwich, dragoons were stationed in the market place, where the crowd, 'growing more furious, provok'd some to fire among them, whereby 3 men, 2 women and a Boy were killed and many more dangerously wounded'.[78] Bloodshed was even higher during London's most devastating riots in 1780 when the army was only called in during the later stages of the crisis.

But confrontations rarely resulted in deaths. During the myriad riots of 1714–16, not one fatality was put down to the army, and throughout the next few decades the same was usually the rule. This was partly because to cause civilian deaths could be construed as murder, with soldiers being put on trial, as occurred to Captain Porteus in Edinburgh in 1736 and to soldiers in London during the Wilkes riots of 1768. Although all men were acquitted, such examples helped restrain the trigger-happy. But officers also often tried to restrain their men in their dealings with crowds. Such was a case in Leeds on 10 June 1715, when Lieutenant Parcier's detachment confronted a crowd of 500 people with Jacobite sympathies. Parcier ensured his men's muskets were not loaded with balls, kept his men under his direct supervision and ensured that they did not become entangled with the crowd. His quartermaster noted, 'The Troop was very civil and only was call'd to preserve the Town from Damage'.[79] Even when there was some physical conflict, it was relatively restrained, such as in Manchester in 1715, when Major Wyvill said that fighting had resulted in some of the crowd having received 'a good cudgelling and broken heads'.[80] The soldiers were not always successful; in Glasgow in 1725, the two companies of infantry sent there were outnumbered and when the mob armed themselves with the contents of the town's magazines, they were obliged to retreat to Dumbarton. Initially they had loaded their muskets with only powder, but this did not calm the situation, and only lethal firepower temporarily cowed their opponents.[81]

Troops sometimes acted in conjunction with the militia. One instance was when workmen rioted against Irishmen in Spitalfields in the summer of 1736. Magistrates called out the militia, but also 'in the meantime the deputy lieutenants wrote to the commanding officers of the Tower, to send to their assistance such a number of the guards as they could spare; upon which an officer, with about 50 men, was sent by major White'. It was a success, 'Upon the appearance of the guards, the mob retired ... and gave no resistance'.[82] Soldiers did not always find such riot duty amenable; Wolfe commented as such in the 1750s. Their very use against their own also did nothing to improve the army's reputation among their fellow countrymen.

Smugglers were another problem facing the forces of the law, and the customs officers were not always adequate to deal with the dangerous gangs on the coasts. Again, the army could be used. The southern and eastern counties especially needed patrolling, and it was usual to employ mounted troops for increased mobility. Some units were given anti-smuggling duty often. In 1739–42, 29 per cent of the time of the 4th dragoons was employed on this activity. Yet soldiers on such duties were often spread thinly. When a cavalry regiment was deployed against smugglers in Norfolk and Suffolk in May 1739, there were 262 men to be spread over forty-two towns, an average of six in each.[83]

General orders from the War Office were directed to a troop of dragoons and usually phrased thus as occurred in March 1732:[84]

to march forthwith from their present quarters ... to Canterbury, there to be aiding and assisting to the civil magistrates and officers of our revenue in preventing the owlers and smugglers from running of goods upon that coast, and in apprehending the said owlers and smugglers, and seizing their goods.

In April 1745, 15 smugglers were captured at Hawkshurst in Kent, 'by some officers of the customs, assisted by a party of Wade's Horse'.[85]

Todd recalled an occasion in 1753 when he was part of a group of thirty-four men led by a lieutenant who went to Kerry to take Murphy O'Sullivan, a notorious smuggler. There was a firefight, and the smuggler was shot dead. Silver spoons were found in his house and the soldiers divided between themselves.[86] However, sometimes too few soldiers were available, as in June 1744, when customs officers and five dragoons tried to arrest smugglers at Pevensey. There were 100 smugglers, who disarmed their opponents.[87] More successful was the case in 1735 where 'five custom house officers with as many soldiers and a sergeant from the Tower were arm'd and bringing to Town 14 boxes of tea which they had secur'd and put in a coach were attacked at Lewisham, Kent'. The attackers were dealt with, two being shot dead and one taken prisoner.[88] More routine tasks included the prevention of a jailbreak in St Martin's, London, in May 1744, when a rescue attempt was made on the parish roundhouse, 'But a detachment of Horse Guards and Foot Guards coming up, 4 of them were taken'.[89] Soldiers could also undertake guard duty. When the Earl of Barrymore was arrested at his house in Cavendish Square in February 1744, 'a file of musqueteers was posted in it'.[90]

Soldiers were regularly required to retake deserters who had been taken by the civil authorities. An instance was an order of 15 March 1730, where a sergeant and three privates of the Coldstream Guards were ordered to march from London to Spalding, 'there to take a deserter and then return'.[91]

Ceremonial and guard duty was the lot of troops in and around London, who were usually guards regiments. On 20 May 1730, an officer, four trumpeters and thirty-two troopers of the Horse Guards were told to 'march to Richmond, there to remain until further orders and attend as a Guard upon His Majesty's Royal Person during his stay there'. Earlier that month, troops from the Foot Guards were to be reviewed at Hyde Park.[92] The Rev. James Woodforde (1740–1803) noticed their ceremonial functions in London in 1786, recording in his diary, 'we walked down to St. James' palace and saw the Guards being relieved'.[93] Boswell referred to 'The sight of the Parade and the splendid Guards' in 1763.[94] Troops stationed in Oxford in 1716 helped celebrate the anniversary of George I's coronation and the King's birthday.[95] Troops also appeared at great state occasions, such as on the funeral of the Duke of Marlborough in 1722, as Gertrude Saville (1693–1757), a London spinster, recorded, 'All the souldiers and officers of the Camp attended him'. She also saw the troops exercising in Hyde Park and firing in platoons. The King often oversaw these reviews and spent a great deal of time with them.[96]

In cases of emergency, large numbers of troops could be gathered together in an encampment near or in London, in order to deter insurrection. James II gathered together forces at Hounslow Heath in the later 1680s. The like occurred under George I in 1715 and in 1721, when Jacobite conspiracies were feared. These camps were formed in Hyde Park. Gertrude Saville confided the following in her diary:

> In May there was a camp form'd in Hyde Park, of about 3 or 4 Thousand Men ... it was the finest Sight in the World ... There was also a camp upon Hounslow Heath and one near Salsbury. These all continued till after Michaelmass.[97]

Although there were few barracks in mainland Britain, garrison duty at home and abroad was another staple for the soldier in peacetime. Garrisons abroad included those in Gibraltar, Minorca, the Caribbean and Ireland. Between 1718 and 1739, eight of the army's forty-one infantry battalions were stationed in garrisons around the Mediterranean.[98] At home, there were a number of castles and barracks which needed troops, especially after 1715. These included Berwick, Chester, Edinburgh, Stirling, Forts William and Augustus, Ruthven Barracks and Portsmouth. Troops marched from one to another. Many troops were billeted in inns in towns.

The eighteenth-century British army was recruited on a voluntary basis. Men were persuaded by recruiting parties to enlist, though in times of war and rebellion, prisoners awaiting trial could be enlisted as well. For officers, a mixture of interest, seniority, purchase and merit determined promotion prospects. In peacetime, soldiers were involved in garrison duty, at home and abroad, and in quelling smugglers and rioters. During times of war and rebellion, however, a soldier's lot was far different and dangerous and it is to that which the next chapters will address.

2 THE ARMY ON CAMPAIGN

Most of the efforts of the men of the regular army during the Jacobite campaigns, as on campaign overseas, was not taken up with the deadly business of siege or battle. For the commanders and men it was the far more mundane business of marching, eating and sleeping which took up most of their time, but these were imperative in order to ensure that they were capable of combat. In these, the direct authority of a general was limited, however, even if he were a captain general as Marlborough had been, or was a King's son. The general had control of operations, tactics, training and discipline. Yet commanders had also to deal with civil authorities, and these loomed especially high when the campaign was on home soil. The Treasury, answerable to Parliament, supplied money, the Ordnance supplied arms and ammunition, and the Cabinet decided on overall strategy. Their representative figures included the Secretaries of State in London, paymasters and commissaries, judicial officials, the county elites of the lieutenancy and justices of the peace, and right down to the level of parish constable. It was upon these civilians that the army depended for its pay, provisioning, billeting, transport and intelligence, such was the superiority of the civil arm to the military. Put simply, the army could not operate in the domestic context without the cooperation of the civil state, though this was less apparent overseas. This is quite apart from the direction and guidance given to commanders in the field over strategy and goals. The military system of the eighteenth century was complicated in order that no one man could be in complete control, but political liberty came at the cost of military inefficiency. Much, therefore, depended on the capability of the commander-in-chief, on his determination, diplomacy and drive. With a capable man at the head, the system worked well enough, but if not, the troops were the first to suffer and thus the outcome of a campaign was imperilled.

We should also note the unusual circumstances of the campaigns of 1715 and 1745, which ran from September to February and from August to April respectively. These were exactly the months in which conventional armies of Western Europe did not campaign. (In 1743 the campaign on the Continent began in May, and in April in 1745.) Rather, the troops went into billets and the generals engaged in diplomacy and politicking. The cause of this inactivity was that food for the men, kindling for warmth and fodder for the horses was in very short supply. Roads, such as they were, were rendered even more difficult because of autumnal rains, winter snow and spring showers. So, because roads were reduced to quagmires, movement of artillery and supply wagons was extremely difficult. Crossing rivers was all the more fraught due to their being swollen, and ports became frozen. Accommodation was all the more difficult, too, as conventionally the inclement weather debarred makeshift sleeping arrangements.[1] Thus the regulars faced an additional burden, campaigning, as they did, in this season.

To state the objective of the British state is one matter: it was the defeat of the rebellions. It is quite another to determine the military means which were taken to combat them, and these were different in 1715 and 1745. Internally, the former posed more difficulties, because of the more complex nature of the threat, although externally Britain was at peace, whereas in 1745 there was far less strife in Britain, but the country was at war, and its principal enemy was also a major maritime power capable of launching an invasion. These differing situations needed differing responses. We shall examine the issues posed by the Fifteen first, and how troops were deployed against it.

Manpower

The defeat of the rebellions required troops. The onset of any fresh military challenge, whether war or rebellion, meant an expansion in troop numbers, above that needed for routine peacetime duties of maintaining internal order. Because Britain had been at peace since the Treaty of Utrecht of 1713, the armed forces had been vastly reduced, there now being no external enemy. At the beginning of 1715, throughout Britain (excluding the Irish establishment) there were three regiments of foot guards, six troops of horse guards, two regiments of horse, six regiments of dragoons, seventeen battalions of infantry and sixteen companies of invalids (chiefly employed in garrison duty); about 25,000 men if all the units were up to strength, which they were not, and of whom about one-fifth were cavalry. In April 1715, this force cost £425,900 14s 6d.[2] As a contrast, at the peak of the War of Spanish Succession, there had been eighty-four battalions of infantry and sixty-five squadrons of cavalry, throughout the world.[3] There were always more regular troops than Jacobite forces in total, but whereas the latter could be concentrated, the former could not be. As with any regular army dealing with insurgents, only a fraction of the former will make up the field armies while the majority are tied down in garrisons. This could often result in localized numerical inferiority, at least for temporary periods.

Units were very variable in size. The Royal Dragoons and Stair's, two regiments of dragoons, numbered, in 1715, 166 and 161 men respectively. Forfar's, the Royal Fusiliers, Shannon's and Montagu's battalions of infantry numbered 246, 263, 328 and 201 men.[4] These numbers would have been inflated by the officers in each battalion; for the infantry, this would be three officers per company. The infantry units under Argyll had seventeen or eighteen sergeants and between eight and eleven drummers in each. However numbers of sick per battalion were between four and fifteen.[5]

Since July 1715, the government had been aware that a major attempt was to be made to restore James Stuart, following numerous riots throughout England. Steps were taken to increase the manpower at the state's disposal. Commissions were given in order that new regiments be formed; in all, these were thirteen regiments of dragoons (about 3,000 men) and eight battalions of infantry (about 4,000 men). Six of these dragoon regiments were employed in battle in England under Wills and Carpenter. How efficient they were is another question, for the units had only been formed for three months before they were being deployed on active service. There would have been little time for training or accustoming the men to working together, and none to gain any prior experience. On the other hand, it is possible that some of those employed had seen service in the late wars; certainly this was the case with some of the officers. Some officers, though, such as the newly appointed Captain Henry Pelham, certainly had no prior experience. The guards regiments were also strengthened. All officers were ordered to return to their posts and half-pay officers were told to be in readiness for service.[6]

Forces were moved to bring them to where they were needed. Many of the Crown's forces were stationed in Ireland as a garrison, but they could be used as an emergency reserve elsewhere if necessary. Troops were sent from Ireland in 1715. James Stanhope (1673–1721), a Secretary of State, wrote on 11 October: 'We shall be impatient of hearing the Regiments from Ireland landing with you. Some squadrons will be ordered to the north of England.' As matters transpired, four battalions of infantry and two regiments of cavalry were sent from Ireland in 1715, out of a total of twenty-nine regiments.[7]

There was an insufficient garrison in Scotland to quell a full-scale rebellion. Major General Whetman, commander-in-chief in Scotland, complained that on 16 August 1715 he had too few men under his command to even arrest leading Jacobites.[8] A week later the situation was no better, as he wrote: 'The forces we have here are so few, 'tis very dangerous.'[9] By 28 August there were less than 1,000 regular troops gathered at Stirling; comprising of two regiments of infantry and two of cavalry, although more were on their way from Ireland and England.[10] These reinforcements could not arrive quickly enough, as the Duke of Argyll, who replaced Whetman as commander on 14 September, wrote: 'I am sorry to find you have been so dilatory in obeying the orders you received to march with the utmost expedition to Scotland.'[11]

Argyll inherited the same perceived shortage of manpower. Most of his letters to Townshend and Stanhope in that year were of this strain. From the outset, he declared, 'if the enemy think fit to act with the vigour that men of common sense would in their case, the handful of troops now in Scotland may be beat out of the country before my small reinforcement can joyn them'.[12] By the time he had arrived at Stirling, he found he had 1,400 men under his command, but even when another two weak regiments of dragoons arrived this would only amount to 1,750. Argyll believed Jacobite strength was 10,000 men.[13] He also adopted an angry tone, on 21 September, writing:

> I am extreamly surprised that notwithstanding the alarms you have had from hence we have heard nothing either from Lord Townshend or you ... His Majesty's ministers still persist in thinking the matter a jest, and that we are in a condition to put a stop to it ... this country is in the extreamest danger.[14]

He also pointed out that he felt it odd that the only place where there was a Jacobite army was in Scotland, yet out of a total strength of 42 squadrons of cavalry and 22 battalions of infantry, only eight of the former and six of the latter were with him in 1715.[15]

By the end of the month, Argyll was beginning to wish that he was relieved from command, that 'these matters are put into the hands of others'.[16] A few weeks later, on hearing that this would probably happen, soon, he found the plan 'most agreeable'.[17]

Further reinforcements arrived in the next few months. Therefore, on 4 November, Argyll, now with 3,300 soldiers, could write: 'We are now strong enough to prevent the rebels from ever passing this river [the Forth].' Yet, given the enemy was about 7,000 strong or more, to advance against such numbers was impossible, until the Dutch troops promised could arrive.[18]

Even after the battle of Sheriffmuir, Argyll was concerned about the disparity of numbers between his force and those of the Jacobites. He told William Pulteney, Secretary at War:

> they will infallibly, notwithstanding their loss, be able to advance with the same numbers very soon, if we are not reinforced in a very few days. I believe everybody here is of opinion that this kingdom will be lost. People in England have always treated these rebels on the foot of the mob but they have found means to form themselves into a regular strong army.[19]

It does not appear that new regiments were raised during the invasion scare and very brief rebellion in 1719, though as will be noted, troops from friendly powers were sent for, and arrived.

The situation in 1745 was rather different. The total numerical strength of the armed forces was far higher than in 1715, but thirty-five regiments and three troops of horse guards were on active service abroad. In 1745, the estimates for troops at home were £15,768; for those abroad it was £28,107. Most of those in Britain were engaged in garrison duties, in Ireland, Scotland and around London. There were enough men to maintain internal order but there were too few to constitute a field army of sufficient strength. The perceived defenceless state of the kingdom was much remarked upon, though it should not be exaggerated. Horace Walpole wrote, 'I don't conceive what should hinder the Pretender from being immediately master of everything' and that Wade remarked that 'England is for the first comer'.[20] John Murray of Broughton, a Jacobite, wrote that there was but 7,000, 'a body no more sufficient than to protect the seaports from smugglers, far from being capable to prevent an Insurrection in that part of the Country had any been intended by the Chevalier's friends in that part of the Island'. However, the real number seems to have been almost 20,000 men, though they were scattered throughout the country.[21] As in 1715, the commander in Scotland highlighted his vulnerability. Sir John Cope (1690–1760) wrote in July: 'As this affair seems very serious, I need not mention the absolute necessity there is of a reinforcement of troops from some part or other.' As matters stood, he had only fifteen companies of infantry and two regiments of dragoons that could take to the field in Scotland.[22]

However, unlike the case in 1715, there was little concern about English Jacobitism as a military threat, and any that might exist could be dealt with by the county militia and volunteer troops. Much depended on the extent to which France would support the rebellion. Many in government circles certainly thought so. Horace Walpole wrote as early as 6 August, 'The French are certainly coming' and a month later wrote, 'the French ... are every day expected from Dunkirk'.[23] Richmond shared these views, writing 'I shall enjoy no ease till troops are in England. I have not the least fear of the young Gentn in Scotland, 'tho to be sure his being there ought to be look'd to, butt my great apprehensions are from a French invasion which I look upon as certain, if not timely prevented'.[24]

Newcastle kept the Duke of Cumberland (1721–65) informed on the situation in Scotland, but did not initially suggest troops being brought over. However, as early as 26 July he informed him that 'a number of English troops may be necessary' for 'the number of our land forces is very small'. A week later, Cumberland was told to have transports ready for dispatch of troops if necessary.[25]

However, he did insist that Antwerp be kept secure 'in order to preserve a Communication with this Country'.[26] The situation was fluid and on learning that the Jacobite army had eluded Cope and was marching on the Lowlands, there were fresh concerns in London, and demands for additional manpower as soon as possible. Andrew Stone, Newcastle's secretary, told the Duke of Richmond his master's latest thinking: 'A Messenger was despatched last night [4

September], with orders for ten Regiments to be sent immediately to England from our Army in Flanders: Sir John Ligonier is to come to England with them.'[27]

Yet for all the concern in London, those soldiers on the Continent, facing the French armies, saw priorities in another light. Ligonier wrote, 'are you aware that the enemy [the French] has 70,000 men against our 30,000 ... and yet you speak of our having a corps to spare to defend England?'.[28] Cumberland wrote similarly to Newcastle from Wilvorden on 6 September:

> I make no doubt but that you who are on the spot have your reasons & very good ones too for recalling troops from hence. I assure you that if England wants them I am intirely of opinion that this country & even the whole alliance ought not to be considered comparatively with our own Country, but the detaching from hence at so critical a juncture may be so fatall that I have sent to the King for immediate orders ... on the whole I hope that my friends will forgive me if I don't see the danger at home so imminent.[29]

No troops were therefore dispatched immediately, though consternation was growing, with Stone writing about their lack of arrival on 12 September and hopes that this would not be long delayed. Two days later, Newcastle wrote: 'I am afraid that they will not be very expeditious in sending our ten regiments from our Army. We have an Account that they are coming, but they don't seem in haste. I have desired this day, that an Express may be sent to hasten them.'[30] Richmond was for the immediate recall of the whole army, 'there is no retrieving it, nor any safety to ourselves, without the Duke & our whole army being sent for home immediately to defend us against the French.'[31]

Eventually the troops were sent, though Cumberland was not entirely convinced it was necessary. On 20 September, he wrote:

> I am heartily sorry for the occasion of this great detachment from our army but will do our utmost endeavour not to be devoured by the army who will now become so much superior. So ever I am rather rejoiced than frightened at the pretender's son being got between Sir John Cope and Edinburgh since I see no retreat left them & I hope that Great Britain is not to be conquered by 3000 rable gather'd together in the mountains but should they dare to advance I will answer man for man for the ten battalions Sir John Ligonier will bring you. As he is coming over I think it is my duty to assure you he is not the man you take him for. If his advice is ask'd, he will give it according to his opinion & generally I have found it a good one. In short the service I have had from him this campaign are too great for me to neglect recommending him to you as one who may be very useful at this conjuncture.[32]

Thus on 23 September, ten infantry battalions arrived in England; three of whom were guards, bringing the nation's troops up to 25,000 men. Yet even this force was felt to be inadequate, now that Cope's army had been destroyed at Prestonpans. The government's military committee decided:

> We are of the opinion that orders should be sent to His Royal Highness the Duke
> of Cumberland to hold nine squadrons of Horse and dragoons, and six battalions
> of Foot in readiness to embark if it should be necessary at the first notice, and that
> transports with provisions etc. should be sent over forthwith.[33]

On 26 September, it was deemed necessary that the forces in readiness in Flanders would only be sent once the French were in winter quarters.[34] Finally, on 30 September, Cumberland was told to send even more troops back, to the tune of 6,000 men above the numbers already requested.[35] On 25 October, two regiments of cavalry, four of infantry and the remainder of the guards battalions came. Cumberland himself appeared in England on 18 October. A month later, additional cavalry regiments, amounting to 2,500 men, also arrived.[36]

As well as recalling existing troops, the committee decided on additional steps to be taken for increasing the army's strength. Firstly, it was decided to allow men to enlist for only a year's service. General Folliott was convinced that this would increase companies of infantry from seventy to one hundred men. Richmond was impressed by the scheme and wrote, 'would augment the army 14 or 15,000 men with little expence, & great expedition. I have talked of it here & I find every body is opinion that now the harvest is over, a prodigious number would enlist'.[37] Constables in and around London were given orders to 'impress all loose and disorderly Persons, who have no Visible Ways of getting a Livelihood, into his Majesty's Service'.[38] Secondly, noblemen in England were given commissions for raising new regiments of infantry and cavalry; thirteen infantry and two cavalry units being raised. In Scotland, commissions were sent out to raise twenty independent companies; in all, 13,408 men were raised by this method. However, their military capability is to be doubted because they were newly raised and so had minimal training and no experience of battle, Cumberland writing, 'they will rather be a hindrance than a service to me ... neither men nor officers know what they are about so how they will do before the enemy God only knows'.[39]

By the end of October of 1745 all this resulted in one sizeable field army in England. This was formed under Field Marshal George Wade's command at Newcastle. It was composed of twelve battalions of regular infantry, eight battalions of Dutch, four squadrons of horse and seven of dragoons. This amounted to 11,800 infantry and 1,380 cavalry. There were twenty-four guns and ten mortars, which were attended by some regular gunners. This was one of the largest military formations seen in Britain since 1688. However, two of the battalions of infantry and four squadrons of dragoons were detached in early November to reoccupy Edinburgh.[40]

Yet the second army was not assembled until late in the following month, and this when the Jacobite army was marching through England. Initially under the command of Ligonier, by the time it was assembled in the Midlands in late

November it was under Cumberland. There were three battalions of Guards, nine regular battalions and six newly raised ones (at least 10,500 men). For cavalry there were three of dragoons and one of horse, and two newly raised dragoon regiments, totalling 2,200 men. The artillery was composed of two six pounders, fourteen three pounders and two howitzers.[41]

There could also be shortages of specialist troops. As Cope told the Marquis of Tweeddale, Secretary for Scotland, 'There were no gunners in Scotland'.[42] Lieutenant General Henry Hawley had similar problems, writing in January 1746:

> The heavy artillery is still at Newcastle, for want of horses, which were sent to Carlisle for no use. The major of artillery is absent through sickness. I suspect his sickness to be a young wife: I know him. I have been obliged to hire a conductor of artillery and 70 odd men to act as his assistants for the Foot Artillery. I was three days getting them from the castle to the Palace Yard and now they are not fit to march.[43]

As well as quantity, quality should also be considered. In 1715, many of the troops engaged in the campaign were those who had fought in the recent wars. They were even in the same units as they had been for years. Other veterans joined the newly formed regiments. In 1745 the situation was similar, with the bulk of the regular troops having fought at Dettingen and/or Fontenoy, or had been on campaign for several years. Most of the officers had had years of experience in both warfare and the low-intensity peacetime soldiering in Britain or abroad.

There were others, too. The units in Scotland had only been raised in recent years and had not seen previous active service. Murray of Broughton referred to one detachment in August 1745 as 'raw and new raised as they were said to be', 'without officers of Conduct and Resolution'. Of Cope's command in Scotland he wrote that 'these not the best in the service'.[44] These included Gardiner's and Hamilton's dragoons, who behaved so badly at both Prestonpans and Falkirk that Cumberland decided, on 30 January 1746, that they were to be left at Edinburgh while he advanced to Stirling.[45] Argyll also had problems with one of his reinforcements in 1715: 'The condition in which I found Mr Echlin's regiment which lately arrived in Scotland, is so extraordinary ... The men, my lord, are many of them old and little, the horses generally wrong turned and ill sized.'[46]

Apart from the regular troops of the Crown, the militia and other irregular forces, there was another source of manpower which was called upon on these occasions. From 1689 to 1815 Britain used contract troops in its wars, but also at home in times of emergency such as rebellion or when invasion was feared. These forces were usually from Holland or from the smaller German states, Hesse in particular. The use of Hessian forces in the American Revolutionary Wars is well known, for over 18,000 were employed, making up over a third of the Crown's total forces. In 1742, 16,000 Hanoverian and 6,000 Hessian troops were in British pay on the Continent.[47] German and Danish auxiliaries had been under British pay in the 1700s, too, though Marlborough had to constantly negotiate on their use.[48] But contract troops were also used on home territory in 1715–16, 1719, 1744, 1745–6 and beyond. Their employment has been overshadowed because none of them were employed in any major engagement and those who saw any serious combat were the few Dutch companies at Glenshiel.

The use of such forces was commonplace in eighteenth-century Europe. Prussia and France did likewise. In Britain's case they were particularly important. Britain was a leading European power, but had a mere 6 million people in 1700, so was vastly outnumbered by France, Russia and Austria. Furthermore, Britain had an anti-militarist tradition stretching back to the seventeenth century, both these factors militating against large standing armies, especially in 'peacetime'. Yet Britain, since the 1690s, had considerable financial muscle, with a superior system of taxation and the ability to borrow money at low rates. Thus she was able to afford to employ foreign troops both at home and abroad, in order to overcome the objections mentioned yet at the same time provide formidable military strength.

Diplomatically, Britain and Holland had been allies since 1689, with a common enemy in France. The Anglo-Dutch Treaty of Barrier and Succession of 1709 promised Britain Dutch military aid if the Hanoverian succession was threatened, provided that Britain promised to support a number of barrier fortresses to defend Dutch territory against the French. This was renegotiated in 1713, signed in 1715 and guaranteed again in 1717 as part of the Triple Alliance.[49]

The arrival of these troops was not immediate. It was in August 1715 that they were requested. There were delays made by the French, who assured the Dutch of their pacific intentions.[50] Horatio Walpole and General Cadogan were dispatched to the Hague to negotiate for their arrival in late September.[51]

It was not until mid-November that any arrived on British soil, ironically just after the two battles of the campaign had been concluded. The entire force numbered about 7,000 men, including servants and camp followers, and was comprised of five battalions of Dutch infantry, five battalions of Swiss infantry and a regiment of dismounted dragoons, under the command of Lieutenant General Reiner Vincent van der Beke.[52] They eventually arrived in Scotland in late December and proved a sizeable reinforcement for Argyll, who wrote on 27 November '[I] think the sending of the Dutch troops northwards a very right measure. I wish to God for His Majesty's Service they were here now.'[53] Such troops came at a price, of course, amounting to £126, 033.[54]

In contrast, the five battalions of Dutch troops dispatched in 1719 arrived in plenty of time for some of them to see action. They were in Britain by April and some saw active service at Glenshiel.[55] Additionally, six battalions of Imperial troops were dispatched from the Austrian Netherlands to Britain.[56]

Likewise, with the bulk of regular forces on active service on the Continent in 1745 during the War of the Austrian Succession, the regency in London initially decided to try to keep the disruption to the war effort to a minimum. Newcastle asked Robert Trevor, Envoy Extraordinary in Holland to make a formal request for troops on 13 August. He wrote 'this may be done without any inconvenience to the republic, or the common cause by the states allocating for that service their troops that were in garrison at Tournai ... which by the articles of capitulation, cannot well be employed upon any other service'. The Dutch troops in question had surrendered to the French in June and had been released on the parole that they would not fight against France or her allies until 1747.[57] However, this was hotly contested by the French, who argued that their being used in such a manner was contrary to the terms of their parole. Yet they were employed, although as we shall see, not for long.[58]

As in 1715, a sizeable force was sent. The Count of Nassau was in command, but while the force should have numbered 6,000 men, in October 1745, when the force had arrived in its entirety, it numbered only 4,200. This was made up of five battalions of Dutch and three of Swiss, all infantry.[59] However, there was initial enthusiasm about their arrival, the Earl of Malton (1693–1750) writing, 'I rejoice to hear the Dutch Troops have landed'.[60] Richmond believed that the best policy was 'to send all the Dutch against the Rebels'. This was because they could not be used against the French for reasons already outlined.[61]

By December, their usefulness was at an end. France had given diplomatic backing to the Jacobite venture. Furthermore, they had sent over a number of units to Scotland. Trevor tried to persuade the Dutch deputies not to withdraw their forces, and explained to Newcastle, 'I urged to the Deputies the ill effect, I apprehended, the Recall of their Troops ... just at this critical juncture, might operate upon the minds of the King's subjects in England, but they appealed to the known circumstances, and conditions, under which they had been obliged to send them over.' The Dutch troops played no further part in the campaign and returned to Holland in the subsequent spring.[62]

Fortunately, by the terms of another treaty, other troops could be sent for. On 5 June 1745, George II and Frederick I of Sweden, who was also Landgrave of Hesse, had made a treaty, the seventh article of which stated that troops from Hesse could be used in Britain's defence.[63] Richmond looked forward to their arrival, writing of the need for more men, 'send for 10,000 more Foot, be they Hessians, Hanoverians or Deviles, if they will butt fight for us'.[64] The force was commanded by Prince Frederick William of Hesse and numbered 5,068 men and 655 horses, divided into six regiments of infantry and a weak force of hussars.[65] They arrived in February 1746 and came under Cumberland's command, remaining until the end of the rebellion.

It took several months, in both 1715 and 1745, before the full force of the British state could be deployed; not until December of each year. Fortunately, the Jacobites had been unable to bring their forces together and strike effectively either, nor to mobilize their expected allies in England and France; though this was arguably a rather close run matter.

General Orders

Once troops were assembled, the next step to take was to appoint commanders and to issue general orders. In the case of Scotland, this was straightforward because there was already a commander-in-chief: Major General Whetman in 1715, although soon superseded by Argyll, and Cope in 1745. There were a number of major commands in England in 1715: Cadogan in London (initially), Wade in the West Country, and Wills and Carpenter in the north. In 1745 the first major appointment was Wade for the command in the north east, then Ligonier for the army based in the Midlands, though he was superseded by Cumberland. Cumberland was to have overall military campaign control from then on, a command denied to any of the generals of the previous thirty years.

The aim of the regular forces during these campaigns had a simplicity that those on the Continent or elsewhere often lacked. It was to bring the rebels to battle and defeat them decisively in order to disperse them as a military force capable of challenging royal authority. Carpenter was told by Pulteney, on 14 October 1715, to 'march into Northumberland and the Borders of Scotland without loss of time ... repair to those parts and march with these our forces or such part of them as you judge sufficient and attack the rebels wherever you find them'.[66] Similarly aggressive orders were addressed to his subordinate, Major General Wills, two weeks later: 'immediately repair to Manchester and give orders ... to march upon the first orders'.[67] These were obeyed, Stanhope writing:

> Lieutenant General Carpenter with the Regiments under his command has positive orders to pursue and attack the rebels of Northumberland who have now joined those of your country: by a letter we received from him this night he promises not to lose an hour in getting up with them.[68]

Soldiers were usually impressed with the notion that they should bring the rebellion to an end as soon as possible. This was despite the difficulties that field commanders often believed faced them. Townshend told Argyll on 6 January 1716 that he should be 'putting in Execution, without the least loss of time, the project I then mentioned'.[69]

Similar orders were issued by Newcastle thirty years later, to Wade who was posted at Newcastle upon Tyne: 'you will equally take care not to let the rebels escape you and get into England, if you can prevent it'.[70] Two days later, Newcastle wrote, 'as soon as you shall know the Route the Rebels shall have taken you will make the best Disposition to come up with them'.[71] Cumberland was given the following order:

> You are immediately to take upon you the command of our said Troops; and to march both them and any other of our Troops ... in order to stop the rebels ... and by all possible means to prevent their further progress.[72]

Newcastle told Cumberland on 2 February 1746, 'the speedy Extinction of the Rebellion and the Re-establishment of the Peace and Tranquillity of every part of this Kingdom' was his aim.[73] This was total war, quite unlike the 'limited' or 'cabinet' wars which typify some of the eighteenth century's conflicts. It was more akin to the American Revolution or later wars than to the wars of the Spanish or Austrian Succession. Only one side could emerge as victor and in order to do so had to achieve complete victory over the other. Not for nothing have these conflicts been termed the 'wars of British Succession'.

Generals in the field often needed assurance, as well as orders, from their political masters. Townshend wrote to Argyll on 4 October, 'all here are very sensible of the great Difficulties your Grace has to struggle with, but we still hope your Grace will be able to overcome them'.[74] But there were also concrete assurances, too. Stanhope told Argyll, 'We have this day received the good news from Holland that the states have agreed to send over 6,000 men immediately'.[75] Congratulations were given in the event of victory. Townshend passed on the King's thanks to Argyll after hearing the results of the battle of Sheriffmuir: 'hearty thanks for the good service you have done His Majesty and your country by this victory you have obtained over the rebels'.[76]

However, the exact execution of these orders was left to the commanders. Townshend told Argyll on 26 September, 'concerning positive orders. None of the Lords here think it practicable at such a distance, to give orders to a General, how he shall act.'[77] On 24 October 1715, generals in England were given the following instruction to use their initiative and not await specific orders:

> Upon notice they shall have of any insurrection in their parts, they without waiting for further instructions, shall march with the forces under their command, or such part of them as they shall think sufficient, wherever they hear such insurrection is; and suppress the same by force.[78]

Cope was told: 'It is impossible at this Distance to give any particular Directions; your Judgement and Conduct will enable you, to make the best of the circumstances that may occur.'[79] This was only sensible, and it is difficult to see how a campaign could have been conducted otherwise, especially as the government was 300 miles from its commanders in the field. Initiative was thus required. Therefore, when Edinburgh was menaced by a flanking manoeuvre in October 1715, Argyll had to waste no time but to lead part of his forces from Stirling there to secure it, which he accomplished, and thirty years later Handasyde reoccupied Edinburgh without awaiting specific orders from London.

One thing that the generals in the field could not do, however, was to engage in diplomacy with the enemy, as would have been commonplace on the Continent. The Jacobites were deemed rebels, not regular enemies as in conventional warfare. This dictated the army's responses to them. When Argyll suggested negotiation with the Jacobites after the battle of Sheriffmuir, Townshend told him: 'It is not consistent with the Honour and Dignity of his Crown ... that any treaty should be entered into ... upon other Terms or Conditions, than surrendering themselves at discretion.'[80]

Strategy and Movement

We shall now examine the specifics of these campaigns, which, of course, varied with the perceptions of the Jacobite threat, which was seen as different on different occasions. The Jacobite rebellions are often seen as wholly, or at least principally, Scottish phenomena, but this view only holds force if viewed with hindsight and if only the battles are focused upon. The regular troops campaigned throughout England as well as Scotland. Not all faced the Jacobite armies; many were involved in essential policing duties. Jacobite risings were expected throughout England in 1715, and so it was here that the bulk of the troops were then deployed. The Rev. Peter Rae of Dumfries, a contemporary historian, outlined the government's official stance:

> Wherefore the Government, being well apprized of all their secret Machinations, took such prudent Measures ... For, instead of sending the Forces to Scotland, for suppressing the rebellion there, they were dispersed thro' England ... where they might be useful ... and all was done in such a manner, as that but a small march, the Troops might upon any Alarm, be drawn into considerable bodies to assist one another.[81]

Therefore the menace was seen as being multi-headed. At Bath, it was reported, 'This place has all the summer been a nest of Tories and Papists ... I never met with such a Jacobite crew.'[82] News from France that autumn read, 'The adherents of the Pretender, whose numbers are much increased for some months past no longer conceal that they have a revolt all ready to break out in England in favour of that of Scotland.'[83] Officers from Frank's regiment were sent to Chester and officers from General Elliot's and General Evans' regiments were dispatched to Carlisle, in order to help train the militia and volunteer forces there. General

Erle was sent to Portsmouth with two battalions 'to reinforce the Garrison ...
there having been some Report of a design to surprise that important place.'[84]
Stanhope wrote: 'We begin to hope that the troops which have marched towards
the West will check the rebellion which was certainly ready to break out there.'[85]
The key strategy was to hold cities, therefore.

London was the financial, commercial and administrative capital of Britain.
Should London fall, then so would the regime, as occurred to Charles I in the
previous century. In 1685, James II had been careful to keep sufficient troops
near the capital and sent initially only a small force to monitor the Monmouth
rebellion of that year. Furthermore, London had been the scene of serious Jacobite rioting earlier that year. Thus General Cadogan was put in charge of an
armed camp at Hyde Park. This was composed of three regiments of foot guards
and three troops of horse guards. There was also artillery with the camp, as had
been the case in the winter of 1688 to deter additional anti-Catholic rioting.[86]
They remained there until December.[87] The West Country was another cause
for concern. Two regiments of infantry and one of cavalry were stationed there.
The Lord Lieutenant also went to Bath to take charge and 'took all the necessary precautions to secure that important Town.'[88] In October, another cavalry
regiment was sent there. General Wade had two cavalry regiments stationed at
Bath, where a number of conspirators, horses and arms were subsequently seized.
The effect was electric. As a newspaper remarked, 'at the sight of [soldiery] the
papists and Tories skulked like a parcel of disappointed traitors.'[89] On Coronation Day, the soldiers went through their exercises in public, fired volleys and the
officers attended a loyalist ball in the evening. These served 'not only to animate
and encourage our real friends, but to deter and shame our enemies.'[90]

Another reputed Jacobite stronghold was Oxford. General Pepper took a
regiment of cavalry there, on 5 October, though ostensibly en route to Bath or
Bristol. However, instead of resting at night, they marched through the night
and arrived at the city at four in the morning. The soldiers guarded the main
avenues of escape as well as public buildings. A number of Jacobite conspirators
were taken prisoner and the soldiers left. Following later Jacobite disturbances
there, another regiment was stationed in the city from 27 October until the following year, 'who kept all things quiet for a time.'[91] At Oxford, scholars cried out
Jacobite phrases in the soldiers' earshot, 'Upon which two musquetts were fir'd
after them, but without doing hurt. This happ'ning the first night has struck such
a terror, that I believe will contribute much to our future peace.'[92]

The north of England only became a concern when a Jacobite insurrection
broke out in Northumberland on 6 October. Four regiments were dispatched to
Newcastle after orders were given on 11 October 1715 to defend the city against
the Jacobites who had risen in Northumberland, but they were also given aggressive orders, and three took part in the last phases of the battle of Preston.[93]

Although the Scottish Jacobites began to gather in arms in September, the government was still convinced that the major danger would be in England, 'the weight both my Lord Townshend and you [Stanhope] lay upon continuing all the troops in England'.[94] Their military decisions were made accordingly, with a relatively small force being concentrated under Argyll at Stirling, with the bulk of the remainder of their forces scattered throughout England. Argyll, facing the only concentration of enemy soldiers, with numbers he deemed inadequate, complained throughout the campaign. To which Townshend replied, on 24 September:

> The situation of our affairs here, is such as makes it impracticable to spare anymore Regular Troops from hence, without apparent danger and hazard to the whole, the security & preservation of which, your Grace will agree with me, ought to be our main and chief business ... they are resolved to put it to the push, and do lay their account with a very great Rising in this Country.[95]

Scotland was second priority to England, because if it fell, it could always be retaken from England, whereas the reverse was hardly true, but such a verdict did nothing to reassure Argyll. Stanhope had to reiterate the situation, two days later, while writing 'I wish it were as easy to send you more Troops'. Intelligence from numerous sources, including that from the Earl of Stair, Minister in Paris, made it 'evident that a general insurrection is intended to be begun at the same time, in several counties of England. Bristol is to be their place of Arms. They reckon themselves sure of all the west of Wales, of Staffordshire, Worcestershire, Derbyshire, Lancaster'.[96]

Even when reinforcements arrived, Argyll deemed them too little, as he told Marlborough on 7 October 1715, 'had those troops my lord which are now ordered from Ireland, been sent over a month agoe I think I could not well have failed of doing His Majesty some service'.[97] However, we should remember that all of Argyll's troops were veterans, unlike those of Carpenter and Wills, who were mostly newly raised and so deemed less useful in battle.

There was even the suggestion that Argyll had been deliberately kept short of troops in order to engineer his downfall at the hands of his political enemies, as suggested by Lady Cowper:

> Lord Townshend, Baron Bernstorff, Mr Walpole and Lord Sunderland, were all afraid of the Duke of Argyle, whose favour with the Prince [of Wales] made them fear that one day he would get the better of them; so to lessen his Reputation, he had been sent to Scotland with very few Troops, and even those that were to go with him, by the secret Orders of the Duke of Marlborough, were so long a coming, that the Earl of Mar had Time to strengthen himself. This made the Duke of Argyle fly out prodigiously. He complained loudly of the Ministry.[98]

Some of this suspicion can be traced back to the War of Spanish Succession, when the two had been at loggerheads, Argyll complaining that he had been deliberately put in danger by his commander. Argyll was also used to leading more troops. At Oudernade in 1708, he led twenty battalions of infantry; seven years later in Scotland he commanded less than half this number.[99] Yet it was not only Argyll who thought the troops insufficient in number. Dudley Ryder, a supporter of the government, wrote on 22 September, shortly after Argyll's arrival at Stirling, that he 'has not men enough yet to make a stand against the rebels ... they have but few men there yet'.[100]

Additional forces could only be spared for the Scottish theatre after the English Jacobite threat had been dealt with at Preston, but even then, this was minimal. Two regiments of dragoons were sent to join Argyll, arriving on 19 December.[101] By January 1716, Argyll had six regiments of dragoons, nine of infantry and eleven battalions of Dutch (about 9,000 men), along with twenty-four cannon and four mortars, a formidable force indeed, though it had taken several months to be assembled, and then only when strategic priorities altered.[102]

Foreign invasion was not feared in 1715, but was in 1719 and 1745. Troops were stationed near the coast on both occasions. In March 1719, seven squadrons of horse, eight of dragoons and four battalions of infantry, about 3,000 men, were sent westwards.[103] Four battalions from Ireland were sent to the West Country too.[104] Scattered throughout Devon, Wiltshire, Somerset, Gloucestershire and Herefordshire, were 8,000 men.[105] These were to repel an expected Spanish invasion, though one never occurred. In December 1745, eight infantry battalions and a cavalry regiment were distributed in various towns in Kent to counter a feared French onslaught; as in 1719 it never materialized, yet in both occasions the danger was real enough.[106]

The initial decisions of the campaigns were political. Newcastle wrote to Argyll on 1 August 1745, thus, 'send directions to Sir John Cope to assemble the troops in proper places; and order the dragoon horses to be taken up from grass. Sir John Cope is also to concert with the Lord Chief Justice and the Lord Chief Advocate what may be proper to be done for securing the publick peace, and Tranquillity, and Disappointing these Designs'.[107] Cope was nothing if not punctual in obeying orders, and two days later, told Tweeddale that he had ordered the horses and for the officers to return to their posts.[108]

These were militarily sensible first steps to take, in order to concentrate the limited troops at Cope's disposal. In July 1745, there were two regiments of dragoons, four battalions of infantry and five other companies from other infantry battalions. All were scattered throughout towns and cities in the Lowlands; it was rare in peacetime for whole units to be concentrated together.[109]

The army was given its first instructions in 1745 on 13 August, when orders were issued from the War Office, 'for all officers belonging to His Majesty's land forces in England and Scotland to repair to their respective posts'. Cope ordered all officers to their posts and summoned all pensioners to Edinburgh or to be struck off the list.[110]

This followed Newcastle receiving a report from the Duke of Argyll who had informed him earlier that day that Charles Stuart had arrived in Scotland and was raising men. He told Richmond that 'Proper Directions are sent down to Scotland: Sir John Cope will march immediately, with such force as He can get together, to the Place, where they shall have their Rendezvous'.[111]

The next steps proved more controversial. They were the same as occurred, and with success, in 1719, but differed radically to the defensive strategy of 1715. Tweeddale told William Harrington, another Secretary of State, on 13 August what this was to be: 'I am persuaded a little rigour shown in the beginning will very soon give a check to this insurrection'.[112]

Tweeddale was supported in this view by the Lord Justices who governed the country while the King was abroad, who, on 16 August, gave orders for Cope to 'march forthwith'.[113] The reasoning behind such a view was thus: 'the most effectual way of putting a stop to a wavering people joining with the disaffected, so as to make a formidable Body, was, immediately to march and stop their progress'. They were to march to the chain of forts from Inverness to Fort William. Cope discussed this with the Lords Advocate and President and later declared, 'Agreeable to this Opinion, I made my disposition and did not lose a moment in putting it into execution'.[114] As said, not all agreed with such a strategy. Argyll wrote, on 19 August, 'Cope will march as he is ordered though I am not sure that such a march is practicable ... the advantage those Highlanders will have in the mountains inaccessible to regular troops may produce very bad effects'. However, he did think that the arrival of 1,500 regulars at Fort Augustus, 'will cast a great damp on the rebels, though even in that case he cannot pursue them through the mountains'.[115]

Decisions were often made by the calling of senior officers at critical junctures of the campaign. At Dalwhinnie on 27 August, Cope called the general officers together, 'desiring to have their opinion what was proper to be done'.[116]

On 20 September 1745 there was a cabinet meeting to decide on strategy, presumably on the assumption that Cope might not be successful against the Jacobite army, either in battle or that they might march southwards into England unmolested. Cope was given orders to pursue them into England if the latter transpired, and not to be restrained by his present commission which was restricted to Scotland. To assist him, Major General Oglethorpe was to disembark the Dutch units which had been sent immediately northwards at Burlington Bay, and these were to link up with Cope. Newcastle upon Tyne was seen as a key city to hold, as it was in 1715. Therefore Major General Huske was sent there to take charge, and two of the four Dutch battalions recently arrived at Gravesend were to be shipped there.[117]

In the meantime, on 19 September, the government decided to concentrate its troops in Lancashire, a county known for the strength of potential Jacobite support, due to the numbers of Catholics and Nonjurors, and perhaps because that county had, in 1715, supplied the highest number of Jacobite recruits. Furthermore, this could be a potential destination for any invading Jacobite army. The three regiments of Dutch troops whose arrival was imminent were to be sent there, as were five companies of Blakeney's Foot, a regiment of dragoons and one of horse. General Wentworth was appointed to command them.[118] Events overtook this decision and the troops were soon moved elsewhere.

Strategy had to evolve rapidly on the news of Cope's catastrophic defeat at Prestonpans. On 24 September, Wade was given the premier role in combating the Jacobites. He was given the command of the entire Dutch force, a battalion of regulars, two regiments of horse and one of dragoons, a rather more substantial force than that of Cope's. Meanwhile, a military committee of Wade, Field Marshals Ligonier and Stair and the Count of Nassau was formed 'to meet immediately and take into consideration what numbers of regular troops there now is in this kingdom, and what disposition may be proper to be made of them; and particularly, what part of them should be sent northwards, to suppress the rebels, and what troops should remain near London'.[119]

Additional forces were allocated to Wade's command; the ten companies of infantry at Newcastle and the two regiments of dragoons who had fled at Prestonpans.[120] Wade's force would be further reinforced by two battalions of infantry who had arrived from Ireland at Chester and two battalions recently arrived in London to be marched northwards. Later that day, eight battalions and three dragoon regiments there were earmarked for Wade's command, some of whom had just arrived from the Continent.[121]

That part of Wade's force, which was to travel by land, was to initially rendezvous at Doncaster, to await developments and initially it was envisaged that the army might move north-west to Lancashire or northwards to Scotland.[122] The seaborne arrivals were eight battalions of regulars and three squadrons of dragoons from Flanders.[123] Wentworth was sent to Doncaster a few days in advance to prepare ground for the troops' encampment and to locate sources of forage for the horses. By 4 October he had accomplished this. Wade departed from London and was in Hertfordshire by 6 October, hoping to arrive in Doncaster soon. The final destination of the army was still uncertain: 'as occasion shall offer'.[124] Given that the Jacobite army did not immediately march towards Lancashire, the decision was taken to march to Scotland via Newcastle because that was where units were being shipped to. As matters transpired, the march to Scotland halted at Morpeth on 3 November because of uncertainties over Jacobite marching intentions.[125]

Defence of northern strong points was another priority for the government in the autumn of 1745. On 24 September, Huske was appointed as commander at Newcastle, 'a place of such great importance'. He was to command the ten companies of Fraser's Foot there, as well as the Dutch battalion, and provisionally the two regiments of dragoons from Berwick, though these were countermanded. He was to train the local militia and to try and augment the numbers in the ten companies under his command. Other troop dispositions in the north-east included moving the Dutch forces from Berwick to Newcastle, although allowing the dragoon regiments to be retained at the former.[126]

The second army to be formed was largely composed of the troops who arrived in England in October and November 1745. It took some weeks to assemble, partly due to initial shortages of arms, as units were ordered to the Midlands on a piecemeal basis during these weeks from 28 September to 26 November. It was not until 28 November that they were commanded by Cumberland.[127]

As we have seen, the defence of the capital was seen as important in 1715, with a military camp being formed in Hyde Park. A committee of politician and generals which had been formed decided that 'The Rest of the Troops to remain about London' and this consisted of sixteen battalions of infantry, two regiments of dragoons and three troops of horse.[128]

This was a substantial force, given that Britain's total military strength at home at this time was twenty-nine battalions of infantry (including the eight Dutch, seven of guards, three of independent companies) and sixteen squadrons of cavalry (three regiments of dragoons, two of horse, two of horse guards and one of horse grenadiers).[129]

London was under threat from the Jacobite army marching southwards in early December 1745. Richmond made a suggestion to counter this: 'I do advise a Camp to be formed immediately upon Barnet or Finchley Common or some where thereabouts, & immediately else you will be too late.'[130] Yet such had already been decided on, for on 1 December, Newcastle had written, 'We shall assemble our Army about London, in expectation of them', and this consisted of ten battalions of infantry and three units of cavalry.[131]

Although the Jacobite army retreated from Derby on 6 December, there were plans for Wade and Cumberland to bring them to battle in northern England. They were unable to do so, and a new danger appeared. A French invasion was threatened in December 1745 and thus a campaign on two fronts was feared. Newcastle wrote to Richmond thus on 12 December: 'We are under the greatest Alarms of an immediate invasion from France.' There were even reports of a landing in Sussex. Newcastle told Richmond, 'For God's sake, hasten to us, for if they should come before Legonier with his Foot, we shall not have 6000 men to oppose them ... London is the great Object and must be prefer'd to all other considerations.' There was even talk of the whole of the forces under Cumberland being sent southwards. Almost all of the infantry were sent southwards.[132]

Cumberland did not send his five regiments of cavalry southwards as they were in pursuit of the retreating Jacobites, but, as Richmond stated, 'if the invasion really takes place our Cavalry even now will be too late to help you'.[133] This concern had potentially decisive effects on the campaign, for Cumberland halted his men for three days at Preston and thus was unable to bring the Jacobites to battle in the north of England. Richmond wrote: 'Never was an army so disappointed as this by so positive an order to retire, had the Duke had butt a discretionall pour, he had destroyed these rebells to morrow.' In the meantime, Wade had been unable to march his army across Yorkshire and into Lancashire to block the Jacobite retreat so only sent his cavalry in pursuit while the infantry marched back to Newcastle.[134]

However, the French invasion did not occur, but even so, the bulk of Cumberland's army remained in the south. The task of defeating the rebellion was left to Wade's army, which was commanded by Hawley in December 1745–January 1746, then by Cumberland. Reinforced by an additional three battalions of infantry and one of dragoons, it was this force which concluded the campaign in April 1746, marching from Edinburgh to Stirling, then Perth and then Aberdeen, to wait for better weather and a fordable river Spey before the final advance to Inverness.

Military and Civil Relations

The army depended on the civil state for much that was essential, including intelligence, accommodation and transport. However, relations between the two were often tense. This can be traced back to the Commonwealth of the 1650s and James II's rule of 1685–8, for on both occasions the army had been paramount as a major adjunct of the state in peacetime. As well as political considerations about liberty, there were also financial concerns about the upkeep of the soldiery, especially when the latter were at home. Tension usually arose when troops were quartered in towns, there being very few barracks. They tended to be billeted on public houses, and the longer the stay, the less accepted they generally became.

An example of such hostility occurred in Oxford in 1716, when the city was garrisoned by a regiment, as they had been since the previous year. The mayor wrote that he intended to 'use my utmost endeavour to assert the power of the Civill Magistrate in opposition to the illegal proceedings of the Soldiers here'.[135] After three companies of Clayton's Foot had been stationed in Leeds for three months in 1712, John Lucas, a schoolmaster, noted, 'For though the officers had

the character of very civil men, yet the generality of the soldiers were the profan-
est, debauchedest, wickedest men that I ever saw'.[136]

Yet soldiers were not always unpopular with civilians, especially in times of
emergency. Richard Kay, a Lancaster doctor, and his family were eager to see
the army march on their pursuit of the Jacobites in December 1745. This was
not just out of idle curiosity (he also went to see the Jacobite army, too), for he
wrote, on seeing the regulars, 'Lord, let our Forces go forth conquering and to
conquer'. On the next day, he wrote, 'It gives Abundance of Joy to good People
to all true Protestants to see such a number of Fine Forces; and question not
but of hearing of them hath given Abundance of Terror to the proudest of our
Enemies'.[137] Likewise, the soldiers at Hyde Park in 1715 drew the crowds, who
watched the men go through their drill. Dudley Ryder wrote admiringly, 'I was
mightily pleased to see how such a body of men moved with an exact regularity:
it looked like a huge machine in motion'.[138]

Intelligence

Commanders were reminded of the need to know where the enemy were and of
their plans. Newcastle reiterated to Wade the importance of such, writing to him
on 2 November, 'you will get the best intelligence possible of their motions'.[139]
He also urged him 'to spare no expense, for getting the most exact and constant
intelligence of the motions as well as the numbers of the Rebels'.[140] Other commanders were asked for, 'accounts from you of what passes where you are'.[141] The
army depended on numerous sources for information about the enemy and their
movements.

Sometimes generals sent men out directly. Carpenter wrote, 'I have constant
spyes out'.[142] Wills also had spies. One told him about the Jacobite activity in
Preston prior to his attacking them there.[143] Cope sent out men to monitor the
Jacobites around Edinburgh in late September. On 24 September, he wrote, 'I
have people out to Coldstream, Dunse, Kelso, Dunbar and Haddinton to bring
me intelligence, most of who, I expect here two or three hours hence'.[144] Four
days later he sent another civilian northwards.[145]

There were also semi-regular agents. A particular government spy was one
Weir. He had been employed by the army in the previous year and then was used
in 1745, too, although was not in disguise. Apparently he had been at Edinburgh
when the Jacobites had been there. When they had marched southwards, he had
kept one step ahead of them 'to give intelligence of all his [Charles's] motions'.[146]

Other sources were mostly irregular and initiated by the intelligence pro-
vider, presumably motivated by ideology or hope of reward. One such, on 24
August 1745, was described thus:

A person arrived at Edinburgh this day from the Highlands, hath made affidavit before a magistrate, that he was five days in the camp of the rebels, near Fort William, that he could not form a certain judgement of their numbers, but that their encampment took up about a mile square, and consisted of two divisions, one French; the other Highlanders; that there were many persons of figure and distinction among them, including the son of the pretender, to whom they all shewed the highest respect; they had plenty of money, provisions and warlike stores.[147]

Friendly magnates could help. Lord Glenorchy informed Colonel Yorke, a staff officer, in April 1746 that he had 'his people ... out for intelligence'. One man had information about hostility between different Jacobite clans.[148] The Whig mayor of Dumfries collected information about Jacobite activity in Scotland and sent it to various postmasters in northern England.[149] Dr Waugh of Carlisle, a clergyman, was also a justice of the peace. At a meeting of JPs of Cumberland and the Lowlands in August 1745 turnpike roads were discussed, but also that they would exchange information about Jacobite activity if the need arose.[150] From 14 September to November, a number of Scottish informants, chiefly the aforesaid mayor of Dumfries, sent information to Waugh. He then relayed it to Newcastle, who could then disseminate it to the army. This information included numbers of men in the Jacobite army, their intentions, an account of the battle of Prestonpans, the state of Edinburgh and information about contributions levied by the Jacobites on Glasgow.[151] Waugh wrote on 9 November, 'I have been up most of the night settling the Dispatches'.[152] Lords Lieutenant, such as the Earl of Cholmondeley, sent information to London. In his case, he told of Jacobite activity, forwarded to him from customs officers in Wales, Lancashire and Cheshire.[153] Similar information was sent by other local officials.[154]

Postmasters were often called on for information. John Norris wrote on 31 March 1719, 'To all postmasters and collectors on the western coast of England, were directed, upon on any certain news or sight of the enemy, to fire embarkations and send me the accounts, it might be very much for His Majesty's service'.[155]

Walter Grossett, Collector at Leith, was another example of an official who passed intelligence to his masters in London and was amply rewarded for his trouble and dangers. The Lord Justice Clerk and various generals commanded his services throughout 1745–6, as Fawkener stated, 'That he was almost constantly employed in ... getting intelligence thereof to the generals officers both before and after the Battle of Prestonpans'.[156]

Then there were more irregular sources. Dr Henry Bracken of Lancaster sent information to Wade in November 1745 of Jacobite troop numbers passing through the town. He also sent a cache of captured Jacobite letters to London.[157] Another civilian source used in order to procure news of the Jacobite forces was William Cotesworth. In 1715, Henry Liddell, a London coal merchant with interests on Tyneside, and loyal to the government, called on fellow merchant, Cotesworth, of Gateshead. Liddell had been approached by a senior minister, possibly the Lord Chancellor:

> Could [he] recommend any notable person in your parts who could be trusted and on whose intelligence one could depend ... I knew none so capable in every respect as yourself. Can you have any intelligence from Scotland?[158]

Cotesworth sent information about the Jacobite rebellion in Northumberland, of movements, numbers and personnel, and he also gathered information from others in the north of England and south of Scotland, as he wrote, 'We are a club of us who have sent messengers throughout these counties to enquire of our friends what appearance the enimie makes'.[159] Townshend wrote directly to Cotesworth declaring that he was 'much obliged to you for the information you were pleased to send me relating to the Rising in your parts'.[160]

Troops could be used to garner intelligence, especially cavalry. Wade posted the men of Hamilton's and Ligonier's dragoons at Wooller and Whittington among other places, 'to observe their motions'.[161] Cope gave 'Directions to the officers quartered in those places [in garrisons or forts] to procure intelligence of all that was passing in these parts, and transmit the same to me'.[162] Another instance of troops providing intelligence was in April 1746, just as Cumberland was approaching the River Spey. Two officers were sent ahead of the army to locate the fords in order to discover the best places to cross. One man was disguised as a Highlander and wore the Jacobite white cockade. He rode up to hovels and asked the inhabitants where the crossing places were. He returned unsuspected. The other officer spread rumours of pontoon bridges being about to be used across boggy ground, thus distracting Jacobite forces.[163]

However intelligence was not always easily procured. Yorke wrote on 13 February 1746:

> The melancholy part of all the story is that there is no trusting to any people in this whole country to give intelligence; for they all abuse each other to indifferent people, but hold together in the national part of being Jacobites, or at least luke warm. The Presbyterian ministers are the only people we can trust.[164]

His commanding officer agreed, writing, 'I am now in a country so much our enemy that there is hardly any intelligence to be got'.[165]

Without intelligence about the whereabouts of the enemy, armies sometimes were inactive. Wade was uncertain about where the Jacobite columns were destined for; whether Carlisle or towards him at Newcastle. By 7 November, he learnt that the Jacobite army was destined for Carlisle. But it was not felt that it could be certain what the Jacobite intentions were. Later, when the Jacobite army was in England, on 12 November, he received news from the postmaster of

Penrith. He told Wade that the Jacobites had passed Carlisle and were marching for Appleby, further south.[166]

This was incorrect; the Jacobite army was besieging Carlisle. Intelligence could not always be relied on, as Cope wrote on 28 September, 'I don't pretend to answer for the intelligence I send you'.[167] Cumberland also misread intelligence reports on 2 December. Hearing that the Jacobites were advancing on Newcastle-under-Lyme, he concentrated his forces on Stone. However this was a feint as the Jacobite force marched to Derby, leaving London vulnerable. It was only two days later that Cumberland learnt the truth, though he was confident that the Jacobites could be intercepted.[168]

Earlier, Argyll had written, 'I have this morning intelligence that the clans are making towards Argyllshire and that the main body of the rebels at Perth design to move towards the Forth, but I am not yet certain of either'.[169] Information sources such as these dried up as Jacobite forces moved through northern England. Waugh wrote, 'Nothing that can be depended upon with the least degree of certainty has come to my knowledge since ... yesterday'. This was because informants had fled.[170] Nor was news always of use, as Argyll once wrote 'I heard of their march yesterday morning ... [it] was too late, for us to intercept them'.[171]

Supply

Money was and is a key ingredient for military success. Without it an army cannot exist, for it must be paid and fed. Armies operating without their own jurisdiction, could requisition cash or supplies, but such could not be levied legally in domestic territory. Britain was known for its financial muscle from the War of the League of Augsburg, during which the 'Financial Revolution' had occurred which led to far more efficient measures of borrowing and taxation, leading to greater yields. This did not guarantee smooth financing of Britain's armies, however.

The government could either provide credit facilities or provide specie, in other words, hard cash. The Treasury Commissioners were deputed to these tasks. On 1 September 1715, £10,000 of credit was lodged at Edinburgh for Argyll's use.[172] Local credit facilities were, however, lacking. By 1 October, Argyll reported that the Bank of Scotland was closed and that specie was needed immediately 'and that will admit of no delay'.[173] Yet economy was also urged, with reference in January 1716 'to prevent the great and unnecessary charge of sending more money to Edinburgh than the service there absolutely required'.[174] Alternatively, a certain lump sum could be entrusted with the commander. On 2 October 1745, Sir William Yonge, Secretary at War, told Wade that he would be given £12,000 for immediate expenses and that he 'will omit Nothing that may contribute to the Good of His Majesty's service'. On the other hand, great care was recommended, 'you will manage the above sum with ... the utmost Economy and Frugality'.[175] Yonge also asked him to be 'acting in the utmost regard for economy for the publick'.[176]

It appears that this sum was insufficient for a force of just over 13,000 men. Wade told Newcastle that a sum of at least £20,000 would be needed, adding 'unless you send a military chest in specie, it will render us liable to a thousand inconveniencys and be a great impediment to the service ... dangerous consequences may ensure if this is neglected'.[177] This would be insufficient, for the costs up to 25 November amounted to £22,145 14s and total costs by the end of the year were £41,207 10d.[178] Some of this money was taken from local receivers of taxes.[179]

Wade's subordinates were not convinced that there was sufficient cash, as Wentworth wrote, 'the want of money for supplying the troops may be attended by the worse consequences'.[180] Treasury parsimony was not entirely to blame, and was partly due to local inflation caused by inclement weather and high demand, as Wade's secretary noted, 'in a winter campaign the soldiers' pay will not suffice to his wants, things here being not so cheap as one would imagine'. Basic commodities, such as beer, beef and bread were selling at inflated prices, with two pence for a pint of beer and two pence per pound of meat. Bad bread was dearer than good bread in London.[181]

It seems that each general had to renegotiate with the Secretaries of State shortly after appointment. Hawley complained on 15 January, 'I have not as yet received the money your Grace mentions, but I hope the paymaster will arrive with it in 10 days'.[182] Wade pointed out at the outset of his involvement in the campaign that

> all necessaries should be taken in time, to prevent the inconveniencys that may arise from the want of provisions for the forces under my command ... a quantity of biscuit and cheese sufficient to subsist 10,000 men for 3 weeks or one month, to be sent to Berwick.[183]

Supply difficulties could delay marches. Shortly after Cumberland arrived in Perth on 10 February 1746, he wrote, 'As soon as we can lay up our magazines of bread, we shall march northwards'.[184] Four days later, he reported the grim tale:

> I am sorry and almost ashamed that I am still forced to date my letters from this place [Perth]. But greater difficulties than we have, it is hardly possible to encounter. No contracts or any sort of agreement for bread; but all turns on one Gomes Serra ... a man no way if an equal capacity for such an undertaking, tho' I hope honest, for I am obliged to furnish him money.[185]

All this obliged Cumberland to return to Edinburgh to settle the issues of money and bread. He met with Sawyer, the Deputy Paymaster. Cumberland informed Newcastle thus:

> it appears that we are fully provided for this month. But, if some stop is not put to the northern country receivers in their practice of remitting their money to London by private hands, which they do because they get half per cent by it, we may be under the same difficultys we have so lately got through. But at worst I have had the satisfaction to find that the Lord Justice Clerk would have been able to procure £20,000 in specie which he locked up in the Bank. I have also had with his assistance got a sufficient quantity of flour here and to go along with us, for to make 15 days bread and have embarked from Montrose and Aberdeen 20 days more.[186]

Cumberland had, by 19 February, more money than his predecessors and more on its way. There was a military chest at Edinburgh of £12,500, £12,000 just arrived from Newcastle, £2,000 at Perth and was due £20,000 from London on 26 February. Furthermore, Pelham assured him of another £30,000 from London.[187] Sawyer promised Fawkener on 12 April that he would 'punctually honour' bills drawn on him and that a sloop would bring another £20,000 for Cumberland.[188]

Even when supplies were gathered together, delays in marching persisted. On 3 March, Cumberland reported, 'I persuade myself the King will not think me dilatory in not marching forward faster than we do, but as I am forced to carry magazines of all sorts of provisions with me, it encumbers and retards us, so that we can move forward but very slowly'.[189]

Perhaps one of the most important considerations for any commander is how to feed his men while on the march or in camp. The Highlands of Scotland were barren and sparsely populated so supplies would have to be gathered together before any march could be contemplated. It was a commander's duty to appoint men to supervise these tasks. Cope had Major Caulfield his quartermaster general; Major Morrison his ADC and Paymaster, and Major Griffiths his Commissary of stores and Provisions.[190] Wade confirmed this later in the year, writing, as the army was about to cross the Forth, 'The difficulties in this case, will be how to provide this army with bread and forage, these being the greatest scarcity of both in that part of Scotland'.[191]

This meant that most armies had to have supply trains carrying food with them. This entailed halts of every four days so field ovens could be established so bread could then be baked. Bread contractors were employed. These were often Jewish. Then there were smaller dealers, sutlers, supplying meat and drink.[192]

One of Cope's officers noted:

> As the country we were to march through could not afford subsistence for the troops, it was absolutely necessary to carry a stock of bread along with us; this the general

caused to be provided at Leith, Stirling and Perth. As soon as it was got ready, we set out for Stirling, where the men were assembled. It was as well for us that we had a suttler well provided, and a butcher with a drove of black cattle (which he killed for us from time to time) along with us, without this precaution we had starved upon the march.[193]

Even when this was accomplished, not all the army could be supplied. Glenorchy wrote, 'he was forced to leave the dragoons behind for want of forage on the road'.[194]

Yet supplies could not be assembled instantly. Cope reported that it was ten days before sufficient bread could be baked before his little army could march from Stirling. He also declared, 'The ovens at Keith, Stirling and Perth were kept at work, Day and Night, Sunday not excepted, to provide Biscuit, which was no other way to be got'.[195] The Leith bakers produced 10,000 weight of biscuits by 12 August.[196]

Hawley had to negotiate for bread supplies. He made an agreement in January with Messrs Thomas and Lawrence Dundas of Edinburgh for a million rations of forage, costing a halfpenny per ration, and had to advance £1,000. Yet this was a verbal contract only; Hawley had no authorization to sign a contract unless he had the power to do so from the king or the lords of the Treasury.[197]

Supply often dictated strategy. When Cope was at Dalwhinnie, it was stated that there were only two day's supply of bread left, so it was imperative that the army move. The supply state was due to the lack of horses to pull the carts and so much of it had had to be left behind on the march.[198] The lack of supplies brought a march to a halt in November 1745 when Wade marched from Newcastle to Hexham en route to try and relieve Carlisle. Lieutenant Robinson wrote, 'the men … wanted both straw, firing, forage and meat'. The reason, he believed, was 'either through the bad conduct of the commissary or the impossibility of his executing his contract in this very terrible season [there had been hard frost and deep snowfalls]'.[199] Cumberland's march in the Highlands in February 1746 was also held up for similar reasons, as Yorke wrote, 'The want of several necessaries has obliged us to stop here [Perth] ever since, but I hope we will be able to move forward'.[200] It certainly reduced marching speed. In the Highlands, Cumberland noted, 'I am forced to carry magazines of all sorts of provisions which encumbers and retards us'.[201]

The War Office was also meant to provide supplies of equipment. When supplies were not forthcoming, complaints were in evidence. On 31 October 1745, Wade implored that they be sent to his forces as soon as possible, for

the tents of the Flanders regiments which came from Williamstadt, are not yet arrived from London, and the poor soldiers, from long marches and bad roads, are many of them bare footed, though we have taken all possible pains to provide them with what the country can afford.[202]

The difficulty persisted in March 1746, retarding marching so that the army was only, a month later, in or near Aberdeen. Yorke wrote:

> It has been a great misfortune to the King's affairs in this country that we have not been able to move with more rapidity after the Rebels, because it would most likely have put an end to the affair before now: but the poverty of the country, which made it absolutely necessary to provide every kind of subsistence for the army before we could move from place to place, has delayed the putting an end to the Rebellion at the critical minute ... and still continues to retard our further progress.[203]

A volunteer in the army noted instances when supplies were limited. One occurred at Stone in early December 1745. He wrote, 'victuals and lodgings were here extreamly scarce: we were glad of a little straw, strewed on the floor ... and bread was so scarce, that it was rare to get a loaf; and Beer, in its turn, was as difficult to procure'.[204] Matters were no better at Berwick later that month, 'We found it extream cold and dirty, and could get no victuals nor Drink for a long time, and then with much difficulty, which I impute to the town's being so full of forces'.[205] Finally, in Scotland on 1 February, 'it was a hard frost ... we could get neither victuals nor drink for our money, the rebels having consumed all the provisions'.[206]

By the end of the campaign, supply questions had been settled to the men's satisfaction, as trooper Enoch Bradshaw of Cobham's dragoons wrote, 'for we had certainly all been lost for want of food, had it not been for his [Cumberland's] care to bring ovens and bakers with him ... had it not been for our Dear Billy we had all been starved only for ye good loaves he ordered for ye army and some provisions that came by shipping ... I am well and we have bread and brandy in plenty'.[207]

Commanders applied for supplies throughout the campaign. Wade wrote that the commissary had purchased 'all the meal and flower that can be purchased'.[208] As in the War of Spanish Succession, the commissary was in the hands of a small number of Jewish merchants. In 1746 Gomez Serra was the commissary general. He was tasked to buy up all the bread and forage he could. Yet doubts were expressed as to the ease of this, 'which, I believe, will be scarcely sufficient to satisfy so many mouths'. As to forage, 'it will be impossible to find it anywhere', unless it could be transported from England by sea 'but it could not be done but at a vast expense'.[209]

It was not only food which could be lacking. Wade wrote that his troops 'are in immediate want of shoes and stockings'.[210] Ligonier reported on 15 December 1745 that his men were in 'extreme want of shoes' and there were shortages of straw and fuel.[211] In October, the War Office acknowledged that equipment had to be sent to Wade's army, as the Secretary at War acknowledged, 'I am very sensible that the regiments which came from Flanders must be in want of tents and

camp necessaries'. They agreed to deliver 990 tents, 960 kettles and 680 tin kettles. Furthermore, 2,500 pairs of shoes and 2,000 pairs of stockings were ordered
to be delivered to them.[212] Ligonier was told to make contracts with those who
could supply shoes and stockings and was advised to check for fraud and quality.[213]

The newly raised forces were also in dire need of uniforms, arms and other
equipment. Gower's regiment was ready to march on 10 November 'as soon as
we have arms and clothing part of which are come and the rest on the road'. They
had still not marched until 16 November.[214] When they did march, on the following day, it was stated, 'their clothes and arms are to follow them'.[215] Similarly,
it was not until 19 November that 'The Duke of Bedford ... has but just got his
arms and clothing'.[216]

Arms and ammunition were also needed. This was especially the case concerning the artillery. At first, for Argyll in 1715, this was not a major worry; his
major concerns were the size of his forces and the money needed to keep them
supplied. However, after the battle of Sherriffmuir and the gradual shift of the
balance of forces from Mar to Argyll, the campaign could now move onto the
offensive, as Argyll was increasingly urged to do. Since the dwindling Jacobite
army was entrenched at Perth behind fortifications, this meant that artillery was
now urgently required. According to Cadogan, 'we only want artillery to put it
into execution'.[217] Argyll requested it, but none had arrived by late December.[218]

The artillery had been ordered from the Tower, but bad weather kept the
ships in the Thames. Instead, on Cadogan's initiative and Marlborough's intervention, guns from Berwick and Edinburgh were sent for, and Brigadier Petit
was sent on 3 January to organize the guns from the latter. It was a formidable
sounding array, of 'twelve battering guns', of eighteen, twelve and nine pounder
cannons, plus six smaller guns of three and six pounders. Horses to transport
these and other supplies were called for by Cadogan on 8 January.[219] However,
it is uncertain how well manned the guns were, with Argyll claiming there were
only sailors, who were not 'versant in leading the artillery'.[220]

Once Wade's command was beginning to be assembled, orders for his artillery train were also underway. Instructions to the Board of Ordnance were first
issued on 25 September for 'a sufficient train of artillery to be got ready with the
utmost expedition'. Eleven days later the train's components were specified; six
six pounders, twenty-four three pounders, howitzer and coehorns for 'immediate service'. The Board was also told to 'appoint officers, artificers, ministers and
others to attend the same'.[221]

On 9 November, Ligonier's train was ordered to be formed. It was to be
composed of two six pounders, fourteen three pounders, two howitzers, eight
pontoons, and fifty balls per gun.[222] It was not only guns which were needed for

the artillery, but also crews to man the guns. Hawley wrote on what was almost the eve of battle, 7 January 1746:

> As to artillery, there is not a gun here can move for want of gunners, the same at Berwick there is but one; the rest are voters, never intended for any other use. And as Major Belford is left by His Royal Highness at Carlisle, the team from Newcastle, nor any one gun, can march without him. There is only a boy of 18 with those here and nobody at all with those at Berwick and for want of horses, part of those at Newcastle are to be left there.

Four days later he wrote 'relating to his great want of gunners and other officers of the artillery'.[223] Even when gunners were available, they could become ill, as did Captain Michelson in March 1746, so Cumberland asked the Board for Major Belford and Captain Desaguliers to be sent.[224]

Assistance was often given by the county authorities. When Wade's army marched back to Newcastle, 'the Marshal sent General Huske to the magistrates to desire, if possible, they could find cover for his men and which was very happily effected'.[225] Accommodation was also provided at Macclesfield 'with great chearfulness and readiness'.[226]

There was voluntary assistance by the London Quakers to the army of waistcoats to keep the men warm in winter, which is often quoted as being a helpful measure. Yet a volunteer remarked that they 'did more harm than good'. This was because the men wore them at all times, so became overheated, and then removed them. This led them to being cold and feverish.[227]

Cumberland's army was provisioned by a number of civil authorities on their march to Scotland in December 1745. Liverpool's mayor asked if provisions and transport would be usefully supplied by them, 'for the more speedy march of the Army'. They sent eleven carts laden with biscuits on 12 December. They were thanked for their 'very considerable zeal on this occasion'.[228] At Lancaster, the army was given seventy-seven bags of bread.[229] Farmers dug up barrels of beer previously hidden from the Jacobites and treated the soldiers.[230] Friendly landowners and others who lived near the route of march could also provide food and drink for the passing soldiers. Private Taylor recorded that at Cullen in April 1746, Lord Findlater gave each company a guinea. A few days later, Lord Bracco gave the army 300 guineas to spend on drink.[231]

All this could take time and so delay the march. Cope had to wait a full day at Crieff for 100 horseloads of bread which had not been ready when they had left Stirling. According to him, 'I was in hopes to have been able to begin our march from Stirling some days sooner than I did, but the Delays I met with in thus Article, made it impossible'.[232]

Arms and ammunition was also needed. These were the responsibility of the Board of Ordnance, under the control of the Master of the Ordnance. Artillery was most difficult to supply. Hardwicke wrote of his concern to Newcastle on 25 September: 'I don't remember that anything has yet been said relating to a field train of artillery for this body of men which is to match northwards. The preparations for that will take up some time and a number of horses must be provided'.[233] Even when it was provided, difficulties did not cease. Richmond also commented on the difficulty of transporting the artillery, writing 'the carryages of the artillery are so disabled in these cursed roads that I am very much afray'd wee shall have butt little or rather no help at all from it'.[234]

Men often arrived with inadequate equipment. Argyll complained in 1715:

> the cloathing the very worst I ever saw, tho' not old. The accoutrements both of men and horse unfit for service ... have been worn these six years. The arms very bad, and the numbers incompleat ... not above 24 men a troop the strongest corps included.[235]

The scarcity of provisions could lead to the arrival of additional troops being seen as more of a hindrance than a valuable additional asset. This was certainly the case in February 1746 when there was the imminent arrival of a contingent of just over 5,000 Hessian troops. On 2 February, Cumberland wrote, 'I don't know what use the Hessians will be here, for if I had them, it would rather increase than lessen difficulties, for cover and provisions are so scarce'.[236] However, Newcastle, doubtless mindful of the financial cost of these forces, wrote, 'give a very particular attention to the providing the Hessian troops with all manner of Necessaries'.[237]

Transporting supplies was to be carried out with the cooperation of the county magistrates. As the military committee in London decreed on 26 September 1745, the Lieutenancy were:

> to assist the march of Marshal Wade's army: and as a large number of carriages may be wanted for the more expeditious march of these troops, that they be directed to provide a sufficient number for that purpose; and also to facilitate the quarters and accommodation of the said army.[238]

High Constables were required to provide horses or oxen, and carts or wagons, in order to move army baggage. Advertisements in Northumberland in the county press called for those wishing to supply transport to apply in writing to the justices of the peace, via an inn in Newcastle. This became the venue for meetings between JPs and potential contractors in order to come to terms.[239] Those providing carts with four horses were to be paid 12d per mile; those with carts with three horses, 9d per mile. These expenses would be repaid by the county's clerk of the peace.[240] Although this was meant to be voluntary, there may have been an element of compulsion, with petty constables being asked to list those who had refused to send carts and horses.[241]

There was disagreement over the effectiveness of this system. On the whole there were complaints when matters went amiss, but nothing complimentary if the reverse were the case. Wade found it difficult to obtain supply wagons: 'We can neither purchase nor hire except at very exorbitant rates, if we can find them at all.'[242] On another occasion, he wrote, 'if the country don't disappoint us of our carriages which they have often done'.[243] Robinson found that this was not always effectual. He wrote, 'Our train has suffered extremely this last march; near half our carriages are out of order and our horses are all knocked up.'[244]

Cope's Highland march was beset by a number of difficulties with his transport. Many of the horses were stolen in the night-time, despite being guarded, or their drivers deserted with them. Horses needed to graze at nights in the open country, making embezzlement and loss easy. On one occasion, 200 horses were lost. This resulted in many bread bags being left at Trinifair. The Duke of Atholl's steward promised to send them on once transport could be procured, but he never did so. Likewise at Dalnacarloch, the lack of horses resulted in 100 supply bags being left behind. The deputy sheriff agreed to have these sent onto the army, but few reached them.[245]

The county authorities seem to have taken more attention depending on the commander. Cumberland, as the King's third son, had a greater and more positive impact than a less exalted personage. Yorke wrote, 'The Duke's coming down has a very good effect in the Country and makes everything go on in a march more expeditious manner; and to do 'em justice here, they are very alert in doing their best to serve the government'.[246]

Supply could also reach the army by ship. Taylor wrote that in 1746, 'We had a Fleet of Boats and small vessels at the same time coming round with provisions under a Convoy of the Fox sloop of war'.[247] Yet supply by sea was not always effective, as Hawley complained on 15 January, the poor weather making it unpredictable.[248]

Commanders had to pay careful attention to transport, as did Cope. He declared, 'I contracted with proper persons for Horses to carry a small train of field pieces and four cohorns (the country horses being too small for that purpose) and with a butcher to carry some cattle along with the army, to kill upon the march'.[249]

Despite the state's overwhelming financial resources in relation to its enemies, this could not always easily be translated into the operation of an efficient supply and transport system for its armed forces. Rather, a process of constant negotiation with numerous individuals, which took up much of a commander's time, was necessitated. Unlike the Jacobite army, goods could not be requisitioned where found.

Accommodation

Given that there were very few barracks throughout Britain, troops were often quartered on the civilian population. This was especially important because much of these campaigns occurred in inclement weather, when troops would normally not campaign. Newcastle reminded Pulteney, who had forces in Hull, 'take care to have them quartered and dispersed so as to be useful and as little burdensome to the town as possible'.[250]

Billeting was not always popular with civilians. In 1690, Henry Prescott noted the situation in Chester, 'A column of Danish soldiers is assigned to our common people to be received with hospitality. This new and unaccustomed situation causes fright to those who live their lives in a quiet recess'.[251] Later that year, a similar demand was met with little enthusiasm and it was only with, 'great difficulty' that they were 'received in the billets'.[252] This could have been because they were foreign. A Newcastle resident observed fifty-five years later, 'the people of the place have so great an abhorrence of the Dutch that I do not believe any private person will be prevailed upon to receive any of them: an English battalion might be quartered there easily'.[253]

Yet there was often enthusiasm for billeting troops. Major General Bland wrote on 27 November 1745 on the situation in the Midlands, 'all the people of the country seem extremely zealous, and quarter our men in private houses, giving them victuals and drink Gratis'.[254] Oglethorpe wrote likewise from Newcastle, 'The zeal and loyalty of all the people is ... almost incredible ... the middling people [invite] the soldiers to their houses'.[255] A volunteer wrote appreciatively:

> When we came to our quarters, yet I have a great deal of pleasure, as well as fatigue in their journies, for we are received mighty kindly wherever we come, and the old women along the road sides with uplifted hands, constantly pity, pray for and bless us as we go by: when the public houses are too full, we are taken in by the gentlemen and tradesmen, who kindly entertain us with civilities that I was before unaccustomed to meet with in our campaigns in Flanders.[256]

At Chester, when troops were about to arrive: 'We are boiling of beef, and getting beds and other necessary refreshments ready for the poor men.'[257] In Scotland, Hawley reported similar assistance, even after Falkirk: 'The country did all they could to raise the spirits of the soldiers and keep them warm by furnishing them with great quantities of blankets and treating them with meat and drink.'[258]

However, in December of that year, it was a different story, as Wade wrote, they 'have absolutely refused to receive them in their private houses'. He claimed that this was because 'the zeal of this part of the country for the accommodation of the troops, increases or diminishes in proportion to their apprehension of danger from the approach of the Rebels'.[259]

Morale

This seemed to be generally good throughout. The anonymous officer of Cope's wrote, 'notwithstanding the very many difficulties we met with in it, and the many forced marches we made ... yet such was the heartiness of the troops for the service, that no body was heard to complain upon the whole march'.[260] Similar remarks were made by Yorke, two months later, and he provided a reason why,

> after all this [inadequate encampments] our men bear their fatigues with great mag-
> naminity and patience; nor have their spirits as yet fail'd 'em in the least, but they vow
> revenge to he cursed authors of it ... They have a just Contempt of the Enemy they
> are running after.[261]

Private Linn agreed, writing that there was 'a good will to be att them & no won-der, considering the fatigues we have undergone this winter by hunger & cold & marching, night & day, after them'.[262]

Yorke looked forward to combat with gusto: 'they will be, I flatter myself, hack'd to pieces on the spot'.[263] Richmond also looked forward to combat, writ-ing, that he hoped the Jacobites would attack: 'I wish they would, for then I am sure wee may do what wee please with them'.[264] Cumberland referred to forced marches from Aberdeen on 8 April, which included the men wading through the Spey at waist level, but added, 'they all went on with great chearfulness'.[265]

On occasions, Cumberland was aware that the men's morale needed improv-ing and took steps to deal with this. One was the terrifying attack of the Jacobites:

> his royal highness had taken great pains to undeceive his men, and convince them,
> that a regiment of English foot, with musket and bayonet, was much superior to a
> highland regiment, notwithstanding their pistols and targets – This had accordingly
> so good an effect, that the highlanders could not break 'em.[266]

The March

The Jacobite campaigns were conflicts of movement. Forces rarely marched together unless a battle was thought imminent, in order to ease transport, sup-ply and accommodation difficulties. For example, the ten battalions of infantry which marched from Newcastle to Edinburgh in January 1746 did so in three columns, with an interval of about a day between each.[267] Likewise, when the army was encamped, it would be divided. In March 1746, six battalions of foot and two of dragoons were at Strathbogie, three battalions and four guns were at Old Meldrum and six battalions of infantry, one of dragoons and the remainder of the guns were at Aberdeen, as was Cumberland.[268] It was only on 11 April, at Cullen, that the three commands came together. Four days later, they halted for a day at Nairn.[269]

Division of forces could make them vulnerable to be potentially destroyed piecemeal. Yorke outlined how Cumberland's men were dispersed in the Midlands in December 1745, 'I observed our leaders were a little uneasy least the rebels by their intelligence be enabled to beat up some of our quarters, at too great a distance, most of 'em, to support other'.[270]

Marching speeds were variable. Cavalry regiments took three days to march 100 miles in mid-December 1745.[271] However, this was unusually rapid. The march from Preston to Northampton took twelve days in the same period, with three days of halts.[272] Long marches were rarely welcomed. Robinson wrote, 'we have the prospect of a long and bad march before us'.[273]

Later he wrote, 'the only thing I grudge is the fatiguing the men to run after 'em'.[274] A volunteer wrote of 'our men though extreamly harassed, bear the fatigue of marching with great chearfulness'.[275] For those eager to see the campaign resolved, marching was deemed too slow. Richmond commented that many Londoners probably complained of the army not coming to grips with the Jacobites, and wrote that if the armies were only separated by Hounslow Heath, this would have been a reasonable point, 'butt it is not to be conceived what a cursed country this is for marching, & wee can move butt slowly'.[276]

Bad weather could also delay marches or inhibit them if they proceeded. This was especially so during these campaigns, most of which were conducted in late autumn and winter. Armies rarely campaigned in these periods, but retreated to quarters before commencing in Spring. Thus snow and swollen rivers held up the progress of the campaigns on several occasions. Argyll noted in November 1715, 'I see no other reasonable project at this time of year when it is not in the nature to keep any time in the fields'.[277] Worse was to come. In January 1716 it was necessary to march to Perth to attack the Jacobites there. Apart from difficulties caused by logistics, the weather made matters worse. There had been heavy snow. On 19 January, Argyll wrote, 'the weather here is extremely severe, the frost is great and there is deep snow upon the ground, so that the roads that are most frequented ... are pass'd with great difficulty'.[278]

Six days later, he took a party of 200 dragoons to reconnoitre and found 'a vast depth of snow, so much that we were obliged to march the whole way one horse after another, and for the most part up to the horses' bellies'.[279] Country people were ordered to work on the roads, but even so, 'we are seldom able to march two abreast'.[280] Although Argyll marched towards Perth on 30 January, all the heavy artillery had to remain at Stirling.[281]

Yorke complained in March 1746 that 'the snows have been so deep for some days past that it has rendered the ways very impracticable', although he hoped that this would not be a difficulty for much longer.[282] Weather and poor roads often meant that artillery and supply wagons had to be abandoned. Wade complained in November 1745:

We have been obliged to leave the three pounders and several artillery wagons at Newcastle, the roads in our last march to Hexham were so broken, the carriages were damaged and half the drivers deserted. I received His Majesty's order to the Lords Lieutenants ... for repairing the Roads through which we may pass, which I fear can have no effect from the bad condition they are in and the length of time it must take to put them in order.[283]

In order to avoid the roads, the seas could be used instead. Troops could also be transported by sea, as were supplies. Half of the Dutch troops sent in 1715 were shipped straight to Scotland.[284] The Hessian battalions arrived in February 1746 near Edinburgh. In March, Bligh's battalion arrived at Aberdeen from Leith.[285]

Yet travel by sea was not all plain sailing. As ever, even without hostile warships, there was still the weather to contend with and the effect it could have on both the speed of the voyage and the health of the men. According to Rae, 'a sudden storm arising and the winds being contrary, one of the vessels and 28 of the men were lost; and the rest were forced to put into Harwich, Yarmouth and some other harbours'. Many of the men were unused to sea travel and the case was put that they should march the remainder of the route. Artillery was planned to be shipped from the Tower to Scotland at this time, but was delayed by a frozen Thames.[286]

Le petit guerre

Apart from the clashes between formed bodies of troops, as discussed in the following chapter, small bodies of troops were often dispatched to make raids on the enemy. This was especially the case when the main body of troops was stationary for a period of time, as Argyll was at Stirling in 1715–16 and as was Cumberland at Aberdeen in March 1746. This occupied the troops and helped weaken and unnerve the enemy, if successful.

Troops under Argyll's command in the autumn of 1715 made at least two excursions against the Jacobites. One took place on 26 September when a party of Jacobites were proclaiming James as King. Dragoons, under the Earl of Rothes, 'prevented them, by entering the Town, sword in hand, and putting them to flight'.[287] Although this encounter may have been the result of chance, another, about a month later, was planned. News that a party of Jacobites would be quartered in Dumferling, Argyll sent Colonel Cathcart and a regiment of dragoons on 24 October to surprise them. His men came to the town at dawn, and captured seventeen prisoners, after killing and wounding several others. All this for the loss of one man injured and a horse missing.[288] Next month, thirty soldiers were sent by the governor of Berwick to retake Holy Island castle, which had been briefly held by the Jacobites, and retake it they did.[289]

Another instance was when Cumberland's main body was at Aberdeen in March 1746:

> The day after his royal highness came hither, he detach'd Lord Ancrum with 100 dragoons, and Major Morris with 300 foot under his command, to a castle at the head of the river Don, 40 miles from hence, call'd Corgarf, and situated in the heart of the rebellion, in order to get possession of a quantity of Spanish arms and powder which were lodged there: his lordship took them without resistance, the rebels having quitted the castle upon our approach: but as they had driven the horses out of the country, he was forced to destroy most of the arms, and 30 barrels of powder.[290]

Later that month, but less successfully, he sent Bland and Brigadier Mordaunt, with four battalions and four guns, to attack Roy Stuart's men at Strathbogie. However the Jacobites caught wind of his plans and abandoned the town before they could arrive and fell back across the River Spey, though the pursuit had to be called off.[291]

Attacks on Jacobite property were another exercise carried out by the troops in early 1746. Major La Fausille marched to Clova and Glen Esk, where Jacobites were disarmed. Furthermore, 'The seizing all the cattle, and demolishing some of the habitations of those in Lochaber, who were out in the rebellion, has had a very good effect, as of the rebels of that country have deserted to go to their own houses'.[292] Yorke was convinced that many weapons had been delivered and that the expeditions would 'frighten that part of the country into their obedience'.[293] However, Colonel Conway, who took part in Bland's raid on Strathbogie in March 1746, wrote 'I have been out on an expedition against the rebels as foolish as anything because it achieved nothing'. Indeed, the Jacobites, though surprised, escaped and darkness inhibited pursuit.[294]

Generalship

The most important single figure in an army is the general in charge. On his shoulders rest the success or failure of his command. Not all entrusted with such a responsibility were successful. Senior officers were censured and praised by their peers and subordinates.

Although the Captain General in 1715 was the newly reinstated Marlborough, there is very little evidence for his activity at this time. Certainly none of the generals in field – Argyll, Cadogan, Wills and Carpenter – had overall responsibility for the conduct of overall military operations either. It was different thirty years later, although only in November 1745. The man given the overall military command of the campaign was the King's youngest son, the Duke of Cumberland, who had been appointed Captain General in March 1745 and had experienced two campaigns on the Continent. He was respected for his bravery. Cumberland's performance and inspiring qualities were highly admired by both officers and men. Yorke wrote that he was able to lift the men's spirits. Apparently, 'What contributes to keep up their spirits up is the presence of the Duke who is justly their darling; for they see he does whatever the meanest of them does and goes thro' as much fatigue'.[295]

This was reciprocated, as Private Taylor wrote, 'He that had seen him reviewing the lines on their march, would have seen pleasure in his eyes'.[296] A volunteer wrote of him, 'whose presence greatly encourages all of us; so that we desire nothing more than to see the enemy'.[297] Horace Walpole stated:

> It is certain that the army adore the Duke, and are gone in the greatest spirits; and on the parade, as they began their march, the guards vowed that they would neither give nor take quarter. For bravery, his highness is certainly no Stuart, but literally loves to be in the act of fighting.[298]

Cumberland exposed himself to the same dangers and hardships as those he led. When an advance guard of troops prepared to force its way over the River Spey in April 1746, Taylor noted that his commander headed them himself, and when the Jacobite force retreated, 'The Duke and his advanced Guards, passed the river and pursued them'. Cumberland also regularly rose before his men did, as Taylor also observed, that he 'was up in the Morning before general beat, giving the necessary orders for the day'.[299]

After Falkirk he replaced Hawley in command in Scotland, as Newcastle told the latter on 24 January, 'in order to animate the troops and ... the King has been pleased to direct the Duke of Cumberland to go to Scotland'.[300] On the march, Cumberland encouraged his soldiers in the following ways:

> When the Duke marched from Aberdeen, he endeared himself exceedingly to the soldiers (if it was possible to increase their affection for him) by walking with them most of the way on foot, generally using one of the soldier's tenttrees for a staff and never going a yard out of the way for a bridge or any burn they met with, but wading through at the nearest.
> Of a long march of near 20 miles from Old Meldrum to Banff the following little accident much delighted the spectators. A soldiers wife carrying a young child, grew quite faint and entreated her husband, who was near with the Duke, to carry the child for a little way; the fellow said he could not for he was burdened with his arms. The Duke overheard, took the soldier's gun and carried it hi0self for some way and ordered him to ease the poor woman of the child for a while.[301]

He also showed his consideration to the men under him in other ways. Following the battle of Falkirk, Hawley had decided to hang a number of soldiers for desertion and cowardice. On his arrival in Edinburgh, Cumberland decided to reprieve them all. As he told Newcastle, 'I thought it better to pardon all the private men, to give a sort of mark of favour to the corps'. He praised the men, telling them that he relied 'upon their future courage and good conduct', that he had 'a pride in commanding them' and that he was 'convinced [they] will support the King to his honour and which they so often and justly acquired'.[302] Wolfe wrote, on the day before Culloden, 'We wanted to have fought the 15th, His Royal Highness' birthday, but his charity for the men after many marches prevented it'.[303]

Not all generals were so well thought of. Lord Tyrawley, one of Wade's senior officers, had a low opinion of almost all his colleagues and his superiors. He wrote 'Nassau very little better and Schwartzenburg ... stupid'.[304] However, it was Wade himself for whom he had most criticism. He declared that his superior was 'infirm and feverish, for he is so both in body and mind, forgetful ... perplext, snappish ... sometimes at the expense of good breeding'.[305] Wade was also criticized by Yorke thus, 'we have not yet had any accounts directly from him which makes me a little angry with my old master, considering how much depends on it; if he should be there [Halifax], the Rebels must move to him or us'.[306]

Wade was well aware, that at seventy-two, he was not best suited for a winter campaign: 'I hope His Majesty will please to appoint a General more active and capable than myself of undergoing so great a fatigue both of body and mind, which my age and constitution cannot support'.[307] On another occasion, he wrote, 'My age and infirmity render me incapable of writing'.[308] Bad health affected others; Richmond wrote of Ligonier, 'I have the highest opinion of him, butt his health is excessively bad still'.[309]

It would seem that Wade shared a failing with Phillip II; the inability to leave details alone while neglecting the bigger picture. Tyrawley noted,

> Wade is wholly taken up with trifles below his notice, a kettle and a tent is a morning's discussion and nothing else determin'd upon, when he could leave these things to the under officers whose business it is ... he would have time to think of greater matters, which are neglected ... All these procrastinations may be very fatal to us ... no line of battle is drawn, but on paper.[310]

Wade eventually begged to be relieved of his command and this was granted in late December 1745. Another instance of generals at loggerheads concerned Argyll and Cadogan, the latter being an ally of Marlborough. Argyll allegedly challenged Cadogan to a duel in 1716 as Wills and Carpenter were also to do.[311]

Generals can lead a lonely existence, but the holding of councils of war could dilute this. Wade held a number of councils of war throughout November and December 1745. These involved Wade and his lieutenant and major generals, plus the two senior Dutch officers. One was held on 7 November, after news that the Jacobite army was approaching Carlisle; the decision reached was to await further news before deciding to march.[312] Eight days' later another council was held, again to discuss the next course of action and on this time, the decision was

taken to march against the Jacobites on the next day.[313] There were others. Cope
and his officers held a council of war at Dalwhinnie on 27 August to decide
whether to take aggressive action or not; they decided against it.[314] Other officers rarely if ever held such conferences; neither Argyll nor Cumberland did so.
Councils were held when important decisions had to be made, presumably as a
way of creating shared responsibility.

Dealing with auxillary troops posed additional questions, especially for
Wade in 1745 and Cumberland in 1746. In part this was because although more
men meant an addition to their fighting capacity, it exacerbated already existing
problems of finance and supply. Wade wrote, 'I am sorry to observe that they
are daily making fresh demands of money on various pretences'.[315] Operationally
there were difficulties, too. The Dutch were accused of slowing down Wade's
forces on the march. Conway wrote:

> I know that he [Wade] is obstructed and hampered in every step he takes by the dead
> weight of Dutch troops and their generals, whom he must drag after him, and there-
> fore he cannot act with that expedition and spirit that he ought, and that the time and
> our present circumstances require.[316]

This was in reference to the ultimately abortive march from Newcastle to Carlisle. In the following month, the French allies of the Jacobites insisted that the
Dutch adhere to their capitulation agreement and desist in their present operations, which they did and so ceased to be a factor in the struggle. Cumberland
had difficulties with the Hessian troops who refused to march against the Jacobites when Cumberland would not allow them to enter into an agreement with
the Jacobites concerning the exchange of prisoners of war. Cumberland insisted
that the Jacobites were rebels and not legitimate enemies, but Frederick of Hesse
deemed otherwise and so deadlock was reached.[317]

Reliability

Desertion and, rarer, mutiny, occurred to an extent in most armies in the eighteenth century, even when there were no ideological or religious clashes of loyalty.
In the early eighteenth century, Britain's soldiers would have had their loyalties
tested as there was a rival claimant to the throne. In 1688 there had been some
high-level desertions from the army led by James II against William of Orange
and these had proved fatal to undermining the former's resolve to fight. Thus the
loyalty of the troops was of critical importance, especially as it has been recently
asserted that there were 'conspiracies within the British Army' during 1745–6.[318]

Certainly some contemporaries believed this was the case. Lady Nimmo, a
Scottish Whig, wrote in March 1746, of her concerns for Cumberland: 'I trem-
ble for his life when I consider how many of his own officers are Jacobites ... I am

convinced the rebels are either assured of some mischief amongst ourselves.'[319] She was not alone in this, in both 1715 and 1745. Jacobites certainly thought so in the former year. Information from France alleged:

> That the army itself is divided and that the King cannot trust it. That both officers and men are both disgusted with the Dutch troops being brought over. A certain Ecclesiastic has written to one of his friends on France that the Pretender has no need of troops to defeat the English army. His presence alone will suffice, and a single pathetic address would make them throw down their arms.[320]

There was a Jacobite plan in 1715 to appeal to the army that they could avert bloodshed if they quit George I's service and joined the Jacobites. If they did so, they would be given the same rank as that they had left, with full pay and arrears to be paid, and further rewards were promised.[321] In 1715, the Earl of Derwentwater, seeing the advance guard of the regulars, cried 'they are all for us'.[322] James Maxwell, a Jacobite officer, wrote, 'The general discontent it [George II's alleged partiality in 1743 for his Hanoverian troops] had occasioned among the British troops, seemed very favourable to the Prince's scheme'.[323] The Jacobites also thought that if many of the influential Jacobites declared for Charles in 1745 'it is probable that it would have had great influence upon the army itself, perhaps have occasioned a considerable defection there, and been a vast resource in case the war had continued'.[324] According to Lord Elcho, a Jacobite officer, Charles himself believed 'the regular troops would not fight against him, because of his being their natural prince'.[325]

Concerns were expressed among loyalists, too. This was especially the case in 1715, when many of the officers had been selected or promoted during the previous Tory administration. Some had been removed from their posts in 1714–15 when George I entrusted patronage to the Whigs. According to Rae, fourteen colonels of the Guards and other officers were dismissed 'on suspicion that they were in the Pretender's interest'.[326] But there were fears that popular Jacobitism, as espoused by crowds throughout England, might have proved contagious along the lower ranks. Dudley Ryder wrote, 'Mr Winoom thinks we must call in foreign forces to assist if the Pretender makes an invasion, that we cannot depend upon our English troops, the common people are so poisoned with Jacobitism and so much set against the present government'.[327]

There were certainly a number of instances of disloyalty among the officers and other ranks. At Manchester, a centre of Jacobite rioting, in June 1715, a soldier was jailed for shouting the Jacobite cry, 'Down with the Rump'. However, after he was released by the rioters and offered money to join them, he refused unless he had his commanding officer's permission.[328] In the following month, Cornet Sadler of Cobham's Dragoons, also stationed in Manchester, was arrested, 'for speaking seditious and scandalous words'.[329] When some of

Colonel Kirke's men caused disorder in Berwick in December 1715, it was said that they were 'disaffected persons and Irish papists'.[330] After a Jacobite riot in Worcester on 20 October, a clergyman reported that 'some of the officers in the Army were in opinion with the people and many soldiers when drunck up to a pitch would declare themselves likewise'.[331] A soldier helped Jacobite prisoners escape from Chester Castle in the winter of 1716.[332] At Oxford, 'the soldiers were seduced to it by four scholars', as Wadham's Jacobite scholars had 'form'd a design to corrupt the soldiers by giving them money, and entertaining them in their butteries and kitchens'. They even were guilty of 'drinking Ormonde and Bolingbroke's healths, and confusion to their officers'.[333]

There were also instances of attempts made to turn soldiers from their allegiance. George Berkley wrote on 3 September 1715, 'There was yesterday detected a new scheme of villainy of the Pretender and his agents. It was no less than to Debauch the Guards and the rest of the army'.[334] Colonel Paul of the First Foot Guards, was found to have recruiting papers on his person and had been enlisting men for the Jacobites, assisted by others of the same regiment.[335] A sergeant and nine men of Honeywood's Dragoons were accused of sedition and were escorted from Chelmsford to London.[336]

Such dissension was feared in later years. The Rev. John Tomlinson reported in June 1717: 'The officers of Newcastle never go to Church, but play at cards on Sunday. Some of them have publickly drunk its confusion and yet many of them say that they will fight for him that gives them the most, they will fight for the [Pretender] if he will give them 3½d a day more.'[337] In 1719, a man addressed the soldiers at the Tower, asking them if they would 'rebel' against 'their lawful sovereign, King James'.[338] Three men from the foot guards were punished for 'using scandalous reflections on his Majesty's person and government'.[339]

There were similar fears expressed in 1745, mostly centred around the Scottish and Irish troops. Oglethorpe thought this might be the case, writing, 'there are great doubts of their integrity ... suspected to be false, and the first [the Scots] not disposed to fight against their own countrymen'.[340] There were also rumours about Irish dragoons deserting, possibly as many as 450, but the reality was far different. Three soldiers deserted while at Berwick and there were two army deserters in Richmond jail in November 1745. There was an advertisement about deserters in the Newcastle press in December 1745.[341] In Chichester, corporal John Mackintosh of Lowther's marines, and a Scot, were heard, in a pub, to declare that Scotland was ill used and that there ought to be a King in Scotland every three years.[342] All this did not amount to very much, however, affecting as it did a very small number of isolated individuals.

Some of the Scottish troops were less than reliable, with Cope pointing out that on his march north, the two companies of Murray's 'mouldered away by Desertion'. Potentially more dangerous was after Prestonpans where the rank and file, amounting to over 1,000 men, were offered the opportunity to enlist with the Jacobites. Few did so, and of those who did, according to Elcho, 'most of them followed the Example of their officers: those that enlisted mostly all deserted'.[343] Some deserters were found among the Jacobite ranks after Culloden, and of these forty were shot, though many of these had deserted while the army had been on the Continent.[344] It is impossible to ascertain precisely how many men deserted from the regulars; clearly not many re-enlisted with the Jacobites, perhaps less than 100, which, given that many were Scottish or Irish, is a very low proportion of the whole indeed.

A more potentially dangerous defection occurred on 8 September 1715, when Jacobites tried to seize Edinburgh castle by a coup de main. A former ensign corrupted one sergeant William Ainsley, a member of the garrison. This was not due to ideology but of 'Money and promises of preferment'. Two privates were given eight and four guineas to let down ropes in order for the Jacobites at the foot of the walls to climb up the walls.[345] The attempt failed, but had it succeeded, the Jacobites would have gained solid advantages in taking Scotland's principal fortress and the arms stored there.

Despite fears by both government supporters and the hopes of Jacobites, the regulars were a reliable force. Although there were some desertions and some instances of verbal Jacobitism, these were on very small scale. More importantly perhaps, not a man of distinction deserted. The army, as in 1685, fought the rebels with zeal. Unlike the case in 1688, there were no defections among the senior ranks.

Conclusion

The regular army had the unusual experience of campaigning on British soil in 1715–16, 1719 and 1745–6. They were facing an enemy whose tactics were unconventional, and were facing military threats from potentially a number of different sources and directions. It was also campaigning in seasons outside the unusual campaigning season, which posed additional difficulties. Logisitics were an additional hardship, on which much else hung. Finally there were initially insufficient troops available.

These issues took time to resolve. It was only towards the end of each of the two major campaigns that they were successfully dealt with. Argyll only had enough troops by the end of December 1715; almost four months after he took command. Cumberland was still facing questions of finance and supply towards the end of February 1746. Generals had to constantly lobby the Secretary of State to have their men properly supplied and had also to rely on civilian support for intelligence, accommodation and transport; and this was given with varying degrees of enthusiasm.

Politicians and generals did not always agree. In 1715 and 1745 the Secretaries of State saw England and London in particular as vulnerable and so their defence was foremost, whether from internal English Jacobitism in 1715 or a Franco-Jacobite twin-pronged threat in 1745. Neither Argyll in 1715 nor Cumberland in 1745 saw these dangers as paramount; rather they saw the immediate enemy of primarily Scottish Jacobite armies before them. Yet both were deprived of troops in order that the potential dangers elsewhere be guarded against. Although it is easy to sympathize with the generals over the politicians, this is only so with hindsight. There were very real fears, especially in 1745, that these dangers would materialize, and were London to be lost, as it was to Charles I in 1642 and which James II took good care to secure in 1685, as did Parliament in the 1640s, then total defeat was surely close. Yet to deny troops to the generals meant postponing victory in the field; there was in reality no best option, only a perceived least bad one.

Yet though overall strategy was outside the generals' hands, at least they did have control of day-to-day tactical decisions. This was only common sense because letters from London could take two or three days to arrive and dictation from London in such matters was not sensible. This gave some control to the generals in choosing when and where to fight. As we shall see in the next chapter, the battlefield was their domain. The campaign was the iceberg beneath the surface; that mountain of effort required to bring an army to battle with a reasonable prospect of success.

3 THE BATTLE

There has been much written about the battles of the Forty-Five; indeed there has been one book written about Prestonpans, another one on Falkirk, but these pale into significance to those on Culloden, with seven in recent decades alone, making it one of the best-known battles in Britain, as well as being the last. They also feature heavily in narratives of the campaign.[1] Although the Fifteen has been neglected in comparison, the two battles loom large in the books on the topic[2] though Glenshiel is even more neglected.[3] This chapter concentrates, not on the familiar narratives, but on an analysis of the battles of the three eighteenth-century campaigns.

There were five battles (Preston, Sheriffmuir, Prestonpans, Falkirk and Culloden) and two major skirmishes (Glenshiel and Clifton). Although this was a relatively large number in three campaigns, all were comparatively small affairs. Of the battles, all concerned fewer than 20,000 combatants, and two involved less than 10,000. Battles on the Continent were invariably far larger. At Blenheim, Marlborough had 52,000 men under his allied command alone. However, during the conflict in the American colonies in the 1770s, field armies were far smaller and more akin to those employed in the Jacobite campaigns, though in 1778, there were 25,000 regulars in the colonies, only a fraction were ever assembled together to fight a battle. Cornwallis at Camden in 1780 had only 2,000 men at his command. We should remember that the numbers in the Continental battles were high because they consisted of men of different nationalities. Germans and Dutch as well as British fought under Marlborough; often the latter were a minority and were never more than half. Hessian troops fought alongside the British in America.

The regular army, too, faced enemies who were mostly not regulars, and this posed different and more difficult challenges than on the Continent. Similar difficulties faced the British army in colonial campaigns in America in the Seven Years War and in the War of American Independence. Adaptation to different tactics often was a difficult and painful process, sometimes beginning with defeats.

In some of these battles, the regular army was on the tactical offensive; at Preston, Glenshiel and Clifton. Jacobite forces had chosen a defensive position; often a built up area, to defend and so the fight had to be brought to them. But during the four main battles, the Jacobite doctrine of a rush to combat with hand-held weapons, after, perhaps, cannon fire and musketry, meant that the initial tactics of the regulars were to stand on the defensive, in order to use their superior volley fire to attempt to overcome the Jacobite rush. We shall examine the battles and skirmishes of the period by looking at them, not as is usual in a narrative fashion, but by the different stages which made up these actions.

The Decision to Fight

Battles are risky affairs. Much could depend on variables that a commander could not ascertain in advance. Bad luck, bad weather and acts of God cannot be taken into account. Within a few hours or less, the loser would usually lose his artillery and baggage, as well as territory and his reputation, if not his liberty and life. Furthermore, both victory and defeat meant the loss of a considerable number of soldiers, who could not usually be replaced quickly or cheaply. At Blenheim, the allied victors lost 12,500 men, about a quarter of those involved; the losers lost 20,000 men or about 40 per cent. Although sieges could also be costly, casualties were spread out over weeks or months and were seen as less of a gamble, while losses on the battlefield all occurred on a single bloodstained day and could cause a political outcry.[4] Care was thus required before a battle was embarked upon. Even those commanders, such as Marlborough, who had a penchant for battles, once writing that a victory was 'of far greater advantage to the common cause than the taking of twenty towns', he only fought four battles and two major actions, but over thirty sieges in nine years.[5]

Charles XII was another general who was enthusiastic for battle, though he was deemed rash and ultimately fell to disaster at Poltava in 1709. As seen in the previous chapter, commanders were urged to seek out the Jacobite army and engage it in battle. Certainly Cumberland looked forward to battle, fearing only he might be cheated of one, for in previous weeks the Jacobites had avoided fighting. Writing to Newcastle on 26 January, he was concerned that the Jacobites 'won't give us fair play but will retire towards the Highlands'.[6] He was confident in the ability of his troops to achieve victory, then having, with fourteen battalions of infantry and two of cavalry, 'enough to drive them off the face of the earth, if they do their duty which we must expect'.[7] He had had a similar view in the previous year, writing, 'our whole body together and then to advance directly up to them in which case I flatter myself the affair would be certain in our favour'.[8] There was contempt for the Jacobite enemy. Hawley wrote on 11 January, 'I do and always shall despise these rascals'.[9]

Hawley was also eager for battle, writing on 15 January, 'I am resolved to strike while the iron is hot', and Cumberland had encouraged him, writing four days previously, 'you proceed marching onto Stirling' in order to relieve that besieged castle. Neither thought the Jacobites would stand and in the previous two months they had certainly avoided confrontation. Cumberland believed 'that despicable enemy' would flee from Stirling on seeing the King's troops and Hawley agreed that the 'rascally scum ... will go off or they are mad'.[10] One reason for a battle was that Hawley did not believe Stirling castle could hold out, 'The rebels are busy at Stirling, but I hope they'll find it a tough nut, tho' I fear we can't be in time to save it'.[11] Generals Wills and Carpenter were also eager for battle against the Jacobites in England in 1715 as was Wightman in the Highlands four years later.

However, some generals were reluctant to enter into battle. Argyll was one, before Sherriffmuir, and Cope declined a possible engagement at Correyarick in 1745. Both had good reasons for such hesitation. Argyll had but a fraction of the numbers of the Jacobite army, so was understandably shy of combat, and, furthermore, was awaiting reinforcements. Cope and his officers decided that to attempt the pass before them was too dangerous; neither was willing to risk the only British army in Scotland. As an officer later wrote:

> Formerly several of these officers had marched over that ground and all of them unanimously agreed that to force the rebels in it was utterly impracticable. It must inevitably be attended with the loss of all our provisions, artillery, military stores and indeed of the troops: that giving the rebels any success upon their setting out, was by all means to be prevented, as that might be attended with by bad consequences to the service.[12]

Battles were conventionally attritional affairs. Each side would pound away at the other, with artillery and then with infantry volleys. Victories were not always decisive. Armies who technically won, by retaining the field while the other retired, might lose higher casualties, such as the Allies at Malplaquet in 1709 or the French at Fontenoy in 1745. The victor might not be able to mount a successful pursuit, as was Cornwallis's lot at Camden in 1780, thus enabling the loser to regroup.

Troop Numbers

Relatively small numbers of troops were present at these battles. This was especially the case in 1715, 1719 and in the early stages of 1745. In the first two conflicts, the number of troops overall was at low peacetime levels; in the second, much of the army was initially on active service on the Continent or was deployed against a potential French invasion. It is also worth noting that only a fraction of the total number of troops at the state's disposal was used in battle.

This was commonplace. For instance, in 1685, James II had almost 9,000 men in his army, but only a quarter were available at Sedgemoor.

At Preston there were six regiments of dragoons and horse and one of infantry. No official returns are available, but estimates vary from 1,100 to 2,000, and the real figure is probably somewhere between the two.[13] Yet they were joined on the next day by three regiments of dragoons, but even so, this reinforcement only numbered about 500, though as shall later be noted, they made a decisive psychological impact. An equally small force was present at Glenshiel; possibly about 2,000 men.[14] Likewise, at Sheriffmuir, Argyll had about 3,730 men, made up of eight battalions of infantry (2,880 men) and five regiments of dragoons (850 men).[15]

Larger forces were available in 1746, though not much more. Hawley's numbers of regulars as counted four days before the battle of Falkirk were thus: twelve infantry battalions totalling an estimated 6,368 and three of cavalry, numbering 772; little more than 7,000, though these were supplemented by various militia units.[16] At Culloden, numbers were about the same, with fifteen battalions, making up 6,419 infantry. This included 330 officers, 329 sergeants and 225 drummers.[17] There were 787 cavalry in three regiments and several companies of militia.[18] The numbers of their opponents varied considerably, too. Often they were roughly even, as at Preston, Glenshiel, Prestonpans and Falkirk, though at Sheriffmuir the Jacobites enjoyed a more than 2:1 numerical superiority. It was only at Culloden that the regulars had a clear advantage in numbers, and then only by 3:2, and this was only because a sizeable portion of the Jacobite army was missing, such was their need to forage for supplies. We should also bear in mind that there were militia and volunteers alongside the regulars at all these battles, though the proportion was relatively small, and their role will be discussed in Chapter 7.

Yet despite this, generals often thought they had enough men. Hawley wrote, after the setback at Falkirk, 'We had enough to beat them'.[19] Had he waited a few more days he would have had two additional infantry battalions and forty-eight additional gunners, and as we shall see the latter were sorely needed.[20] The one exception to this rule was Argyll, who, as stated in the previous chapter, continually bemoaned his lack of manpower. The others all considered they had enough men to finish the job.

Generalship

The role of the general was widely held as being supreme, as was noted in 1745: 'It is most certainly true that the commander in chief is the main spring of action; as he is dull or active, the machine moves accordingly.'[21] The destinies of his men and his King lay, to a large extent, within his hands. Marlborough was certainly an active commander. Dr Hare, who accompanied him at Blenheim, wrote, 'My Lord Marlborough is everywhere in the action to encourage our men and exposed to infinite dangers'. He massed units when they were needed and placed guns where necessary. He led them to the attack and encouraged them. He also worked with his subordinate generals. Not all commanders followed this model.[22]

The generals of the Jacobite campaigns were mostly experienced officers who had seen many years service in senior command. However this was not always sufficient for a successful battlefield command. Cope had been a colonel in 1732, a brigadier in 1735 and a lieutenant general in 1743, and had led the second line of troops at Dettingen. Yet he had never had an independent battlefield command until Prestonpans in 1745. Likewise, the generals of the Fifteen, though equally experienced, never had hitherto had independent commands, either, and all were successful in battle. Ironically it was the least experienced commander of the Forty-Five who was the only one who had hitherto led an army into battle, and that was Cumberland. He was also the most effective.

If it were known that battle was impending, a general met with his subordinates. Cope met his junior officers when at Correyarrick. Another instance was on the evening of 15 April 1746. Cumberland had already given the orders for how the army should march on the following day. The colonels were summoned and he:

> told 'em the possibility there was of coming to an action the next day with the Rebels, the method he would have everyone of them observe in the leading up of his regiment, and what he expected of them, and assured them of victory if they obeyed his orders.[23]

Communication with the troops was also needed. Before battle could be joined, the commander made a speech to the troops within earshot. Cumberland was well versed in this; before the fight at Clifton he addressed the men:

> His Royal Highness made a short speech to the troops before the Action, in which he took notice of the Honour they had acquired by their intrepid behaviour at the battles of Dettingen and Fontenoy, intimating that he had no doubt of their shewing the like on this occasion.[24]

At Culloden, Cumberland rode along the front lines and addressed the men. One version, whose final two lines recall part of Shakespeare's *Henry V*'s Agincourt speech, is as follows:

> My brave boys, your toil will soon be at an end; stand your ground against the broadsword and target; parry the enemy in the manner you have been directed, be assured of immediate assistance, and I promise you that I will not fail to make a report of your behaviour to the King; and in the meantime, if any are unwilling to engage, pray let him speak freely, and with pleasure they will have a discharge.[25]

Cumberland's efforts were successful. Michael Hughes, a volunteer in the ranks, claimed, that the speech was, 'followed by a full acclamation of all the soldiers, testifying their intire satisfaction and Loyalty'.[26]

Cope was much criticized after his defeat at Prestonpans. However, he had certainly been diligent enough on the field, though energy alone was not always sufficient, one officer there later wrote of 'the diligence and activity which the general behaved himself. He first order'd the right to form, and then gallop'd to the left, and brought the dragons there up to their ground; from thence I saw him hasten back along the front of our line, to the right, upon his observing that the rebels were advancing to attack it'.[27]

The commander's role was also to encourage and to praise. Taylor wrote, that at Culloden, the men were 'being encouraged by the Duke and Generals Example, they doubled their Efforts'.[28] Colonel Harrison wrote, 'above all, the great Example of his grace, the Duke of Argyle, whose presence not only gave Spirit to the Action, but gained Success as often as he led on'.[29] Likewise, Cope wrote, 'I returned again the same way to the right, encouraging the men as I went along the line, to do their duty'.[30] Leading by example was undertaken by Argyll, for on the night before Sherriffmuir, he 'sat in a sheep cote, upon straw' so the men had little to complain of.[31]

A general needed to survey the battlefield and his enemy's dispositions. At Sherriffmuir, Argyll rode up to the top of a hill with some of his officers. He remained on this hill for several hours, until 11am, partly because he could not see all of the Jacobite army. From what he eventually saw, he changed the order of his army to avoid his outnumbered forces from being surrounded or flanked.[32] He also led by example, 'His Grace was everywhere in person, made as good a disposition as possible in his circumstances, and charged at the head of several regiments by turns; for nothing but extraordinary courage would have broke the rebels'.[33] Yet Argyll allowed himself to be too involved in one sector of the battle, as a contemporary stated, 'The Duke who was upon the right and saw not what passed upon the left wing thowght he had got ane intire victory till coming back from the pursuite'.[34]

He needed to be seen and to be able to direct. Therefore, at Glenshiel, General Wightman placed himself in the centre of his small command, 'where everyone had free access to him for their orders'.[35] Likewise, Cumberland moved cavalry to cover the right flank at Culloden. During the artillery exchange he put himself on the army's right, 'imagining the greatest push would be there'. Later, at the climax of the battle, Yorke noted 'for the Duke's piercing eye, discerning how hard the left was pressed, sent me thither to order Major General Huske to remedy it from the second line'.[36]

A general needed to rally the troops if the battle was going awry. Cope was accused of neglecting this duty at Prestonpans, 'The General was the first who abandoned the field, and leaving his troops to the mercy of the enemy, retired with the utmost precipitation to a place of safety'.[37] Andrew Henderson, a contemporary historian, on visiting the battlefield at Prestonpans, recorded, 'what was become of Cope? And they all, but especially the English Soldiers, spoke most disrespectfully and bitterly of him'.[38] Yet Cope did try. He later reported, 'Seeing the dragoons go off in this manner, I went to the Foot, to try by their means to retrieve the affair ... I endeavoured all I could to rally them, but to no purpose'.[39]

Major Talbot reported, 'He and the rest of the officers did everything in their power to stop the men running away, but all to no purpose'.[40] Earlier, 'I recommended it to the men to keep up their fire, and be attentive to their officers'.[41] It was also reported that Hawley tried to rally his men, too, 'General Hawley drew his pistol and endeavoured to rally them but thereafter fair words would not do for they never stopped until they got to camp'.[42]

Argyll is credited with the ability to deceive. On the afternoon of 13 November, the remnant of each army faced one another. Argyll disguised his weakness in numbers by keeping his forces behind mud walls, having them only two ranks deep and having flags distributed along the ranks. There were about 1,000 men, but to the Jacobites it seemed there were 2,000–3,000 and so were deterred from attacking.[43]

At the end of the fighting, and at the moment of victory at Culloden:

> When the action was over, his royal highness rode thro' the army and thanked the officers and soldiers, in his majesty's name, for their firm and vigorous behaviour. There was a general shout, and Flanders, Flanders! repeated, We'll follow your royal highness against any enemy.[44]

Linn recalled Cumberland's behaviour at Culloden: 'The Duke Rode through our front line just befor we began & desired us not to be afraid, & after it was over he Rode along the same line & Returnd us a great many thanks for our good behaviour & said he never seed [*sic*] better ordered or better done'.[45] Bradshaw later wrote, 'had he been at Falkirk these brave Englishmen that are now in their graves had not been lost, his presence doing more than 5000 men'.[46]

Even in the case of a defeat, those troops that had done well were in the receipt of a general's pleasure. A soldier of Barrell's later wrote after Falkirk, 'Brigadier-[Cholmondeley?] was pleased to express his satisfaction at our Behaviour, by kissing our men and making us a present of 10 guineas'.[47]

Hawley came in for severe criticism. An officer present at the battle wrote to Lady Elizabeth Hastings thus:

> I am alive and well at present though, it is only by God's blessed will than our general's conduct. For he drew only 400 dragoons, sword in hand, up against 1,000 of our enemy and we had orders not to draw a pistol or fire and as soon as he had given

these orders to the rest of the officers he moved away from us and we never saw him move until the next morning. We lost the day for we were all sold to our enemies by treacherous general Hawley, for we could have got the day if he had done us justice or let us fight like Englishmen as we are. I wish the Duke had been with us.[48]

The figure of 400 is a gross underestimation, however, as will be noted in troop figures at the end of the chapter. Bradshaw wrote, 'General Hawley does not love us because the regiment spoke the truth about Falkirk jobb'.[49] Hawley, of course, claimed 'nobody will lay many faults' at his door.[50] Yet not everyone condemned Hawley. Cumberland wrote, 'The King is entirely satisfied with your conduct on that disagreeable occasion. I can assure you that I think that you have done wonders in coming off so after such a pannick was struck into the troops'.[51]

The March to Conflict

Troops were rarely concentrated until the moment just before the battle. This was partly for reasons of supply and accommodation. Cumberland, writing from Litchfield on 28 November 1745 explained his troop dispositions:

> That part of the army which is already come up, is canton'd from Tamworth to Stafford, with the cavalry at Newcastle in our front. By this position we endeavour to be equally at hand for the preservation of Derby or Chester.[52]

Argyll's march to battle was determined following intelligence that the Jacobite army was about to march on Stirling. He wrote, 'I design to pass the river and meet them'.[53] Cumberland's men had been marching for several days before Culloden. Before the final step, there was a halt of a day 'in order to refresh our men after the fatigues of several long marches'.[54]

It was between 4 and 5am on 16 April that the army marched from Nairn to Culloden. (Marching at an early hour was not unusual; the army marched at 1am at Fonteony.) They were composed of three columns, each of five battalions of infantry, and a further column of three regiments of dragoons. Guns and baggage followed the first column of infantry. After eight miles of marching, the advanced guard of forty dragoons and a number of Highlanders saw movement among the Jacobite army. The whole army formed into battle formation but with no further aggression on their enemy's part, reformed into columns of march and proceeded to within a mile of the enemy.[55]

It was important to reconnoitre the route to conflict. Before Cope moved his forces from Haddington towards Edinburgh, he sent Colonel Whitefoord ahead. He found that the direct road to Edinburgh was unsuitable and dangerous, for if they were attacked, defiles and enclosures would prevent the cavalry from forming up for action.[56]

The soldier's view of the march was different, as Private Linn told his wife:

And upon Wednesday the 16th instant we Marched from Nairn pretty early & it was avery bad day both for Wind & Rain, But thank God it was straight upon our Backs. We marched 10 long miles befor we came up with the Enemy & upon a long Boogie Muir 2 miles from Inverness.[57]

The weather and the proximity of the enemy caused additional woes. Private Taylor wrote that 'We also had great Difficulty in keeping the Locks of our Fire-locks dry: which was absolutely necessary: for the day was very stormy, and the Rain was violent'. However they were able to accomplish this. Then, for fear of attack, they had to march part of the route with fixed bayonets, 'a very uneasy Way of marching'.[58]

However the march enabled the army to arrive before their enemies and deploy accordingly. Conway later wrote, 'Our march was ordered so as to come just upon their front, which was so well executed, that we came up exactly over against 'em and in the best order imaginable'.[59]

Likewise, Wills's march to Preston on 12 November began at daybreak; they had eleven miles to cover before reaching their destination.[60] Caution was also employed by Wills in his approach towards the Jacobites at Preston. According to Robert Patten, a contemporary historian and participant in the battle, 'he proceeded with Caution, and caus'd the hedges and fields to be view'd and ways Laid open for his Cavalry to enter'.[61] Reconnaissance prior to battle was common. On the day before the battle of Falkirk, it was noted, 'the Report of several persons who were sent out to recconoitre, they [the Jacobites] were observed to be in motion early in the morning ... but it was not confirmed that they were in full march till about one in the afternoon'.[62] The night before Sherriffmuir was a difficult one for the soldiers, for they had to 'lay all Night on our Arms' because the Jacobites were three miles away, and this after a march from Stirling.[63] Furthermore, because the plan was to go into battle on the next morning, no tents were pitched by anyone, as enforced by the officers, who also stood with their men. 'And thus they lay in an extreme cold Night, without either tent or cover'.[64] Similarly, at Prestonpans, the troops lay at their arms all night. Major Talbot posted outguards and they brought intelligence to Cope frequently all night. They especially kept watch to the east.[65] Just before the battle, ammunition was dispensed to the soldiers. Between 12 and 2 on the morning of 13 November, Argyll gave orders that the soldiers be given enough musket balls to make their totals up to thirty each.[66]

Choosing the ground on which to fight was of crucial importance. Cope managed to do so at Prestonpans, as an officer stated, 'The general therefore thought it proper to chuse the first open ground he found, and a better spot could not have been chosen for the cavalry to be at liberty to act'.[67] Likewise, James Johnstone, a Jacobite officer, wrote, 'the position of which was chosen with a great deal of skill ... a position inaccessible on every point'.[68] The field was a mile long, protected from the east by a morass, from the north by the sea and the west by park walls. The army could not be outflanked and could use all its three arms. According to Cope, 'There is not in the whole of the ground between Edinburgh and Dunbar, a better site for both Horse and Foot to act upon'.[69]

A good site was also selected by Argyll in 1715. The ground near Dunblane was more suitable for his cavalry than that at the head of the Forth. Furthermore, the river was frozen and therefore could be crossed in many places and so could not be properly guarded with the relatively small number of troops under him.[70] Later in the battle, the regulars used defensive works, for the first and last time in these campaigns. Although they were at the bottom of a hill, they had earth works and ditches which were breast high.[71]

Good scouting work provided valuable intelligence for the commander in guiding his ultimate disposition of the troops. Two or three people had been sent to spy out the Jacobite army. Their news led Cumberland to suspect that they might try and fall on his men while they marched along on the main road to Inverness. According to Yorke:

> This information was enough to determine HRH what method to take to disappoint their design, and make it turn to his own confusion. He with great skill and military genius changed in an instant the disposition of the march, and leaving the great Inverness road on the right, continued moving over the hills, called Gladsmuir, till we came within a mile and a half of the enemy, when we drew up again in order of battle, and marched forward.[72]

It was customary to form the army into two lines, with cavalry on the flanks. At Sheriffmuir, there were three squadrons of cavalry on each flank of the front line, with six battalions of infantry in the centre. The second line was weaker, with two infantry battalions in the centre, and two squadrons of cavalry on each wing. However if there were few cavalry they were all posted on one wing, as at Falkirk and Prestonpans.[73]

However, not all of Argyll's army was formed and part was still on the march as battle was imminent. James Keith, a Jacobite officer, wrote, 'His [Argyll's] army was not yet entirely formed, the rear, which was to have formed his left wing, was yet on their march, and shows us their flanck'.[74]

Battle sometimes commenced at first light. At Prestonpans, Cope's patrols noted Jacobite movement at 3am on 21 September. Battle began as day broke.[75] The first shots at Culloden were fired just after noon and Sherriffmuir late morning. However, the skirmishes at Glenshiel and Clifton occurred at about 5pm, and the battles of Preston and Falkirk in the late afternoon. They were usually over in a relatively short spell of time.

Just before the battle, soldiers handed their valuables, such as 'cash, rings and watches' to officers' servants, who would then retire to the rear to keep the valuables safe for the men, or in the event of their deaths, their dependents.[76]

Morale

One of the crucial determinants of a battle is morale. Setbacks and losses can lead to a collapse of morale, leading to retreat, rout and surrender. Good leadership could supply the defect, as, Patten notes, occurred at Preston. He wrote that the regulars were 'for the most part raw men, new-listed men and seemed unwilling to fight, yet the Bravery and good Conduct of experienced officers, supplied very much that Defect'.[77] Yet casualties discouraged the men, as another Jacobite wrote of the same battle, 'they never durst approach for the dragoons were all raw men and those that came within shot never returned'.[78]

It is uncertain whether those who were wounded and taken prisoner, however, were downhearted. According to Patten, none refused to switch sides, 'not one Man belonging to the King's forces but would not die in their Country's Cause'.[79] However, another Jacobite claimed 'all the prisoners lookt upon the affair as lost'.[80]

Colonel Gardiner was very unsure about the men in his regiment on the eve of Prestonpans, as he confided in Dr Carlyle: 'I have not above 10 men in my regiment whom I am certain will follow me. But we must give battle now and may God's will be done.'[81] However, others thought differently, with Lascelles noting 'the troops always perform'd with great spirit and the utmost exactness'.[82]

Stories spread about the Highlanders had undermined the soldiers' morale at Falkirk, as Hawley commented in retrospect:

> I can impute their pannick to the prepossession imprinted in them by the constant topick in all discourse from the first, and best of the King's subjects doune to the lowest and worste who are Scotchmen, of the desperate men the rebels are. This is no rational thing they can't help it, and from this the men when they found their arms would not prime, were terrified with the notion of the rebels' swords, which made hem give way.[83]

Panic there undoubtedly was. Hawley wrote, 'such scandalous cowardice I never saw before. The whole second line of Foot ran away without firing a shot.' Attempts at rallying were ineffective: 'every officer did their duty; and what was in the power of man to do, in trying to stop and rally the men and they led them on, with a good a countenance'.[84] Having seen their comrades flee, as at Prestonpans and Falkirk, reduced the morale of the remainder considerably. However, when this did not happen, and under commanders that the men had confidence in, such as Cumberland, morale was high.

We shall now examine the role of the army's three arms.

The Artillery

Given that the reach of the artillery was further than that of any other arm, it would be imagined that they would make the opening salvo in any encounter. Yet of the encounters, artillery was only employed in action in only two of the battles and one of the skirmishes, though was present, but unused in another two. The forces employed at Preston did not include any artillery. This was probably because this was a campaign against a mobile enemy and guns would only slow their forces down. The same can be said for the Clifton skirmish. This was a case of pursuit by an advance guard chiefly composed of cavalry against a rear guard, and again, speed was of the essence. At Falkirk, Hawley's guns were never deployed; likewise with Argyll's at Sheriffmuir. Part of this was due to the lack of trained gunners available. The Royal Regiment of Artillery was not founded until 1716 and even then, the civilian component of the personnel was high as drivers of the teams of horses who brought the guns to the battlefield were civilians.

Field artillery had an effective range of 600 yards; far more than musketry. Solid shot would be used at this range, and the calibre of the gun would be measured by the weight of the shot it fired. Small calibre guns only were employed. There were three pounder guns at Culloden, for instance, and one and a half pounders at Prestonpans. They were used in conjunction with infantry battalions as close support. However, such small guns could be manhandled if there was a need for them to be moved in battle, or by two horses, which was not the case for higher calibre guns. At short range, 250 yards, canister was used instead of ball.[85]

However, when guns were employed, they would be the first to be in action against an enemy. On the night before Prestonpans, 'we could only content ourselves with a small train of six gallopers, to throw a few shot amongst an advanced party of theirs'. A few men were wounded.[86] At each discharge, the gunners cheered, hoping to discomfort the Jacobites.[87]

Artillery was deployed differently in these battles. At Prestonpans it was deployed together, on the left of the army, about 100 yards in advance of the main body, guarded by 100 infantry.[88] This was later criticized: 'why it was put to the hazard of suffering the cannon to be detach'd from the main body during the night, seems perfect infatuation, and such kind of generalship as not to be met with in history'.[89] At Culloden it was placed in twos between the battalions in the front line, with six coehorn mortars positioned between the two lines of infantry battalions.

Moving artillery into position was not always easy. At Falkirk it never reached the field of conflict. At Culloden, they became stuck in the morass in the field, but they were dragged out and were able to be of use.[90]

Artillery fire was variable in effect. At Prestonpans, the Jacobites, 'after receiving the discharge of a few pieces, almost in an instant and ... seized the train'. Its role was over almost as soon as the battle was begun, having fired but one ball each.[91] However one account states that this single discharge 'broke the ranks of the rebels and obliged them to divide into small parties as they advanced'.[92]

Although there were six cannon and two mortars there, there were no trained gunners to fire them. This was because there were none to be had in Scotland. The only man who knew how to fire them was a veteran of at least 40 years' standing from Edinburgh Castle. Cope had little choice but to bring him along, as well as three other fellow veterans. At Prestonpans, sailors from the transports which had ferried Cope's forces from Inverness to Dunbar, were brought into use. These men were less than useful, for they were 'generally drunk upon the march; and upon the day of Action, ran away before the action began, and he could never have any dependence on them the two days they were with him'.[93] Moreover, 'as soon as the action began, the others ran away with the powder flasks, which hindered him from firing so many cannons as he would have done'.[94]

Furthermore, the drivers ran off with the artillery horses, so could not be moved.[95] Colonel Whitefoord, who was in charge, managed to fire five of the six guns, the last being unprimed. This had minimal effect, as Home wrote, 'which killed one private man and wounded an officer in Lochiel's regiment. The line seemed to shake, but the men kept going on'.[96]

Cope had made other attempts to find trained gunners. On 20 September, he sent one Lieutenant Craig to Edinburgh castle to ask General Guest for gunners. At 11 that night, he made the request for the castle's Chief Engineer. Guest said he could not spare the man, but offered him a bombardier and four gunners. They disguised themselves as tradesmen to avoid Jacobite patrols, but were too late to take part in the battle.[97]

He also tried to redeploy two of the guns on the day of battle, from the right to the left flank. 'I sent Major Masson to the right, to Colonel Whitefoord, for cannon immediately to annoy them'. However, the artillery horses had run off and so the order could not be carried out.[98]

Similar difficulties arose at Falkirk, as their commander was only too ready to acknowledge two days before the battle, writing, 'the train is more for show than for use'.[99] Captain Cunningham had ten guns, including four pounders and one and a half pounders, but his personnel were highly inadequate: a young lieutenant, a bombardier, fourteen inexperienced matrosses and a dozen countrymen were hired to drive the limbers forward. Most of the artillery officers and men were still at Carlisle and Newcastle, though the latter were on their way to Edinburgh and did not arrive in time.[100]

On the day of battle, the guns were linked to the horses and the train was to the left of the main body of the army at 1pm, but unlike the case at Prestonpans, there was not an artillery guard. Hawley had not given Cunningham any orders and time elapsed before a staff officer could be found to instruct Cunningham 'march the artillery up to an adjacent hill in the rear of the rear of the front line of the army'. The roads were 'very bad and intricate' and they failed to keep pace with the infantry, falling behind the second line of advancing troops. Two heavy guns stuck in a bog and could not be dragged out, so were abandoned.[101]

So, with only two four pounders and a one and a half pounder, the artillery plodded forward. They then heard firing and saw most of the infantry fleeing the field. The drivers then deserted with the horses and all but one of the matrosses followed them.[102] A soldier noted, 'the carelessness and cowardice of the people belonging to the horses, who cut the traces and made the best way to save themselves'.[103] Lacking an artillery guard, Cunningham could not prevent their flight. With the battlefield in a state of chaos, he concluded, 'In such a situation, deserted by his men and the rebels within 20 paces of him, it was impossible for him to do any service with three guns, he thought it most prudent to order them down the hill'.[104] Hawley blamed Cunningham: 'one who ran away with all the horses and was the first man in Lithgow. I have ordered a court martial.'[105]

Cannon fired roundshot at several hundred yards range. Individually the guns were not very deadly at such ranges, but after time a number of them could be. There is much dispute over the length of the opening cannonade at Culloden, the one battle of the campaign in which artillery were effective. Linn states it was three quarters of an hour, and a fellow private thought it lasted 'half an hour or more'. Yet Yorke thought the duration was far shorter, that the Jacobites charged after only a volley or two of artillery fire.[106] Maxwell wrote that it 'was admirably well served' and was aimed at the Jacobite cavalry at first, possibly because they were an easier target or because they thought Charles was there. He added that the Royal Artillery 'had infinite advantage in cannonading'.[107]

It was also used to fire canister at short range against infantry and here artillery fire was deadly. Private Linn recalled that at Culloden, '2 or 3 of our cannon gave them such a Closs with grape shott which galled them very much'.[108] Maxwell, who was on the receiving end, agreed, writing, 'their cannon, which were now charged with grape shot, did a great deal [of damage], particularly an advanced battery on their left, which outflanked the Athol men'.[109]

Mortars were used at Prestonpans, but rather more effectively at Culloden, where recent archaeological evidence from 'The Field of the English' shows that they were fired at charging clansmen.[110] When the enemy were in retreat, artillery still had its uses, as Linn wrote, 'our cannon & a few royalls sent them a few small bomb shells & cannon balls to their farewell'.[111]

Artillery was part of Argyll's army at Sheriffmuir. There was a train of six three pounders and eighteen gunners. These were to be placed at the centre of the army in three small batteries. However, such was the speed of the rush to contact on both sides, that there was insufficient time to deploy them. Two of the guns were unlimbered and pointed towards the Jacobites, but by then both sides were engaged in melee. The other four were slower, due to a steep hill they were required to navigate, and when in position, were forced to retreat because the left wing of the army was in retreat: 'So that it was impracticable to use them, either in the Right or Left, without doing damage to their own men, as well, as the Rebels: so that the Officer that commanded, got them very narrowly off, without the Opportunity of firing one shot'. However, at the end of the day, with the remnants of both armies facing one another, two of the guns were drawn up facing the Jacobites, but given no attack occurred, they saw no service. That having been said, none of the Jacobite guns were brought into play, and most were captured by the end of the day.[112]

Sometimes the artillery was faulty. At Prestonpans, it was uncertain whether the mortar shells were breaking. This fear was because they had been in store at Edinburgh Castle for a long time and many of the fuses were faulty.[113]

The perceived purpose of the artillery was 'to make the Highlanders leave the ground where they stood, and come down to attack the army'.[114] However, although artillery could help win a battle it was not the decisive arm; victory was possible without it. It had been absent or negligible at Preston and Sheriffmuir, and its presence at Prestonpans had been of very limited use.

The Infantry

The bulk of any army at this time was made up of the infantry. At Culloden, infantry made up almost 90 per cent of the regulars; though at Sherriffmuir, they were about 80 per cent and unusually at Preston, about 25 per cent. The rank and file carried a flintlock musket with a socket bayonet; officers, sergeants, standard bearers and drummers did not. They would march to the battlefield in column and then deploy into lines, usually three deep, in order to maximize firepower. Effective range was 100 feet. Regular troops fired volleys, platoon by platoon, usually against enemy infantry, who would return fire and victory usually went to the side which could longest withstand the other.[115] Melee was uncommon, unless troops came across each other accidentally or if there was fighting over defensive works, but the threat of it could be decisive. The Jacobites were often well armed with muskets, but for them, melee (or the threat of it) was crucial, unless standing on the tactical defensive such as at Preston and Glenshiel. Thus the regulars had to demolish the potential chargers. Hawley issued the following directive on 12 January 1746:

The sure way to demolish them is at 3 deep to fire by ranks diagonally to the Centre when they come, the rear rank first, and even that rank not to fire until they are
within 10 or 12 paces but If the fire is given at a distance you will probably be broke
for you never get time to load a second cartridge ... if you will but observe the above
directions, they are the most despicable Enimy that are.[116]

The Jacobites were also aware that volley fire by the regulars could be deadly.
Colonel John O'Sullivan noted, 'there are no troops in the world but what they'l
overcome in firing'.[117] Likewise, Cumberland, writing on 30 January, on changing the army's order of battle: 'I put all the cavalry in the third line, because by all
accounts the rebels don't fear that, as they do our fire, and on that alone I must
depend.'[118] Cumberland had already seen what disciplined volley fire by British
regulars could do to their enemy at both Dettingen and Fontenoy.

The breakdown in morale was crucial in battle. At Prestonpans, this was
deemed to have been decisive, but it was not initially irretrievable. When the
Jacobites advanced, Lascelles noted that his men, 'were crouching and creeping
backwards, with their arms recovered, occasioned by a continual irregular fire
over their heads, which I soon set right, by my example and reproaches, and kept
them firm by continuing at their head'.[119] Men did not fire volleys as they should.
Instead, as Henderson reported, 'They [the Jacobites] received some platoons,
which some of the soldiers, without orders, discharged for their own safety'.[120]
Colonel Whitney later wrote, dismissively, 'the fire of the Foot began, which
was rattled off'.[121] This was also put down to the fact that 'a great number of
new raised men among them, they fired too soon'.[122] An officer later concluded,
'Neither officers nor general can divest men of dread and panick when it seizes
them, he only can do that who makes the heart of man. To their being struck
with a most unreasonable panick and to no one thing else, this disgraceful event
is owing.' He added that Cope and his officers did all they could:

the whole body became posses'd with the same fatal dread, so that it became utterly
impossible for the general, of the best intentioned of his officers, either to put an end
to their fears, or stop their flight, tho', he and they did all that was in the power of men
to do, and in doing it, exposed themselves in such a manner to the fire of the rebels.[123]

However, it was also argued that the senior officers had let down the men. One
contemporary letter stated, 'Our men had orders not to fire till they had the
word from their officers, but that no orders were ever given by the general, or he
seen after the first fire. The general officers being gone, the men fired at random,
some one shot, some more, not any above two'.[124] Likewise: 'We learn no account
but that the general officers being run away with the first fire of the Highlanders,
the men were almost left to themselves, made little resistance, and submitted
and it was all over within a quarter of an hour'.[125] It was also alleged that the
men's bayonets were not fixed.[126] The 100 infantry who acted as the artillery

guard were charged by the Jacobites. According to Kerr: 'upon which the artillery guard fell into confusion ... and gave a very irregular fire.'[127]

Yet not all the infantry behaved badly. Sir Peter Halkett, a captain of Lee's battalion, 'acted a distinguished part on this account; for after the rout he kept his company together; and getting behind a ditch in Tranent meadow, he kept firing away on the rebels till they were glad to let him surrender on easy terms'.[128]

The infantry were affected by the action of their own cavalry at both Prestonpans and Falkirk. At the former, 'The dragoons began first to reel and give way, and their example was soon followed by the foot, who likewise took to their heels'.[129] When the dragoons had been repelled at Falkirk, they were swiftly pursued by their enemies, and 'the English cavalry, falling back on their own infantry drawn up in order of battle behind them, threw them immediately into disorder and carried the right wing of their army with them in their flight'. At the same time, other infantry units fled on seeing what had happened and also the charge of the Camerons being directed upon them.[130] Sir John Clerk of Penicuik wrote, 'whole regiments ran off without firing or receiving fire from the enemy ... who had behaved well in Flanders'.[131]

Hawley wrote, 'Such scandalous cowardice I never saw before'.[132] Cumberland was surprised at their behavior: 'they did not use to run away formerly'.[133] The like occurred at Falkirk, too, as a private from Barrell's regiment reported, 'At the running away of —'s regiment, like a catching infection, the whole front follow'd, and likewise the rear, not one regiment being left in the field but ours'.[134]

At Prestonpans, the infantry only managed a single and ineffective volley, 'and received a very regular fire from them' as Elcho wrote.[135] Twenty men, including six officers, rallied at one point and fired upon the Jacobites, but their resistance collapsed when Lord George Murray confronted them with 100 men.[136] Home wrote, 'none of the soldiers attempted to load their pieces again, and not one bayonet was stained with blood'.[137] Part of this was due to seeing their comrades' actions around them. According to Home: 'The soldiers, confounded and terrified to see the cannon taken, and the dragoons put to flight.'[138]

The battalions on the left wing at Sheriffmuir gave way when attacked by the Jacobites and routed. However, this was not wholly due to a collapse of morale. It was partly because the troops were not properly formed up for battle and the Jacobites were hidden because of the terrain. Wightman further wrote, 'the Right of the Enemy's Army ... was fallen upon the Left of our Line with all fury imaginable'.[139] Hawley estimated that only 1,000 shots had been fired by his army on that day; perhaps about three volleys from a single battalion.[140] As he wrote, 'the whole second line of foot ran away without firing a shot.'[141] In part this was because the rain made gunpowder wet; a soldier reported, 'it being one of the most turbulent rainy days I ever saw, a fourth of our pieces missed fire'.[142]

Yet when the infantry did stand firm, they could and did repel the enemy. Long range fire was not effective, as Maxwell noted, 'Their musketry did no great execution at first'.[143] As the private in Barrell's wrote:

> we took their ground and maintained it in spite of the rebels ... we gave them a volley
> of shot, and kept a reserve, which caused them to halt and shake their swords at us;
> we gave them three huzzas and another volley, which caused them to run; we pursued
> them and took a few prisoners.[144]

Likewise, infantry fire was effective at Culloden as Linn wrote, 'we gave them so Warm a Reception that we kept a continuall closs fireing upon them with our small Arms'. He claimed that musketry continued for a quarter of an hour.[145] Taylor wrote that 'the thunder of our fire' resulted in the Jacobites falling back.[146]

There was only one instance when the regulars were outgunned by the Jacobites in a firefight. That was at Preston, where they faced opponents who had the protection of barricades and houses while firing. One contemporary claimed that at one barrier, the Jacobites 'made a dreadful fire upon the King's Troops, killing many on the spot' and forcing the others 'to make a Retreat'.[147]

Hand-to-hand combat for the infantry was relatively rare. Usually one side or another would break before this stage of fighting was reached. For example, at Glenshiel, the defending Jacobites were 'driven from rock to rock, our men chasing them for above three hours'.[148]

However, on those very rare occasions when morale on both sides was high, it did happen and was bloody in the extreme. At Culloden, Barrell's and Monro's battalions were involved in melee. Huske rode up to Barrell's regiment at Culloden, 'bidding the men push home with their bayonets, was so well observed by these brave fellows, that hundreds perished on their points'. Lord Robert Kerr, a captain of the same unit, was 'killed with his spontoon in the heart of a rebel'.[149]

Other accounts attest to the ferocity of this stage of the battle, in which Barrell's battalion lost seventeen men killed and 108 wounded, about a third of the total, and Monro's had fourteen men killed on the spot and another sixty-eight injured. Of these casualties, eleven were those of officers.[150] It was reported, 'There was scarce a soldier or officer of Barrell's or Monro's which engaged, who did not kill one or two men each with their bayonets or spontoons'. Of Barrell's, it was said, 'After the battle there was not a bayonet in this regiment but was either bloody or bent'.[151] An officer of Monro's attested, 'Our lads fought more like Devils than Men'.[152] According to Elcho, Jacobite losses were greater because 'it was the more easy as they had no targets, for they would not be at the pains upon a march to carry them'.[153]

Yet it is arguable that it was massed volleys of musketry fire that proved decisive. Despite the bloody hack just mentioned, many Jacobite troops burst through the two battalions. They were checked by three battalions of the second line, 'who made great havoc of 'em, and the greater for them being (unusually) fifty deep'.[154] William Oman, who was in one of these battalions, wrote, 'The perpetual fire of our troops made for five minutes', which 'beat them off, and obliged them to turn their backs and run away'.[155]

Those on the receiving end thought so, too, with John Daniel recalling, 'our hopes were very slender from the continual fire of musketry that was kept up upon them from right to left'.[156] O'Sullivan wrote, 'the enemys musquetary begins, & continues as regular & as nurrished a fire as any troops cou'd. Our men advances, but slolly, & really it is not possible yt any troops yt cant answer such a fire as the enemy kept can do otherwise'.[157]

It was thought that the regulars had the advantage over the Jacobites in a firefight. Maxwell recorded, 'Lord George Murray was very sensible that regular troops must have the advantage in Highlanders in the use of firearms'. So, at Clifton, he ensured his men were lined behind hedges and ditches.[158]

Many soldiers on the battlefield were never engaged at all. According to Linn, at Culloden, 'Note there was only 3 or 4 regiments of foot in the front line that were engaged; our centre & rear lines were not engaged att all; the battle was only on the left of the front line: the regiments that were engaged were Barrells & Monroes & ours'.[159] The infantry were the battle-winning component of any army. If the infantry stood, the battle would not be lost. At Mollwitz in 1741, the Prussian cavalry had been routed by the Austrians, but Frederick's infantry stood firm and won the day. So it was the case in these campaigns.

The Cavalry

There were two types of mounted soldier in the British army at this period; horse and dragoons. The latter were originally mounted infantry and were also trained to fight on foot, though rarely did so (except at Preston and Clifton), so there was little difference in effect between the two, though the former were fewer in number and better paid. Cavalry were divided into regiments and subdivided into squadrons, usually two or three, each with two troops. Their purpose was to act as mobile shock troops and to charge with sword, primarily against enemy cavalry, and also to pursue fleeing enemy at the end of a successful action, or to cover a retreat. Dragoons were also armed with carbines if they had to fight on foot.[160]

Yet the battles of the Jacobite campaigns were different, for in most of the actions, the role of the Jacobite cavalry on the field of battle was negligible and their numbers minimal, so were usually kept in reserve; Sheriffmuir being the single exception to the rule.

Cavalry often perturbed the Jacobites. The Master of Sinclair reported that in 1715, concerning the Grey Dragoons, 'tho' not two hundred men, they were a greater terror than all the others'.[161] At Falkirk, Daniel recalled, 'Here, I must acknowledge, that when I saw this moving cloud of horse, regularly disciplined, in full trot upon us down the summit, I doubted not but they would have ridden over us without opposition (I mean the front line) and bear us down without difficulty in their impetuous progress'.[162] It was said that the Jacobites were fearful of cavalry. Glenorchy remarked, 'the people of that country dislike coming southward and fear dragoons more than double the number of foot'.[163] Henry Conway agreed, writing in 1746, 'They [the Jacobites] cannot defend themselves against the force of our cavalry'.[164]

Their effectiveness could be blunted if either horses or men were inexperienced. The dragoon horses at Prestonpans were unused to musketry, and so 'would not stand fire, and had immediately fallen into disorder, that soon after they saw many dragoons flying, some one way, some another'. Fowke noted:

> I found many of the horses backs not fit to receive the riders, many of the men's and some of the officers' legs so swell'd that they could not wear boots; and those who really were to be depended upon, in a manner overcome for want of sleep.[165]

They could have had a decisive effect, as one commentator noted:

> Had the squadron of Colonel Gardiner's dragoons that covered the train [of artillery] advanced and put that party that attacked it into confusion, which they might easily have done, we by that means would have gained as complete a rout over the rebels as they did over us.[166]

They could also be used in a scouting capacity, in front of the army, as at Prestonpans. Cope had placed 'out-guards of horse'. On seeing the Jacobite advance guard, they called out, and hearing no answer, 'perceived what they were, and rode off to give the alarm'.[167] As an officer later related, 'Here, to do the dragoons justice, they were very alert, and their patrols brought good intelligence the whole night, of every motion the enemy made'.[168] The cavalry were deployed in the same way at Falkirk, reporting that the Jacobite army was on the march.

It was usual for them to be stationed on the flanks of the infantry, as at Sheriffmuir and at Culloden, though were only on one flank, the left, at Falkirk. They could also be stationed in reserve, as at Preston. Two regiments were posted on the left of the line at Culloden, 'to endeavour to fall upon the right flank of the rebels'. Cavalry could also be used defensively. With the advance of the front line there, a morass on the right was passed and so this 'left our rank flank quite uncover'd to them; his royal highness thereupon immediately order'd Kingston's Horse, from the reserve, and a little squadron of about 60 of Cobham's which had been patrolling, to cover our flank'.[169]

Argyll used cavalry at Sheriffmuir to great effect. He later explained:

finding them [the Jacobites] not entirely formed, I judged it was necessary to lose no time and accordingly I began the action on the right with the dragoons, charged both their horse and foot without firing one shot, and tho' they received us with a very good countenance, and gave us their fire pretty close, we broke thro' them.

The Jacobites were driven three miles backwards, across the river Allan and

we could not but judge it an entire Rout and thought of nothing but pursuing them as long as we had day light.[170]

His cavalry on the left flank also charged the enemy as soon as possible and carried off a Jacobite standard, but afterwards could only help cover the infantry's retreat.[171]

Cavalry could be employed to devastating effect, or could be thrown away to not only negative effect, but also serving to demoralize the infantry. This was certainly the case at both Prestonpans and Falkirk. In the former, morale was critical, yet this was not apparent until the last moment, for as Colonel Whitney later wrote, when the army wheeled to face the foe, it was, as his cavalrymen were concerned, 'done with all the coolness, silence and Resolution that I could wish from brave men'.[172]

Whitney was ordered to have his dragoon squadron to charge:

to march his squadron out of the line, in order to attack them in the flank, before they come up to the cannon. On which he immediately marched out, and wheel'd his squadron, and got within pistol shot of their flank; when, on a few shots coming from the flank of the Highlanders, the men stopt and could not be got away any further, notwithstanding that all that Lord Loudon, Colonel Whitefoord and the other officers could do; and immediately the rear rank began to run away, and the rest followed.[173]

Indeed, Whitney was wounded by a pistol shot in his sword arm. Gardiner's dragoons, on the left, fared no better. His squadron also received a few shots and followed suit. 'The dragoons on the left, about the same time went off, also without ever being attacked, and so did the two squadrons which made up our corps de reserve'. All the cavalry halted by the edge of the park walls, but could not be prevailed on to rally.[174] It was alleged, but denied, that Gardner shouted at them, 'What, dragoons, are you going to desert me?'[175]

It was also the horses who were frightened. Henderson wrote, 'the young horses on the wings ... affrighted at such a noise [of gunfire] in the Morning, fell a capering, fell a capering, fled off all at once'.[176] Whitney's subordinate also had problems with his horse, as Whitney recalled that he ordered him to order the men to charge, but 'having a wild mare horse, he fell a plunging and never ceased till he threw the lieutenant on his back on the ground, by which means a second lucky occasion ... was lost'.[177]

Richard Jack, who was present at the battle, noted the decisive importance of the cavalry's role, writing, 'Had the squadron of Colonel Gardiner's dragoons that covered the train advanced, and put that party that attacked it into confusion, which they might easily have done, we by that means would have gained as compleat a victory over the rebels as they did over His Majesty's Troops'.[178] Whitney thought likewise, 'otherwise I thought I had the fairest opportunity of doing a notable piece of work'.[179]

The three regiments of dragoons were the first to be thrown into the fray at Falkirk, unsupported. According to Elcho, 'The Dragoons drew up in Battle opposite to the Prince's right wing, and after having made several motions to intimidate the Highlanders, at last came down in a line at a full trot & attacked them sword in hand'. However, the Jacobites fired 'within half pistol shot of them, gave them a full discharge, which kill'd a great many of them, & broke the rest'.[180] Some of the cavalry did reach the Jacobite lines and 'some of the Highlanders that were in the front line were trod down'.[181] However, the Jacobites seized dragoons by their clothes and dragged them down to be killed with their dirks.[182]

Archibald Butler claimed that 'It is certain from undoubted authority, that Ligonier's dragoons began the attack a great deal too soon'. He wrote that 'The occasion of this precipitous charge and our hasty attack was to wipe off the dust and odium of Gladsmuir [Prestonpans]'.[183] Hawley was angry at their flight, writing 'they ought to be decimated' and emphasized that they were 'Scottish and Irish sheep'.[184] Cumberland considered that the same dragoons fled at both battles, and so on the second time it was a case of 'escaping the first time, made them like safe methods'.[185]

There were attempts made to rally the cavalry at both Prestonpans and Falkirk. At the latter it was unsuccessful, for there was a second fire directed against Gardiner's dragoons, and once they fled, Hamilton's did likewise.[186] However, at Falkirk, one regiment, Cobham's, joined those infantry battalions still standing; but although the regiment made aggressive moves towards Charles's entourage, they did not attack.[187]

Dragoons could be dismounted to fight. This occurred at Clifton and they 'behaved extremely well', but as we will see, they were pushed back by a Jacobite charge.[188] It was also the case at Preston. Four of the five dragoon regiments were dismounted, as was the regiment of horse. This was because Wills's force consisted of six cavalry regiments and one infantry regiment, and he had to take a held town. Cavalry would be of no use if the Jacobites were defending barricades and houses, which they were here. Dismounted dragoons fought as if they were infantry, with firepower alone. Only one regiment of dragoons remained mounted, presumably in the case of any attempted break out.[189] Similarly, at Clifton, some of the dragoons were dismounted and others stayed mounted.[190] This was rarely successful, however. At Clifton, the dismounted dragoons were in melee with the Jacobites and were pushed back.[191]

Once the Jacobite attack at Culloden had faltered, the cavalry were employed to great effect:

> The cavalry, which had charged from the right and the left, met in the centre, except for two squadrons of dragoons, which we missed and they were gone in pursuit of the runaways; Lord Ancrum was order'd to pursue with the horse as far as he could; and did it with so good an effect, that a very considerable number was killed in the pursuit.[192]

Rigorous pursuit was also the order of the day at Sheriffmuir, as 'Our dragoons gave no quarter for some time, which made the slaughter the greater'.[193]

Yet the cavalry concentrated on the easy targets. Maxwell wrote, 'They made no attack where there was any body of the Prince's men together, but contented themselves with sabering such unfortunate people as fell in their way'.[194] On one instance, a body of cavalry gave way to allow a retreating Jacobite body to escape.[195]

Sometimes, two or more of the three arms were used in conjunction. We have noted that artillery and infantry acted together against the charging Jacobites at Culloden. At Sheriffmuir, as Wightman wrote, 'the Horse on our right, with the constant fire of the platoons of Foot, soon put the Left of their Army to rout'.[196] While the cavalry pursued the Jacobites, the three battalions on the right of the front line advanced towards them as quickly as possible, too.[197]

As with the artillery, the cavalry were not the decisive battle-winning troops. However, they could turn a victory into a decisive victory. Fatigue and darkness could prevent any vigorous pursuit. Lacking cavalry meant that an army could not pursue its defeated foe, as did not occur at Brandywine in 1777, thus enabling the American rebels to retreat and fight another day. A vigorous cavalry pursuit would have made all the difference, turning a victory into a decisive one. This happened at Culloden, and to a lesser extent at Sheriffmuir.

The Aftermath

After the battle it was time to count the cost. This was in terms of lives lost, prisoners taken, but also in terms of trophies: standards, cannon and baggage. The loser would usually have taken the most casualties and have lost the most trophies. Victory usually meant far fewer losses in manpower. Linn wrote that, at Culloden, 'We lost very few men of our Army, only a few wounded; our loss is about 200 men Wounded & Killed. Thank God we lost not one man of our Regiment, only a few wounded, we never had such good Luck befor'.[198] The enemy's loss was the victor's gain. At Culloden, twelve standards, twenty cannon, 2,320 muskets, 190 swords, twenty-two ammunition wagons and thirty-seven barrels of gunpowder were taken, as well as a number of high-profile prisoners, including the Earl of Kilmarnock. Jacobite dead were in the region of 1,000.[199]

This was not always the case, for the regulars lost twenty-one dead and 121 wounded, from a force of about 2,000 men at Glenshiel; yet the Jacobite force was dispersed and the Spanish laid down their arms on the following day, having suffered minimal casualties.[200] Likewise the regulars lost far more casualties at Preston four years previously (at least fifty-six dead and ninety-two wounded) and victory went to them. As with Glenshiel, this battle was won due to a collapse of morale among their opponents. Carpenter later wrote:

> the chief prisoners assur'd me and others that as soon as they saw my detachment from the steeple the Lord Widdrington who was in the churchyard said very loud that their men that they were all undone, and upon that they consulted to ask termes, which they did in 4 hours after my arrivall.[201]

Defeat was another matter. According to Elcho, at Prestonpans, £2,500 in the military chest and all the baggage was lost, along with 'a great many Colours and Standards ... and some horses'. Elcho claimed 500 men were killed and 1,400 taken prisoner, though the real number was lower, it was still substantial; perhaps 1,036 captured and 364 killed and missing.[202] There were similar losses at Falkirk, though proportionately far less, with 280 killed or wounded among the infantry and at least eighty casualties among the cavalry. Material losses at the latter were seven cannon, three standards and other flags and the camp's baggage.[203] Defeat was a demoralizing experience. Whitney wrote that at Prestonpans, 'I observed the field in their rear covered with Runaways', who had thrown down their weapons and left their officers behind.[204]

Yet victory and defeat were not always clear cut, and the former was not always greeted with wholehearted enthusiasm by the successful commander. There was a great deal of disquiet over the conclusions of both of the battles of 1715, although both were victories for the regulars. Argyll wrote on the day after the battle, 'The Victory we have got is owing to Providence, for my own part, I pretend no further merit than to have done my duty'. In part this was because of his high percentage of losses.[205] Argyll lost about 670 men, killed, wounded and captured, too, which was a far higher percentage of his troops than the Jacobites had lost, as well as 1,500 stands of arms. On the other hand, the Jacobites had lost 800 men (far less proportionately), fourteen standards, four cannon, ammunition carts and bread wagons.[206] A costly victory was a tragedy. About 148 regulars were killed or wounded at Preston; about a tenth of the total.[207] Colonel Forrester, after the battle of Preston, wrote, 'the loss of soe many brave gentlemen, takes off a good dale of the joy I should have had, in gaining so considerable ane affair'.[208]

At Culloden, the casualties were relatively minor. A total of fifty men, including four officers, were killed outright and 259 were wounded. Of these, many would have died of their wounds – the total number is unknown. Casualties were not divided evenly between the fifteen battalions of infantry, three regiments of cavalry, Highlanders and artillerymen. Seven of the infantry battalions suffered no fatalities (and two recorded that none were wounded either), as did a regiment of cavalry (and none wounded), a militia unit and the artillerymen. Six units only lost one man killed outright. On the other extreme, one battalion lost seventeen killed and 108 wounded; another fourteen dead and sixty-eight wounded.[209] Casualties were lamented. After Culloden, Cumberland returned to the scene of battle and walked there alone. He was apparently in deep meditation, laid his hand on his breast, and with eyes lifted to Heaven, said, 'Lord! What am I! That I should be spared, when so many brave men lie dead upon the spot?'[210] Yet a victory was to be celebrated, as Bradshaw wrote after Culloden, 'No history of battles can brag of so singular a victory and so few of our own men lost'.[211] God was often thanked for victory, with Private Linn writing 'I give you the trouble of these to acquaint you what great things God almighty hath done for us'.[212]

Meanwhile, an officer would be dispatched with the news; after the Jacobite surrender at Preston, this task was entrusted to Colonel Maurice Nassau; after Glenshiel it was Ensign Hugh McKay. They were chosen as a reward for their services on the field; the latter for his 'good service in battle'. Both were rewarded on arrival, respectively with £500 and £100.[213]

There could also be dissension among the protagonists after the battle. Although that at Preston was a victory for the regulars, Generals Wills and Carpenter argued. Wills took 'on him great command' and so Carpenter, who was his senior, 'us'd him very freely'. Carpenter even considered putting Wills under arrest, but was dissuaded from such an action. Given that the Jacobites had not yet surrendered and Wills's command was the larger, 'itt might have proved fatall to His Majesty's service'.[214] After the surrender, Carpenter was still aggrieved and still wanted to have Wills arrested. Yet his troops had been sent to Wigan to recuperate after a long march. One reason why he was so angry was that he thought that Wills's attacks on Preston on the 12 November had been costly and fruitless, writing, that he had 'made a rash attack, highly blameable, by loosing so many men to no purpose (of which you will hear more), except to serve his own ambition by ending it before I came up'.[215] He was also unhappy because he feared that Wills would gain the credit for the victory, not himself, 'I find the prints give him all the power and applause, I suppose by his own or some friends' direction, and I fear that his Majesty may be under that mistake also'. He wrote to Townshend and Marlborough to ensure that his part in the victory was not overlooked.[216] The two men had been rivals for several years already, and almost fought a duel in Hyde Park in the following year, which was only called off at Marlborough's insistence.

It was not always the case that defeated troops were downhearted. A soldier of Barrell's, a unit which had pushed back the Jacobites immediately before them at Falkirk, in contrast to much of the rest of their comrades, was not downcast, writing, 'We expect in a few days' time to give them another meeting which I pray God it may be attended with a better opportunity'.[217] The lack of success at Falkirk was not acknowledged by some. Wolfe later wrote, ''twas not a battle, as neither side would fight ... Though we can't have been said to have totally routed the enemy, yet we remained a long time masters of the field of battle'.[218] Hawley, too, wrote, 'I can't say we are quite beat today, but our left is beat and their left is beat', yet he was clearly not deluding himself, for he continued, 'We had enough to beat them for we had 2000 men more than they'.[219]

Captain George Fitzgerald of Monroe's battalion later recalled, 'I was knocked down by a musket ball which went through my hat and wig and graz'd my head, but I rose again being only stunned by it'. On trying to join the battalions which were holding firm, he was attacked by 'a party of the rebels, who cut me in the head and knock'd me down a second time, when they began to rob me'. However, though he feared death, a French officer intervened when he called to him. Another wounded soldier, an unknown dragoon, recalled his experiences calmly in a letter after the Clifton skirmish: 'I am wounded in the right shoulder with a Ball, and am shot through the first finger of my right hand, but am in a Fair way to do well, and hope to do my Duty with the Regiment in a few days time.'[220]

Pursuit could lead to far more serious casualties for the loser, as has been noted as happening at Sherriffmuir and Culloden, but could be prevented by terrain, as at Glenshiel, when the moutainous terrain made the Jacobite escape possible.[221]

To the victor, the spoils. After the battle of Preston, the Jacobite prisoners were deprived of their baggage, their money and their linen by the victorious soldiery. This was initiated by their commander: 'General Wills, as soon as the action was over, and the rebels secured, gave the troops engaged in it, the plunder of the rebels, amongst the leaders of whom they got a good booty, as well as some others in the town, who appear'd fond of the rebels'.[222] It could have been worse, as Forrester wrote, 'it has been lucky for them that I was here, else they would have been very ill used by our people'.[223]

There was also some looting of property in the town itself, too. According to Henry Paton, a Jacobite, 'they with force and armes broke open doers and locks of chambers and closets, and the moneys, plate, goods, and chattels of most of the inhabitants of that towne' were stolen. Even those loyal to King George had their houses pillaged.[224] Henry Prescott wrote 'Wee are disturbed with Accounts of the barbarous behaviour of the soldiers of the popish gentlemen's houses'.[225] However, this behaviour was short lived, as a Lancashire Quaker noted, 'They then plundered several Papists' houses and then there was some little quietness'.[226]

On the field of Culloden, the victorious regulars took their revenge, as Henderson noted:

> The Field was clear, and the Victory being compleat, the soldiers, warm in their Resentment, did Things hardly to be accounted for; several of their wounded Men were stabbed, yea some who were lurking in houses, were taken out and shot upon the Field, tho' others were sav'd, by those whose Compassion was raised at the sight of so many victims.[227]

He attributed such behaviour as follows:

> the Rebels had enraged the Troops, their Habit was strange, their Language still stranger, and their way of fighting was shocking to the Utmost degree: The Rebellion was unprovoked and the King's Troops had greatly suffered by it; the fields of Preston[pans] and Falkirk, were fresh in their Memory, they had lost a Gardner, a Whitney, a Munro besides other officers ... their mangled corpses could not but stir up the soldiers to revenge. Therefore, if, when they found Vengeance in their Power, they violated the stricter rules of Humanity, some allowance ought to be made for the Passions they were inspired with at that time.[228]

Spectators were also not immune from the victorious soldiers. Michael Hughes later wrote, 'many of the inhabitants, not doubting of success, who came out of curiosity to see the Action, or perhaps to get plunder, never went home again to tell the story: for their being mixt up with their own people, we could not know one from another'.[229] Soldiers also helped themselves to the spoils of war, as a contemporary historian observed, they were seen 'strutting about in rich laced waistcoats, hats, &c'.[230]

However, there was no universal massacre following the battle. Private Linn wrote, 'we send out every day Strong parties of foot & Horse ... & they bring in great heaps of prisoners every day'.[231] Troops were also rewarded for captured weapons and standards brought in.[232]

Conclusion

Land battles could be decisive. Culloden was, but so was Preston and Glenshiel. Sheriffmuir was, too, though only in retrospect. Poltava in 1709 led to the destruction of the Swedish army and the end of Sweden being an offensive power in the Great Northern War, though even so, fighting continued for a decade. The Boyne was a victory for William III, and led to the flight of James II, though the conflict continued for another two years. Five years earlier, the latter's army brought Monmouth's rebellion to a bloody climax. But this was not always the case; Falkirk was not. Even renowned battles on the Continent were rarely knockout blows. Leuthen and Rossbach in 1757 were crushing victories by Prussia over Austria and France respectively; and Blenheim in 1704 was a great victory for Marlborough over the French. Yet none of these victories led to the ending of the wars for the victors. Saratoga in 1777 led to the capitulation of a British army, but although it encouraged France to ally with the rebellious colonists, it did not immediately lead to the war's end. Killiekrankie was a famous victory for the Jacobites in 1689, but it led nowhere.

The question is to explain why some of the battles on the Jacobite campaign were decisive. In 1746 the Jacobites had but one field army. It suffered heavy casualties; at least 1,000 dead and several hundred made prisoners, with loss of artillery and baggage. It was no longer in a position to wage conventional warfare and this was obvious to Charles who fled and without him, formed resistance was effectively over. At Glenshiel, Jacobite casualties were relatively light, but morale collapsed and the Spanish troops surrendered on the following day while their Highland allies fled. At Preston, too, morale of the English Jacobite leaders collapsed after a day's fighting and reinforcements for the regulars arrived. This was despite the fact that the Jacobites got the better of their enemies on the first day of fighting and had inflicted greater casualties. With the Jacobite army encircled it had to surrender, with the loss of all its men.

Sherriffmuir was a tactical draw. Neither army was destroyed: both withdrew to potentially fight another day. It was the subsequent developments which were of equal importance. As Argyll received reinforcements, Mar's men began to drift away. Yet it was two and a half months later that another decisive state was to be taken in bringing the campaign to an end. However, without the battle's result, the latter would not have been possible.

Although Prestonpans and Falkirk were defeats for the regular army – and the former more so than the latter – neither were ultimately decisive in altering the campaign's conclusion, though this is not to infer that victory for the regulars was inevitable. Rather, in the first instance, only a very small portion of the forces available to the Crown had been destroyed, and they not the best. At Falkirk, a rather larger battle, the majority of the regulars survived to fight another day and within a fortnight of the battle were talking the offensive again, under a new leader. In part this was because the Jacobites failed to rigorously pursue and so exploit their victory to the full; which was to occur in the reverse to the British armies in several battles in America three decades later.

Why were the regulars successful and why did they occasionally fail? Numbers alone did not supply an answer, as they had at Fontenoy in 1745 or

Hastenback in 1757. Indeed, of the four victories, in only one, Culloden, had the regulars had a numerical advantage, and arguably this was not the decisive factor. At Glenshiel and Preston the numbers were roughly equal, but at Sherriffmuir, the Jacobites had an advantage in over 2:1. At Sherrifmuir and Culloden troops were used at the key point in the battle, and then two or three arms of the army were effectively combined. Argyll concentrated infantry and cavalry offensively against the left wing of the Jacobites; whereas Cumberland saw to it that artillery and infantry turned the Jacobite advance into a retreat, while the cavalry turned the retreat into a bloody rout. This was not only a great material loss for the Jacobites in terms of men and material, but just as importantly it led Charles to give up the struggle and begin his flight to France, thus ending any realistic chance of further Jacobite resistance. Glenshiel and Preston were less dramatic, and it was a case of the regulars holding firm in the face of setbacks, while the Jacobite morale sank, leading to retreat and surrender respectively.

Defeat at Prestonpans was largely due to inexperienced troops facing an unconventional and aggressively offensive foe. The cavalry refused to charge and fled; the men operating the guns did likewise and the infantry fired too soon. At Falkirk, the precipitate use of the cavalry, the lack of any artillery and bad weather affecting the infantry's musketry led to a collapse in the morale of the majority of the infantry. Only the presence of mind of Huske and Cholmondely prevented the same happening to the battalions on the right flank.

In all these battles, morale was crucial. In conventional warfare, this was the case, too, as lines of infantry and artillery exchanged fire until one side began to falter and then might collapse in the face of a determined advance, supported by cavalry. Morale was a factor of effective combat and maximizing enemy casualties. Experience was important, and so was leadership, with haste leading to disaster at Falkirk, but caution to victory at Culloden.

4 THE SIEGE

One of the major components of eighteenth-century wars – perhaps the most important of all – was siege warfare. After all, Marlborough took far more strongpoints than he won battles (thirty major sieges to four major battles) during the War of Spanish Succession. Possession of these fortifications meant that the surrounding countryside with its supplies could be controlled and denied to the enemy, and capture of them in itself was a measurable achievement. They were useful bargaining pawns at treaty negotiations. Furthermore, there were psychological and prestigious reasons for taking or holding onto a place. The decision not to besiege or to fail to take a place could have dire consequences, as lines of communication could be threatened if an army left a fortress untaken in its wake. They were formalized and predictable, unlike battles, and were seen, albeit often erroneously, as cheaper in terms of human losses. Yet siege warfare was not cheap; in the sieges of 1708–11, the Allies lost 50,000 men, compared to 44,000 during the major battles of the war. The length of Marlborough's sieges varied from six days to four months, averaging at thirty-six days. They were, then, a potentially great drain on limited resources of men and time, even if successful. Sieges could provoke battles as an army marched to the relief of its besieged compatriots or allies, as occurred at Fontenoy in 1745 or Falkirk in the succeeding year.[1]

It should come, therefore, as no surprise that there was concern over the holding of fortresses during the Jacobite campaigns, as Cumberland wrote to Newcastle on 28 November 1745:

> By a letter of Lord Cholmondeley to General Ligonier of this day's receipt, he expressed apprehensions as to the possibility of defending the town of Chester and seem'd to have taken a resolution of abandoning that, of sending away the two new regiments and of retiring into the castle (which they are putting into as good a condition as they can) with that of Bligh, but as I look upon it to be of the utmost consequence to preserve the town, as well as the castle of Chester, I have written to him to desire him to hold out both as long as possible, and promised to march to his relief if the rebels should attempt to besiege him.[2]

For the attackers, as John Murray observed in August 1745, 'the chiefs were of opinion that the barracks at Ruthven ought to be taken not only to have the country free, but on account of the quantity of oatmeal that might be found there'.[3]

The Jacobite campaigns saw a number of sieges take place, though almost all occurred in 1745 and 1746. Before these can be examined, and the differences and similarities between more conventional Continental warfare can be surveyed, we need to say a little about the nature of fortifications and sieges both in Europe and elsewhere.

In the Middle Ages, towns and cities of any significance were walled for protection, as were the seats of magnates and monarchs. Defences were built of stone and walls and towers were high. But by the fifteenth century, the use of artillery was commonplace and such fortifications were deemed obsolete in the face of modern guns. Greater internal security, partly brought about by more centralized states with standing armies, also reduced the need throughout many states for costly private or municipal defences, though many towns and cities retained their old walls.

However, such castles were not wholly obsolete, as was proved in the Civil Wars, when castles and manor houses had withheld assaults for months or years. Their walls were thick and so able to withstand all but heavy artillery. The latter needed many horses to pull them among poor quality roads, so the time, trouble and cost of using such prohibited their employment and so many commanders preferred not to use much artillery at all, which led to more traditional defences withstanding sieges.[4]

However, there were significant changes in the way that new fortifications were constructed from the sixteenth century onwards, which was part of the much vaunted 'military revolution'. Walls became lower, and were built as earthworks, with bastions providing platforms for defensive artillery. Engineering became a specialized form of the soldier's trade, especially in France from the later seventeenth century, where Vauban became the greatest exponent both of fortifications and siege craft. Fortifications were mostly built along troubled borders in the Low Countries, in parts of Italy and along the Austrian frontier with the Ottoman Empire. All these were highly expensive undertakings, so were not carried out lightly, but only for essential military reasons.

Taking fortresses was as much an art as holding them. Elaborate measures were taken to besiege fortresses. The besiegers had to isolate the garrison from the outside world, to prevent supplies or reinforcements arriving. Trenches were dug around the fortress, being dug closer and closer to the outer defences. Siege artillery – guns of far higher calibre, and far heavier, than those used on the battlefield – would be sited and bombardment commenced at one or more places in order to make a breach in the defences. The enemy would then be summoned to surrender. According to convention, a negotiated surrender would then take place. A bloody conclusion by storm was rare. Even without this, a siege could be both lengthy and costly in terms of men and money.[5]

Of course, because Britain is an island, a superficial assessment might deem that such fortification was not deemed necessary. However, because Britain was a player, at various degrees of intensity, in the great power game of Europe, it could not wholly rely on the wooden walls of the Navy, but had to invest in fortifications. These primarily were built on coastlines, and were initiated by Henry VIII along the south coast and on the Scilly Isles. The important naval base at Portsmouth was defended thus, as were others on the Thames estuary.

Yet there were also internal threats to consider. Perhaps the most significant was England's northern neighbour, who was at war with England under both Henry VIII and Elizabeth. Berwick upon Tweed was fortified at great expense under the latter, along the lines of modern fortress designers. Elsewhere there were castles which were garrisoned by regular troops; at Edinburgh, Stirling, Chester, Hull and Carlisle, for example. This was usually to the extent of two or more companies of infantry, under the command of the lieutenant governor (the post of governor was usually a sinecure). Some cities were still walled, such as Newcastle, Chester, Carlisle, York and Hull. In 1726, there were 31 garrisoned forts in Britain, including nine castles, but excluding the barracks and forts to be built in Scotland in the decade. Most were coastal and in the south and east of England.[6]

The Civil Wars led to a number of castles and cities being pressed into service for use by each side. Few new fortifications were built, however. Defensive works were built around both London and Oxford, the headquarters of the parliamentary and royalist causes respectively. These were largely dismantled and neglected after the 1640s, and a number of towns and castles had their defences slighted by the 1660s. However, the Cromwellian period did lead to a number of barracks and fortifications being constructed in Scotland. Although there was conflict with Holland and then France in the later seventeenth century, this did not lead to an overstretched Treasury investing in additional fortifications. The first Jacobite rebellion in 1689 led to Edinburgh castle being held by troops loyal to James II, in opposition to those of William of Orange. A major new fortress was built at this time, however, on the west coast of Scotland, and was named after the new monarch; Fort William. It was in a strong position, with the sea to the west and mountains and morasses to the north. Initially it was made of earthworks topped by a wooden palisade, with two entrances and bastions at each corner. It was however strongly garrisoned by 1,200 men, but with only twelve guns. This was the only purpose-built fortification standing in Scotland until after 1715.[7]

Existing fortresses were strengthened, however. After 1689, gun embrasures were rebuilt at Edinburgh Castle on its east side and new artillery batteries were created at Stirling. The latter had all but the main entrances closed.[8] However, the attempted invasion of 1708 led to further improvements to Edinburgh castle. Captain Drury had five gun emplacements built on the west and south side.[9] Likewise, at Stirling, there was a construction of massive outer works, incorporating parts of the mid-sixteenth-century artillery platforms. Low-set outer defences were built in order to absorb any artillery bombardment. At the north end there were straight walls pierced by a single gateway, with flanking batteries. More artillery were mounted there.[10] Meanwhile, Fort William's bastions were rebuilt in stone, and there were new powder magazines and barracks built.[11]

Thus at the dawn of the eighteenth century, Britain possessed a patchwork quilt of fortresses, of varying vintages. These were scattered and concentrated in Scotland and the north of England, relics of former border warfare and of the more recent Cromwellian state. They were centres for the state's authority, but were not geared up for conventional warfare, as fortifications on the Continent were.

After the Fifteen, four barracks were built in Scotland. This was a novelty, for troops on mainland Britain usually lived in billets provided by the civilian population. These were at Kiliwhimen, near Loch Ness, Ruthven, Bernea and Inversnaid. The first two were built on rising ground; the second of these on the site of a former castle. They were built to a simple design, with Ruthven being made up of two barrack blocks and a parapeted wall enclosing them, to accommodate 120 men, though Kiliwhimen could hold three times that number. Stables were later added at Ruthven.[12]

Captain Burt, writing a decade later, was critical, writing, 'Barracks were built at a very great expense'. Yet all this was to no avail. This was because, although the soldiers stationed there were meant to keep the peace and inhibit rebellion, 'The regular troops were never used to make such marches, with their arms and accoutrements; were not able to pursue the Highlanders'.[13]

Barracks were also built at Berwick from 1717–21; the only ones then existing in England. They were on a more extensive scale than those in Scotland, costing £5,000 to build and accommodating 36 officers and 600 men. None of these barracks would have been able to resist the attacks of an enemy armed with siege artillery, but since the Jacobites had not had such support in 1689 or 1715, this was not seen as a problem. Instead, they were viewed as being able to resist attacks of lightly armed troops.[14]

Ironically, at the same time, the number of guns at the existing fortresses was being reduced. Edinburgh Castle's complement fell from fifty-four to forty, Fort William's from sixty-eight to thirty, but Stirling Castle only lost two.[15]

In 1724, Major General Wade was sent to Scotland. He was also critical of the state of the defences there. He made two main criticisms. Firstly, each barrack held but a weak company of about thirty men. This was inadequate for their given role. Burt wrote, 'if the number of troops they are built to contain, were constantly quartered in them ... they might be of some use to prevent the insurrections of the Highlanders'. Secondly, 'two of the four are not built in a proper situations as they might have been'.[16]

What was needed, decided Wade, was a chain of properly garrisoned forts and barracks in the Highlands, together with a road network connecting them to each other and to the Lowlands. Their purpose would be to prevent a Jacobite descent into the Lowlands and to provide quarters for sufficient troops to inhibit or contain any insurrection. Newcastle wrote in 1725, that the forts would 'be of the greatest use for restraining the Highlanders'.[17] This entailed building two new fortresses. One was Fort Augustus, near Loch Ness and the other was Fort George at Inverness, thus, with the existing Fort William, making a chain of three fortresses. There had been a plan of making Fort Augustus the chief of these, run by a governor, with lieutenant governors at the other two, but this never materialized. Likewise, though there was accommodation for a battalion at each, these troop levels were never realized.[18] Once all this was underway, Wade was confident in the effectiveness of these measures. He wrote, 'the Pretender's interest in the clans is so low that I think he can now hope for no effectual assistance from that quarter'.[19]

Because fortifications are inherently static, they stand on the defensive. Almost all the siege warfare of this period pitted the regular troops as the defenders against the besieging Jacobites. The exception, as we shall see, was the siege of Carlisle in December 1745, but this was a matter of retaking a stronghold previously lost. To take a fortification usually needed either time or expertise and siege artillery, or a garrison with low morale. It is worth noting that fortifications had their limitations. Forts could be bypassed, as those built by the Spanish in New Mexico in the late seventeenth century. Nor were they impregnable, even to irregular opponents as occurred in America in 1764 during the Pontiac War. Others had to be abandoned.[20]

Although it is traditional to concentrate on the battles of the period, it is worth noting that the following were under siege in 1745–6: Edinburgh, Stirling, Carlisle and Blair castles, Ruthven Barracks, Forts Augustus, George and William, and it was feared that a number of other places would be under attack (Chester, Hull, Portsmouth, Newcastle and Berwick), but never were. Although there was an attempted coup against Edinburgh castle in 1715, there were no sieges during this year; nor in 1719. This chapter examines the condition of the defences of castles, forts, barracks and towns, how these were prepared for potential defence and how effective these were.

Fortresses must not be viewed in isolation. None were impregnable and given time and resources, all could fall. Rather, they need to be viewed in the context of the wider struggle. As contemporary commanders realized, they were part of a defensive network in which field armies were also crucial, and that the fortresses were of limited use without a vigorous stance on the part of the more mobile troops of the field army.

The Condition of the Defences

The siege worthiness of the state's fortified places in 1745 was variable. Decades of internal and external peace do not bode well for military spending, except for that which occurred in Scotland as already noted. At Carlisle, for instance, according to Johnstone:

> The fortifications are in the old style and have been entirely neglected for several centuries, in consequence of the cessation of the long wars between the two countries, and the final union of the Crowns ... The castle was formerly a place of considerable strength, but at present its walls, like those of the town, are falling from age into decay.[21]

Colonel Durand, given the task of defending the place, agreed with him. Arriving on 11 October, he concluded, 'I found it in a very weak and defenceless condition; having no ditch, no out works of any kind, no cover'd ways, the walls very thin in most places, and without proper flanks'.[22] General Folliott, the absentee governor, later observed, 'it was in a very weak condition, there being neither ditch, covered way, no flankers ... he went up on a part of the Rampart between the town and he castle, he was advised not to go too near the wall for fear it should break down'. The defences had not been repaired since about 1737.[23]

A similar story was apparent on the other side of northern England. When Cope surveyed the defences of Berwick at the end of September, he was most critical, writing, 'This place is far from being in a posture of defence' and referred to it as being 'a defenceless place' and in a 'wretched condition'. To be exact, the gun platforms were inadequate, walls and parapets were decayed, the moat was dry and difficult to water, and the ground before the fortress provided cover for any attackers.[24] The town's mayor, Thomas Watson, agreed, 'Our fortifications are in great disrepair'.[25]

On the other hand, there was the recently completed Fort George, of which Johnstone wrote:

> The castle of Inverness was fortified in the modern manner, being a regular square with four bastions, and it was advantageously situated on the top of an eminence which commanded the town ... and has ever since been kept in good repair with the view of enforcing the subjection of the Highlanders.[26]

Fort George also seemed a tough nut to others. O'Sullivan described it thus: 'too well fortified for one small cannon, & yt it would be no easy matter to escalle it because of a double enstinte it had, but discovered a place just under the Bastion yt faces the Bridge, where it could be undermined'.[27]

Fort William was one of the strongest fortresses in Scotland, Stirling and Edinburgh Castles apart. Yet in September 1715, the governor wrote, 'I could wish I had found this place in a better posture of defence, for besides that we have no drawbridge, the parapets here are not completed'.[28] Thirty years later, Maxwell described it thus:

> the strongest fortress in the north of Scotland; it's situated on the western coast, at the mouth of the river Nevis; it's partly defended by that river and by the sea, and that side which is accessible from the land has a good wall, ditch, counter-scarp, and bastions at proper distances, and a kind of ravelin before the gate. It seemed impossible to take such a fort with six pounders.[29]

Yet this view was not universal. Two days later, Alexander Campbell, in charge at Fort William wrote, 'the inner gate which was pulled down some time ago not yet rebuilt'.[30] Furthermore, on the south east side of the fort there was a hill, where guns there would be able to bombard the inside of the fort. One of the bastions, too, projected so far that it could not be covered by the fire from the others.[31] When John Russell, an engineer, arrived on 4 March, he also noted the defences were less than perfect, 'they are not in so good repair as I could have wished, the parapet being too low'.[32]

Ruthven Barracks was also deemed strong, as O'Sullivan noted, they consisted of:

> two buildings upon a sugar loaf, joined together by a very high rampart with a parapet, wch formed a square & flanked at every corner; there were stables detached from the barriks, & surrounded by a wall brest-high, & the ramp inaccessible in a manner. Sullivan judged it to be unatackable with highlanders, & without Cannon.[33]

Yet, as with Fort William, it was far from impregnable, especially to attackers with artillery. As it was situated on top of a hill, the defenders' guns could not be depressed enough to fire upon attackers at the foot of the hill – Fort George had a similar weakness.

Another contemporary was less sure about Fort Augustus, writing that it was:

> a new thing where the public money has been thrown away profusely. They say it cost £30,000 on spacious buildings, a governor's house etc., but it is no fortress and one would be amazed at the folly and profusion that appears there. Twas this year erected into a Government with an establishment for gunners etc ... half their garrison is left out of the new fort and quartered in a barrack a quarter of a mile from them.[34]

Cumberland was not impressed by the fortress's strength, either. He wrote 'by the plan I have seen of the fort, it was impossible it should defend itself long, as

the curtain was comprised of council rooms and lodgings for the principal officers of the garrison'.[35]

Apart from the castles and forts, there were also city walls. Daniel Defoe, on
viewing York's Medieval defences, wrote:

> The old walls are standing, and the gates and posterns; but the old additional works
> which were cast up in the late rebellion [the Civil Wars] are slighted; so that York is
> not now defensible as it was then. But things lie so too, that a little time, and many
> hands, would put those works into their former condition, and make the city able to
> stand out a small siege. But as the ground seems capable by situation, so an ingenious
> head, in our company, taking a stricter view of it, told us, he would undertake to make
> it as strong as Tournay in Flanders ... But this is speculation.[36]

Edinburgh's city walls were also less than suited for defence, as Richard Jack
explained in 1745:

> that from a certain infatuation, to give it no worse name, they were neglected to such
> a degree that it was impossible for the town to stand out for a few hours tho' within
> it they should be thrice the number of the rebels. The principal defect was that the
> parapets of the embrasure was so low, as not to cover any man of a middling size above
> his thighs ... so that the whole chest of a man was exposed as a mark to the enemy.[37]

On the north wall there were low parapets, with doors and windows as part of
the walls where they incorporated the hospital and college church. According to
Jack, this was 'The weakest part of the Town'.[38]

It was not only the state of the defences that gave cause for thought. Fortress
commanders were less than optimistic concerning the strength of their garrisons.
On 9 August, the officer in charge at Bernea Barracks reported thus, 'in case they
attempt ye Barrack we cannot hold out long they being well armed' and that they
could make but a 'small defence'.[39]

Each of these fortified places was garrisoned; anything from five to two
companies of invalids. These men were usually old soldiers, best suited for less
energetic duties than those of the younger soldier on campaign. However, their
numbers were usually inadequate. At Fort William in 1715: 'there's about 70
men in the outposts, nor is it expected they can be fully conformable to the
establishment'. In all, the garrison numbered 300 men.[40] Edinburgh castle had
only a garrison of 100.[41] Major Wentworth, the governor of Fort Augustus in
1745, was concerned as to the condition of the defenders, writing:

> Our men have very hard duty; having both the old and new barracks to defend ...
> Here is a very good train of artillery; but I cannot find one man, who knows how to
> point a Gun, or even saw a shell fired out of a Mortar. There being only two gunners,
> and they not having been much accustomed to it.[42]

Similarly, at Carlisle in 1745, there were only two trained gunners, and of these, one was very elderly and infirm, which left one man to handle twenty guns. To try and rectify this, eighty townsmen were designated as gunners, but clearly this was not a solution as they had next to no instruction.[43] Likewise, Cholmondeley, governor of Chester castle, complained on 21 November 1745, that there was a 'great want he is of a number of gunners and matrosses, there being only two on the establishment, and the guns mounted on the castle walls being 19'.[44] At Berwick, Handasyde noted 'that there are neither engineers, nor gunners in that garrison'.[45]

Fortifications needed more than sturdy works and a competently sized garrison. Artillery had to be adequately mounted and supplies laid up. Cholmondeley, despite his lack of gunners, stated, 'The castle walls are in a very good order, and the artillery mounted in good order'.[46] Clifford's Fort on the Tyne had twelve eighteen to twenty-four pounders.[47] Provisions were often scanty. At Edinburgh castle in September 1715, there were only four days' provisions.[48]

Britain's fortresses were not in a fit state at the outset of the Jacobite campaigns for defence against a properly equipped besieger. In various states of disrepair, undermanned and lacking in provisions, they presented a sorry state of defence, due to years of neglect caused by the lack of any perceived necessity, and by the political importance of keeping taxation low.

Steps Taken to Rectify the Defences

With the outbreak of rebellion and with the threat of invasion, in 1715 and 1745, measures were needed to put defences in order, as much as it was possible. Given the various deficiencies in the defensive preparations, steps were taken to alter this state of affairs. Tweeddale wrote to Cope as early as 2 August 1745, 'that he should dispatch proper orders for the security of the Forts and Barracks in the Highlands'.[49] At the important naval dockyard at Portsmouth, General Thomas Erle, the governor, was overseeing work on the defences. On 1 August 1715, he informed Brigadier Michael Richards, chief engineer and Master Surveyor to the Ordnance:

> We work here daily (Sundays not excepted) with the few hands and materials we have upon credit. We are endeavouring to place as many guns as we can where they may be most usefull for the defence of the body of the place to the best of Mr Edwards and my judgement.[50]

Chevaux de frises were placed at the foot of those curtain walls thought most vulnerable. Old palisades found at the docks were used to help defend the bastions. Yet Erle found these to be insufficient. He needed more of both these commodities, as well as an extra £300 of credit. He wrote, 'I shall by Saturday next have done all that I can doe here towards putting the place in a position of defence, without further directions as well as assistance both of men and mony'.[51]

In 1715, Colonel Pollock made steps to rectify Fort William's defences. He had logs placed on top of the parapets. Turf was used to enable the garrison to fire from the walls.[52] Yet his attempts at repairs were not always successful. In early November, forty yards of the bastions facing the land collapsed, and with them their battery of guns. All hands were required to make repairs.[53]

Newcastle upon Tyne was hastily put into a posture of defence in October 1715. Patten wrote that, apart from manning the city with militia and posse:

> Newcastle ... has an old and very strong Stone-Wall about it, and good Gates to
> defend it, though they have no cannon planted: the Gates also were walled up with
> Stone and Lime in case of any Attempt; so that without cannon they could not have
> assaulted the Town.[54]

Another report states that cannon were mounted by the only two gates left open.[55]

Commanders were not always confident. On 23 September, the new governor of Berwick, Cope, declared, 'I am endeavouring to strengthen this place all I can, which very much needs it'.[56] Rush was the order of the day, as Cholmondeley wrote 'they are in the greatest hurry imaginable in putting of it [Chester castle] in the best posture of defence that so short a time will allow'.[57] Commanders reported that they were trying to obey such directives. Campbell wrote, 'all hands are now being at work to make it [Fort William] up'.[58] The gates and bridges were repaired, the ramparts and stockade were palisaded. Thirty-six workmen were employed in these tasks. The twenty-two cannon and two mortars were 'in good order' and there was 'plenty of ammunition'.[59] The proximity of the enemy always served to stimulate additional efforts. The said fortress was further strengthened in March 1746 in anticipation of an attack. The parapets of the walls where an attack was anticipated were increased in height to seven feet. Even when the siege was underway, pioneers raised the glacis so that the Jacobites could not see the foot of the fortress walls. Drains near the walls were dammed up so that, should there be rain, the beginnings of a moat would be created.[60]

Likewise at Edinburgh, efforts were made. The parapets were built up with turf and gates were blocked up with lime and stone. Musket batteries were erected to flank Dr St Clair's gardens. Yet, though 100 workmen were employed, it was too much to be done in too short a time. Jack concluded, 'Had we got 2 or 3 days more respite the whole south part of the time would be in the same manner repaired'.[61]

Food supplies were another issue. At Fort William, in August 1745, there was a 'tolerable quantity of meal and a small parcel of malt and nothing else but five or six cast of salt herrings'. Furthermore, the brewery was outside the walls and the ship bringing malt did not arrive.[62]

When siege seemed imminent, an order was sent to Chesterfield in Ireland, 'to send directly to Fort William a sufficient quantity of arms and provisions'.[63] However, Andrew Fletcher reported that at Edinburgh castle, on 25 September, there was 'not much above a fortnight's provisions' and the Lord Advocate believed the Jacobites might lay siege to it 'to starve the castle who have but a month's provisions'.[64]

Newcastle was shocked at this state of affairs, though said nothing until it was a matter of urgency, after the defeat of Prestonpans. He told Fletcher on 3 October, 'It was a matter of great surprise here, to find that the castle of Edinburgh was so ill supplied with provisions, considering the notice there was to provide for the defence of that important place, from the beginning of the rebellion in Scotland'.[65]

This apparently slack state of affairs was because in the past the castle had been given provisions from the city on a day-to-day basis, and this routine had been maintained. After the Jacobites had left the city, and it was reoccupied in November by Handasyde and several battalions, steps were taken to lay down stores of food and drink. Handasyde informed Newcastle, of the 'care taken to erect places for keeping either provisions or stores'. None had been made hitherto, he learnt, so he bought 800 boles of oatmeal flour, 40,000 weight of biscuit and 10 tons of malt, together with salt pork and butter, in order to stand a siege. In all, food for at least three months was laid in. Another 800 boles of oatmeal, 30,000 weight of biscuit and fourteen hogsheads of spirits were also ordered.[66]

Other preparations were made. At Edinburgh, cannon were taken from ships at Leith and mounted on the walls.[67] Similarly, breastworks and cannon were mounted at Whitehaven in early November.[68]

Sometimes men with specialized knowledge or training were at hand. Professor Colin MacLaurin assisted at Edinburgh.[69] Cholmondeley reported that he was guided by Brigadier Douglas and two engineers in rectifying Chester's defences.[70]

One of the difficulties was that suburbs and other buildings had grown up beyond the city walls, often in places which would assist a besieger and impede defensive fire. This sometimes resulted in conflict between the civil and military authorities. There was conflict over the extent of defensive preparations that should be taken. At Carlisle, Durand wanted all the city gates blocked up, but was told that this 'would be an infinite prejudice to the city', presumably because it might disrupt trade, and as the city magistrates were merchants, this would be a major concern. He also wanted to demolish the houses standing outside the walls, but again the corporation resisted: 'they objected, and said it was private property, and they could not do it'. These houses were valued at £150, and were they to be destroyed, the corporation would have to reimburse the owners at the very least, and for such an illegal action there might be further consequences for them. Durand felt he could not press them too far, 'for fear of disabling the town, upon whose inhabitants I partly depended for my defence'.[71]

This was not always the case. Captain Philips, an engineer, wanted some demolition work to the outskirts of Berwick in 1715 since that this was 'absolutely necessary' for the garrison's security. The corporation agreed, deciding at a guildhall meeting that property in Castlegate and the Green 'must indispensably be destroyed'.[72] Several owners 'readily assented' to the proposal, perhaps thinking it necessary for the safety of the town against a possible Jacobite threat. They were also reimbursed from the Treasury, eventually, too, to the tune of £841 10s.[73]

There was even suspicion in some quarters that magistrates were of dubious political loyalty. MacLaurin, who had departed Edinburgh for York, was asked by the corporation of the latter to inspect the walls, 'to consider if they were defensible'. He reported 'that they were, but supposed from the behaviour of some of the magistrates there that they did not mean to defend them'.[74]

The Provost of Edinburgh was later accused of disloyalty, too. But in his defence it has to be stated that efforts were made to reinforce the city's defences. On 14 September the city walls were inspected and a document produced at the time recorded:

> The copping is taken off the bastion at the head of Rules' Yard near the west point, also all of the walls and bastions around heriots gardens and the poor house yard, further they have noticed there are already 6 timber stairs made for walking up to the parapets on the head of the walls.[75]

Some efforts at defence were taken at York. Matthew Wharton was reimbursed £1 14s 9d 'for workmen's wages in paring the ramparts in several places'. Stones from a ruined priory were used to shore up gaps in the walls. Work commenced on the city's gateways and the ground below the walls was dug. Yet the foundations for the walls were only three feet beneath the surface, so the amount of work which could be done to make the city less vulnerable was limited.[76]

Similarly, at Newcastle, the municipal authorities were active in striving to rectify years of neglect. Matthew Ridley, the mayor, told Malton on 25 September 1745:

> We are doing all that the situation of the place will admit of to make it tenable, having got a number of ships' guns planted on our gates and in the gateways when they are built up, and have placed other cannons on stations in the walls by the direction of the officers of His Majesty now in this place.[77]

One observer believed this had been effective, writing, 'the town is tolerably well fortified'.[78]

Orders had been given as early as 17 September to make the city defensible. All gates, except for Newgate and Sandgate were to be blocked up. The building committee gave orders for those parts of the city walls which were in a ruinous state to be repaired. Property adjoining the walls was to be destroyed and all trees and undergrowth about 100 yards before the walls was likewise to be cut down, thus allowing the cannon and musketry a clear field of fire if necessary. The cannon were manned by sailors from Sunderland, though there was a shortage of cannonballs.[79]

The one identifiable weak point was Clifford's Fort, which lay on the mouth of the harbour. This was not deemed defensible from the landward side, as it was designed to defend against seaborne enemies. Furthermore, its forty cannon might fall into Jacobite hands and be used against the city. Ridley suggested they be either removed or nailed up. Huske agreed and had them brought into the city to add to the cannon already there.[80]

There were other steps taken to render the town secure. A mayoral proclamation of 18 October announced that citizens living outside the walls should surrender their ladders, arms, shovels and picks to the town's yard, behind the hospital. Guns were not to be fired at night, nor cannons approached after dark, on pain of imprisonment. Furthermore, the annual October fair was cancelled.[81]

Such measures were expensive. The farmers of the great toll lost considerable sums due to most of the gates being blocked up. They were given £140 from the municipal coffers. Those whose property outside the walls had been demolished petitioned for redress. Provided they carted away the rubble from their buildings, this was granted although not until 1747, and the city paid out £300 5s in total.[82] Huske lauded their efforts, informing Newcastle, 'the great zeal of the magistrates for His Majesty and the publick good is beyond what I can express, and by their prudent conduct I make no doubt but the people here will follow their good example'.[83]

Although Cope was despondent about his achievements at Berwick, and his successor wrote, 'He has done as much for the defences of the garrison as such a heap of ruins would allow of'[84], Newcastle's response was upbeat: 'His Majesty was very glad to find by your letter that Sir John Cope has used so much diligence in putting that place into a state of defence.'[85] A volunteer seeing the fortress at the end of the year was impressed, writing, 'The fortifications are very strong, especially in the Scots side, where it very much resembles the fortifications abroad, having fossas full of water and very broad'.[86]

Lack of money could be another inhibitor. Cope told Newcastle that, at Berwick in 1745, 'it is necessary to lay out a good deal of money about it – for Repairs – and to employ a good number of hands. I will be as frugal in these matters as I possibly can without starving the service.' He was fortunate that Ridley could offer public money, and that he had his own personal credit. He needed at least £2,000, and when he left the town, he left £1,800 in unpaid bills.[87]

Commanders needed the support of the civilian magistracy and could not afford to alienate them. Cope and the mayor of Berwick brought in supplies to the town in the case of siege; corn, hay and horses. Ridley supplied them with 170 sacks of meal and 1,000 bushels of wheat. These all seem to have come from a four-mile radius of the town.[88] Likewise, at Chester, Cholmondeley had the justices of the peace gather in hay, oats, straw and wheat to stand a siege. He also warned that commissaries would be needed to deal with it in order to 'prevent combinations among the farmers'.[89] Not all fortresses were as well stocked. After a few weeks' siege, it was feared that the 'provisions and firings were almost consum'd'.[90] It was noted that in Edinburgh Castle's case, that the King was surprised that 'so small a quantity of provisions, notwithstanding the notice he [the castle's governor] must have had' had been laid in store.[91] Newcastle told the mayor and the chancellor of Carlisle that the newly appointed garrison commander should count on their support.[92] Civilians assisted in rectifying defences – Cope employed between 100 and 150 at Berwick.[93]

On occasion, supplies could be brought into the fortress during the siege itself. This occurred at Fort William in March, where command of the seas meant that such was possible. On 23 March, vessels brought provisions, and the garrison's artillery fired upon the Jacobite guns. Two days later, parties from the garrison sallied out and brought back bullocks – twenty-nine on the first occasion – and there were other expeditions, some using boats to do so.[94]

Enough troops and other military support were also required. Additions to manpower were often made when a place was endangered. Campbell wrote, 'I'll take all the care I can with the few troops I have to prevent a surprise, had I a strong reinforcement it would overawe the Highlanders from joining the enemy, whereas without it they certainly shall'.[95] On another occasion, he remarked, 'there were by far too few men to defend the fort'.[96] At Chester there were only Gower's newly raised battalion, who had only been issued with arms a few days previously, and Bligh's.[97]

Additional troops were sent to garrison Portsmouth in 1715; firstly five companies of foot guards and then these were replaced by Dubourgay's regiment of foot.[98] In late February 1746, there was intelligence that Fort George would be thus strengthened, 'a proper supply of men was put into the garrison at Inverness, viz a company of Grants and a company of Ross'.[99] However, when governor Campbell asked that the sloop The Serpent remain near Fort William, the captain wished his vessel to depart, but eventually orders were sent for the captain to 'keep his present station'.[100] Concern that Fort William might be in danger led Cumberland to strengthen the numbers there. He wrote to Newcastle:

for fear the same should happen at Fort William, I have sent Captain Scott thither, & have appointed him to command the garrison, which at present consists of 3 companies of Guise's but I shall send 3 subalterns that were at Edinburgh and 50 men of that regiment who were to have gone to Fort George.

He then pointed out the strategic importance of the place and other concerns:

I have been so anxious about this particular fort is, that from thence the Lowlands would be open to them & that the fort were taken by the rebels might cause us much trouble before we retook it & the lieutenant governor Alistair Campbell is by all accounts no way fit for a thing of that importance.[101]

Yet there was not always enough men to defend a place. Cope told Newcastle that the length of Berwick's walls was too long for all his troops and townsmen to properly defend.[102] When Cope was replaced by Handasyde, he stated, 'One thing necessary to mend was no more in his power than mine, the reinforcing of the garrison with a battalion of Foot, for unless that is done, our present numbers will not be half sufficient to do the duty of the place'. Nor were there any engineers or gunners.[103] At Carlisle, no troops were sent, but a garrison commander was dispatched, Colonel Durand, who was told on 3 October, to 'immediately repair to Carlisle'.[104] When Cholmondeley learnt that Ligonier's camp was to be at Coventry, thus a considerable distance from Chester, he wrote 'defence of this place impossible'.[105]

At the end of all these efforts, some were still unconvinced that they would be able to withstand attack. John Raper, the Lord Mayor of York, was one. He certainly did not think the city was capable of much of a defence. In this he was in agreement with the Lords Lieutenant of the county, whose loyalties were above doubt. Malton wrote, 'The officers unanimously agreed the town was not tenable with our force an hour, above three miles of wall, quite ruinous and not one cannon in the place, so this scheme must be laid aside'.[106] The only possible defence was 'against a straggling party', but against artillery, 'as is very obvious to everyone … they could not be maintained an hour'.[107]

Yet some commanders, despite earlier misgivings, were confident in their ability to withstand assault. Cholmondeley wrote on 30 November 1745, 'The castle walls are in very good order and the artillery mounted in good order'.[108] Handasyde wrote on 1 November, about Berwick, 'I have almost put the garrison beyond the apprehensions of being surprised' and the ongoing works 'would inable any garrison to defend the place against 20,000 men'.[109] He also looked forward to an attack, 'I wish the villains would come here … I doubt not but His Majesty's troops will give a good account of them'.[110]

The Effectiveness of the Defences

When an army, or part of one, approached a fortress, convention demanded that the besiegers summon the garrison to surrender. Almost always, the garrison commander would refuse. So, it would have come as no surprise that, when the Jacobites summoned General Blakeney to surrender Stirling Castle in January 1746, he should have responded thus, 'That he was always look'd upon as a man of honour, and the Rebels should find he would die so'.[111] At Carlisle, the answer was more than verbal: 'On which the Garrison thought proper to confine the messenger, and returned no answer but from the mouths of their guns.'[112] Once this ritual of polite warfare had been accomplished, hostilities proper could begin and each side usually looked to its artillery.

The first attempt made on any fortified position in 1745 was at Ruthven Barracks on 29 August. A party of 300 Jacobites under O'Sullivan summoned the commander, one sergeant Molloy, to surrender. Molloy only had a dozen men at his back, but he replied, 'My answer was that I was too old a soldier to surrender a garrison of such strength without Bloody Noses'. He was then threatened with being hanged along with his men when the barracks fell to the attack, but remained resolute, 'I should take my chance'. On the following day, 150 men tried to set fire to the main entrance, using barrels, but the man charged with lighting them was shot dead and so the attack failed. There was another parley and this time a conditional surrender was proposed, but Molloy turned it down as well. The Jacobites left at 8pm that evening. Molloy wrote satisfied, 'I shall give them the warmest reception my weak party can afford, I shall hold out as long as possible'.[113]

Much, of course, depended on the effectiveness of the besiegers, their skill and the calibre of their artillery. At the siege of Carlisle in November 1745, the Jacobites had only twelve guns, and all of small calibre. Johnstone noted, 'we did not discharge a single shot, lest the garrison should become acquainted with the smallness of their calibre, which might have encouraged them to defend themselves'.[114] There was only one siege in the campaign when adequate artillery was brought to bear by the Jacobites, and that was at Stirling in mid-January, when there were two eighteen pounders, two twelve pounders and two six pounders, all of which arrived from France.[115]

But these were more a hindrance than a help, as Johnstone observed:

> Who could have imagined that the six pieces of heavy artillery, sent by the court of France to our assistance, would become our ruin? And yet they certainly were our ruin, for without them we would never have dreamed of laying siege to Stirling Castle, as no one could have thought of a siege without artillery.[116]

Small calibre guns were of little use, too. Murray pointed out that Edinburgh Castle was virtually impregnable, given Jacobite resources. He wrote, 'it was impracticable to take it without cannon, engineers, and regular troops'.[117] The two Jacobite four pounders which were assigned to take part in the attack on Blair Castle in March 1746 were inadequate to blast through seven feet thick walls, and the making of a mine to blow up the walls was impossible due to there being no men skilled in this work.[118] Likewise, at Fort George, Colonel Grant found 'that his cannon were too small to do the walls of the fort any harm'.[119] Jacobite artillery used against Fort William was also less than effective. They were positioned on a hill known as the Sugar Loaf, about 800 yards from the fortress, 'which, because of the distance, did no execution, the greatest part of them falling short'.[120]

Weak defences could fall even to guns of modest calibre, as occurred at Fort George, near Inverness, in late February 1746. Maxwell wrote:

> Tho' the Prince had left his heavy artillery, there was no difficulty in reducing the fort; as the little mount on which this castle is built is contiguous to the town, one may go to the foot of the mount without being exposed to the fire of the Castle. It was immediately resolved to undermine and blow it up; and the work was begun upon Major Grant's refusal to surrender ... when he found the work was going briskly on, and that in a few days at furthest he must be blown up, he chose to surrender himself and the garrison prisoners of war on the 25th after a few days siege.[121]

Grant had been summoned again to surrender once the mining had commenced. He had asked the Master of Ross to inspect the work, but this he could not do. Grant then had the fort's guns fire on the house near the mine, but they did little damage. O'Sullivan noted, 'it was too low, that they cou'd point their Cannon, on the windows or doors'. Grenades were thrown down the mine, too, forcing those working on it to abandon it. These either ran out or did insufficient damage, and so Grant was obliged to capitulate.[122]

Likewise, when the Jacobites moved against Fort Augustus on 3 March, as Maxwell wrote:

> He attacked the old barrack without waiting for the artillery and carried it; the soldiers behaving with surprising intrepidity on this occasion. The 3d March, a trench was opened before Fort Augustus, which held out but two days. What hastened the reduction of the place was, that some shells had been thrown into it had set fire to the powder magazine and blown it up'.[123]

The engineer in charge on both occasions was one Mr Grant, an able soldier. However an inept engineer could ruin a siege. On 6 January 1746, Monsieur Mirabelle de Gordon, a French engineer and chevalier of the Order of St Louis, oversaw the siege of Stirling castle. Unfortunately, his arrival was not to prove a blessing for the Jacobites. Johnstone remarked:

It was supposed that a French engineer, of a certain age and decorated with an order, must necessarily be a person of experience, talents, and capacity; but it was unfortunately discovered, when too late, that his knowledge as an engineer was extremely limited, and that he was totally destitute of judgement, discernment and common sense. His figure being as whimsical as his mind, the Highlanders, instead of Monsieur Mirabelle, called him Mr Admirable.[124]

Mirabelle was consulted by Charles, following remonstrations against the plan of attack made by Grant. He undertook to open trenches on hills to the north of the castle, but here there was only fifteen inches of earth before rock was reached. This necessitated men hauling sacks of earth and wool to be brought there. Fire from the castle was directed against these men and resulted in fatalities, sometimes as many as twenty-five per day.[125] Progress was slow, even with the siege being interrupted on 17 January due to the battle of Falkirk being fought on that day. It was only on 30 January that any of the Jacobite cannon were able to fire, and even then, only three of them, and with this proviso: 'our guns, being pointed upwards, could do no execution whatever'.[126]

Regular troops were the best forces for laying siege. French and Irish troops under Brigadier Stapleton were present at the sieges of Forts George, Augustus, William and Stirling in 1746. Jacobite Highlanders were less enamoured of siege warfare. Maxwell admitted:

> it is hard to make Highlanders do the regular duty of a siege, though they are excessively brave in an attack, and when they are allowed to fight in their own way; they are not so much masters of that sedate valour that is necessary to maintain a post, and it is extremely difficult to keep them long in their posts, or even in their quarters without action.[127]

Able management of the defence was also crucial. Johnstone wrote admiringly of his enemy's skill at Stirling:

> Justice ought to be done to the merit and good conduct of General Blakeney, who perceived our ignorance from the position of our battery and did not disturb us while constructing it. Convinced that we could do him no injury from that quarter, he remained silent, like a skilful general, and allowed us to go on ... Well he knew that he could destroy our battery whenever he pleased, and level it in an instant to the ground.

This is what happened. Blakeney's guns were more elevated than the Jacobites', so his gunners could see the Jacobite gunners very clearly. Their fire dismounted the Jacobite guns in half an hour and no one dare approach them, for to do so risked certain death. This ended the siege and led to a Jacobite retreat, abandoning all their heavy siege artillery.[128]

The guns of Fort William were also effective against the besieging Jacobites two months later. On 23 March:

the garrison all at once discharged eight 12 pounders, two six pounders, two bombs, and several cohorns against their battery, which were all so well levelled, that not only was a great part of their battery was beat down, but they visibly occasion'd the greatest confusion amongst them. The men from the ships saw several rebels fall.

Three days later, counter battery fire resulted in dismounting one Jacobite gun, and on 27 March, one gun was silenced and later the battery magazine was set on fire.[129]

Effective action on the part of the defenders could involve a sally, as in the successful defence of Fort William. This began even before a formal siege could commence, but as soon as news came that parties of Jacobites were approaching the vicinity, and bringing with them artillery. Soldiers and their naval counterparts met to decide upon a combined course of operations.

in consequence therefore, early this morning [4 March 1746] Captain Askew of the Serpent sloop, sent his boat with 27 men in it, another boat of the Baltimore's, with 24 men, and a boat belonging to Fort William, with 20, down the Narrows, where they all arriv'd by daylight. Captain Askew's men landed first and were immediately attacked by a party of rebels, who fir'd upon them, without doing any damage; and upon the rest of the boats coming up, the rebels fled. Our people pursued them, burnt the ferry houses on both sides of the water, and a little town with about 12 houses in it, a quarter of a mile distant from the ferry house on the north side, and destroyed or brought off all their boats. Two of the rebels were killed in this affair, and several wounded. It was very lucky that our boats went down as they did, for there was a boat with a party of militia in it, which was coming hither from Stalkirk castle, which would have fallen into the hands of the rebels, but for the skirmish aforementioned.[130]

Additional aggression was displayed by the defenders of Fort William before the siege proper could begin. On 15 March, soldiers and sailors took to boats once more, in order to destroy Killmady Barns. The Jacobites were ready for them. Swivel guns from the boats were employed against them, and there were exchanges of small arms fire. A sailor was killed and three of his compatriots were also hit. However, the tide was also against them – the impact of the natural elements on these campaigns was a factor constantly making itself felt – and so the expedition was forced to retire, their task unaccomplished. It was later found that this raid did have one beneficial result – Grant, the Jacobites' principal engineer, was wounded and so unable to carry out his work, leaving it to the lesser Mirabelle.[131]

Undeterred by this setback, a further attempt was made against the same target on 18 March. This time, the attackers were assisted by The Baltimore sloop, which would use its cannon and mortar to deter the defenders. However the Jacobites were numerous, well entrenched and the sloops' cannon were only four pounders, so could make little headway against these stout defences. Four Jacobites had been killed, nonetheless, though a landing could not be made.[132]

Much of this kind of action had occurred before the risk of a siege began, anyway. On 22 February, the governor was told to 'send out parties to burn and destroy all the country belonging to the rebels'.[133] This was to use the fort as a forward base for the government's forces to harry the Jacobites wherever they and they sympathizers – or their property – could be found. This was part of a more general strategy practised in February and March 1746 whose aim was to weaken the main Jacobite force by inducing clansmen from the affected areas to leave the main army.

Once the siege proper had begun, on 20 March, the garrison continued to make sallies. Two Jacobite villages of the Appin Stewarts were burnt on one raid, and four prisoners were taken on another. Elcho wrote:

> On the 31 [March] Captain Caroline Scott, at the head of 150 men, Sallied out from the fort and attacked the works at the craigs, beat the men of from it with the loss of two or three men on both sides and took the three Cannon and carried them with him after demolishing the battery.[134]

According to Maxwell, forty-seven cannon and two mortars had been lost; government sources listed three four pounders and two coehorns, and the spiking of two cannon and two mortars which made up the remainder of the battery. There were another eight cannon and seven mortars.[135]

This action proved decisive in bringing to an end a lacklustre siege. Maxwell wrote:

> Besides the loss of the artillery, the ammunition was almost exhausted, and there was no prospect of reducing the fort: it was a rash undertaking from the beginning. The besieged were little inferior in number to the besiegers, and might be reinforced from sea at pleasure. But nothing less than this attempt would satisfy the Highlanders that live in the neighbour-hood of Fort William, and the Prince would not refuse them.[136]

Failure to take fortresses meant leaving bodies of the enemy in the rear. When the Jacobites marched towards Edinburgh, 'The garrison at Fort William sallied out, when the Prince was gone, seized what had been left there, burned some of the people's houses and carried off their cattle'.[137]

Similar strong-arm tactics had been advised at Edinburgh in the previous year. Tweeddale sent instructions to Lord Mark Kerr, governor of the castle, reminding him that 'the security and preservation of the castle of Edinburgh being of the utmost importance to His Majesty's service at this juncture'. Kerr was to tell Guest:

> to declare to the magistrates and inhabitants of the town that if they do not furnish him with such provisions as shall be necessary for the Garrison, he will distress and annoy them by all means in his power, particularly by destroying the reservoir.[138]

During the fairly lax siege of Edinburgh castle in the previous autumn, the defenders took a number of Jacobite sentinels prisoners.[139] When a blockade of the castle was proposed, General Preston acted vigorously, in the words of Elcho: 'General Preston sent word to the City that if they did not send up provisions to the Castle as usual he had orders from court to fire upon the town.' Initially the Jacobites refused this request, despite pleas from the townsmen. So, on 1 October, the castle 'fired their Great Guns upon the Weigh house and wherever they saw any of the Princes soldiers. There was some of the towns people kill'd & some houses damadged.' Following successful sallies, the townsmen made other pleas. Charles threatened to destroy Preston's house in Fife, but was told were this to occur, Weemys castle would be burnt. Further firing from the castle led to the blockade being lifted. The results were that the castle's guns fired to celebrate George II's birthday on 30 October, and as soon as the Jacobite army left the city a week later, it was once again in the government's hands.[140] Guest had been given instructions how he should act if his supplies were endangered, 'he should threaten the town; and, in the extremity, put his threats into execution; but in such a manner as to oblige the town; effectually to comply with his demands, and if possible, without executing these orders in their full extent'.[141] Fletcher was able to report to Newcastle thus, 'General Guest has behaved well in baffling the attempt of the rebels on the castle of Edinburgh'.[142]

Starvation by effective blockade was another technique to take a fortress, but it required time, so was not conducive to a campaign of movement. Some Jacobites thought Edinburgh castle 'would be obliged to surrender for want of provisions ... I was sure we were not going to stay long enough to bring them to any straits'.[143]

Relief forces could make a difference. In the case of Fort William, the Serpent and the Baltimore sloops prevented it from being wholly invested, so supplies and communication were maintained.[144] Hessian forces relieved Blair Castle, otherwise the Jacobites might have starved the garrison into surrender.[145]

Morale, as ever, was vital, even in strongly fortified places. When the Jacobites summoned Carlisle to surrender, on 10 November, the summons concluded, ominously enough:

> But if you should refuse us Entrance, we are fully resolved to force it by such Means as Providence has put into our hands, and then perhaps it will not be in our power to prevent the fatal consequences which usually attend a town's being taken by Assault.[146]

On 14 November 1745, the defenders of Carlisle, 'seeing the trenches pretty near them and the cannon ready to be mounted upon a battery, they hung out a white flag ... they were told, to frighten them the more, that the battery would fire red hot balls upon the town next day if they did not Surrender'.[147] According to Henderson, though some wanted to fight on, 'The Terror of the Highlanders storming the Town, sword in hand, in the Night Time, having raised in their Minds a dreadful Prospect of Blood, Slaughter and Rapine, it was resolved to deliver the place'.[148] Yet the Jacobite guns were not in a position to do much damage, as Durand noted:

> I said everything to encourage them to do their duty, assuring them it was nothing but a poor paltry ditch, that did not deserve the name of an entrenchment; that the rebels had no cannon large enough to make a breach in our walls ... it was only done to intimidate them.[149]

However, another factor in weakening the morale of the defenders was that there was no prospect of relief and they knew it. Wade, whose army was at Newcastle, had been contacted, but Wade wrote back to say that the Jacobites could not possibly take the city with the guns they had but would march around it, and concluded with 'I wish you all imaginable success'. Therefore he would not march to their succour. This was conventional military wisdom but applied to an unconventional campaign.[150] When Durand did his best to raise the spirits of the county militia and armed townsmen who made up the bulk of the defenders, on 14 November, they 'all declared they would do no more duty, nor would they stay and defend the castle upon any account whatsoever'. Despite entreaties by the militia officers, by 8am on 15 November, they had all fled.[151]

Durand was only left with the two companies of invalids. He needed between 500 and 600 men to adequately defend just the castle. As he wrote, 'we remained with only our few Invalids, who from their great age and infirmities, and from the excessive fatigue they had undergone, occasioned by the frequent false alarms we had which had kept them almost continually upon duty, were rendered in a manner of no use'. Surrender swiftly followed.[152]

Likewise, at Fort George, Major Grant surrendered before 'the mine was not far advanced'.[153] According to Henderson, this was 'solely owing to Grant, whose cowardice and bad conduct cannot but reflect Dishonour upon himself'.[154] John Millross, a soldier of the garrison there, wrote to criticize the commander. According to him, the defenders' artillery was used against the Jacobites, 'and would have fired more, but the governor, Mr Grant and Lieutenant Minclan were very backward and hindered them from firing'. Earlier, the governor could have ordered the guns to have fired on the Jacobites while they were in Inverness, 'they might have done much more execution to the rebels'. He accused the governor of defeatism, for, once the mining had commenced, 'both of them proposed to surrender'. This was against most of their men's wishes 'But they were obliged to submit to the governor'. Minclan was allegedly drunk at this time. Lieutenant Grahame of Guise's regiment wanted to fight on, and 'came boldly up and called to the private soldiers to stand by him and he would stand by them, as long as he had a bit of life in him, for that he was ashamed to see so little done in defence of the castle'.[155]

Luck could also play its part. The siege of Fort Augustus was over quickly, despite the small calibre of the Jacobite artillery. According to Elcho, 'by means of Coehorns, Mr Grant blew up the magazine and destroy'd all the roofs of the quarters'.[156]

Finally, numbers and artillery could also tell, even against stout-hearted defenders. In February 1746, Lieutenant Molloy's garrison at Ruthven was once again summoned to surrender. However, on this occasion, the Jacobites had artillery, which the fort was not proof against. Molloy duly surrendered, but was not court-martialled for this as was Grant over Fort George.[157]

The results of these sieges were material and psychological. It was noted, in the case of Stirling:

> His R.H. is pleased to commend extremely the behaviour of Major General Blakeney, who, by his conduct, as well as his courage, has sav'd the castle of Stirling, which is a place of the greatest of importance, from falling into the hands of the rebels.[158]

Cumberland was shocked at the fall of Forts George and Augustus, especially the former. He told Newcastle, 'the bad news of Fort George having fallen into the rebels' hands, I am no ways able to explain how or by what neglect it is so, but a silly affair it is'. Newcastle agreed, writing, 'The Lord Chief Justice has sent the Duke of Argyll some particulars, which do not do great honour to the garrison'.[159]

The only siege the British state was required to undertake in these conflicts was that at Carlisle. This was because the fortresses which the Jacobites took in Scotland were demolished. As we have seen, Carlisle was not inherently strong. Cumberland additionally said of it, 'An old hen-coop, which he would speedily bring down about their ears, when he should have got artillery'.[160]

As would be expected, he conducted the siege conventionally enough. The garrison was called upon to surrender on 21 December 1745 and they refused. The town and castle were surrounded. Bland and 300 men from St George's Dragoons were posted on the north side. Major Adams, with 200 infantry, were stationed by the English gate. Major Meriac and another 200 soldiers guarded the Sally Port. The bulk of the besieging forces, including Sir Andrew Agnew's 300 soldiers, the foot guards and the regiments of horse, were cantoned a mile or two from Carlisle. In all, there were about 4,000 men, against about 400 defenders.[161]

However, there was no artillery immediately available to the besiegers. Cumberland's force had been put together for speed, in order to pursue the retreating Jacobites. There were ten eighteen pounder guns at Whitehaven, and these were called upon. Newcastle gave instructions to the Board of Ordnance to assist with artillery and supplies[162] To attack without artillery would be costly, as Cumberland wrote, 'to expose ourselves to any considerable loss against an enemy such as these'.[163] While the guns were being awaited, preparations were made. Trenches were dug and wood was cut to make batteries on 24 December.[164]

Yet all was not well among the besiegers. Yorke wrote, 'We have many inconveniencies to struggle with, the wetness of the season, which makes it difficult to raise the earth, the badness of the ways for conveying artillery, the want of engineers, artillery, etc'.[165] Likewise, Richmond wrote, 'Our situation here is a very disagreeable one'. Laying siege would take time and assault would be costly.[166]

However, the civilian population, under the direction of the justices of the peace, assisted the besiegers. Thomas Robson, constable of Grinsdale, produced a cart and three men to help carry artillery for the siege. Eighteen people from Cockermouth carried cannon and ball from there to Carlisle. The constable of Blackhall instructed that hay and corn be sent from there for the army's horses. Fifty men from Dalston worked on the siege batteries; twenty men from Weatherall worked on the trenches. Horses were pressed to pull carts carrying guns from Whitehaven.[167]

Four of the eighteen pounders arrived on Christmas Day. Further progress was apparent on 27 December. Reinforcements from Wade's army, including Major Belford, a gunner, and Captain Scott, an engineer, together with sixty gunners, arrived. So did the remainder of the eighteen pounders. Ten coehorn mortars from Wade also arrived, with 300 shells.[168] Their commander inspected the works, 'the Duke came around to our side of the River to reconnoyter & went down by himself to view the castle and the city'.[169]

It was on 27 December that the mortars began to lob shells into Carlisle, with about twenty-five being fired: 'brought a very hot fire upon the place'.[170] Meanwhile, the heavy guns were mounted and made ready for service. On 28 December, at about 7–8am, six of them began to fire, focusing on a four-gun battery on the west of the town. Cumberland was confident in their effectiveness, writing, 'I persuade myself the thing will now be soon over'.[171] This was not to be, for the ammunition ran out at about noon.[172] Fresh supplies meant that the bombardment could recommence on 29 December and was 'renewed very briskly for two hours'. Furthermore, by now all eighteen pounders were in operation. It seems to have been effective, with Richmond writing, 'there is a good deal of their wall beat down and a great crack made in it'.[173]

There was a little more firing on the next day, before a white flag was seen hanging from the walls. This was the signal for a cessation of hostilities. Negotiations now followed. The Jacobites called out that they would then send out two hostages. Cumberland sent messages to the besieged, delivered by Colonel Conway and Lord Bury. The first read, 'His royal highness will make no exchange of hostages with rebels, and desires they will let him know by me, what they mean by hanging out the white flag'. Bury's ran 'To let the French officer know, if there is one in the town, that there are no Dutch troops here, but enough of the King's to chastise the rebels, and those who give them any assistance'. This was a reference to the fact that the Dutch troops were forbidden to fight the French due to the terms of their capitulation at Tournai earlier that year.[174]

Colonel Hamilton, the Jacobite governor, replied, stating that the purpose of the white flag was to 'obtain a cessation of arms for concluding such a capitulation' and wanted to know 'what terms His Royal Highness will be pleased to give them' on surrendering the city and castle. Cumberland replied thus:

> All the terms his royal highness will or can grant to the rebel garrison of Carlisle are, that they shall not be put to the sword, but be reserved for the King's pleasure. If they consent to these conditions, the governor and principal officers are to deliver themselves up immediately, and the castle, citadel, and all the gates of the town, are to be taken possession of forthwith by the King's troops. All the small arms are to be lodged in the town guard room, and the rest of the garrison are to retire to the cathedral, where a guard is to be placed over them. No damage is to be done to the artillery, arms or ammunition.[175]

These terms were agreed to, 'recommending themselves to his royal highness' clemency, and that his royal highness will be pleased to intercede with them'.[176]

Cumberland's views were rather different, as he informed Newcastle later that day:

> I wish I could have blooded the soldiers with these villains, but it would have cost us many brave men and it came to the same end as they have no sort of claim to the King's mercy and I sincerely hope will meet with none.[177]

It may be worth noting that Hamilton, along with a number of officers and men from the garrison were later tried for the treason of levying war against their rightful monarch, found guilty, and executed. On the Continent, this type of behaviour between regular armies was almost unheard of. At Tournai in May 1745, the Dutch garrison had surrendered the fortress to the French and had then agreed not to take part in warfare against the French King and his allies for the next eighteen months. The difference here, which was clearly not realized by Hamilton and his officers, was that this was not a conventional war between sovereign states. The British government saw it as an act of rebellion, of high treason, by subjects against their legitimate King and government. Their foes were not deemed soldiers and honourable enemies, but as rebels and traitors, who were criminal, and whose acts fell under criminal legislation. As Chesterfield wrote, 'They are not enemies, but criminals, and we cannot be at war with 'em'.[178]

The result of successful sieges was partly material. When Fort George fell, 'We found no mony, but a good quantity of arms and ammunition; a great quantity for such a garrison, of meal, salt beef, Cheas, bear, Wine &c but there was a very ill acct given of it for most of it was plundered'. Prisoners were also taken, to the number of 200 men. Forts were usually demolished rather than being held; these included Fort Augustus and Ruthven Barracks.[179] Yorke was told that the failure of the Jacobite bid to take Fort William had led to 'coolness' between the MacDonalds and Camerons over their joint failure to deal with the sally made by the garrison, each blaming the other.[180]

Ironically, after Culloden, when Fort Augustus was abandoned and Fort George being left to decay, a new state of the art fortress was built several miles from Inverness. Also named Fort George, this was the largest and most expensive military architecture in the British Isles. The estimated cost was £120,000 and the actual cost £160,000. It covered fifteen acres, and had eighty guns, four bastions and could accommodate 3,000 men. Under the ramparts were bombproof apartments and bombproof powder magazines were located inside the walls. Construction was not complete until the following reign, when it was noted, 'The usefulness of Fort George is not now very obvious' and it never heard a shot fired in anger.[181]

Another question is to consider how important these sieges were. Although that of Stirling led to the battle of Falkirk, it also led to a potentially more significant encounter, for on 30 January, on arrival in Edinburgh, Cumberland resolved:

> I thought it of the utmost importance to move to the relief of Stirling Castle, which we are under some pain for, tho' the rebels have as yet mounted but three guns … but I believe they propose to themselves to retire to Perth without coming to blows, if they can take the castle before we come up.[182]

The price of failure could be severe. Major Grant, for his failure to hold Fort George, was court-martialled and found guilty, with the verdict that he would never again hold a commission in the armed forces. Yet Durand was court-martialled, too, but found not guilty. Sergeant Molloy, though, following his successful defence of Ruthven Barracks, was recommended by Cope for a commission and was duly made a lieutenant.

Conclusion

Siege warfare was more prevalent in the Jacobite campaigns, especially that of 1745, than has usually being acknowledged. The forts in Scotland were meant as a key part of the strategy, after 1716, to contain the rebellious Jacobites. Yet in this they failed because they were unable to prevent the Jacobites gathering in arms and marching in force against the King's troops, due to a lack of manpower. It was all they could do to hold out, and even then the results were variable. Edinburgh and Stirling castles were held for the Crown, while Carlisle fell and was subsequently retaken. Forts George and Augustus surrendered, while Ruthven Barracks withstood one assault but not another. Fort William and Blair Castle also held out. The sieges were, in all cases, short, lasting from two days to three weeks, in contrast to sieges on the Continent, which lasted weeks or months.

These sieges were usually small-scale affairs, certainly compared to major sieges on the Continent. At Tournai in 1745, the Dutch garrison numbered 7,000. But this is to be expected because the size of the campaigning armies was far smaller.

Their importance should not be exaggerated, however. The holding of Ruthven Barracks in September 1745 did not led to any setback for the Jacobite advance on Edinburgh. Although all of the fortresses in Scotland were in the government's hands in 1745, this did not prevent the Jacobites being virtual masters of the kingdom. Similarly the taking of Forts George and Augustus and the said barracks in February and March 1746 did not significantly strengthen the Jacobite position. It can be argued therefore that these sieges were relative sideshows to the main confrontation between the contending armies. Likewise, had Argyll been defeated in battle in 1715, the retention of Stirling and Edinburgh castles would not have altered the situation in a decisive manner. It is uncertain whether the loss of Fort William in March or April 1746 would have had a major impact on the campaign.

Yet the conflicts over fortresses were not wholly without impact on the overall campaign. The struggle over Stirling castle in January 1746 resulted in the battle of Falkirk and could have led to a decisive clash shortly afterwards. It also led to the decision of the Jacobite army to remain before Stirling following their victory at Falkirk, which enabled the regulars to regroup and thus nullify the result of that battle. Had Carlisle held out a few more days, Wade might have been able to march to its relief and a decisive battle might have then been fought.

Contemporaries certainly thought that fortresses were important to take or hold. Cumberland believed that Stirling and Fort William must be held and marched to the relief of one and reinforced the other. Likewise, Jacobite attempts at taking fortresses indicated a similar desire and recognition of the conventional nature of this type of warfare.

These sieges indicate the weaknesses of the post-1716 security strategy in Scotland, with two fortresses and a barracks falling to the Jacobites in a matter of days in 1746. Nor were they effective in stemming the progress of the rebellions; nor could they, due to the overall number of troops in Scotland. Garrisons alone were of limited effectiveness unless supported from outside. Pollock's garrison at Fort William in 1715 was too weak to deter the Jacobites marching towards Mar at Perth. Yet the retention of Stirling and Edinburgh in 1745–6 served to respectively hold the Jacobite army in a fixed position for three weeks and allowed Handasyde to regain control of the Scottish capital with two battalions and two regiments of dragoons without a fight. This enabled Hawley to establish his forces in Scotland following the Jacobite retreat there. Yet it was not impregnable and without Cumberland's relief in February 1746 it would have fallen. Carlisle fell in 1745 to the Jacobites because Wade failed to march to its relief. The new Fort George, built after 1746, showed that the lessons had been learnt; it was sufficiently large to be defensible and to hold a garrison which was potentially capable of offensive action, too. Ironically, though, and with the benefit of hindsight, this impressive structure was built too late.

5 THE FORMATION OF THE MILITIA AND POSSE

Warfare in this era was not restricted to conflict involving regular troops and their opponents. Indeed, there was no hard and fast rule differentiating combatant and non-combatant. This was true especially in time of civil strife, where civilian forces were often raised in the localities as well as centrally. Some were raised in support of the established government, such as loyalist militia in the American colonies in the 1770s or by the insurgents to supplement the more or less 'regular' forces, such as the American Patriot Militia. They were not primarily envisaged as being responsible for defeating the main Jacobite army either in battle or in siege warfare, but were seen as playing a secondary role in support of the Crown's regular forces, though this key distinction has not always been recognized. This chapter will, then, examine the state's other formal military forces. These were the militia and posse, to see how they were raised, officered, manned and armed and how they were trained. Their successes and shortcomings in their formative stages are important to understand before we proceed to Chapter 7, which will rate their effectiveness in the tasks in which they were deemed able to perform or those they had to deal with due to the circumstances of the wider campaign.

This chapter will concentrate on the militia raised in 1745–6. This is because there is far more material available for the later conflict. Partly this is because more evidence was created as they were in service far longer, but it is also because more information has survived. The chapter will argue that despite a host of difficulties, significant numbers of men were formed, both in England and Scotland, into numerous militia units in both 1715 and 1745.

Although the militia frequently feature in most histories of the Jacobite rebellions, relatively little attention is paid to them, and certainly not to their formation. As James Ray wrote in the foreword to his *History*, his account was to be 'a particular and succinct Account of the several Marches and Counter Marches of the REBELS, from the Young Pretender's first Landing on the Island of Sky, until his Retreat at Culloden'.[1] Most authors have subsequently followed Ray's lead. Some writers do allot space to the militia, however, though often only cursorily. Linda Colley and W.A. Speck, though they both spend time in discussing militia and other forms of loyalist activity, do not spend much time in considering how these units were raised.[2] Yet both take a positive view of them, with Colley writing, 'when a Stuart restoration might – just – have been on the cards, large numbers of men from commercial as well as landed backgrounds took an active part in raising money and in taking up arms on behalf of the existing order'.[3] According to Speck, 'These activities were apparently genuine demonstrations of a determination to crush the rebellion'.[4] Although Duffy and McLynn spend a little time discussing them, their sketches, too, are necessarily brief.[5] McLynn is mostly scathing about civilian opposition to the Jacobites in 1745, harking back to a golden age that never was, thus 'The older tradition of civic and martial responsibility was almost dead'.[6] His comments elsewhere are a little more considered, concluding:

> The problems encountered in Carlisle, which proved fatal to the defence of the town when the Highlanders invested it in November 1745, were merely more dramatic in form than elsewhere though completely typical of the chaos and disharmony prevailing in most towns in the north of England. Newcastle, Liverpool and Nottingham were the sole exceptions to this general tendency.[7]

It is the less well-known local studies, mostly appearing in academic journals, which spend time describing how the militia were brought together and organized. Those in York and Yorkshire have earned themselves a number of studies, by historians such as Collyer and Oates.[8] Their equivalents on the other side of the Pennines have been attended to by Jarvis and the aforementioned Oates.[9] And there are a handful of other studies of similar forces across the country.[10] These tend to give a more positive account, partly by stressing the difficulties in their being raised and discussing to what extent these were overcome. However, there has never been one single survey on a national level before, as these local historians naturally focus on particular localities, chiefly in the north of England.

The only book to focus solely to the eighteenth-century English (not Scottish) militia had disappointingly very little to say about the first half of the eighteenth century, concentrating on the latter half of the century. The author suggests that the militia were in a state of terminal decline from the 1670s to the 1750s. He writes:

> In the sleepy Walpole era, the whole organization seems to have sunk into inanition. In 1745, even in 1715 ... it seems to have been as easy in most places to have raised a body of volunteers from scratch from among the friends of the government as to call out the militia ... The militia had really lost the advantage that could be set against its military inefficiency – namely that it was a force always in being.[11]

This chapter will cover a wider remit by surveying the militia raised throughout Britain against the Jacobites in this period. Firstly, the militia will be defined, paying particular attention to their legal status. Then we shall examine how these forces were raised, led, paid for and armed. Training will also be discussed, as will uniforms, if any, and the men who made up the officers and rank and file. The difficulties in the creation of these forces will be examined, and the extent to which these were solved will be stated.

The principal military force in Britain after 1660, apart from the relatively small regular army and the Royal Navy was the militia, which was an older military institution than the regular army. Its origins lay in legislation dating back from the last year of Mary's reign, which stated that a Lord Lieutenant be appointed to each county who would raise and lead the militia in times of unrest. It had occasionally been called out in subsequent reigns. By the eighteenth century, the militia were governed by legislation made shortly after the Restoration of 1660 and was in part a reflection of the fear of standing armies following the period of Cromwell's military rule, but it was also a response to the need for armed force to put down insurrectionary movements, such as the recently quashed Venner revolt of 1661. What was needed was a military force which would be effective but would not be politically threatening, either by ambitious generals or would-be absolutist rulers. Standing armies were viewed with suspicion; and even more so after 1685, when James II expanded the army in peacetime in order to further his political and religious goals, which were abhorrent to the majority of the political nation.

In 1662 the Militia Act became law in England; and the Scottish Parliament passed a similar law in 1663, both remaining in force, with modifications, until the New Militia Act of 1757. They stated that the King, acting via the Secretaries of State, could authorize the lords lieutenant of the counties to call out the militia in time of invasion or domestic rebellion. The lord lieutenant would then work through the county authorities to summon the men, horses and arms necessary to make up the county force. He would lead the militia and his deputy lieutenants would provide the officer corps. No formal military training or experience was needed at this level; the lieutenants were appointed for their political loyalty and landed position. They were usually noblemen. Where towns or cities were outside the remit of the lieutenancy, as were most sizeable ones, the provost or mayor would be invested with these powers. In order that the men be ready for militia service, they would theoretically have attended an annual weekly training period, overseen by an experienced soldier. Landowners would provide men and horses, depending on their income, and the parish constables would maintain and supply arms and ammunition for the men. A landowner with an estate worth £6,000 or who had an annual income of £500 was to provide a man and a horse; those with estates worth £500 a foot soldier. Initially the men were to be supplied with pikes, armour and muskets, but in 1715, the infantry were to be armed with musket and bayonet. There were references to the men being uniformed, too. Unlike the regular forces, the militia was employed for home defence only and was geographically restricted. In England the militia could not be obliged to march outside their county; in 1588 the Dorset militia refused to march to London, though in Scotland, the Militia Act declared that a force of 22,000 men could march to wherever in England or Scotland that the monarch desired. However, in 1708, the Scottish Militia Bill did not receive the Queen's consent, thus rendering the militia in that country defunct, at least in theory.[12]

Militia theorists spoke highly of the effectiveness of such county forces. They drew their readers' attention to citizen armies of both antiquity and Medieval times. For instance, the Republic of Rome's civilian soldiery were applauded, as were the Swiss pikemen who defeated the professional armies of their Austrian enemies in the fourteenth century. As *The Craftsman* pointed out in 1733, 'Militia are the strongest and most proper Defence of Countries'. Unlike standing armies, they were not in the pay of the government, but under the control of the county gentry; cheap, effective and politically safe.[13]

Yet one practical problem, ignored by the theorists, was that by the early eighteenth century mainland Britain had enjoyed internal peace for many decades. Even in the late 1630s, when Britain had also enjoyed a similarly lengthy period of tranquility, Charles I had great difficulty in raising forces to fight the Scots; with the militia south of the Trent being most unwilling to march northwards. In any case, few of the gentry had any military experience, equipment was scarce and there was very little training.[14] After 1660, there were only two battles in England between formed armies, whereas in Scotland there had only been five between 1660 and 1715. Even clan warfare was unknown after 1688. It was noted, in 1745, that the Edinburgh Trained Bands 'had not appeared in arms since the Revolution [of 1688]'.[15] Peace brought flourishing trade and Britain's wars had been fought on the Continent, while after 1688 the weather and the Royal Navy had prevented invading forces from landing (saving a very small Spanish force arriving in Scotland in 1719 and a French force in 1746). The militia were only occasionally brought into being; and then only during rare emergencies, such as in 1696 in Cumberland.[16] Training was rare, but not wholly unknown, with William Stout, a Quaker merchant of Lancaster, writing in 1682, 'the [Lancashire] militia raised a week or 10 days every summer, which was a charge to the country'.[17] All this meant that very few men, except professional soldiers, had any experience of armed conflict. Ploughshares, not swords, were more familiar to most Britons. As Maxwell, noted, 'the use of arms and practice of war, both of which the common people of England are utter strangers to'.[18] Furthermore, with the militia system atrophying, training and the upkeep of arms was neglected. Edward Montagu MP, wrote, in October 1745, harking back to a golden age that never was, 'it will be some time before these companys can be raised, and made usefull, which would not have been otherwise, if the militia had been kept up and exercised as the law directs instead of being ridiculed and rendered contemptible these last 50 years'.[19] Even by the late seventeenth century, this had led to mixed performances. On one hand, the action of the militia in the south-west of England against Monmouth's rebels in June 1685 was generally unimpressive, but on the other, London's trained bands had successfully helped quell rioters in London in 1688. In both cases, however, regular troops were also brought into play.

Furthermore, the key figure in this system, in each county, was the lord lieutenant and much depended on him. This post was for life and the choice was made on political, not military grounds. In England, once George I had become King, loyal Whigs were installed as lieutenants, replacing Tories; for instance the Earl of Scarborough replaced the Bishop of Durham, Nathaniel Crewe, as Lord Lieutenant of Durham, while Viscount Irwin replaced the Earl of Carmarthen in the East Riding. In Scotland, however, none were appointed until as late as 27 August 1715, when Stanhope appointed the Earl of Roxburgh as Lord Lieutenant of Roxburgh and Selkirk. Stanhope listed his duties; to name and appoint 6–12 deputies, to appoint militia officers, to arm and assemble men in companies and to obey the commander-in-chief's orders. Like appointments in Scotland were also made at this time.[20] Arguably this was rather tardy.

Yet the situation in Scotland in 1745 was even worse, for then all the Scottish counties lacked lieutenants. This was because the political system which dominated Scotland, was controlled by the politicians at Westminster. The factional nature of politics in both countries meant that the Scottish MPs could hold the balance of power in Parliament. To appoint lords lieutenant might upset the delicate balancing act, and successful political manoeuvres were seen as more important than military necessity. None were appointed. In peacetime this was fine, but in other times it was potentially disastrous.[21] Sir John Clerk made the following observation:

> there was little or no care taken to provide against the impending storm, no lords lieutenants were appointed as in 1715, for by the contention of two factions in Scotland, and even amongst the Ministry in London, it could not be agreed who should be intrusted with lieutenancies, and therefore nobody was named. The heads of the factions were the Duke of Argyll and the Marquis of Tweeddale.[22]

Alexander Brodie, writing on 20 August 1745 was quick to note the problem, writing, 'I am glad to find the yachts are gone for the King but surprised to find they have appointed no lords lieutenant'.[23] Yet none were, despite urging by Andrew Fletcher, Lord Justice Clerk, on 5 November, who recommended that various noblemen be appointed in the Lowlands.[24]

Even in England, where each county had a lieutenant appointed, some were absentee during both the Fifteen and the Forty Five. In 1715 the Earl of Carlisle, Lord Lieutenant of Cumberland and Westmorland, was resident in Yorkshire as was his successor in 1745; whereas in that latter year the Lords Lieutenant of Northumberland and Durham both spent the crisis in London. The departure of the Earl of Tankerville from Northumberland did not go unnoticed, with a newspaper remarking, 'We are all in confusion here, as the LL is not here, nor has left any orders to raise the militia'.[25]

The lieutenants were criticized for other failings, too. In 1745, Henry Vane was not supportive of Edward Chandler, Bishop of Durham and Lord Lieutenant, 'I shall not say anything of the behaviour of our Lord Lieutenant the bishop only [that it is] obvious to everyone, how unfit a clergyman is for Head Office [sic]'.[26] Chandler was not unaware of his incapability in this sphere, writing, 'fearing His Majesty's service may suffer by reason of my many infirmities, I entreat your Lordship humbly to beseech His Majesty in my name to appoint a fitter person be his lieutenant'.[27] Yet absentee lieutenants were able to direct affairs as in the case of Cumberland and Westmorland in 1715, with Carlisle appointing Viscount Lonsdale as his chief deputy.[28]

Leadership in the north-west of England in December 1745 came in for severe criticism – lieutenants being absent in light of the earlier advance of the Jacobite army – as Colonel Yorke wrote:

> The Country people are enraged against 'em [the Jacobites] to such a degree that if the country gentlemen had had the least grain of spirit to have headed them, they would never have come so far, nor I believe will never again.[29]

There was initially a lack of leadership among loyalists in Scotland in 1745, too. 'But such was the situation of the Nobility of these countys, that no such thing could have been expected of any of them.' They were either ill or lacked the landed authority. The Earl of Aberdeen did not think it 'prudent to have tried to raise the Friends of the Government', perhaps because a poor showing would expose the level of disaffection. The Duke of Gordon was 'prevented by his indisposition' and the Earl of Findlater's 'sickly constitution quite disabled him', Duncan Forbes 'had by no means an estate suited to his ability' and Lord Salton 'had no weight in the country'. Of the gentry, 'many were selfish, many were careless who governed, and many were timid and fearful, so that the few who were resolute had not sufficient strength nor influence to make a stand'.[30] What was needed was firm leadership from a powerful magnate and the presence of regular troops, and neither were prevalent until early November 1745.

The militia was not the only type of official civilian force to be raised in this period. Another formal force was the posse comitatus. This was under the jurisdiction of the county sheriff, and involved the calling out of all able-bodied men aged between sixteen and sixty. On the whole, though, it was rarely summoned into being, except in several counties in 1715, such as in Northumberland, Cumberland and Westmorland, and, briefly in the two former counties, and possibly Durham, too, in 1745.[31]

We shall now turn to the raising of such forces during the Jacobite rebellions. The first to be raised in these times were usually in those places which were in immediate danger. As early as 28 July 1715 (five weeks before the Jacobite standard was raised at Braemar), but shortly after the official proclamation about the danger of invasion and insurrection, the Edinburgh magistrates noted that they had 'ordered the wholl train bands of the City to march out to Bruntisfield links tomorrow to have their Arms viewed'.[32] Likewise, it was on 27 August 1745 that the decision was taken to raise the Edinburgh volunteers and militia.[33] In England, it seems that the militia at Berwick was the first to be raised in 1745, with the corporation making the order on 14 September 1745, with Yorkshire, Newcastle, Carlisle and Liverpool not being far behind.[34]

The raising of irregular forces in Britain was far from uniform, especially in 1715. Although several were raised among the loyalist Highland clans, in the Lowlands of Scotland and in the seven northern counties of England, their appearance elsewhere was sketchy. Very few irregular forces were raised in 1715 in the Midlands and southern England. Exceptions included the formation of dockyard workers at Deptford and Woolwich into units of militia, another was the four companies of militia summoned in Berkshire.[35] During the Forty-Five, such forces were far more geographically widespread. Apart from those in Scotland and the north of England, there were several militia units raised in Hampshire, and militia and volunteers were called out in Essex and Kent. However, much of southern England; including Berkshire, Surrey, Middlesex, Hertfordshire, Essex and Cambridgeshire, preferred to raise money to help with army recruitment, rather than raise men for the militia or armed associations.[36] The reason for this geographical diversity is clear. Most Jacobite activity occurred in Scotland and northern England and so it was these places which needed loyalist action to deter them. It was correctly envisaged that these precautions were not needed in much of southern England, except during a handful of invasion scares.[37]

It was customary at the outset of the Jacobite attempts on the Crown for orders to be sent from the centre to the counties for the raising of the militia. On 5 September 1745, an order was issued from the Privy Council to each lord lieutenant, 'to cause the whole Militia of the said County to be put in a Readiness fit for immediate Service'.[38] The next step was for the lieutenant to call a meeting with his deputies and then call the militia into being. Clearly the government saw these forces as being of some potential use.

Thirty years earlier the procedure was straightforward. The order from London was written on 16 September 1715. In the case of Cumberland and Westmorland, which had a single lord lieutenant for both counties, the order went to the Earl of Carlisle who was absent from the counties throughout the crisis (not unusual; his successor in 1745, Viscount Lonsdale was absentee then, as were his counterparts in Northumberland and Durham, even though all were on potential routes of the Jacobite army). He appointed the foresaid Lonsdale as his chief deputy, and in turn he contacted his fellow deputies on 25 September. Fourteen of them met on 4 October. Men were chosen as captains for the militia companies and each then had to send an order to the high constables of each ward in the counties. Each petty constable then had to summon three men aged between twenty and twenty-five to report for duty. The constable also had to supply weapons for the men.[39] They were then fit for duty and would be told to report to their respective captain.

Although it was easy to issue orders from London, putting them into effect was far more difficult; especially in 1745. This was because the Militia Act, which had to be renewed annually, had expired in 1734. Thus it was illegal to raise a single militiaman until a new Act had been passed, which could not happen at once because Parliament was not yet sitting (it was to be passed on 14 November, when the Jacobite army was already in England). As Chandler pointed out, 'they are not legally empowered as the law stood to draw them out'.[40] Understandably, some did not want to break the law, but equally some did not want to wait until Parliament would reconvene and alter the law.

Eighteenth-century Britain was, in some ways, a very law-abiding society. Those in authority did not care to break it lightly. This was a difficulty in both England but especially in Scotland. In 1715, when associations were being proposed against the Jacobites, one David Stewart wrote that an association

> is against an express Act of the Parliament in Scotland that stands yet unrepealed. It is the 4th Act of the 1st parliament of King Charles II intitled An Act asserting His Majesty's Royal Prerogative in making leagues and the conventions of the subjects whereby this design of association so necessary to our present constitution stands condemned.[41]

There were similar concerns in 1745. The Lord Advocate of Scotland, Robert Craigie (1685–1760), advised Lord Glenorchy that it would be illegal for any civilians to resist the Jacobites by force.[42] Others whose loyalty was above suspicion agreed. Duncan Forbes (1685–1747), Lord of the Sessions Court and a leading loyalist in the Highlands, was very doubtful, too, and he was a staunch supporter of George II. He wrote on 8 August 1745:

> I do not know that there is at present any lawfull authority that can call them [the militia] forth to action, should occasion require it. In 1715 lieutenancys were estab-

lished in all counties, if any such thing now subsists, it is more than I know. In that unhappy year, the King's friends in the Highlands (tho' few) were armed, whereas at present they are not.

He also pointed out that private gentlemen had had to foot defence costs in 1715 'out of their own pockets' and had not been reimbursed, therefore, 'It is highly improbable that at present men will not be so ready to put their hands in their pockets'.[43] The Duke of Argyll also noted, 'it is not yet lawfull for any person in the Highlands to defend the government, or his own house, family or goods, though attacked by Robbers or Rebells'.[44]

When Glenorchy told Lord Hardwicke, the Lord Chancellor, of this objection, the latter wrote:

> This was the first time I ever heard that my Lord Advocate was of opinion that there was any difficulty in point of law as to arming the King's well affected subjects to suppress a Rebellion, and I can't help being surprised that no method was ever proposed to deliver the government from that difficulty in time of danger, nor the objection (so far as I remember) ever mentioned from that quarter.[45]

John Home, a later historian of the Forty-Five, discussed how the legal issues were dealt with in Edinburgh. A meeting on 27 August:

> recommended to the Provost and Magistrates to name a standing committee of the Town Council, with the addition of some other citizens, to consult the Justice Clerk, the crown lawyers, and such of the Judges as were in town, what other steps the community might legally take to frustrate the Designs of His Majesty's enemies. The committee was named, and met with the judges and lawyers, who informed them that it was necessary to apply for His Majesty's warrant to raise a regiment; and such an application was immediately prepared and forwarded to London for the King's advocate.[46]

However, with news that the Jacobite army was at Perth, some Edinburgh citizens petitioned to form a regiment of volunteers, and another meeting was held, on 7 September, but the outcome was very different. According to Home:

> he [Provost Stuart]consulted the King's advocate and the solicitor, whether or not it was lawful for the council to grant the desire of the petition: these gentlemen gave their opinion in the most positive terms, that it was lawful for the Town Council of Edinburgh to authorize the inhabitants to take arms for the defence of the city.[47]

Home commented that the lawyers consulted on both occasions were the same men, and that they gave different verdicts to the same question. It was believed that some of the lawyers who advised caution were being deceitful, 'some of the magistrates have taken up an evil spirit of law that it was treason to take up arms in defence of themselves and the government'.[48] What clinched the case was the arrival of the King's instructions allowing the raising of companies, thus sanctifying the raising of volunteers with legality.

Yet in some counties the militia was raised, notwithstanding the legal difficulties. These included Lancashire (at least initially), Cumberland and Westmorland. In the latter counties, Lonsdale simply wrote to his subordinates to raise the militia, and on 21 September, Newcastle gave him permission to do so, even though this was illegal. His deputies seemed to have concurred in all this, with Lonsdale writing that they 'have proceeded in this service with great chearfulness'.[49] Difficulties only surfaced twenty-eight days later, when it was thought that the militia would have to disband without permission to raise further funds. Newcastle then became cautious and wrote, 'I could advise them to do nothing which was contrary to law'. Yet with the Jacobite invasion threatening to be imminent, the deputies were worried about what to do and thought that the militia's disbandment 'may be of ill consequence, and therefore we beg your lordship's advice'. Newcastle gave Lonsdale the following nebulous advice, 'I am persuaded your lordship will do everything in your power to prevent this'. In the end, the clerk of the militia was asked to raise the money and pay the men.[50]

There was no militia raised in the Scottish Highlands until towards the end of 1745. Unlike the case in Cumberland, money was easier to come by. The Argyllshire militia were supplied with money from London. In February 1746, Mr Bruce, agent to the lieutenancy there wrote to Newcastle, 'desiring payment of several sums of money, as well for purchasing oatmeal, for the use of the militia officers and soldiers raised in that county, for His Majesty's service, as for two months pay for their maintenance and support'.[51] Money, to the tune of £4,000 was sent up to Loudon from London in October 1745 by ship. In the interim, money was advanced by magnates, such as Forbes, who wrote, 'I have subscribed out of my own pocket' because the militia 'officers could not in their own private credit find money'.[52]

The forces were usually organized on conventional military lines, with infantry in companies and cavalry into troops, each led by a captain, with junior officers and NCOs beneath him. A number of companies would form a regiment under a colonel. Each company usually consisted of 50 privates. In February 1746 it was noted that the Argyllshire militia was composed of 13 companies. Each was officered, as in the regular army, by a captain, a lieutenant and an ensign, with three sergeants, three corporals, a piper and between thirty-five and sixty-seven men, totalling 765 men of all ranks. The Earl of Loudon's independent companies were similarly organized.[53]

Men enrolling into the militia and volunteers often had to swear an oath of loyalty. The men of the Berkshire Militia in 1715 had to swear the following:

[I] do sincerely promise and swear that I will be faithful and bear true allegiance to His Majesty King George: so help me God ... I do swear that I do from my heart, abhor, detest and abjure as impious and heretical that Damnable Doctrine and position that princes excommunicated or deprived by the pope or any authority of those of the see of Rome may be deposed and murthered by their subjects.[54]

The most important matter to distinguish these civilian forces from other civilians was their being armed. In a largely unmilitarized society, arming these men was often a very difficult task, because there were usually insufficient arms in the localities and those which existed were often unusable. Hardwicke noted in a speech in 1756 that England was a 'nation of merchants, manufacturers, artisans, husbandmen ... The weaning of the people since the days of Elizabeth from arms to trade, arts, manufactures, had been the origin of the national greatness and prosperity'.[55] The scarcity of any arms, let alone those which were in serviceable order, was widespread. Joseph Crisap referred that in Newcastle in 1715, to 'the generall Scarcity of Ames, along the well affected'.[56] In 1745 Lord Reay wrote, 'The long disuse of wearing Arms, has been the occasion that we have few'.[57] Likewise, Lonsdale noted in the same year:

The Militia throughout is ill armed, but I don't know how that can be remedied at present, for they can't be provided with better ones in this country and it will be a long time before new ones can be had from London. We have ordered them to throw away their pikes and get firelocks in their place, and also to put the arms they have into the best condition that is possible.[58]

There may have been an exception to this rule. Joseph Symson (1650–1731), a Kendal merchant, told a correspondent, 'Ours and the Cumberland militia both horse and foot are up ... and well armed and strictly disciplined every day'.[59]

There were similar complaints to Lonsdale's among Scottish loyalists in 1715, too. In August of that year, both the Lord Justice Clerk and the Principal of Glasgow University told the government that without being sent weapons, the men who would otherwise be raised against the Jacobites could only stay at home. Likewise, later that month, James Stuart wrote, 'how destitute our country is of arms ... they have the men, but no arms'.[60] However, elsewhere, the situation was mixed. In Inverary, the Rev. John Anderson wrote, 'The clans here have graly muskets, but few swords, which are the arms they mostly depend on'.[61]

It was often alleged that more volunteers would have come forth if arms were ready for them. James Nimmo wrote in 1745 of a plan to raise the Lowlanders as a fighting force: 'but of what use they will be without Arms is more than I conceive. I wish this may open the eyes of the Ministry to see of what use the country people might have been had they been armed.'[62] It was complained that the lack of weapons was holding back a rush of volunteers. Yet when Cope marched through Scotland that month, none of these 'loyal' Highlanders joined him except for 200 Monroes, so these assertions should be treated with caution, at least.

In 1745 the situation in Scotland was even worse. Although Scotland was generally less of a commercial society than England, various methods taken after 1715 to weaken the Jacobite cause had, ironically, resulted in weakening the capacity of loyalists to defend themselves. The Disarming At of 1716 had made the carrying of weapons in the Highlands illegal. In the following decade, further legislation decreed that all weapons be surrendered to the government. Only those clans loyal to the government made any attempt to obey this, and those with Jacobite sympathies handed in, if anything, obsolete arms, retaining the ones which worked.[63]

On 17 September 1745, Andrew Fletcher stated the matter to the government thus:

> This Act has been found by experience to work the quite contrary effect from what was intended by it, and in reality proves a measure for more effectually disturbing the peace of the Highlands and of the kingdom ... for all the disaffected clans retain their arms and ammunition concealed them at the first disarming, or have provided themselves since, at the same time that the dutyfull and well affected clans have tamely submitted to this measure of the government and Act of the Legislature and are still disarmed or have no quantity of arms amongst them.[64]

Yet the carrying of weapons in Scotland, even in the Highlands, was not as common as was once believed. It is worth noting that the Jacobite army in 1745 was only partially armed with modern weaponry until after their victory at Prestonpans. Despite Fletcher's fears, the Disarming Acts had not resulted in the Jacobite clans all being armed to the teeth. Elcho wrote, 'The Prince's Army, when it pass'd the Forth, Consisted of 2000 foot – the half Compleatly armed, the others with pitch forks, Scythes, a sword or a pistol, or some only a Staf or Stick'.[65] Likewise, John Murray wrote that the MacDonalds of Skye 'had not arms for above one half and so of the rest, by which means they all in general when spoke to, declared they were not Armed'.[66] This was, of course, little consolation to the loyalists. Those who wanted to join the McLeods were parlously armed. Some 'could get nothing but pistols they proved of no service'. Others 'could get no firearms' and this 'had caused make a number of spears with iron heads, for them'.[67] However, some loyalists in Scotland did have arms. On 26 September 1715 it was noted that in Glasgow, 'We have now in this toun of well armed men about 800'.[68] In England the situation was not always helped by legislation, with a reference in 1715 to 'the late disarming of the people by our wise game laws', though how extensive this was and how far it had been carried out is questionable because there is no other reference to it being a hindrance to arming anyone at this time.[69]

Modern weaponry for use in the field consisted of muskets and bayonets for infantrymen and these were in short supply, because these weapons were not used for civilian purposes, such as hunting, but usually only by the army. Some cities had municipal armouries, but these were seldom adequate. For instance, the corporation of Liverpool discovered that the town's armoury only held 220 muskets, 154 pistols and 25 swords.[70] Edinburgh had 1200 bayonetless muskets for the volunteers.[71] Elsewhere, the situation was even bleaker. Lonsdale told Newcastle on 9 September 1745, 'The arms are extreamly bad and it is impossible to gain new ones in so short a time as they shall probably have'.[72]

If the localities could not supply adequate arms, then the centre might. After all, the Tower of London was the country's main arsenal (Edinburgh Castle also had one, too, though it was less well stocked) and application could be made to the Board of Ordnance to dispatch weapons from there to the provinces. Major General Campbell set sail for Scotland bringing arms from London.[73] They were sent to Scotland, first, with Argyll writing as early as 11 August, 'I am very glad there are arms ordered for Scotland, though I fear it will be late before they come'. These amounted to 500 muskets, broadswords and ammunition being sent by sea to Inverrary.[74] Sometimes this could run smoothly. The City of Carlisle was swiftly supplied, once a request had been sent by the deputy mayor, Thomas Pattinson. Even so, it does not appear that the men were actually armed until 11 November, by which time the Jacobite army was threatening Carlisle.[75]

In 1745 Scottish loyalists looked to the government for weaponry which they lacked at the outset of the rebellion, too. Hardwicke noted on 15 August that 5,000 arms had been sent to Scotland; presumably to Edinburgh castle.[76] The Castle supplied 200 muskets, bayonets and cartridge boxes to the volunteers in September 1745 as requested.[77] Edinburgh castle supplied 1,000 arms for the Glasgow militia in late November 1745.[78] A Royal Navy sloop, *The Saltash*, supplied arms and money to Lord Loudon's forces in the same month.[79] In 1715, the Earl of Rothes took 500 arms from Edinburgh for men he was raising in Fife and Aberdeenshire.[80] The irregular forces were thus armed from numerous sources, resulting in the men bearing a diverse assortment of weapons; some with modern muskets and bayonets, others were antiquated and faulty firearms.

Those not supplied from London were annoyed; Sir George Bowes writing, 'I think it is my duty once more to represent to your Lordship the great want we have of arms in this county [Durham] ... we cannot but think it is a little hard that the other counties should be indulged every request'.[81]

On 3 August 1715, in Aberdeen: 'The counsel recommends to the provost to buy 200 stand of arms, viz., guns and bayonets for the use of the towne with all convenient dilligence'.[82] Another method of acquiring arms was to make an appeal to the public. Advertisements were placed in the Newcastle press to ask that weapons for the county force be sent to the Morpeth bailiffs, the Alnwick chamberlains or to Messrs Wilkinson Kersopp and Bell in Hexham.[83] Weapons confiscated from Catholics were also used, as accounts relate to repairing Catholic weaponry.[84] In Aberdeen the order came to 'seize and take up all the powder from the merchants of this towne', though the merchants were paid.[85] Hand-to-mouth methods were used in Newcastle in 1715. Joseph Crisap wrote, 'your Petitioner industriously apply'd himself to diverse Masters of ships and officers of his acquaintanceship, and borrow'd of them 94 firelocks and blunderbusses and 31 swords or cutlasses'.[86] At this time in Durham, Edward Blackett was 'very free' in lending arms for the militia.[87] In the West Riding the Earl of Burlington, the Lord Lieutenant, agreed to pay for the 600 muskets, bayonets, swords and other accoutrements required for the militia, which, together with the cost of moving on vagrants, came to £800, on the condition he was repaid by the county treasurer.[88]

Constables were called upon to supply weapons and ammunition, and to have these in working order. This occurred in Lancashire in 1715 as well as in other counties. The constable for Formby spent money in repairing muskets, at the cost of 5s 4d. He provided belts and cartridge boxes at the cost of 10s 4d, had a halberd cleaned for 2d, and put two swords and a pike in order for a shilling. The Tarleton constable did likewise, for muskets and halberds. He also advanced money for the three parishioners who were sent to join the militia.[89]

If this is a representative cross-section of the arms in the hands of the militia, then they were clearly armed with a mixture of seventeenth and eighteenth century weapons; pikes had been wholly abandoned by the regulars in 1704. A diverse selection of arms were used by irregular forces in Kent in December 1745; as well as swords, pistols and muskets, some had blunderbusses, pitchforks, fowling pieces and cutlasses.[90]

Even when the militia was armed, not all had weapons which were in good order. Of the 282 known men of the Cumberland and Westmorland militia, fifty-seven were without swords, seven lacked muskets, fourteen were without bayonets and nine men were totally unarmed. Almost half those who had muskets, had faulty ones and seventy-two men had swords which were in poor condition.[91] The quality of weaponry with which the men were armed was certainly diverse. In December 1715, it was said that the Frasers and Grants 'are extremely well armed' but that the men from Murray 'are but indifferently armed'.[92]

The consequence of the lack of arms could mean that the force raised ceased to exist. Tweeddale told Robert Pringle on 27 October 1715, 'I have now reduced our Foot Militia to 400 men pretty well armed, being forced to disband the other half for want of arms'.[93]

Yet if arms were a problem, uniforms were probably viewed as a luxury. Volunteer units in 1745 were sometimes provided with uniforms, although the militia were rarely uniformed, and there is no reference to any being thus clothed in 1715. This could have been because of the relatively short time frame between the Secretaries of State ordering the calling out of the militia in September and the surrender of the Jacobite army at Preston on 14 November, as well as the expense involved being seen as prohibitive.

Similarly, in 1745, none of the militia who were embodied were uniformed, certainly not those in Durham and Northumberland; and likewise those in Cumberland and Westmorland. However, there is a reference in Lancashire to some form of uniform. Sir Henry Hoghton referred to the men being dressed in blue, brown, red and white cloth, but there is no further mention of this, so how far this constituted a uniform is uncertain.[94] He wrote to the Earl of Derby, Lord Lieutenant of Lancashire, thus, 'Many of the Foot are likely fellows but [have] poor bad Cloathes. I have spoken to several, and I hope it would not be thought much of if yor Ldship thought fit to order each man to have a coat without lining, only facd and turned up at the sleeves; if the cloth were brown would be cheapest'. It seems uncertain if this wish was acceded to, for Derby informed Newcastle, 'As to the cloathing, I know not what to say to it: an uniform seems necessary, and yet if it be paid for out of the private Subscriptions, a less number of men must be raised, and I fear this is not the time for it'.[95] There is no record of whether the volunteer regiment raised in Hampshire was uniformed either.

Training was another issue. Musketry and drill had to be learnt if the men were to effectively use their arms, and to march and manoeuvre in a recognizable military manner, and that meant instruction was required. Very few of the officers and men enrolled in these formations had ever used weapons before, and even if this were so, this had not been as part of a disciplined military unit, so they had no knowledge of drill. Tweeddale reported of his men in 1715, 'few or none of them had ever fired a gun or a musquett'.[96] Sometimes this could be rectified. Half-pay officers were sent to various places in Britain in 1715 to help train militia and volunteers. They were sent to Newcastle, Berwick, Hull, York, Carlisle and Chester, and to Stirling where many of the militia were concentrated. William Cotesworth wrote that those sent to Newcastle would be useful in leading the militia there.[97] In Cumberland, Lonsdale, wrote of the posse and/or militia there, 'by the assistance of some broken officers of General Elliott's regiment (who were extremely diligent) they were put in a very tolerable order'.[98] Half-pay officers were also directed to Scotland 'so that they might be in readiness to encourage, exercise, and command the Militia on any Emergence'.[99] Similarly, Colonel William Maxwell helped train loyalists in Galloway.[100] Yet many men were wholly untrained and even those that were lacked any experience of campaigning. Likewise, in 1745, training was sometimes provided by veteran soldiers. The Earl of Hume and two troops of dragoons helped train the Glasgow militia in late November 1745.[101]

Yet these were the exceptions; most irregular bodies received no training whatsoever, probably because there were insufficient half-pay officers. The
Hampshire deputy lieutenants, for instance, complained that they needed half-
pay officers to train their men, but it does not seem that any were ever sent, and
there were similar complaints in the north-western counties in that year.[102] In
1715, Mr Stirling of Glasgow wrote, 'the friends of the government seem somewhat concerned that no officers have been sent by the government to these parts
with orders to be assisting'.[103] The Glasgow militia in 1745 were well rated, 'they
are now doing duty by detachment with the regular troops to the satisfaction of
everybody who sees them ... they will behave more like soldiers than militia'.[104]

Leadership in the field was also required, so the provision of officers was
another issue to contend with. Except those involved in training as noted above,
some of whom also helped lead the volunteers, very few of the Lords Lieutenant
or their deputies had any military experience, yet it was they who were expected
to lead the county forces. Again, as with the Lords Lieutenant, political loyalty
was seen as key. As Stanhope noted in 1715, they had to 'not only be the most
capable [but also] of the greatest and most known zeal, before our accession to
the Crown and for the Protestant Succession'.[105] Yet this was not enough in the
field. John Murray's remarks about the Edinburgh officers in 1745 may be more
universally applicable. According to him, after describing the poor state of the
men, 'they had no officers to head them who were better versed in military matters than themselves'.[106] There were a few exceptions. One was George Bowes,
who led the Durham Horse Militia in 1745 and had once served as a cavalry-
man.[107]

Yet even when there were half-pay officers to lead the men, they were not
always welcomed by those under them. Henry Prescott wrote of the Cheshire
militia in 1715, 'The Militia seems unanimous and promote a saying, All of a
Mind, which is interpreted, Not to be Exercisd by half pay officers, nor to march
but under command of their proper officers'.[108]

Most of the officers were amateurs, though. Of the Lieutenants and their
deputies, some were physically unsuited to active command. Sir James Lowther,
a deputy lieutenant of Lancashire, wrote that he was 'of a great age and much
disabl'd in my limbs with the gout'.[109] In Edinburgh, the captains of the volunteer
companies included two former provosts, a baronet, a former Baillie and a town
councillor. Merchants and craftsmen officered the Edinburgh trained bands.[110]
The officers of the Dumfries Volunteers in 1715 included tax officials, merchants
and a schoolmaster.[111] The Aberdeen militia in 1745 was mainly to be officered
by councillors and merchants, but there were also three advocates, a pewterer,
a goldsmith and a shipmaster.[112] In some places, the pool of gentlemen to draw
on was thought to be limited, with Derby thinking that in Lancashire there was

only one Whig gentleman who would make a good officer; a very high proportion of gentlemen in that county being either Catholic or Tory.[113]

Clergymen were often involved with the militia. Bishop Nicholson of Carlisle rode with the Cumberland posse on Penrith in 1715, as did Sir William Dawes, Archbishop of York. As a newspaper noted, 'The Arch Bp of York and Carlisle are very zealous for His Majesty's Interest and are with the Lord Lansdale [*sic*] at the Head of the Volunteers who have risen in Cumberland and the Neighbouring Counties'. Lesser clergy were also present on this instance.[114] The Dumfries clergy were also actively involved with local volunteers, and Mr Ramsey, Minister of Kelso, was jointly responsible for bringing the men together. In fact, in Kelso the initial meeting was held in the church.[115] In 1745, clergy helped recruit men in both Holmfirth and Haworth, as well as gathering money.[116] Andrew Fletcher, on 2 January 1746 wrote that there was a need 'to advertise the country people from the pulpit, whose names we had formerly given in, to be in readiness to come hither for the defence of the City [Edinburgh]'.[117]

The other ranks were often filled with working men and agricultural workers, as might be expected; depending whether the captain recruiting was looking for men in a town/city or in the countryside, Gentlemen often 'recruited' their servants, just as in 1715, the Northumbrian and Lancashire Jacobite gentry took their servants with them or Highland chiefs employed their clansmen.[118] Likewise, in 1715, there was a reference to the West Riding forces being summoned to Pontefract in mid-October, and these were 'a great number of Gentlemen and their Servants'.[119] Tenants of gentlemen were also encouraged to join these forces, with Burlington in 1715 promising to remit part of their rents to any who came along[120] Certainly for these employed in seasonable trades, such as agriculture, the fact that the rebellions occurred in autumn and winter, meant that as these were slack times, work-wise, they could easily commit themselves as they provided a stable income for a few months.

That having been said, there were units which seem to have been manned mostly by men of a rather higher social standing than would be usual in units of the standing army. The Argyllshire militia in 1746 had in their ranks four gentlemen volunteers and twenty men acting as privates but requiring no pay – clearly men of independent means.[121]

The men usually received a shilling a day, which compares favourably to the regulars, who received half that and faced greater dangers. NCOs usually received 1*s* 3*d* or 1*s* 6*d*, depending on rank. Those NCOs raised at Glasgow in 1715 received 6*d* per day, as did some among the Jacobite rank and file; the Argyllshire men received more money if they were serving away from home.[122] To receive regular pay was very useful indeed. Yet the officers were not always paid. Glasgow militia officers in 1745 were 'to subsist themselves'.[123]

But some would-be volunteers were perturbed at the prospect of serving in the militia. In Berkshire, militiamen were warned by the Rev. George Read of Chilton, that 'they would turn to the Rebellion when he comes to be sure for ... they were foolish if they did not turn to the strongest side'.[124] In Scotland in October 1745: 'Some people among ourselves industriously spread false reports in the county that had almost turned the men wild they would on no account enter one independent company'.[125] This was where the officers were crucial. Forbes wrote, 'both officers and private men must be strongly indoctrinated before they leave home & someone, who has authority over them, must necessarily come alongst with them'.[126]

It seems that raising men did not usually take much time. Yet in some instances in 1715, the militia in England were not raised until it was too late, with one Mrs Robinson writing on 26 November 1715, nearly two weeks after the Jacobite surrender at Preston, of the North Riding militia, 'If the party attempt riseing any more they [the militia]'ll be well prepared to oppose 'em'.[127] Likewise, the men in the Berkshire militia were not swearing their oaths of allegiance until 23 and 24 November.[128]

The county sheriffs occasionally called the posse comitatus into being, but this was mainly confined to 1715. John Johnson, county sheriff of Northumberland summoned them into being, raising 407 men in a couple of days. More would have been raised if the Jacobite army at Warkworth had not obstructed loyalists. Furthermore, one Robert Lawson of Chirton refused to send a horse as required, and 'Several gentlemen did not appear on the Posse but on the other hand laughed and discouraged others'.[129] His counterpart in Cumberland had the posse summoned on Penrith Fell on 2 November, and the Westmorland posse was summoned for the following day. There was discussion of Joshua Lucock raising the Cumberland posse in December 1745 and Matthew Ridley calling out that of Newcastle in September 1745, but the later may be a reference to the city militia. In all cases the sheriffs seemed able to summon the posse more rapidly than the militia were called out, though they were only in arms for a few days on each occasion.[130]

Almost all of the irregular forces raised against the Jacobites were infantry, despite the order in Privy Council of 16 September 1715 stating, 'cause the Militia, both Horse and Foot, to be put in such a posture as to be in readiness to March at the first order'.[131] Infantry were doubtless predominant for three reasons. Firstly, few men other than the gentry and nobility and some of their servants could actually ride a horse. Secondly, it was far more expensive to keep a horse and rider in service than just an infantryman. Finally most horses would be unaccustomed to the noise of battle or were being used for other purposes.

However, in some cases, cavalry were raised. In Cumberland and Westmorland in 1715 and 1745 two troops of cavalry were brought into play. It also occurred in Durham and Northumberland in 1715, when James Clavering led a troop of cavalry, who served as intelligence gatherers.[132] During 1745 they were raised in Durham and Northumberland, being 400 strong in the latter county.[133]

The West Riding forces in 1715 were almost wholly cavalry. There were at least three troops of Horse Militia, each with three officers, numerous NCOs and seventy-five troopers.[134] John Lucas described their gathering at Leeds on 12 November 1715:

> 'in the afternoon [Burlington] was attended on Woodhouse Moor by His Honour Wentworth, and his son, Sir John Wentworth, Sir William Robinson, Sir William Ramsden, Sir John Armitage, Sir Rowland Winn, Sir William Lowther and several other knights and gentlemen to the number of about 300 which with the militia and volunteers made betwixt six and seven hundred, all or most of them well horsed and well armed. The foot were about 100'.[135]

These few units of Horse Militia and mounted volunteers formed only a small proportion of the volunteer forces raised at this time, however. The majority were infantry.

In England, in 1715 and 1745, there was time enough to raise the militia before the Jacobite army ever came near to them, though less so in the former year. In Scotland, this was not the case, because the attempts to restore the Stuarts emanated from there on both occasions, resulting in a scenario in which the need for action was imperative, though militia were formed in Glasgow, Edinburgh and in Argyllshire.

Numbers are important because they give an indication, however crude, of the strength of support for a cause. It is hard to know how large the militia raised against the Jacobites were, in part because that number was constantly changing as units were raised or stood down, or as men drifted away. Furthermore, in many cases there are no reliable figures. We shall take two important northern counties to gain an impression of numbers. In 1715, the Lancashire militia numbered about 560.[136] In Yorkshire, there were the fifty men raised in York, the 700 in the West Riding, and those raised in the other two Ridings, whose numbers are unknown.[137]

Yet there was not always a higher turnout in 1745; certainly not in Northumberland's case. In 1715, there were 1,200 in the county militia and an unknown number of city militia companies; over 2,000 men in all. In 1745 the county militia numbered 600, and as before there were and city militia companies; numbering under 2,000 in all. The earlier crisis had led to about 600 more men being raised; perhaps because the threat in 1715 seemed both more immediate and more containable, also in 1745 there were regular troops in Newcastle in large numbers.[138]

The militia were raised throughout Britain in 1715 to assist in the suppression of the rebellion. However, because of legal difficulties in England and Scotland and the lack of Lieutenants in the latter, the militia were rarely raised in 1745. Instead, volunteer regiments were raised, though there was a great deal of overlap between the two forces, as we shall see in the following chapter.

6 THE FORMATION OF THE LOYALIST VOLUNTEER FORCES

It has already been noted that the militia and posse were not seen by many in authority as being adequate, or even legal, during 1745. There was, therefore, a need to bypass these official structures and create others. These forces raised by civilians during 1745–6 to combat the Jacobites had a very similar role to that of the militia, as we shall discover in Chapter 7. Yet their formation was, in some ways, different, yet was not without similarities, as were some of the difficulties faced.

The principal method of evading the legal obstacles was not to call out the militia, but to form voluntary associations of like-minded men and so organize volunteer companies and troops, led by the lieutenancy in the counties or by the mayor in a borough which was outside the county administrative jurisdiction, who would be given blank officers' commissions from the Secretary of State. The lieutenant or mayor would allot the commissions to those he thought would make good officers and these would then raise men to fill their company. The forces would be financed by voluntary subscriptions from among the populace. Yet it seems that this method had been used earlier, as Newcastle wrote to the Lord Lieutenant of Lincoln, 'This method was practised at the time of the rebellion of 1715, and it has been thought proper to revive it upon the present one'.[1]

The men raised would then act as militia in all but name. As Newcastle told the deputy lieutenants of Northumberland:

> the King, thinking it absolutely necessary, That the Lords Lieutenant of those counties should have a legal authority to put them in a Condition of Defence in this time of Danger; his Majesty has ordered me to transmit to your Lordship the enclosed warrants authorizing and empowering your Lordship in the several counties ... to form into Troops or Companies such persons as shall be willing to associate themselves.[2]

Some doubted this would work, with Lonsdale writing, 'no force worth mentioning can be expected to be raised by voluntary subscriptions'.[3] He was to be proved wrong: this system was followed in many counties and towns, including the three Ridings of Yorkshire, Hampshire and in towns such as Edinburgh,

Glasgow, Hull, Berwick, Carlisle and Liverpool, as well as in Scotland. By early October, twenty-four counties had chosen to raise volunteer units.[4] In Scotland, for instance, Forbes was given twenty officers' commissions in October 1745 in order to raise men in the Highlands. These were given to the loyalist clans, including the Monroes, Sutherlands, McKays and McLeods. One reason may have been as much political as military, with Lord Fortrose raising two companies in part to prevent some of his clan from joining the Jacobites.[5] Forbes was told that the commissions were 'to be disposed of to the well affected clans as you shall think proper for the publick service at this juncture ... I am sure they could not be put into better hands'.[6] On 11 September, the Provost of Edinburgh could note that steps would be taken for raising forces 'as is directed by His Majesty's Sign Manual of date the fourth current'.[7]

One criticism of using this method in Scotland was made by the Earl of Chesterfield, who was strongly prejudiced against the Scots. He wrote on 6 December 1745:

> I am very sorry to see any loyal Highlanders are to be arm'd at all ... I both hope and believe that those to whom I see money is given to raise loyall Highlanders will put that money in their pockets and not raise a man. Upon my word, if you give way to Scotch importunitys and jobs upon this occasion you will have a rebellion every seven years.[8]

Loyal Scots had another method of raising irregular forces, as Lord Glenorchy wrote, albeit as late as 6 December 1745:

> As the common people in the Highlands have no idea of the laws relating to the militia, they look upon themselves as my father's men, raised by his order; and the great readiness and chearfulness with which they assembled gave me a handle for reproaching some of the people of this country, which has had such an effect that they declare they will not be outdone in duty ... and that they will go with me wherever I please to lead them.[9]

Similarly traditional quasi-feudal methods had been used in 1715, Rae writing that vassals and tenants of the Duchess of Hamilton and others assembled on 8 September at Lanark.[10] Jacobite forces in the Highlands were raised by men either being forced out or being liable to serve because of the terms of their land tenure and Whig forces in the Highlands were raised by similar methods. This led to desertion on both sides, partly because of the compulsive element but also because kinsmen might find themselves on opposing sides due to the decisions of different members of the chief and his family.[11]

In England, then, associations were formed. Although leadership, in the form of the lord lieutenant or mayor was important, so too was wider political support from among the county elite. Meetings were held, usually at the county town, to canvass such. Archbishop Thomas Herring (1693–1757) of York delivered a speech to a meeting for Yorkshire at York Castle on 24 September and this was described as 'the most numerous ever known'. For Lancashire, there was one at Preston town hall on 3 October when 'an excellent speech [was] made by the Earl of Derby and seconded by Mr Bootle'.[12] That at York was particularly effective, and won plaudits. Horace Walpole wrote:

> Dr Herring, the Archbishop of York, has set an example which would rouse the most indifferent: in two days after the news arrived at York of Cope's defeat, and when they every moment expected the victorious rebels at their gates, the Bishop made a speech to the assembled county, that had as much true spirit, honesty, and bravery in it, as ever was penned by an historian for an ancient hero.[13]

Not all meetings were so successful. At Durham, Bowes wrote, 'What a poor meeting there was at the castle last Tuesday ... I was greatly struck at the absence of some and the coolness of others'.[14] At Lancashire, Derby reported, 'the event has not answered our expectations'. This was due to the recent news of Prestonpans, 'which causes here the utmost consternation', leading some to believe that civil defence was useless.[15]

After a loyal association had been formed, usually by all those at the meeting adding their names to a list of those who supported George II, they would then promise to pay a sum of money. Money was needed to pay the men, to arm and clothe them; for the militia this was paid for out of the county rates levied on the landowning classes and was therefore straightforward. However in the case of the armed associations, money had to be raised. Subscriptions were called upon and those willing to pay would promise a sum and then pay in instalments. The sums promised varied considerably. In Hampshire, for instance, the Duke of Bolton, the Lord Lieutenant, subscribed £1000, the bishop of Winchester offered £200 and Peter Delme, MP, subscribed £100. Humbler people also gave money. In Hampshire these included Mrs Anne Bennett of Fareham (£20) and William Bignell of Lymington, who offered £2 2s.[16]

Certainly these subscriptions were not restricted to those in the elite, but throughout society. An analysis of the subscribers to the fund at York revels that of the 515 male subscribers who can be identified from the 1741 poll book, there were thirty-nine tailors, twenty-eight barbers, twenty-six bakers, seventeen bricklayers, sixteen coopers and fourteen whitesmiths, as well as men from many other professions. Some gave but a few shillings or less.[17] Generally speaking, there seems to have been enthusiasm for making such payments. Ray observed, in the case of Liverpool, 'the chearfulness and Alarcity with which everyone contributed to the forwarding of this noble design; since even the poorer Sort did not refuse to cast in their mite, and the rich were not slack in their giving, according to their Abilities'.[18]

The principal source of money came from those who attended the county meetings; these tended to be the nobility, clergy and gentlemen. But, as we have seen, the net was cast wider to include men and women from the middling and lower ranks of society, too, as these examples illustrate. So other methods were used as well, often by the clergy. Newcastle told the Lord Lieutenant of Lincoln, 'The minister of a parish is desired to notify the matter to his parishoners'.[19]

The Rev. Mark Hildesley of Hitchin, Hertfordshire, promoted the cause in church, as he wrote, 'I should for my part be ready to publish it here on Sunday'. The Rev. John Rooke of Willian wrote that he would ask his neighbours for subscription. The press was also used, with adverts placed in county newspapers. John Allen responded to one such, commenting, 'This is, I think, according to the advert published in the papers'. Posters asking for subscriptions were displayed in market towns where men could be expected to congregate.[20] In Yorkshire, 'almost evry town in the county has rais'd sums ... even the small villages are not behind in their duty'.[21]

It is noteworthy that it was not only the natural supporters of the government who paid into such schemes. The above-mentioned Delme was an opposition Whig and was listed as a man ready to assist in a Stuart restoration.[22] Sir Richard Grosvenor, MP, was another whose loyalties were suspect, yet he subscribed at Chester, to the extent of £2,000. The two Tory York MPs did likewise.[23]

At York, one newspaper related 'even the Roman Catholics contributed, and that very chearfully'. Likewise in Lancashire, 'even the Catholics of the best distinction shew'd their zeal for the government'.[24] This could have been because, as was observed of, 'their Gratitude for the Peace they had long enjoyed under his [George II] mild administration'.[25] But some were sceptical, with Hardwicke writing, 'The subscription of some of the papists is surprising ... it can only be colourable and to procure some Resolution in their Favour'.[26]

Not everyone did subscribe. Drs Francis Drake and John Burton, both prominent Tories in York did not do so[27] Likewise, in Middlesex, Roger Newdigate, a Tory MP for the county, did not do so either.[28] Despite the willingness of Catholics in York and Cheshire, some in Lancashire also resisted demands to contribute towards the volunteer forces, with Robert Patten remarking, 'the property of those towns being much in the hands of Roman Catholics'.[29] Cambridgeshire Tories were also lukewarm, with one observer noting, 'a few gentlemen who subscribed ... put down so small a sum considering their estates'; perhaps because the scheme was in the hands of their Whig enemies, and so they 'look'd upon it, as they gave out, as a party business'.[30] There were some Quakers in Hertfordshire who were also reluctant to subscribe, drawing the ire of others. Hildesley wrote that this was a 'strange return for the extraordinary lenity and protection of the Government they live under' and another clergyman wrote, 'The Quakers would do nothing on a pretence that they are to do it in a body'.[31]

Dr William Webster noted the lack of enthusiasm in some, 'Many of the Church folks had their Excuses, too, but I spared no pains'. This might have been because 'the Poverty of the County is so great at Present'.[32]

Some questioned this system of finance on principle. Humphrey Sydenham, a Tory MP for Exeter, doubted both the sincerity of those who paid and likened it to a tax. He wrote, 'many have been threatened into them, under the pain of being represented as Jacobites' and the promoters were little better, wishing merely 'to recommend themselves to posts under the government'.[33] From another perspective, Malton thought that 'voluntary subscriptions ... fall alone on the honest folks who by their expence protect the states of every scoundrel in the Realm'.[34]

The sums of money raised by these methods varied enormously. The city of York raised £2,556 13s 1d, which was deemed by the archbishop, 'an incredible sum of money'.[35] Liverpool did even better, with one estimate being £6,000.[36] At county levels, sums were higher, with Lancashire raising at least £11,000 and Yorkshire almost £32,000.[37] In Hampshire, about £16,000 was subscribed.[38] Cambridge raised £5,159 8s.[39] These funds were needed to pay the volunteers and to arm and perhaps uniform them. Some were sceptical. Dr John Brown, later rector of St Nicholas's church, Newcastle, wrote in 1755, 'It has been urged indeed, as a proof of that the national spirit of defence is not yet extinguished, that we raised large sums ... This is weak reasoning ... The capital question therefore still remains, Not who shall pay, but who shall fight'.[40] This is a good point, and to one which we shall return, but without money – Cicero's 'the sinews of war' – little could be achieved.

Arming the men was a challenge. In York, the city parishes were able to supply 260 guns, but only forty-two actually worked when tested.[41] So, because the localities could not supply adequate arms, then the centre might do so. After all, the Tower of London was the country's main arsenal (Edinburgh Castle also had one, too, though was less well stocked) and application could be made to the Board of the Ordnance to dispatch weapons from there to the provinces. On 19 September, Malton told Newcastle thus, '[Sir Rowland] Winn is now with us and it is his opinion as well as that of other gentlemen, to desire your Matie to promise us a sufficient quantity of arms and ammunition to be sent immediately to this county [Yorkshire]'.[42] Sometimes this could run smoothly. On 18 October, Newcastle told the Board that 800 arms were to be sent to Liverpool and, eight days later, that sixteen drums and twenty-four halberds would also be dispatched.[43] The volunteer companies of Berwick were armed with 500 muskets out of the King's stores in that garrison town without any difficulty, though these lacked bayonets.[44]

Yet it was not always so simple, as the Yorkshire Lieutenancy and their allies discovered in October 1745. One month after the initial request had been made, the usually placid Herring, wrote to Hardwicke, 'What, no news of arms yet? Do they intend to despite all we can do to defend ourselves, and tell the world so? ... Will they put us ... at the mercy of these ruffians? ... Have we deserved this neglect? ... Are the ministers asleep?'[45] Malton was also exasperated, writing, 'I am in a violent passion and am very desirous to beg all my commissions may be suspended and put into worthier hands nothing restrains me from taking this step but the confusion it must put the affaires of the publick into in this county'.[46] Coming from two leading supporters of the government, these were harsh words indeed. It was only by the end of the month that the arms began to arrive and only in early November that all the men were armed. No wonder that Viscount Irwin wrote, 'The custom and practice of the Office of Ordnance I am a complete stranger to'.[47] At least they were armed by the time the Jacobite army arrived in England. John Graves alleged that in November, the York companies were lacking arms, due to 'a blundering experiment of our corporation'.[48]

If the government could not be availed upon, there were other methods. Private contractors were also used. Robert Watkins of Birmingham offered to supply York corporation with muskets and bayonets at 23s per pair, and 100 were ordered. The corporation also purchased a number of blunderbusses from him.[49]

The irregulars were not always wholly armed. Even if they were, so, their weapons were not all in good order. For instance, of the 141 troopers in the Durham volunteer cavalry regiment, eighteen lacked carbines, twenty-six were without pistols and there were twenty-six too few swords. Others had faulty weapons; to the tune of eighteen carbines, fourteen pistols and twelve swords.[50] Protestants who marched against local Catholics in 1745–6 in northern England were variously armed with axes and cleavers, cutlasses and pistols, though the latter two were carried by sailors, as might be expected.[51] Furthermore, according to a newspaper, the men who gathered at Northallerton in October 1715 were armed with 'firelocks, swords, halberds, axes, scythes, forks and such weapons as they could get to make a proper Defence'.[52]

Some of these volunteers were uniformed. These were almost always blue turned up with red; certainly this was the case in Yorkshire, York and Liverpool. Why this should be so is unclear. Possibly it was because cloth of this colour was readily and inexpensively available. York corporation deemed that its four companies were to be uniformed in coats, breeches, hats and cockades, at the rate of 18s per private, though officers' uniforms were more expensive (a captain's uniform cost eight guineas). City drapers and hatters were given contracts to supply these needs. Flags were also provided for each company.[53]

Thomas Ridge of Portsmouth referred to putting his company of seventy volunteers into uniform, but did not state what the uniforms were to consist of.[54] Sir Gregory Page apparently armed and uniformed 500 men on Blackheath in

October 1745.[55] Two companies raised in Peckham and Camberwell in 1745 were also intended to be given uniforms. Sir Abraham Shard had fifty men of Southwark armed and uniformed.[56]

It took time from the decision to provide uniforms to the point the uniforms were on the backs of the men. Liverpool Corporation decided on 28 September to equip its men 'with new Blew Frocks, Hatts and Stockings'. Orders were placed on 5 October, perhaps after a tendering process had been undertaken to obtain the cheapest quote. It was optimistically expected that 'These goods will be wanted in a fortnight or a very few days'. The order consisted of fifty-two dozen felt hats, with fifty dozen to be bound with white and white metal buttons. Three thousand yards of kersey were needed for the coats, and thirteen Liverpool shoemakers were required to make 626 pairs of shoes at 4s 2d each. Finally fifty dozen white stockings were ordered from Wales.[57]

These were not ready for some weeks. Walter Shairp, a lieutenant in the Liverpool Blues, later wrote, '12th [November] Nothing Extraordinary happened only the Men's hatts, shoes and stockings were delivered to them' and it was not until later that they were fully uniformed, with Shairp writing, 'the 15th when the men were all cloath'd & arm'd'.[58] The Yorkshire companies had their blue coats by October but had to wait two more months for the rest of their uniforms.[59]

Sometimes the men merely wore a particular type of headgear. A company of gentlemen volunteers formed in Newcastle in 1745 wore pink and red cockades in their hats.[60] The company of volunteers in Pickering were also distinguished by their cockades.[61] These were economical compromises.

Wearing uniforms may have helped foster a sense of corporate identity within the unit and also may have helped to impress others with their military appearance, though most wore blue – not the colour of the regulars, but that of the Royal Artillery and the Dutch troops used in the campaign. Yet it would seem that outside Yorkshire and Liverpool relatively few of the other irregular forces wore any type of uniform. This was probably due to the expense involved; perhaps also because of the time it would take. Although there was no Jacobite march into England until seven weeks after Prestonpans, no one was to know this and it may have seemed to those in the very north of England that an imminent descent would not allow enough time for men to be dressed in military garb.

Training was another issue. Musketry and drill had to be learnt if the men were to effectively use their arms and to march and manoeuvre in a recognizable military manner, and that meant instruction was required. Very few of the officers and men enrolled in these formations had ever used weapons before, and even if this were so, this had not been as part of a disciplined military unit, so they had no knowledge of drill. John Murray's comment on the Edinburgh volunteers in

1745 would be applicable to many others. He wrote, 'they was composed of a parcel of raw undisciplined fellows, numbers of whom had never seen nor heard a gun fired'.[62] Unusually, in Edinburgh, the volunteers are stated as practising the use of hand grenades, though how much of this actually occurred is impossible to discern; probably not much.[63]

According to Rae, the volunteers there in 1715 were 'carefully trained up in Military Exercises' and one company in particular was 'exercised often and thereby acquired such Expertise in military Discipline, as made them very useful'. From late July they drilled twice or three times a week.[64] Yet many men were wholly untrained and even those that were lacked any experience of campaigning.

Likewise, in 1745, training was sometimes provided by veteran soldiers. The men of the Liverpool Blues were formed into companies by 11 October and as Shairp wrote, 'Ever after that time we were employed in Disciplining the Soldiers by their Diffr't companys in which they made very great progress'. Further training took place in two days in November by two experienced veteran officers, and they were pleased with what they saw: 'he reviewed them and putt them through the Manuall Exercise and firing with which he was greatly pleased'.[65] In Yorkshire, Major Charles Wedell came forward to help with the East Riding companies, and Colonel Greenwood, a veteran of Dettingen, along with Captain Rowlandson, a former dragoon officer, for the West Riding ones. Malton reported that Greenwood and a sergeant drilled his men in his estate grounds. Three of the seven captains in the East Riding companies had had military experience.[66] Lower down the scale, Irwin had eight Chelsea veterans sent northwards to help train his men.[67]

Yet these were the exceptions; most irregular bodies received no training whatsoever, probably because there were insufficient half-pay officers. The Hampshire deputy lieutenants, for instance, complained that they needed half-pay officers to train their men, but it does not seem that any were ever sent, and there were similar complaints in the north-western counties in that year.[68] Training was variable; although in December 1745, General Pulteney, reviewing the East Riding volunteers, 'expressed himself highly satisfy'd with their behaviour and complimented the officer', and in the previous month Sir Conyers D'Arcy, acting Lord Lieutenant of the North Riding, reported that his companies were 'very ignorant in military discipline and exercise'.[69]

The problem was that there was insufficient time to train the men so that they could proficiently handle their arms, despite efforts been made to remedy this. In Edinburgh on 13 September, 'the volunteers were employed, morning and evening in learning the most necessary parts of the exercise of arms. On the fourteenth, they were employed in the same manner; and they had no time to lose, for before they received their arms, the rebels left Perth'.[70] Since the volunteers never fired a shot in anger, their expertise cannot be known, but it seems unlikely that it was adequate.

Yet there were a few exceptions. The Liverpool Blues were fortunate enough to be led by professionals. As Shairp wrote, these were 'Colonl. Graham and Coll. Gordon two pretty gentlemen & very good Soldiers who came down to command the Regiment by His Majesty's orders'. This was popular among the temporary officers, it being 'to our great happiness & joy at being no longer under the direction of a parcell of Ignorant Aldermen'.[71]

Most of the officers were amateurs, though. Of the lieutenants and their deputies, some were physically unsuited to active command, and few had military credentials. Some would have active commands; although this was less common among mayors than lords lieutenant. If the unit was that of a town, the more junior officers – the captains, lieutenants and ensigns – were usually merchants, office holders and others from the middling ranks; otherwise they would be gentlemen. The officers of the Liverpool Blues included a young Lowland Scottish merchant (Shairp), businessmen, Customs officers, the tide surveyor and shipowners.[72] In Yorkshire, six of the captains in the West Riding companies were baronets. One colonel was the fifteen-year-old son of the Lord Lieutenant.[73] Jacobite officers were usually gentlemen, with some merchants, too, and often those under them were tenants and servants.[74] Social and political position dictated who would lead. Noblemen and gentlemen were used to giving orders and being obeyed, as was the case throughout the social world of pre-Revolutionary Europe. But personal connections were important, as noted, 'The publick service will be carried on more cheerfully and effectually where the men are commanded by their natural leaders and landlords'.[75] Fletcher claimed, 'an officer of family distinction and rank, esteemed and beloved in the country with some inferior officers under him, skilled in the common routine, would be of great use'.[76] Military experience or formal training was seen as no substitute for such, nor as a necessary attribute of commanding officers, though beneath them, it would be useful for the junior officers to be men with some military knowledge. Yet one critic later wrote, 'gentlemen, used to Day Rooms, good fires, warm beds, coaches and chairs, plenty of wine and good sauce ... these associations of gentlemen who cannot bear hardships, can be of no use'.[77]

The other ranks were often filled with working men and agricultural workers, as might be expected; depending whether the captain recruiting was looking for men in a town/city or in the countryside. A unit of volunteers raised in Halifax in October 1745 was made up of '450 working clothiers'.[78] Malton's personal company was made up of his servants.[79] An examination of the York poll book of 1741 and the lists of men in the ranks of the corporation companies enables the occupations of a minority to be identified. They included seven tailors, six translators, five labourers, four joiners and four bricklayers, as well as men from at least another twenty-eight callings.[80] As with the militia, for those employed in agricultural trades, the fact that the rebellions occurred outside the seasons for planting and harvesting meant they could easily commit themselves to the volunteer companies as they provided a stable income at a time when other work was scarce.

However, like certain militia, there were volunteer units which were manned mostly by men of higher social standing than would be usual in units of the standing army. The company of freeholders in Pickering and the company of gentlemen volunteers at Newcastle are both examples of these.[81] There were several companies of such men in Leeds, one apparently being composed of 'either Heirs apparent to Great Estates or considerable Merchants'.[82] Students at Edinburgh University joined volunteer companies in September 1745, one being John Home.[83] According to Ray, 'five Hundred of the chief Inhabitants of the City [of Edinburgh], Lawyers, Writers, Physicians and even Divines, took up Arms for the Defence of the Town'[84] There was a Traders' Company, a Traffickers' Company, a Maltsters' Company and a Shipmakers' Company.[85] Volunteers in Aberdeen included 'some merchants and tradesmen, several students of Divinity and Philosophy and Prentices from both towns of Aberdeen'.[86]

Although Home had joined the regulars for a limited period, it is probable that those who joined the volunteer companies for a similarly limited commitment could have said the same. Certainly volunteer recruiters were sometimes able to be more discerning than recruiting sergeants were. Captain Hall wrote that he had been so inundated with volunteers that he only selected the 'pick'd men, young, tall and strong'.[87] Yet in 1746, it was noted that in the winter of 1745–6, of the East Riding companies, fourteen were sick and one lame, out of 359, though this is only about 4 per cent.[88]

There seems to have been a general agreement that there was an enthusiasm to enlist in these formations; certainly in 1745, and this was attested by a number of contemporaries. Malton noted, in the crucial autumn months of 1745, 'It would be easy to raise thousands more would the money and stores hold out'. This was because of 'the common people being furious in our cause'.[89] A gentleman in Sheffield noted similarly, 'It is not easy to conceive how heartily affected people are here for the government'.[90]

It is not certain what motivated these men. Presumably, for some, it was political or religious considerations. Certainly those armed dissenters under Woods and Walker who joined General Wills on his march to attack the Jacobites at Preston in 1715 were motivated by religious factors and fear of the Jacobites, who had attacked several dissenting chapels in Lancashire earlier this year.[91] In both 1715 and 1745 the defenders of Newcastle could count on the aid of the dissenting keelmen there, too. The maintenance of the Toleration Act by the Whigs was a strong point in their favour; and since the Tories had been eager to repeal this, dissenters were generally opposed to Jacobitism.[92] As William Stout stated, the upholding of the Toleration Act by George I 'gave great satisfaction to all well wishers of the nation's true interest'.[93]

Propaganda from pulpit and the press might also have been influential for some. Many clergy thundered against Catholicism to their congregations. The Rev. James Bate of St Paul's Deptford was but one clergyman, but his rhetoric was common. In a sermon in October 1745 he said:

> the Nation is invaded by a desperate band of hungry popish vagabonds and Cut-throats ... by the help of France and Spain'. Horrors awaited Englishmen because of the 'craving demands of the Pope and the French ... the gaping mouths of his hungry and naked Fiends of the north.[94]

The press, too, was equally strident in its discussion of the crisis. *The Newcastle Journal*, to take one example, told its readers on 21 September that Protestants had been burnt during the reign of the Catholic Mary I and that there had been massacres in Ireland and France in the seventeenth century carried out by Catholics against Protestants.[95] Of course, it is impossible to gauge the impact of the clergy and the press in formulating people's responses, but since most attended Anglican worship and either read or heard readings from newspapers, it seems safe to believe that some did take such words to heart and acted on them.

There were other reasons. Others may have been motivated by the need to defend their property and families. This might especially have been the case for those living in towns which feared an attack, if that town was at all defensible, or at least seemed to be, such as Carlisle, Newcastle or Berwick. Some were persuaded by their social superiors, with the Duke of Devonshire being told, 'as to the temper of the people in the political sense. They are easily determined to act steadily if they have an opinion of the person who will conduct their understandings and whom they can confide in'.[96]

For others, as in all conflicts, the motive was probably economic. The Earl of Warrington told his tenants that if they agreed to fight, and were killed, he would add another life onto their leases – leases of land were usually held for three life times.[97] Herring noted that the rebellion 'has put an absolute stop to trade and business ... the want of business in the W. Riding has made it much easier to raise soldiers there, for the manufacturer has no other way to get bread'.[98] It should also be recalled that the call for volunteers came from September onwards in 1715 and 1745; at a time when the harvest had been brought in and when, for some, time fell heavy on their hands and regular income looked unlikely. Yet in parts of Scotland in 1745, the crop cycle was problematic: 'Their being but now in the throng of their harvest is also a sort of impediment which we must obviate the best we can.'[99]

In the case of one Yorkshireman, and he was probably not alone in this, the financial incentive certainly loomed high. William Todd (1724–91), who eventually became a private in the East Riding companies, explained in his diary how he came to join. At first, on 8 October 1745, he was not particularly interested:

> Captain Grimston of Kilnwick, who is raising a Company of Blues at Beverley came past me as I was sitting at Sutton Salts and he seeing that I was young & likely for the Service Ask'd me if I would Inlist to which I told him I had no Inclination. He told me as the Rebellion was broke out so strong he greatly question's but every one must as able to bear arms & he desired me to consider of it & enter with him.

That evening, Grimston asked one Mr Featherstone to talk to Todd on the matter, and:

> he said that the Turnpike must be given Over, & that all Business would be at a stand until the Rebellion was ceas'd. As he told me, I only should Inlist for two Months, & have a shilling a day, & he would give Either me or my father a Bond of what sum we pleas'd, that I should be at Liberty at two Months End if I chused it. As he said, that both he & everyone that could carry arms should be obliged to go if the Rebels was not stop't very shortly.[100]

The volunteers usually received a shilling a day, which compares favourably to the regulars, who received half that and faced greater dangers. NCOs usually received 1s 3d or 1s 6d, depending on rank. To receive regular pay was very useful indeed. Yet the officers were not always paid.[101] The York city volunteers, being all gentlemen and rich merchants' sons, were unpaid, but their NCOs were. This is probably because they had seen military service.[102] However, officers in the corporation volunteers received 2s per day.[103] Not all approved of this. Irwin remarked that his junior officers, 'embarked on this affair without thought of pay' and that if payments were made to officers, the funds available 'may not be sufficient to keep the companys so long as they must be needed'.[104] Yet the officers in the West Riding companies demanded some form of remuneration, and this is what they eventually got. Not all of the militia/volunteers were paid anything. Those in Berwick in 1715 and 1745 are not known to have received any remuneration.

Others may have been motivated by adventure and comradeship. Malton's fifteen-year-old son, later the Marquis of Rockingham and George III's chief minister on two occasions, went to join Cumberland's forces at Carlisle in December 1745.[105] Home recorded that there was a company of men in the Edinburgh volunteers who either had been or were, students at the University.[106] Several of the officers of the Liverpool Blues were members of the town's 'Ugly Face Club', and as Walter Shairp (one of the club) recalled of his experiences as an officer:

I cant say that ever before spent any time more agreeably and I am sure that most of the gentlemen that were with us will say the same with me ... the mirth & joy that we afterwards had when we got into our Quarters & the constant Harmony that we lived in with one another.[107]

Some probably were involved because of their livelihood. Tax officials, who featured among the officers, probably took part because they owed their livelihoods to the government, and failure to act might have meant them risking their salaries or careers.

But some would-be volunteers were perturbed at the prospect of doing so. Mr Draper of Bridlington noted that some men were 'under such a terror of the highland swords that they were backward in associating' in Captain Boynton's company. So Draper took the step of joining as a private himself and shared the quarters of the volunteers already enlisted. Apparently, this had 'so good an effect that Captain Boynton made his company up to 48 men in two days'.[108] Likewise, Cholmondeley reported that in Cheshire, tales told by the 'disaffected' were discouraging potential volunteers.[109] In Scotland in October 1745, 'Some people among ourselves industriously spread false reports in the county that had almost turned the men wild they would on no account enter one independent company'.[110]

It seems that raising men did not usually take much time. Gertrude Saville wrote, 'dear Sir George had the commission of Captain, and rais'd 50 Men in 3 days'.[111] By 18 October, all Irwin's seven companies were complete – which had taken just over three weeks.[112] However, William Nowell told Winn on 10 November that his company was not at full strength as yet.[113]

Apart from these formal methods of raising irregular forces, there was another way. This was the one used when groups of men were brought together at short notice with the intention of harassing the Jacobite retreat in December 1745. It was simply a case of gathering friends, neighbours and dependants together by word of mouth, and arming themselves with whatever came to hand. Dr Richard Kay (1716–51) of Bury described how this occurred:

This Day this Sabbath Day in the Morning as we were going to Bury Chappel, we met coz. Doctor Kay and his Brother Coz. John Kay from Manchester ... Manchester with the Assistance of the Country People are intending to make a stand against them, Cousins wou'd have me go to Rossendale with them about four Miles from hence to raise the People there, I took a Ride with Them.[114]

Some did raise bodies of horse soldiers. Malton had certainly hoped that cavalry could have been raised; to the extent of six troops each of eighty cavalrymen.[115] Irwin had similar thoughts, at least initially, but soon realized this was not possible, informing Newcastle on 28 September, 'some light horse would have done better but it is indeed true that the difficulty of getting horses to mount the men was not to be got over'.[116] Malton concluded, 'We find our finances would not make any show in buying horses &c proper for a dragoon service, therefore we propose to raise companys of Foot only'.[117]

However, in some cases, cavalry were raised. This happened when the schemes were less ambitious than Malton's outlined above. During 1745 they were raised in Durham and Northumberland. In Yorkshire, a number of young gentlemen and their servants formed the Royal Regiment of Hunters of about 100 men. They were well armed and uniformed thus:

> The Gentlemen who composed the first Rank, were all dress'd in Blue, trimm'd with Scarlet, and Gold Buttons, Gold Lac'd Hats, light Boots and saddles, etc., their Arms were short Bullet Guns slung, Pistols of a moderate size and strong plain swords. The second and their ranks which were made up of their servants, were dress'd in Blue, with Brass buttons, their Accoutrements all light and serviceable, with short Guns and pistols, and each with a Pole-axe in his hand.

To accentuate their military image, they had a standard of green silk embroidered with gold.[118] Other cavalry units were Oglethorpe's Georgian Rangers, clad in green, and Malton's Austrian Hussars, once in Oglethorpe's service.[119] These few units of horse militia and mounted volunteers formed only a small proportion of the volunteer forces raised at this time, however. The majority were infantry.

In England, in 1745, there was time enough to raise volunteer forces before the Jacobite army ever came near to them. In Scotland, this was not the case, because the attempts to restore the Stuarts emanated from there, resulting in a more pressing scenario. The Edinburgh volunteers apart, almost all the Scottish loyalist irregulars were formed in the last three months of 1745.

Numbers are important because they give an indication, however crude, of the strength of support for a cause. It is hard to know how many volunteers were raised against the Jacobites, in part because that number was constantly changing as units were raised or stood down, or as men drifted away. Furthermore, in many cases there are no reliable figures. We shall take two important northern counties to gain an impression of numbers.

It would seem that in 1745 the numbers raised were certainly higher, to take Yorkshire and Lancashire as examples again. In Yorkshire the county forces numbered forty-one companies (twenty-five in the West Riding, nine in the North Riding and seven in the East Riding) of about fifty men in each, plus three officers and five NCOs; in all perhaps about 2,255 men. Then there were the forces raised in York – the corporation's companies and the independent companies – about 428 men in total. Hull raised volunteers to the number of 840 (fourteen companies of sixty men apiece). There were several companies raised in Leeds, perhaps 300 men. The volunteer company at Pickering and the Yorkshire

Hunters are other forces, perhaps numbering 50 and 75 men respectively. Then there were the 450 men of Halifax. We could add the numbers of the crowd who pulled down the Stokesley mass house in December 1745 or attacked the nunnery at York. This would give a total of perhaps about 5,000 men, or about the same number as the men in the Jacobite army in December 1745. To look at another comparison; the Manchester Regiment of the Jacobite army only numbered between 200 and 300 men and not all of these were Englishmen.[120] Yet Yorkshire was England's largest county, no other one remotely approached such an impressive array. Lancashire only boasted a county militia of 500 men and the Liverpool Blues of 600–700. However, we have also to bear in mind those men who attacked the stragglers of the Jacobite army in December 1745 and they probably numbered some hundreds, as did the crowd who attacked the Catholic chapels in Liverpool and Ormskirk in 1746. Perhaps about 2,000 men of this county took up arms against the Jacobites, although some of them might have participated in more than one occasion.[121] These are impressive numbers.

In both Scotland and England, despite myriad difficulties – including a lack of arms, training and experience, even apparently insurmountable legal barriers – in 1745, many thousands of men were raised outside the remit of the regular army and the militia for George II. These numbers alone outnumbered those of the Jacobite army in 1745. Yet for their capabilities, we must look beyond mere numbers. Most had little training in use of firearms and other weapons. They were led by men who were mostly amateurs. They were often geographically isolated from both the regulars and from other units of militia and volunteers – it was rare for such forces to move beyond their county/borough boundaries. Unlike the case in 1688, when the state's existence was also at stake, they were instituted and were ready to act, despite having a relatively short time to come into being. Of course there were great differences between these forces, not only in numbers, but also in leadership and training and some were certainly more 'professional' than others – the Liverpool Blues being one of the best. It was an achievement simply that, despite many difficulties, these forces had been raised in large numbers throughout Britain. For their performance and effectiveness, we now turn to the following chapter.

7 THE MILITIA AND VOLUNTEER FORCES IN ACTION

Once these forces were raised, officered, armed and perhaps uniformed and trained, what followed? The effectiveness of irregular forces in this period was hotly debated both then and since. Many saw them as practically useless; others as heroic defenders of the nation and able to beat regular troops.

These forces have certainly previously been assessed variously. Some contemporaries had poor words for the militia: Jacobite officers writing memoirs almost always implicitly or explicitly denigrate their efforts; in Jacobite code, the militia were known as 'small beer'.[1] Traditionally the eighteenth-century militia has been dismissed, too, with remarks such as 'Until 1757 it remained a decayed and little used force' or being deemed 'a gravely neglected and most useless force'.[2] Furthermore, McLynn asserts that, when faced with the Jacobite army, 'they simply melted away'.[3] An equally dismissive remark comes from Duffy, writing that apart from a few 'the others are usually glimpsed only when they were trying to put all the distance they could between themselves and the Jacobites'.[4] Referring to the militia forces in 1715, Szechi states, 'the government militias and volunteers performed as poorly as could be expected'.[5] A more realistic view comes from Reid: 'their actual and exaggerated failings were in reality no more than a reflection of their circumstances'.[6] A balanced appraisal comes from Jeremy Black, who notes that, 'loyal irregular units in England had little impact', but proceeds to state, 'Possibly the major role of the loyal units was in discouraging Jacobite sympathizers from acting'.[7] None of these historians, however, has examined these forces in much detail, concentrating on the campaigns as a whole.

Local studies have gone into greater depth and reached different conclusions to this rule, and as noted in Chapter 5, it is the local historians who have made the running. Thus one, who concentrated on the militia of the north-western English counties concluded:

> The militia therefore in the various counties withdrew or stood down in the face of the invaders' advance, and to poke fun at them for having done so is to mistake

entirely the situation. The county militia was not mustered to fight any pitched battle or for the military defence of any town ... The militia was raised in the first instance 'to keep the county quiet' ... or if it must engage the enemy, to do so 'by securing passes, by harassing the Rebels in small parties.'

Another, which also studied the impact of the Jacobite rebellions in the north of England in 1715 and 1745, likewise concludes that the militia and volunteers were not meant to oppose the Jacobite armies, but were more of a symbol of political support for the government. Practically they were capable of both quelling local Jacobites and assisting the regulars.[8]

In order to judge their capabilities, we need to examine why these forces were raised. Firstly, there was the obvious reason, as Shairp noted of the Liverpool Blues, 'It was Rais'd to defend the Nation against the attempts made by the Son of the Chevalier de St. George'.[9]

But although this was clearly the overarching reason for these forces being brought into existence, there were divergent views about how this objective could best be achieved. Some suggested that the men should be used for purely local defensive needs, while others thought that a more forward role would be better. Liverpool corporation believed that its unit should 'lye in town to defend it against the Enemy'. This was criticized by Shairp, who wrote sarcastically of 'the Wise Corporation' and 'so Ridiculous a Scheme'.[10] Yet it occurred elsewhere, at York, at Carlisle and at Newcastle, for instance. York corporation stated that the purpose of their volunteer forces was 'For the securing of the ill effects of the Rebellion and the Houses of and within this City and Ainsty from being plundered by those who are now in open rebellion or by any other wicked persons, whether Strangers or living within this City or Ainsty'.[11] In Scotland in August 1715, their use was stated as 'to defend themselves and their neighbours belonging to them from being robbed and plundered by flying parties and stragglers'. As part of this aim they were to 'sett out watches at severall stations' to stop strangers.[12] Richmond was offered other reasons why he should raise the Sussex Militia in 1745 thus:

> it is one of those [counties] that lies most open to Invasion from France; and it is generally supposed, that there is a considerable Number of disorderly people [smugglers] there, who, living on open Defiance of the Laws, may be too likely to countenance and assist such an Attempt.[13]

Newcastle believed that the volunteers could obstruct the Jacobite march by destroying bridges, damaging roads and sniping at the enemy.[14] The Earl of Rothes in 1745 stated that if accoutrements for horses were brought, then armed civilian horsemen would be useful for 'scouring the country and dispersing small parties'.[15] Clearly purely localized motives were uppermost, but these were concerns which were linked to national ones, too.

Economic factors also influenced the decision to raise militia, as did the example of others. Apparently the Glasgow Militia in 1745 was influenced by the example of the raising of the Argyll Militia, whereas:

> The little Town of Paisley having Tasted the Fruits of Trade, and Advantages of a Thread Manufactory, raised a corps of 210 men. The Shire and Town of Renfrew, from much the same Motives, armed in the Defence of the Constitution.[16]

Liverpool, Bristol and Newcastle were all major centres of commerce and all were steadfastly behind the Hanoverian dynasty in 1745, too.

It should be emphasized that these forces were never intended to fight the Jacobite army unaided and alone, though many historians have taken them to task for being unable to achieve that which they never set out to do. Hoghton informed Newcastle to this effect: 'We can keep our county from rising but cant face the enemy except if some regular troops come this road.' Newcastle did not disagree and wrote that the militia should be used 'for preserving the peace and tranquillity there'.[17] In Yorkshire, the thinking was likewise, with Herring writing, 'they cannot oppose a regular force', and Malton observing, 'we of ourselves may be unable to make a real stand'.[18] General Wentworth, when his advice was asked, did not advocate such, only 'manning passes and by harassing the rebels in small bodies from behind hedges and in the night which may be easily done should they enter Yorkshire'.[19] In Scotland, Forbes was advised that his companies should 'live at discretion in the country the rebels shall leave or if it is thought necessary the whole or part may march with you'.[20]

Negatively, Cumberland saw some of the irregulars in the following role in February 1746: 'Sir James Grant's people are in arms in their own country headed by his son Lewis Grant and all I shall expect of them will be to keep his people from joining them and to prevent provisions going into the hills by his country'.[21]

Instead, they could deprive the Jacobites of any internal support. According to Malton, 'I dare say we shall be able to prevent their being joined by any in this county had they any inclination to it'. On a later date, he added:

> we think ourselves capable to prevent and curb any riots or insurrections that so near an approach of the Rebels might encourage, for your Grace can be sensible of how fatal it might be should any tumults cause a diversion of any of the Regular forces necessary.[22]

Herring thought that the forces could 'awe the papists'.[23]

Fletcher's remarks provide a useful summary of the militia's role:

> I admitted we were not to hold to these, fighting a regular battle, but that the great use of them would be to scour the country, restrain stray levying parties, secure and strengthen outposts, get intelligence, bring in forage and provisions and upon occa-

sion act as pioneers ... in short to save the army in 20 different shapes every day, from being very harassed and fatigued before their proper Business, the day of action.[24]

Apart from such practical uses, they also were deemed to have a propaganda value and this was indicated by Herring; the mere existence of such forces would raise the morale of the government and its supporters, to show that they enjoyed a degree of support in the counties.[25] When considering the success or other of these forces, we must bear these criteria in mind, not those foisted upon them by some historians.

The use of such forces falls into three main categories and we will now examine their role in each. Firstly, there is their role in opposing the Jacobite army, or parts of it, more or less by themselves. Secondly, there is their employment as part, usually a small part, of a larger force of regulars. Thirdly there is their use in acting as a form of armed police, in an essentially civil capacity, acting against suspects for example, or in ceremonial duties.

Some were gloomy from the outset of the use of these formations. Lonsdale wrote on 9 September 1745, 'very little service can be reasonably expected from the militia ... I am afraid your Grace will find the militia in the other northern counties much in the same way'.[26] Two months later, a similar opinion was expressed by Sir Conyers D'Arcy, acting Lord Lieutenant of the North Riding, writing 'the new raised companys in this riding, which do not amount to 500 and are but new cloathed and armed, consequently must be very ignorant in military discipline and exercise'.[27] In 1745, Irwin recalled the behaviour of the irregulars, with a degree of disdain, alleging, 'the little effect the militia would be of, unless we could imagine that they would behave better than in the year fifteen'.[28]

Direct opposition to the main Jacobite army was not something the irregular forces were expected to do; certainly not unaided. Yet there were instances in which they, usually not through choice, but because there were no regular troops in the vicinity, formed the main component in confronting the Jacobite forces. This often occurred when major towns, garrisoned by militia, were threatened. Whig volunteers at Perth dispersed bloodlessly with the arrival of a Jacobite advance guard on 14 September 1715 and in the following month, militia left Kelso when it was threatened by advancing Jacobites. Jacobite forces were faced by irregulars at Edinburgh (September 1745), at Carlisle two months later and at Stirling in early January 1746. In none of these cases were the militia able to mount a successful defence for more than a very few days. Other, more mobile forces, such as the Lancashire Militia in both 1715 and 1745, the posse comitatus of Cumberland in 1715 and the Liverpool Blues in 1745, not to mention the Highland companies under Loudon in 1746, retreated in face of the Jacobite army; the last first from Inverness in February and then from

Dornoch in the following month. On a lesser note, in the same month, two companies of Argyllshire militia were surprised near Blair and surrendered or fled. Finally at Inverury on 23 December 1745, Highland irregulars were surprised and retreated after a short skirmish.[29] This sounds like a catalogue of high-profile disasters, which has been given as evidence for the uselessness of the militia and other irregular forces when confronted by a real foe. One might be tempted to agree with McLynn's comment: 'What is certain is that all "loyal" forces set up to oppose the clansmen melted away with amazing rapidity once the prospect of a real fight loomed.'[30]

Of course, for militia to fall back before a more determined, better armed and more numerous enemy was not unique to those in Britain in 1715 and 1745. When Monmouth's rebels faced the Devonshire militia at Axminster in June 1685, it was the militia who dispersed without a fight; while in the American War of Independence, there are numerous examples of the Patriot militia routing before the British regulars. At the battle of Pentland Hills in 1666, at Bothwell Bridge in 1679 and at Sedgemoor in 1685, it had been the regulars who had had to defeat the rebels, rather than the militia.

Why was this? Partly it was because the Jacobite army often greatly outnumbered the irregular forces. With about 5,000 men on the march through England in 1745, the Jacobite army faced small and scattered forces en route; the Liverpool Blues numbered about 600 men, the Lancashire militia about 500, and the city forces and county militia at Carlisle numbered about 700 men in total. To flee or surrender before vastly superior numbers should not be seen as proof of lack of zeal or cowardice; Stanhope's dragoons fled from Preston in 1715 on learning that the Jacobite army's arrival was imminent, as did Hamilton's and Gardiner's dragoons at Coltbridge in 1745, both being badly outnumbered. As Shairp wrote, the Liverpool Blues 'could be of no service in opposing the whole army when there was no forces near us to support us'.[31] Likewise, Derby informed Newcastle, that the idea that 'a raw, undisciplined militia consisting of Foot without anyone that knows how to command, should be able to prevent an army 7 or 8 times their number' was sheer folly.[32] Both noted that, without any substantial military aid from the regulars, resistance was useless. Likewise, as William Fletcher wrote on 17 November, 'the militia [at Carlisle] proposed to keep the Rebels out 8 or 10 days longer *if any promise of assistance in that time*' (my italics) had been given by Marshal Wade; instead Wade wished the garrison 'all imaginable success' and did not start marching to their relief until after the town and castle had surrendered.[33] Likewise, when there was discussion in the same month about throwing the Yorkshire militia into York, Malton declared, 'The officers unanimously agreed the town was not tenable with our Force an hour, above three miles of wall quite ruinous and not one cannon in the place, so this scheme must be laid outside'.[34]

Numbers also played their part in the Jacobite retreat in 1745, as did the reluctance of irregular forces to fight formed units. Irregular cavalry certainly hovered around the flanks of the retreating army in December 1745. Johnstone noted that there was 'a great number of the enemy's light horse continually hovering about us, without venturing, however, to come within our musket shot'. On the Jacobites threatening to charge them, the cavalry, who only numbered about 200–300, fled. A Whig observer wrote, 'But they kept in so compact a Body that we thought the attempt impracticable, especially considering the difference of weapons and numbers'.[35]

Sometimes irregulars made as if to confront the Jacobites in the belief they would be facing but a remnant of the army. On returning to Scotland in December 1745, Elcho reported:

> All the Country people upon the borders were in arms, for they had gott news from Ednr that the Duke of Cumberland had overtaken the army near Lancaster and had given them a total defeat, and that the Prince and the few that had escaped were flying to Scotland, so they had got themselves prepared in case it had been so, to have knock'd all Stragglers on the head.[36]

There were other reasons, too, why these forces were less than effective. In some of these towns and counties there was internal dissension among the defenders. The two main forces defending Carlisle were the companies of Cumberland and Westmorland militia, officered by gentlemen from these two counties, and the Carlisle volunteers, under the city authorities. The whole burden of mounting guard on the city walls, both night and day, had fallen to the county forces. After several days, this led the men to becoming exhausted, being so 'sick with this great Fatigue'. One added, after the siege was over, 'Most of our militia ... generally complain'd of very ill treatment in that place ... many of the inhabitants making them pay an exorbitant price for provisions and they could not, for any money, procure a sufficient quantity of straw to lie on'.[37] Some began to desert. Yet Dr Waugh, speaking for the city, commented, 'Most of the militia officers came to our defence with great reluctance and stayed there from the first with us with great unwillingness'. When a council of war was held, 18 out of the 24 militia officers there voted to surrender.[38] Had the burden of guard duty being fairly shared, there might have been a decision made in favour of continuing to resist. Similarly, lack of numbers and weariness was decisive at Stirling two months later: 'The impossibility of their enduring constant fatigue much longer, since for three days and nights past they had been almost continually under arms.'[39]

Fear of the Highlanders was one reason for a lack of enthusiasm for a fight. These affected Lowlanders as well as Englishmen. The Earl of Rothes gathered together men in September 1715 to defend Perth, but the men were reluctant. According to the Jacobite Master of Sinclair, 'But those in that county having been taught by their experience, that it is not good medling with edged tools, especiallie in the hands of Highlandmen, were very averse from takeing arms'. This, together with the fact that the men were near Tippermuir, the scene of a Highland victory in 1645, 'made them throwe down their armes and run, notwithstanding the trouble that Rothes and his ministers gave themselves to stop them'.[40]

It was also questioned how politically reliable were the irregulars. There are certainly instances which suggest that a minority in 1715 and 1745 were not (many in the South West in 1685 were not enthusiastic in their duties, either). The Cumberland posse are a case in point. They had gathered on 2 November 1715 to confront the Jacobite army. Despite their perhaps outnumbering their enemies, they fled. This could have been due to low morale, but could have been caused by sympathy towards the Jacobites. One account stated that when they ran they called out 'down with the rump', a well known Jacobite cry, and another that some said, 'God save King James and prosper his merciful army', though in the later case, these were men held captive by the Jacobites.[41] This was not just wishful Jacobite thinking. Lonsdale also wondered whether some of the men had Jacobite sympathies, for he wrote:

> I don't know whether this rout proceeded from fear or Disaffection, what makes me imagine it was a thing designed is because most of them came without any manner of arms and though the rebels knew their number to be so great they did not alter their march at all, which I fancy they would have done if they had not depended upon a great many friends who did not shew themselves.[42]

There were also strong doubts cast about the loyalty of the Scots in the autumn of 1745. Lord Glenorchy noted on 7 September of his clansmen, 'they [the Jacobites] having sent out many emissaries amongst them and invitations to their old friends, to which threats have been added. However I flatter myself that they will fail in all these endeavours'.[43] In 1715 the clan had fought for the Jacobites, it should be noted. Similarly, the Hon. Philip Yorke wrote 'Sir John Cope who offered some of the highland lords arms, but was told they could not sufficiently depend upon their people'.[44] This behaviour led some to make sweeping generalizations about Scotland, with Lieutenant Robinson writing, 'pray employ your time meritoriously, as I do, in damning sinking, confounding the whole Scotch nation'.[45] Some took this lack of action to be sign of treachery. Herring was one and he wrote:

> What shall we think of the behaviour of the Scotch nobility on this occasion? Strong marks of treachery, my lord, when they fled their country, which they might have saved, by only standing up in Edinburgh in their own defence, and lending Cope their advice and countenance. Lord Loudon is an exception to this.[46]

Hardwicke wrote likewise, this time about the deserting Scots, 'I never tasted that measure and am now thoroughly cured of any inclination for raising troops amongst what they call the well affected Highlanders. I believe they may fight in Flanders, but they have shewn they can distinguish between cases'.[47]

Desertion was not uncommon both among Scottish irregulars and their Jacobite opponents in 1715, though this was not always indicative of disaffection. Argyll reported on 18 September about the fall of Perth:

> My Lord Atholl's men and about 20 of the townsmen which made about 140 imme-
> diately took their arms upon the first alarm and formed themselves in the market
> place and when the rebels drew up over against them ... the magistrates gave them no
> orders to attack them.

The provost was heard to say 'no blood, no blood'.[48]

The loyalists then dispersed and the Jacobites bloodlessly took the city, which was to be their base for the next four months.

Another instance occurred when Tweeddale sent Sir William Baird with 200 men from Haddington in October 1715, and then ordered their return, in order to confront the Jacobites, 'But most of them deserted having mutinied against Sir William upon his ordering them to march back and telling them that the Highlanders were at Haddington'.[49]

Unreliability among the loyal Highlanders was noted by Yorke, writing about the Argyllshire militia:

> tho' God knows they are not to be supposed to fight), by the connection they have
> with the principal Rebel clans their neighbours, will, I daresay, be protection enough
> for their own country. But should they act contrary to their usual cunning and the
> affection they bear one another in all roguery.[50]

Glenorchy enlarged on this matter, writing that Highlanders would not fight against one another and explaining 'This must appear very odd to your Lordship, but the connections and dependencies amongst the Highlanders are very strong and difficult to break, and indeed may be sometimes dangerous'.[51]

Desertion was not always the same as treachery. The needs of agriculture were also pressing, especially as the year progressed. Lord Glenorchy told Yorke on 10 April 1746:

> I am extremely sorry any of my men have deserted home. I was in hopes Mr Camp-
> bell of Carwhin's presence would have restrained them ... This is the time of year
> for sowing their grounds by which their families are to be supported, which makes
> country farmers very earnest to go home after being six months absent. Great num-
> bers of those stationed hereabouts have deserted home ... I believe this restlessness is
> in the nature of the Highlanders, for 'tis the same thing with those in the Rebellion.
> Their chiefs can never keep them long together ... I don't say this to excuse my men; I
> believe they are like the rest; I heartily wish they were better.[52]

It has to be said that these were the only instances when the irregulars were possibly sympathetic to the Jacobites; in all other cases, their loyalties were firmly against them. Unlike the case in 1685, the loyalties of the militia were less ambiguous; certainly in 1745 and hardly less so in 1715.

It is worth noting that there were divisions among the Whigs over the militia and volunteers elsewhere, too, though because these were behind the front lines, they did not come to prominence. Had it been otherwise, their weaknesses might have become more apparent. One instance in 1745 occurred when commissions to raise volunteers were given to the mayor of Hull and to the Lord Lieutenant of the East Riding. Although Hull is geographically part of the East Riding, administratively it was independent of it. This did not prevent Irwin, as Lieutenant, being annoyed about this, seeing it as an affront to his authority. Irwin was not mollified by Newcastle informing him that mayors of other towns such as Carlisle, Berwick and Liverpool had been granted similar powers. Irwin wrote:

> the power given to the mayor of Hull of granting commissions for associated companies which I find is looked upon as superseding of my commission as His Majesty's lord Lieutenant and Custos Rotulorum of that town and county ... I have reason to complain.[53]

Likewise, there were clashes of opinion between the corporation of Liverpool and the officers of the Liverpool Blues; the former wanting to retain the regiment for the town's defence, the latter wishing to march out. The officers threatened to resign their commissions en masse and so the corporation was forced to back down.[54] Derby and Hoghton had different views of the utility of the Lancashire militia too. In Durham, the horse volunteers were stood down in December 1745 because of a lack of unanimity among the county elite.[55]

There was some friction among the officers of the Liverpool Blues. Shairp wrote, 'Our old vigilant Coll had the Drums beting by 5 nixt morning & threatn'd to putt all the Officers under arrest for not appearing upon the parade as soon as himself without making any Indulgence for the Fatigue we had had the day before'.[56] Later, on marching into Chester, Cholmondeley caused upset among the Liverpool officers, too, as Shairp recorded, 'he had talked very freely of our Regiment in general for which reasons we had contracted a great dislike of him as we looked upon our Regiment as greatly superior to his'.[57] Yet these examples of ill feeling do not seem to have hampered operations.

Morale was another key ingredient in causing the surrender or rout of these irregular forces and their allies. The Carlisle defenders had been in receipt of a declaration from Charles, which included the ominous phrase, 'the fatal Consequences which usually attend a Town's being taken by Assault'.[58] Given that the Jacobite attackers were inching their way towards the city walls, and there was fear of an assault, this was not unreasonable.[59] Morale was also probably the lead-ing factor in the rout of the Cumberland posse on 2 November 1715. When the Jacobite army came into view, according to Patten, 'they broke up their camp in the utmost Confusion, shifting every one for themselves as well as they could, as is generally the Case of an arm'd, but undisciplin'd Multitude'.[60] When Loudon's 1,500 men marched to seize Charles at Moy on the night of 16 February 1746, being fired on in the dark by a few Jacobites, they fled, as Home noted:

> Lord Loudon's men, who thought the whole Highland army was coming, turned their backs, and striving who should be foremost in running away, many of them who first began to fly were thrown down, and trod upon. The panic, fear and flight, con-tinued till they had got near Inverness, without having been in any danger but that of being trampled to death; which many of them were.[61]

Other factors were at play in some circumstances. The Lancashire militia in 1745, apart from being outnumbered, had other difficulties. Summoned into being on 12 November, they were issued with two weeks' pay. By 24 November, with the Jacobite army about to enter Lancashire, there was little chance of pay-ing the men their next instalment of wages, so they could not be kept together much longer.[62] Furthermore, if they were disbanded, their weapons could safely be stored aboard ship so as to prevent giving the invaders a present of weapons.[63]

Yet even when panic played a part, the role of the militia was not always wholly inglorious. In Stirling in early January 1746, although 'nothing but dis-traction and confusion was to be seen among the militia', they 'seeing they could do no more towards the defence of the town, went to the castle ... with their arms, lest the rebels get them'.[64]

Setbacks could result in reduced morale. When outposts manned by Argyll militia fell in March 1746, defeat was total, as Cluny of McPherson wrote, 'We secured, killed and took prisoners every private man and officer upon the dif-ferent commands without the escape of one single person ... Not one of the commands smelt the design till they were fallen upon'. Yet on another raid, resistance was at least fiercer, though the result was similar, with a Jacobite writ-ing that the firefight 'continued very hote on both sides, about half an hour (the fire from the Campbells coming very hard from the windows of the kirk)'[65] On this occasion, five of the militia were killed and seven wounded out of a total of sixty-three.[66]

A retreat also sapped morale. When Loudon pulled his forces back from Inverness in February 1746, desertion was rife. An informant noted, 'Lord Lou-don on his march from Inverness to Sutherland lost the 200 or 2 companies of McKenzies that were with him who all deserted and it was believed most of them joined the rebels'. When part of the force was forced to surrender in the following month, 'Most of the private men taken as above at Dornoch were

Mcleods and my informant was told that most of them inlisted with the rebels'. Yet not all who went over to the Jacobites stayed there, for 'a soldier of Colonel Monro's regiment taken prisoner at Preston by the rebels and enlisted with them but had lately left them and was returning home'. To cap it all, Lady Seaforth enticed 300–400 McKenzies into joining the Jacobite army. Furthermore, Loudon could not keep his men together 'both for want of provisions and also for want of money and ammunition'. In February, in Sutherland, there were 1700 men, by March there were 800 with Loudon and Forbes in Skye.[67]

Cumberland was unimpressed, writing, 'His Majesty must have observed how negligently these Highlanders who are with us do their duty, as well by the surprise of the posts upon the hills as the last affair that happened tells'. Twenty men from another post deserted. Colonel Campbell testified to their low spirits:

> there has been great numbers of the Argyll militia deserted and general discontent, nay even a mutiny, thro' the whole. They complain that they are always sent upon the most dangerous expeditions, that they have much more duty and fatigue than the rest of the troops, that their wives and familys have sent word that there is great scarcity at home and they are starving.[68]

Campbell took steps to raise the morale of his men after some of them taking part in the successful defence of Fort William in March 1746. On 31 March having announced that the widow of a man killed in the action would receive a pension for life, he wrote to his men thus:

> should any of our brave and loyal Argyllshire men meet with a like misfortune I shall take the same care of the widow and make it my study to provide for the fatherless ... Let our brave fellows know that tho' I cannot set their pay regularly I do by this promise that oatmeal and money shall be particularly accounted for it ... After exhorting you all to consider the great honour you will do to the whole body of our brave Argyllshire men by your good behaviour in His Majesty's service and the cause of liberty, I need add nothing further than to desire that this letter of mine may be publickly read or communicated to the private men.[69]

Yet the irregular forces, simply by being under arms and in existence in a town or city, could successfully act as a deterrent, especially against less than ardent opponents. One instance occurred in early October 1715, when the Northumbrian Jacobites rose and expected to take the wealthy and strategically significant town of Newcastle. After all, there had been some demonstrations of Jacobitism there in 1714 and Sir William Blackett, a Tory MP for Newcastle, was believed to be an active ally. However, a number of determined Whigs – Cotesworth, Alderman White and John Johnson, the county sheriff – acted decisively in opposing them. This they did by calling out the county militia, the posse, arming townsmen and dissenting keelmen, and requesting military assistance. As Patten wrote:

the Magistrates and Deputy-Lieutenants having first had some Suspicion, and soon after positive Intelligence of the Designs of the Rebels to surprise the Town, had effectually prevented it, and taken all imaginable Precaution for their Security, raising immediately what Men they could ... arming and encouraging the Inhabitants for their own Defence ... They got the Militia and Trained Bands ... to be taken into its for its better Defence.[70]

The Jacobites did not approach the city and as this was their aim, Newcastle being a key regional and strategic centre, so this was a decisive check to their strategy.

At about the same time, Kemure's band of Lowland horsemen vaguely threatened Dumfries, hoping to take the town by surprise, but once the magistrates there were appraised of this, they gathered able-bodied men from the town and adjoining parishes, perhaps numbering 5,000 in total. The Jacobites decided not to force the issue, but opted for the safer goal of joining up with their allies at Rothbury.[71] Another similar occasion occurred two weeks later. The Northumbrian Jacobites, reinforced with Highland and Lowland Scots, were marching along the borders. On reaching Hawick, a party of cavalry was sent towards Dumfries, with the intention that the rest of the army would attack this wealthy place. According to Patten, the town was only defended by 'some Train-bands, Militia and Townsmen, which would not have been able to hold out'. It seems, though, that the irregulars may not have had a decisive effect because, according to Patten, it was not attacked since 'the English Gentlemen were positive for an Attempt on their own Country'.[72] However, the Jacobites were aware of the preparations being made in the town for its defence, which, according to Rae, were impressive, and it is possible that these helped dissuade the Jacobites from marching on the town.[73]

It was not uncommon for irregular forces to hold a town against the foe. In 1685, the strategic city of Bristol was held by the Gloucestershire militia against Monmouth's force; the former also deterring any local support for the rebels, too. When at last Monmouth was ready to attack, Oglethorpe's Life Guards arrived to reinforce the garrison and so ended all hope that Bristol would fall.[74]

It is also worth pointing out that the courage of the irregular forces – providing the scenario into which they were plunged was favourable – was not always lacking. Shairp noted, after witnessing his men's behaviour during what turned out to be a false alarm:

However, this was of some service to us as it gave us an opportunity of trying the men's Courage, which was very extraordinary as not a man of them showed the least Fear but went all on with the greatest alacrity, altho' I believe evry one of them expected to be attacked that moment.[75]

Irregular forces had their share of success in the Highlands of Scotland in 1715, and fighting was not always required. In fact, the campaign in the northern and western Highlands of Scotland at this time wholly involved loyalist forces and Jacobites engaging in shadow-boxing, although this has often been obscured by historians concentrating on the crucial – and ultimately decisive – drawn out confrontation and battle between Mar and Argyll. Although there was little fighting, the actions of the irregular forces did pin down sizeable numbers of Jacobites and so prevented them from taking part in the campaign to the south. Therefore, as Rae told his readers:

> it may not be improper to acquaint the Reader with the State of the Rebellion in the West Highlands, and the prudent Conduct of the Earl of Islay, and His Majesty's Friends at Inverary, and in some other Parts of Argyleshire; which was of very great Importance to his Majesty's Service at this dangerous and critical Juncture.[76]

Colonel Alexander Campbell prevented the Jacobites from taking Inverary by posting the 400-strong Argyll militia there. On 19 October, a force of 2,400 Jacobites marched to Inverary, in which were now 1,000 militiamen. Islay advised Sir Duncan Campbell, in command at Inverary, to play for time. On 25 October, the Jacobites, unwilling to attack, marched away. Islay wrote of the Jacobites that:

> at large musquet shots distance they halted, finding all our men lying within walls round the town with works flanking every way, and all houses pulled down which would facilitate their approach: They lay most of them upon the hill close to the place these 2 days and after having sent some ridiculous messages, they marched off this morning.[77]

According to the Rev. John Anderson, 'Our close and bold firing mightily discouraged the enemy, the subalterns and soldiers were utterly against attacking this place when they seed our strength'. Yet the irregulars were hardly thirsting after blood, when it came to a pursuit, as Anderson then related, 'We expect our detachment will go no further after they have disperst the camp'.[78]

Campbell indeed followed them with 800 men to overawe any potential Jacobites and convinced Broadalbin not to send his clan of 400 men to join Mar. Meanwhile, the militia at Inverary remained in arms in order to keep the adjacent country secure.[79]

Local agreements between Jacobite officers and irregular Scots officers led to a low level of armed violence, but this was not always popular. A contemporary noted, 'That tratie Isla made with the clans is made a handle at court as dishonourable'.[80] Furthermore, Anderson wrote on 4 November:

> he allowed the enemy after they had march'd on the rear of our own men about 6 miles to go home with their arms upon their parole and not to rise. Our officers and

souldiers were extremely angry at the terms expecting at least their arms should be
taken from them. Many of our men went off through meer discontent.[81]

Yet it had been a success that Inverary was held, as Patten noted:

> The preserving of the Town of Inverary, was a considerable Piece of Service; for had
> the Rebels been Masters of that important Pass, they might have pour'd in their Men,
> either towards Glasgow, or into the Shire of Air, and must have been fought with,
> perhaps, to Disadvantage, as things then stood, or they would have joined the Rebels
> in the North of England at their Pleasure.[82]

The irregulars had mixed fortunes near Inverness in September, Lady Forbes of
Culloden House found it under siege, and when 200 Monroes marched to her
relief, they were prevented by 1,500 Jacobites and forced to retreat. Soon after,
the Monroes themselves were at risk of attack. Lord Sutherland came to their aid
in the following month, but even so, they were outnumbered by the Jacobites,
now 3,000 strong, and so the loyalists retreated to Bonar. Although the Jacobites
marched to join Mar at Perth by the end of the month, the resolution of the outnumbered Grants, whose territory they traversed, ensued that they received no
food supplies from the district.[83]

Lord Lovat took his Frasers against the Jacobites at Inverness. En route,
Clan Chattan and the MacDonalds of Keppoch were persuaded to disperse.[84]
Lovat and the Grants joined forces with Sutherland and on 10 November, they
marched towards Inverness, which was held by Sir John Mackenzie. The Jacobite
garrison was invited to surrender, since they were outnumbered by ten to one.
Mackenzie retired to the castle, and then retreated from there, so that on 12
November, Sutherland was in possession of both town and castle, deemed by
Patten to be 'no small affliction to the Earl of Mar'.[85] In the following month,
Lovat's men forced 200 Jacobites in Inverness-shire to surrender and obliged
the other Jacobites to take to the sea.[86] Lovat claimed his men were resolute to
defend Inverness, though they had received no orders from anyone. He wrote on
17 January 1716, 'We are here maintaining the King's interest with open arms
these two months ... We're resolved to make our graves in the streets rather than
yield this place till it is in flames'.[87] How much of this assertion is hyperbole is, of
course, impossible to tell. However, the loss of Inverness was said by Mar to have
been 'another piece of bad News' and had obliged him to dispatch Lord Seaforth's men northwards, thus weakening the already depleted Jacobite army at
Perth.[88] There were other successes towards the end of the year. General Wightman reported on 29 December that:

> Colonel Finab that commands a body of the Duke of Argyll's clans has taken Castle
> Fenclareck belonging to the Earl of Bradalbin, which is a place of consequence by

reason it stops some of the clans in their retreat and is a great hindrance to Lord Bradalbin's men to joyne the rebels.[89]

There was often, in 1715, a great reluctance among both Jacobites and irregulars to come to bloodshed. Tweeddale and his militia had been garrisoning Haddington in October and later wrote, 'I was forced to abandon Hadington, being the most disaffected place of the shire, upon the approach of the rebels, but did not march out of the town until they were within a mile of yt'.[90]

Thirty years later, the loyalist irregulars in the north of Scotland acted more or less independently, too. Lord Loudon's little army based at Inverness in late 1745, had ambitious plans to frustrate Jacobite schemes in the Highlands. They aimed to ensure the garrisons were well supplied and to prevent Lord Lewis Gordon's Jacobites 'from giving any further disturbances'.[91] Since the main Jacobite army had left Scotland, and four regiments of regulars had arrived at Edinburgh, matters were more propitious for them to act.

Supplies could be seized. On the march from Edinburgh in early November 1745, the Jacobites were obliged to leave some of their baggage at Ecclefechan. Elcho later wrote, 'The people of Dumfries, after the army had passed, took possession of it'.[92]

Scottish irregular forces were an important part of the loyalist response against the Jacobite army after the bulk of the latter had marched into England in November 1745. Loudon helped supply the garrison at Fort Augustus in November 1745. They also attempted to deter Jacobite recruiting in Banff, Aberdeenshire and Elgin. Loudon tried to persuade Lord Lovat, now a Jacobite sympathizer, 'to come to Inverness along with him, and to live there under his eye, until he should bring in all the arms which the clan was possessed of '. However, the wily Lovat managed to escape from house arrest.[93] Even before then, in October, Forbes's men beat off an attack on his home at Culloden one night.[94] When the 200 Monroes left Cope at Aberdeen in September, there was the possibility of a confrontation. However:

> Culkairn himself was under no dread, as his men were good and better armed than Glenbucket's, and therefore marched on very briskly the way to Banff. Glenbucket ... not choosing to wait their coming up he sheered off .[95]

The irregulars were not always successful. On 23 December 1745, the MacLeods, 700 strong, and a Jacobite force made up of French and Highlanders, totalling 1,200 men, clashed at Inverrury. The former were surprised and despite exchanges of musketry, the MacLeods fled, leaving five of their number dead and another thirty prisoners.[96] Yet this was not a complete rout, as one account stated:

The attack was sustained by the Laird of McLeod and Culkairn with great bravery, who finding the superior number of the enemies ... ordered a retreat, which was managed with good advantage, having only seven private men killed and a few taken prisoners ... There was considerable execution done upon the Rebels ... and the Rebels made no pursuit.[97]

The amateur nature of the loyalist forces on this occasion was shown by the fact that they failed to send out patrols and so were surprised by their enemies. Their position was not hopeless. 'But the confusion and surprise of the McLeods at the unexpected coming of the enemy made them neglect all these advantages'.[98]

Yet even if the irregulars were defeated, their efforts were not always in vain. According to Maxwell, commenting on the situation in February 1746:

Lord Loudon seemed disposed to return to Inverness upon the Prince's leaving it; this discouraged his friends from joining, and would discourage such as had joined from marching South, when there would be occasion. Though Lord Loudon had behaved all along as a gentleman, and was incapable of doing anything inconsistent with that character, people did not care to leave their families and effects exposed to the insults of an enemy.[99]

Ray agreed, writing, 'Those Companies much retarded the Increase of the Rebels'.[100]

Loudon's force was eventually routed and dispersed, but by merely being under arms to the north of the Jacobite headquarters, they had inhibited Jacobite recruitment and had distracted part of the Jacobite army which could have been used elsewhere against Fort William or Cumberland's forces.

Yet there were also instances in March and April 1746 when the Highland irregulars were able to score successes off the Jacobites unaided by regulars. On 25 March, Lord Reay noticed the Jacobite *Hazard* sloop run aground on Tongue Bay. There the Jacobites landed men and money – cash which was crucial to the Jacobites' depleted war chest. Apparently, 'Lord Reay's sons, with some other officers, gather'd what men they could together, attack'd those that landed from the Hazard sloop, killing five of them, took the rest prisoners and seized the money, said to be 12,500 guineas'. They then took their prizes to Aberdeen, in case the Jacobites attempted their recapture. This was an important success, because the lack of money led the Jacobite army's supply situation to become so dire that men were paid, if at all, by meal, and this led to increased foraging afar and so a smaller army to face Cumberland at Culloden.[101] Sir John Clerk noted, 'The loss of this little ship of war entirely disconcerted the measures of the rebels for having no money they were obligded to stand the chance of a battle with the Duke of Cumberland on the moor of Culloden, where they were severely chastis'd'.[102] Another success was the ambush near Dunrobin on 15 April 1746.

The Jacobite Earl of Cromartie was surprised; fifty of his men were killed and 164 surrendered.[103]

If it was possible to attack the Jacobites the irregulars did do so. This occurred on the Jacobite march through England in 1745, but more so on the retreat. This meant preying on small parties. On 29 November, a party of Jacobites from Carlisle went to Lowther Hall. Mr Armitage, Lowther's steward, took thirty men from Penrith to attack them. After a firefight, the Jacobites lost one man dead, three wounded and eleven were captured. Yet Armitage was worried that such an action might bring about retaliation.[104] The retreat of the Jacobite army through the north-western counties of England gave the irregulars several opportunities to harass small parties of Jacobites. As Johnstone observed, 'Our stragglers seldom failed to be attacked by the English peasants, who were all implacable enemies of the Prince'.[105] Elcho wrote of the initial phase of the retreat:

> All the Country people were arm'd, and at Stockport they fir'd from a village in the night upon the patrouilles and killd some of them: the rest sett fire to the Villadge. They were quite prepared in case the army had been beat to have knock'd on the head all that would have Escaped from the Battle. Whenever any of the men Stragled or Stay'd behind they either murder'd them, or sent them to the Duke [of Cumberland], and all the way from Carlisle to Darby all the men that were left sick upon the road were either kill'd or were after much abused and sent to jails off the great road.[106]

In Kendal, the Duke of Perth's advance guard found themselves under attack. There was further opposition in the countryside between there and Penrith. The result was that Perth's men had to retreat and join the main Jacobite force.[107] Jacobite stragglers were rounded up by these forces, in one instance in Lancashire, they numbered about forty.[108] Mr Eccles and friends were determined not to be robbed by Jacobite stragglers, so when they found one, they arrested him.[109] Colonel O'Sullivan was shot at and a sleeping English Jacobite was killed.[110] There are many such other examples.

According to Lord George Murray, fear of the militia was a factor in ordering a retreat from Derby. He wrote that:

> upon a misfortune, it could not be supposed one man could escape, for the militia, who had not appeared much against us hitherto, would, upon our defeat, possess all the roads, and the enemy's horse would surround us on all hands; that the whole world would blame us for being rash and foolish.[111]

Yet, for all the sniping noted above, the irregulars were unable to stop the Jacobite army's retreat; had the Jacobites been defeated in battle, it would probably have been a different story. Yet Cumberland was hoping for more of the irregulars at this point. Sir Everard Fawkener, his secretary, thought that the people were willing, but that their local leaders had let them down, and he singled out Derby in particular and his 'irreconcilable Quitting of this County'.[112]

Such behaviour, motivated as it probably was, by the well-founded fear that the retreating Jacobites would be less careful of property and possessions than they had been on their advance south, recalls the behaviour of the Club Men in the Civil War. These were peasants and farmers who combined to protect themselves 'against all murders, rapines, plunders, robberies or violence which shall be offered by the soldier or any oppressor whatsoever'. Although neither were ideologically inspired, both served to be hostile to the side who was menacing their own goods, whether the royalists in 1645 or the Jacobites exactly a century later.[113]

Yet it was not envisaged that the irregulars would act alone. Sir George Warrender wrote that regular troops were needed to act alongside the militia, 'ane regular force is much wanted by reason of the many strangers that resort thither'.[114] Regulars and irregulars were known to fight together against the Jacobites. It is worth noting that there were irregular forces present with the regulars at each battle of the 1715 and 1745 rebellions, though they formed only a minority of the total forces employed. Sixty gentlemen cavalrymen were present at the battle of Sheriffmuir on 13 November 1715 under the Earl of Rothes and were posted behind Evan's regiment of dragoons on the right wing. They may have taken part in the charge against the Jacobite left and the subsequent pursuit.[115] Argyll, rarely complimentary about the irregulars, wrote after the battle, 'The squadron of volunteers commanded by the Lords Rothes, Haddington and Lauderdale deserve His Majesty's favour, they were with me upon the right during the whole action'.[116] Yet most of the militia forces which arrived at Stirling were not called upon to march to meet the Jacobites, their role being to perform routine guard duty. Those 400 men brought by Lord Polworth were assigned to guard Lithgow and then march from there if needed.[117]

A somewhat more direct role was played by the fifty armed volunteers from Berwick who accompanied thirty regulars to retake Holy Island from the Jacobites in October 1715. They marched over the sands at low tide and retook it, sword in hand, though it was hardly a heroic exploit, for there were only two men opposing them.[118] Rather more irregulars were employed at the battle of Preston. Although General Wills welcomed the dissenters joining his force, along with the Lancashire militia, neither took part in the assault on Preston in 1715. This is not to say that they had no purpose, nor that Wills was merely humouring their leaders. Wills had asked Sir Henry Hoghton to inform the dissenting leaders:

> to raise what men I can to meet us at Preston tomorrow, so desire you raise all the force you can, I mean lusty young fellows to draw up on Curedon Green to be there by ten o'clock to bring what arms they have fit for service, and scythes putt in straight polls and such as have not, to bring spades and billhooks for pioneering with.[119]

Although the militia were posted to the south of the river Ribble, it was said 'they were very serviceable in guarding the Passes and several parties attempting to force their way through them, were either killed, taken or beat back'.[120] It is also worth noting that the subsequent Jacobite surrender on 14 November was in part due to the sighting of reinforcements for their enemies; these consisting largely of mounted militia and volunteers from Yorkshire, who, rather unusually, had crossed the county boundary.[121]

Scottish irregulars were present at all three of the major battles of the Forty-Five; and at Falkirk, William Thornton's company of Yorkshire volunteers was with Hawley's army, too. Irregular contributions to the first two battles, however, were of limited consequence. There were sixteen Edinburgh scholars with Cope at Prestonpans, plus some men of Loudon's regiment. The only reference to them is that they were lining the walls of Cockenzie, a mile from Prestonpans, before surrendering.[122] The Argyllshire militia acted as an advance guard on the days leading up to the battle of Falkirk, 'being posted in the Front, kept them in Awe, and effectually frustrated their Intention'.[123] At Falkirk, the Glasgow militia (possibly 800 men) were posted at some farmhouses in reserve, 'where it was thought they might be of use when the action begun, and remain'd formed there', one account read, 'when Hamilton's dragoons gave way, on receiving a brisk fire from the enemy, they bore back on the Glasgow regiment. Lord Hume, who commanded it, ordered some of his men to fire, they did so, and brought down some of their horses'. At least nineteen of them were killed.[124] Thornton later wrote, 'they stood and maintained their ground most heroically, so as to secure, in a great measure, the retreat of the army, at the hazard of their lives and liberties, many of them being cut in pieces'.[125] It is also stated that 1,000 Argyllshire militia were also present, though on the right wing. Some men in the irregular forces, on that occasion, surrendered, such as Thornton himself, and eighteen of his men, albeit escaping a few days later.[126] Yet the behaviour of many regulars at both battles was hardly glorious either, since many fled on these occasions, too.

It was later in the campaign that the Highlanders played an important part. This was at Culloden, where Cumberland's army included Argyllshire militia and some of Loudon's men. Their total numbers may have been about 1,600 men (about a sixth of Cumberland's command). They were involved in the march from Nairn, with the Argyllshire men being in the vanguard, under the quartermaster's command, along with men from Kingston's Horse (similarly, in 1716, 300 of Argyll's Campbells had served as his advance guard as the army marched to Perth. They also formed part of the spearhead of the army when it crossed the last physical barrier between them and the Jacobites – the River Spey – which, it was thought, would be contested, though was not, as it transpired).[127] When Cumberland made the dispositions for the battle itself, most were sent to the rear to guard the baggage (they numbered 501 men and officers). However, some 140 (two companies of Argyll militia and one of Loudon's) were posted to the left of the front line. Here they played a key role in breaking down the walled enclosures. This enabled Hawley's cavalry to threaten the Jacobite right flank. They also took part in the fighting themselves 'which did great execution on our right' wrote a Jacobite. A captain of Loudon's militia and one of the Argyllshires were wounded and later died; along with eight others who were killed or injured.[128] This was more casualties than half of the other infantry battalions on their side. General Campbell wrote, 'The Duke of Cumberland observed the behaviour of that corps of Highlanders, that he commented and said to Colonel Campbell afterwards that they prov'd themselves good men and loyal subjects'.[129]

It was not only during battle that irregular forces worked with the regulars. They often acted as scouting or advance parties, or formed part of them. Sir Andrew Agnew was given 500 regulars and 120 Argyllshire militia on his march from Perth to Dunkeld on 8 February 1746.[130] Forty Argyllshire militiamen formed part of Cumberland's advance guard on the march to Culloden and they also covered part of Hawley's army's retreat from Falkirk.[131] Such tasks were often carried out in conjunction with cavalry, such as in the advance from Stirling on 2 February, with the Argyllshire militia and Cobham's dragoons, or in harassing the retreating Jacobites with Brigadier Mordaunt leading accompanying dragoons.[132] Although Cumberland had his doubts about their use in some tasks, he had none with them acting thus, as he wrote on 20 February, that he would 'keep with me his [General Campbell's] son with about 600 Highlanders to go upon partys, as they are better qualified for that service here, than our troops'.[133] Cope had found irregulars useful, too, 'He has carried some of the Highland comps with about 200 Monroes amongst with him to scour the ground of either side of his march'.[134] Another useful task, this time performed by the Angus militia in January 1746, was to rescue a number of officers (thirty in number) taken by the Jacobites after Prestonpans.[135] Ray commented on this action, 'It was likewise a full Proof of the steady Loyalty and sincere Attachment to the Government, of those who undertook to rescue them, since they did it at a Time when the Rebels were flush'd with their late Advantage'.[136]

Irregular forces were accused of plundering. A Jacobite complained in December 1715 of the loyalist Frasers, 'They have pillaged Sir Robert Gordon's interest and in and about Elgin and in short all places where they come without sparing some of those that called them'. They were clearly triumphant and revelling in it, as the Jacobite continued, 'All north Whigs are mightily puffed up, even those of the better sense, and they hint that they may do as they will'.[137]

Irregular forces could be encouraged by the presence of regular troops. Some of the Edinburgh forces – the four companies of the city guard and the gentlemen volunteers, accompanying the two regiments of dragoons – marched out of the city on 15 September 1745, and 'they gave out they were to fight the highlanders the next day'.[138] The Edinburgh volunteers seemed to be ready to accompany the town guard and the two regiments of dragoons in defence of the city on 14 September 1745: as soon as the bell was rung, as a signal for them to assemble at the Lawnmarket, 'which they did in a body', and on seeing the regulars, 'the volunteers huzzaed'. Despite pleadings from relatives, the volunteers appeared to be resolute, 'neither the arguments of the men, nor the tears of the women, had any effect on these volunteers'. Yet only one company did so, and upon the investigation as to why the others did not, their officers replied, 'very few of their men would consent to follow them' However, 'Many of the private men complained that they had not one officer to lead them'. Instead they agreed to stand on the defensive only.[139]

There was a rather different outcome on 14–15 October 1715, when 600 men of the Edinburgh militia and volunteers had been assisted by Argyll and 500 of his troops in deterring an attack on the city and then in marching out to threaten the Jacobites at Leith.[140] Two regiments of the London trained bands marched out in December 1745 to join the regulars at the camp at Finchley. The arrival of regular forces in Edinburgh on 14 November 1745 encouraged the formation of militia companies in Glasgow and Edinburgh (again) and they gathered at Edinburgh in the following month.[141]

It was not uncommon for units of militia to fight alongside regular armies in this period. Most of the American rebel armies which took to the field against British and Hessian regulars had a strong contingent of militia alongside the Continental troops. The Wiltshire militia were present at Sedgemoor in 1685. Regiments of London's trained bands stood with 'regular' troops against the royalist army at Turnham Green in 1642 and also were present at the battle of Newbury in 1643.

Irregular forces could also be used in siege warfare. When Cumberland's forces were surrounding Carlisle in late December 1745, one of the besieging units was the Liverpool Blues, perhaps making up a tenth of the besieging forces. It was certainly unusual for volunteer forces to travel so far from their town or county of origin. The regiment had been stationed at Lancaster, when an order on 21 December came, to summon them northwards. On arrival, they helped form a blockade, being stationed at Stanwix 'there to defend the Pass & prevent any of the Enemy from making their escape that way'.[142] They were treated as the other soldiers in the regulars were, with posting guards both night and day to watch for any sorties or escapes. Some of the men were in danger of being killed or injured by artillery fire from Carlisle. Their duties were arduous enough, as Shairp noted:

> Our 4 oldest Compys had been now upon duty for 6 Nights running without ever getting any rest or being reliev'd by the younger ones as was at first propos'd at which they made great Complaints & indeed I must say they had Reason for it as they were

now growing sick in great numbers & quite stupid for want of Rest. But there was no Redress for them.[143]

Had the castle had to be stormed, 200 men of the Liverpool Blues were designated to take part. That this did not occur – because the garrison surrendered – was much to Shairp's relief, 'Butt thank God that it hapnend as it did else a good many lives would have been lost'.[144]

An observation in a contemporary newspaper suggests that a reason for the castle's surrender, apart from a breach having been made by heavy artillery, was that the garrison mistook the Liverpool Blues for the similarly blue-coated Dutch battalions under Wade's command, 'had not the Rebels taken the Liverpool Blues to be the Dutch forces, and whereby conceived that the whole Army of Marshal Wade had joined the Duke's, this barbarous Banditti would have completed their [the civilian population's] Destruction by starving them to death'.[145] Irregulars could also be used successfully in defence, with Cumberland ordering General Campbell to have a company or two of his militia in Fort William to help defend it in March 1746 'I have been so anxious about this particular fort'.[146]

Irregular cavalry were able to undertake more adventurous tasks. The cavalry troop of Westmorland militia arrived at Carlisle in late October 1715. They were sent by the deputy governor there to go to Longtown to find out what the Jacobites were doing; they arrested one Graham of Inchbrachy.[147]

The Yorkshire Royal Regiment of Hunters, already mentioned, were also active. They attached themselves to Wade's army at Newcastle initially. Much was hoped of them and Horace Walpole wrote, 'they are to act as a flying squadron to harass the enemy ... and to give intelligence'.[148] They rode in the vanguard of the army when they made an abortive march northwards to Morpeth, but later in November, they were sent to Penrith to spy on Jacobite movements. Major General Oglethorpe was impressed by them, writing, 'the Royal Hunters and Rangers bring me the best intelligence and I have made them send the last to Sir John Ligonier by express'.[149] They also helped disperse and round up Jacobites in December 1745; with Cuthbert Readshaw of Richmond writing, 'They have done well, for being inform'd that abt 2 or 300 of the rebels were at Lowther Hall they went there and attack'd them, killed 10 and dispersed the rest'.[150] Admiral Vernon also heard of their exploits, writing 'their spirit and example must be of infinite value'.[151] Yet there were critics; Ralph Reed telling a friend that 'they might have done good service by watching the rear of the rebel army' for stragglers and Stephen Thompson thought, 'They make more noise than they deserve, their numbers being much magnified'.[152]

At Culloden, once the Jacobite army began to flee, the irregulars took part in the pursuit: 'They were pursued by the horse, the dragoons and Argyllshire men, and it is computed that as many fell in the flight.'[153] They were also involved in the campaign in the aftermath of Culloden. Reay's men took over 100 prisoners and the Munroes killed about fifty fleeing Jacobites. The Grants captured the Jacobite Lord Balmerino and passed him to Cumberland and Lord Sutherland took 800–900 of his men into Fraser territory.[154] When the theatre of operations shifted to Fort Augustus in June, the Argyllshire militia helped scour the district around Fort Mingary in order to disperse any bodies of Jacobites there. Arms from the Camerons had already been surrendered to them.[155] In August, the Argyllshire militia were assisting in the hunt in north-west Scotland and on the Western Isles for Charles himself. Skye militia checked the boats coming from the Isles, convinced Charles was there. The fords between South Uist and Benbecula were guarded by the militia, too, sentries standing within musket shot of each other and their captain examining the passes of all travellers.[156] Although they ultimately failed, with Mcleod militia vainly ordering the boat carrying him to Skye to stop, and then firing on it, they did take some prisoners, including Captain O'Neal, three priests, one of whom was Cameron of Lochiel's brother, and the old laird of MacKinnon. Some of their fellows under Colonel Campbell, took the lieutenant colonel of Clanranalds's regiment, in Moidart. Stores of arms and ammunition were also found.[157]

In 1715, militia took Jacobite stragglers prisoner as about 500 left the Anglo-Scottish army and returned to Scotland. Once they were seen, loyalist gentry gathered local men 'well horsed and well armed and accoutred' and in the hills near Lamingtown found 'upwards of 200 of them in two Bodies besides other small parties, whom they obliged to surrender'. At least another ninety were taken at this time in Hopetoun and Sanquhar, and a few others elsewhere.[158]

In February 1746, Cumberland sent out forces to attack the property of Jacobites who were in arms against his father. Some of the loyalist Highlanders were involved, but there is an ambiguity in their enthusiasm in such work. According to Cumberland, who had his doubts in their zeal, General John Campbell, their leader:

> assures me that they will shew no favour or particularity to the other Highlanders, as he knews them best. He must answer for them greatly, for those who were with us here before me, absolutely refused to plunder any of the rebels' houses, which is the only way we have to punish them and bring them to heel.[159]

However, in the following month Cameron of Lochiel had had different experiences and he wrote angrily, after first discussing the antipathy of the clan Campbell to the Stuarts:

> Nor could we ever form a thought to ourselves that men endowed with reason and commonsense could use their fellow creatures with such inhumanity and Barbarity as they do and of which we have daily proofs by their burning of houses. Stripping of

women and children and exposing them to the open fields and severity of weather, burning of corn, hanging of cattle and killing of horses ... with hearts full of revenge will certainly endeavour to make reprisals and are determined to apply to Royal Highness for leave and order to enter their country with full possession to act at discretion.[160]

Similar work against fleeing rebels was undertaken by the Somerset and Sussex militia in the aftermath of Sedgemoor in July 1685. Indeed, it was these irregular forces that actually caught the escaping Monmouth.[161]

As a general rule, the activity of the irregular forces was limited by geography. They rarely went beyond their own borough or county boundaries. In this they were similar to many of the trained bands in the civil wars, those of London often being reluctant to leave the capital, but differed from the state militias in America in the 1770s, who often marched outside their own state.[162] This made them less useful as a military force. There were exceptions, of course, such as the Liverpool Blues and most of the Scottish irregulars raised in 1745–6.

The role of irregular forces was not always viewed positively by the regulars. In October 1715, Argyll was annoyed to receive a letter from the Provost of Edinburgh, demanding that he send regular troops to help defend the city against Jacobite forces, which led to him detaching 450 of his already small force at Stirling to the Scottish capital. He wrote that he was 'not able by any manner of means to prevail with the vast numbers of inhabitants to defend themselves, tho' well armed'. Although 350 Edinburgh volunteers joined Argyll against the Jacobites at Leith, Argyll was still unimpressed:

our well affected people cannot be persuaded to defend themselves against the very smallest numbers of the rebels till they had arms and ammunition, from all comers of the country, they assured me they would do wonders. Now they have them whenever the smallest number of rebels approaches, they say nothing can be done without regular troops. The faintheartedness of this small number of loyal subjects, excepting a few noblemen and gentlemen, is beyond all sort of imagination.[163]

Argyll also had problems with the militia when he wanted them to garrison three castles, writing that it was 'with the greatest difficulties imaginable' he had prevailed upon them to do so and complained 'what use I either have or can hope to receive of the militia' when he heard they wished to leave their posts. He concluded, 'in short, my Lord, a lamb is not more afraid of a lyon than these Low country people are of the Highlanders'.[164]

Argyll was not impressed by the Lowland militia who marched to Stirling where he and his army were stationed, in 1715. On 10 November, he wrote, 'in truth they are of very little use, excepting the few that are in the castles on this river, which we must do all possible to continue there'.[165] He was not alone in his views. In 1745, General Wentworth thought their best use would be if they could be drafted into the regular army and 'form them to compleat our 10 English battalions' and he later told Malton 'who is under some difficulty how to dispose of his forces to the best advantage ... I have again propos'd to him the reinforcing the old regiments which would perhaps be the only method he can take to make these people really usefull'.[166] When the Edinburgh volunteers requested to join Cope's forces, 'Sir John Cope refused their assistance, for fear of confusing his men'.[167] Mr Herdman, Wade's secretary, was contemptuous of the volunteer forces in England, writing, 'those useless men to whom they allow twelve pence a day to do nothing and upon occasion would fly before the rebels'.[168] However, when Thornton's company of Yorkshire Blues joined the forces under Wade at Newcastle, Wentworth gave them great praise indeed, 'his zeal to His Majesty's Government; his case is so extraordinary that I really think it would be for the King's service that some distinction be shewn him'. Wentworth wanted this company to be made part of the regular forces, 'they are really good men, and deserve a little attention'.[169] Hawley's views were mixed; on being asked if the Edinburgh volunteers could march with the army, he initially suggested another duty, but on being pressed, agreed that they could do so.[170] As noted, Cumberland's views were mixed, writing on 28 February 1746, on the behaviour of Loudon's force:

> When the rebels appeared with an inferior force and yet he abandoned Inverness with the utmost confusion, and some pretend to say that his people will all disband, how far that may prove true I know not, but upon the whole I fear the well affected Highlanders will not do much more than defend their own country.[171]

However, the attitude of regular officers towards Thornton's company of Yorkshire Blues in January 1746 was not at all accommodating. Thornton complained, 'they had never met with very civil usage from the regular officers who seemed not at all to affect volunteers'. On reaching the village of Ellon, the quartermaster 'would not assign Quarters to the volunteer as Officers, and none of the Officers would give orders for it, which and some other things of this kind effectually disgusted them, so that they immediately left the army and returned home'.[172]

Civilian responses to the militia were often more positive. When the Glasgow militia arrived in Edinburgh on 24 December, they were welcomed enthusiastically: 'These were most kindly received by the inhabitants, who were overjoyed to have these near them for their support against an attack which was at that Time greatly feare.'[173]

But it was not just the Jacobite forces which the irregulars were concerned with. Most irregular units did not have to face the wrath of the Jacobite army or even saw their enemy. Some performed practical measures against the Jacobites behind the front line, in order to inhibit them. Cholmondeley told Newcastle that, 'I sent to Warrington last night, for the breaking down of that Bridge'.[174] The men of the Liverpool Blues destroyed the bridges over which it was feared that the Jacobites might march, en route to the rich sea port of Liverpool. Bridges at Stockport and Crossford were also destroyed. This was not always easy, as Shairp wrote, 'it was Mischief however, the Bridge was so well made that our Tooles so blunted that it stood us till six the nixt morning'.[175] Similarly, the Peak miners of Derbyshire destroyed the turnpikes from Whaley to Buxton.[176] Demolition of bridges which were of strategic value to the enemy had also occurred in 1685 when Keynsham bridge was partially destroyed, thus delaying Monmouth's advance party long enough to allow regular cavalry to arrive and thus guarantee Bristol's safety.[177]

Such actions were not always effectual. The breaking of the bridges over the Mersey would have inhibited an advance towards Wales, but not one towards London and the Jacobites repaired bridges near Manchester easily enough. Likewise, Hardwicke noted:

> 'The measure which the Duke has taken with the Duke of Devonshire , for spoiling the road by Buxton, is undoubtedly prudent and right; but will, I fear, have little effect to stop the Highland foot; and, as there are no regular troops on that side, the Rebels may possibly soon be able to repair the damage (which can be done in so short a time), sufficiently for their light cannon to be drawn thro' these roads.[178]

Action against local suspects was another task well within their capabilities. In early December 1745, when there was a scare about York Catholics, the 'Associated Company of Tradesmen of York' guarded the doors of each premises which was searched in that city. Horses and arms were sought and twenty-six of the former were sent to Leeds. Their input was needed because the corporation, who had also raised its own companies of volunteers, refused to sanction such measures.[179]

Rioters or Jacobite sympathizers could be dispersed by irregular forces or loyalists. In fact, it was commonplace for militia or trained bands to perform such tasks, as Pepys noted in the London in the 1660s, but it occurred later in the seventeenth and eighteenth centuries, too.[180] During anti-Irish rioting in London in the summer of 1736, they had been effective, as Newcastle informed the Earl of Waldegrave:

> the mob rose again to a great number; but the militia of the Tower Hamlets being then raised, marched against them; but the mob in the same manner retired before them whenever they came, and gave not the least resistance. The deputy lieutenants upon this wrote to the officers of the Tower that they did not want their assistance.[181]

Part of the Cheshire militia marched to Manchester in November 1715 probably because there had been rioting there earlier that year and they were needed
to prevent a recurrence.[182]

When Jacobites tried to interrupt the celebrations in York for the defeat of
the rebellion, on 9 June 1716, militia officers helped to put them down.[183] Loyal
citizenry stemmed Jacobite disturbances in Sheffield in June 1715.[184] When
200 Catholics rose in Ormskirk, on 25 November 1745, drums beating and
proclaiming Charles regent, while the Jacobite army was marching through the
county, local loyalists disrupted their gathering and arrested a dozen of them.[185]
Maxwell noted, 'the militia were armed in every county for the service of the
Established Government, all passes guarded, and suspected persons watched; by
this means an insurrection would have been crushed before it was well begun'.[186]

There were instances in 1715 in which the county sheriffs were ordered by
Townshend to curb the riots which were frequent in the Midlands that summer.
In Warwickshire, the posse numbered 930 men, both on foot and on horseback,
and were armed by the constables. They were able to quell the riots in Birmingham and arrest the ringleaders, at the cost of £841 9s 3d. Mr Oswald Mosley,
High Sheriff of Staffordshire, did likewise.[187] There had been Jacobite riots in
London in May and June 1715. In July, the trained bands of London and Westminster were ordered to be 'put in a Posture for Suppressing Tumults and Riots,
which at this time were grown up to an unusual Frequency and Forwardness'. In
September and October 1715, the militia brought about 800 Catholics, Nonjurors and other suspects to the magistrates, resulting in some being jailed or
bailed, 'which tended not a little to keep the peace of those populous Cities,
while many other parts of the Nation were disquieted with the Noise of War'.[188]

However, the militia or posse's role in riot duty should not be exaggerated.
There is no reference to their being used against Jacobite mobs in the north of
England in 1715.[189] Similarly, Sir William Williamson, sheriff of Durham was
asked in 1740 to raise the posse to quell economic riots there. Yet Thomas Rudd,
a lawyer, 'said in his opinion that the Posse was by no means an adequate force'.[190]
Similarly, in January 1746, with an outbreak in the county of anti-Catholic rioting, a similar step was proposed by Bishop Chandler: 'It has not been thought
prudent ... to raise the Posse.'[191] In all these instances, regular troops were called
upon to disperse the rioters. In all these cases, it is probable that the men of the
civilian forces were sympathetic to their fellows. Likewise, one reason for the
lukewarm nature of the loyalties of the militia in the South West in 1685 is that
they were reluctant to fight their neighbours or/and shared their concerns. Certainly the latter seems to have been the case for the men of the Lancashire militia
in 1685, as one of its members, Timothy Craggs later wrote, 'our hearts was for
the Duke [of Monmouth]; for when the news came that the Duke was taken,
there was but a poor shout'.[192] Major General Moyle wrote in the aftermath of

the Porteous riots in Edinburgh in 1736 that, 'The town souldiers, instead of resisting, delivered their arms to the mob'.[193]

Potential Jacobite recruits were intimidated into remaining 'quiet' by loyalist militia. The autumn of 1715 saw the militia of Greenock and Carsdyke 'employed in guarding their respective towns, sending detachments to seize and secure suspected persons, to prevent their going to the Earl of Mar and in bring over Boats etc. to the south side of the Clyde, to prevent the Rebels ... from transporting themselves over therein'.[194]

In early December 1745, Loudon's force marched to Fort Augustus and en route, 'intimated to the people of Stratherrick what they were to expect if they joined the Enemy'. A few days later, the Monroes crossed the Spey and moved towards the Grants, who 'retired from thence to defend their own estates to the great Misfortune of the other commanders'.[195]

As Forbes had written, 'We shall be able to check the Rebels' further recruiting'.[196] He later wrote that only 500–600 Frasers and 150–160 McKenzies had been able to join the Jacobite army and 'By this diversion, His Majesty's army will have a much smaller body of Highlanders to deal with to the southward'.[197] This point was also made by John Daniel, who wrote, 'had he [Forbes] been as firm a friend as he was an implacable enemy, we would have seen, instead of the 4000 men who marched into England, an army of 18 or 20,000 men'.[198]

Intelligence gathering was another useful function of the militia. The Durham Militia Horse in 1715 were certainly most active, with a watch being kept at Hexham and Dilston, centres of Jacobite activity. They had been ordered to 'spare no expense for intelligence and the security of the troop it being so much for the service of the publick'. Passes were also watched by these horsemen for signs of Jacobites passing therein.[199] In September 1745, the Edinburgh volunteers gave Cope news of the Jacobite numbers and their arms. Home wrote, 'Sir John Cope dismissed the volunteers with many compliments for bringing him such certain news and accurate intelligence'.[200]

Militia were able to undertake searches for Jacobites and their weaponry. Arthur Jessop, a Holmfirth apothecary, noted in November 1745, the volunteers searched Mr Scot of Woodsome's house for any concealed Jacobites.[201] Nicholas Blundell's house was searched on 13 November 1715, and he recorded thus, 'This Hous was twice sirched by some Foot as came from Leverpoole, I think the first party was about 26'.[202] The properties of other Catholic gentlemen in Lancashire were also visited by the militia in early November, too. Richard Townley's housekeeper recalled that a party of twenty men arrived and said 'they would shoot him ... they fired a pistols into the Room where the master and mistress slept' and were also accused of stealing from another mansion.[203] Loyalists in Liverpool in early November 1715 believed that Viscount Molyneux was sheltering Jacobites and so 'a vast mob of sailors and others were come from Liverpool and had beset the house and threatened to pull it down and burn it if they would not deliver themselves'. Several Catholics therein surrendered to them.[204] In Westmorland, in 1715, the Lord Lieutenant gave 'the necessary Directions to the Proper Officers of the Militia, forthwith seize the Persons and Arms of all Papists, Non Jurors and other Persons that you suspect to be Disafected'.[205]

Guarding prisoners was another task which could be entrusted to the irregulars. Prisoners of war were held at Portsmouth and guarded by Colonel Frampton's battalion of regulars. The troops were needed elsewhere, so the Hampshire volunteers, stationed at Winchester, were required to march to Portsmouth and take over guard duties. They were also asked, two weeks later, to provide escorts for prisoners on their way from Petersfield to Porchester castle.[206] Likewise, men from the North Riding companies guarded prisoners on their way to York in December 1745.[207]

London's six regiments of Trained Bands were called upon to guard the avenues of approach to the City in the crucial weeks of early December 1745. From September, they had manned gateways, patrolled the streets night and day and conducted searches. They were seen as being absolutely essential to the security of the capital, both against invaders and any insurgents from within. Alarms and signals were to be given in the event of any danger. Once sounded:

> every soldier in the six Regiments of Militia without waiting for Beat of Drum, or any other Notice, do immediately on hearing the said signals, repair with their Arms, and the usual Quantity of Ball, to the respective Rendezvous; the Red Regiment upon Tower Hill, the Green in Guildhall Yard, the Yellow in St. Paul's Church Yard, the White at the Royal Exchange, the Blue in old Fife Street, and the Orange in West Smithfields.[208]

Newcastle was pleased with the City's conduct, writing to the Lord Mayor, 'His Majesty was pleased to express a particular satisfaction in the orders given by your Lordship and the magistracy for preserving the peace of the City'.[209] Yet there were reported misdemeanours among some of the men; perhaps the most heinous being that, on one occasion, one of the gateways was found to have been unguarded.[210]

Dealing with such forms of Jacobite outbursts was similar to the action taken by American 'Patriot' militia in the 1770s. In both instances, both the leaderships of the Jacobites and the British regulars expected a great deal of support from the civil population, in England and in the southern American colonies respectively. Little was forthcoming in either case, and in part this can be accredited to the intimidation and control of these localities by the militia. Likewise, the Wiltshire militia's routing of men supportive of Monmouth at Frome denied their joining the main rebel force and prevented their weapons being used by them, either.[211]

Routine guard duty on city walls was a common task for some irregular forces, especially if the city was walled, and therefore, perhaps, not wholly indefensible. At York, the archbishop remarked that the city companies guarded the city's four gates and so, 'none [are] permitted to come in or go out of the city without examination'. There was concern that the men might try to relieve citizens of money or drink. There was probably a rota for the volunteers, for a guardroom was established in Robert Sowerby's schoolroom near the market cross.[212] Despite the defeat of Hawley's army at Falkirk, on 23 January, it was noted that 'the Rebells are far distant from this City the Town quiet, no appearance of Tumults or Disorders & therefore no occasion to keep Guards in Thursday market at the Barrs'; the men would be stood down.[213]

Glasgow and Edinburgh were guarded by their respective volunteers and militia in September 1715, as Warrender told Townshend, 'the magistrats of this place are takeing all imaginable precautions for their saffty by the City guaird New levie and inhabitants ... for the intrest of the Government and peace of the place'.[214]

Another instance of such police duties, though with a rather more violent outcome, occurred in 10 October 1715. Deputy Lieutenants were ordered to have Robert Keith's house searched for arms and horses. Twenty 'Fencible men' accompanied them, led by Sinclair of Herriston and the result was that they:

> came up straight to the house and sent to know if Keith was at home and to acquaint him with his commission and orders. After Keith endeavoured to make his escape out of the back entry and finding he could not ... Keith himself with his sons. Two brothers and servants, came out on horseback, fired their pistols as they came out ... Herriston's offering to return his fire, his pistol snapt, Keith with a broadsword gave Herriston three wounds in the head: The fencible men fyred and Keith's second son was shot dead.

This was the first fatality of the conflict and it had been the work of the militia; though Keith and the others of his party escaped.[215] A less bloody incident occurred in Edinburgh on 9 September. On hearing that the Jacobites planned a coup de main against Edinburgh castle, Cockburne acted quickly: 'I likewise caused several well affected gentlemen who reside here and they frankly went out ... the party from the City Guard came up at the same time and some gentlemen at them who were most usefull.' Although most of the Jacobites escaped after their failed attempt, a few were rounded up that night.[216]

Similar duties occurred thirty years later. The Lord Chief Justice wrote that on 6 September, Mr Napier, the Sheriff of Stirling, had 100 men who watched the county south of the Forth, guarding passes and fords, under the JPs' supervision.[217] In Edinburgh, the city guard was to patrol 'in case of any disturbance or commotion within the city or suburbs'.[218]

It should also be noted that the mere presence of loyalist forces in a town or city meant that the Crown's authority was being upheld and was not interrupted, or at least not permanently, by the Jacobite forces. The latter found that they could only command a place if their forces were physically present. Even in towns and cities where they had been greeted with great enthusiasm by some, once they had departed, the power vacuum was soon filled by their opponents. In Manchester in 1745, the exit of the Jacobites resulted in their supporters there being harassed, and on the return of the Jacobite army, the reception was by a hostile crowd, though it soon melted away. Similarly in 1715, although the Jacobite army passed through towns in the north-west of England, without any conflict, once they had gone, the companies of the Cumberland and Westmorland militia returned to these places.[219]

The Jacobites saw themselves as the legitimate government; but they could only be so when their army was in control. The volunteer forces in Yorkshire and Lancashire in 1745 were spread throughout the county, as were the Cumberland and Westmorland companies in 1715, presumably as a method of emphasizing that the Crown was still in control.[220]

Ceremonial duties were also undertaken by the irregulars. Presumably this was in order to intimidate any Jacobite sympathizers and to buoy up the confidence of loyalists. Prescott recorded that in Chester on 15 November 1715, 'The City and the Wirral Militia exercise and exult in their Hatts, wear the Colour of Victory, Green Ribbands'.[221] In 1745, the four York companies paraded through the city and then drank the King's health on his birthday.[222] The York force who made the search of Catholic properties mentioned above, took part in a parade with two regiments of regular forces outside York Minster on 11 February 1746 and greeted the arrival of the new county sheriff in the following month.[223] If these actions were to impress onlookers, at least one man was taken by them. John Graves of York spoke of the York troops, that they were 'well cloathed and disciplined, in high spirits'.[224]

Clearly the militia was not a substitute for the regular army. Few, if any contemporaries believed it was. After Lonsdale had seen the posse rout in 1715, he told Townshend, 'The Country is entirely without Defence and I am very much afraid these rebels won't be stopped till they meet with a Regular Force'.[225] Cope, seeing the militia guarding Berwick in 1745, wrote, 'the townsmen (tho' they are very zealous) I am afraid little is to be expected in case of attack'. A citizen of the town thought likewise, writing, they would 'do all that an undisciplined Militia can do'.[226] Clerk wrote, 'it appeared very evident to me that 100 Highlanders would have routed 1000 of their militia'.[227]

Yet even some of those who thought like this did admit the militia had some uses. Clerk noted, of the militia in 1715, they 'signified nothing in the military way, the Lowland men being a great deal more unfit for the like expedition than the Highlanders. However, these militia troops were sometimes made a show, and perhaps they served to intimidate those who knew nothing about them'.[228] Elcho wrote that Lord George Murray gave this verdict on them: 'the militia, although they durst never face the army awhile in a body, yet they would have courage enough to putt an end to them if ever they were routed'.[229] Malton gave the following sensible assessment of the value of the irregulars he led: 'perhaps we of ourselves may be unable to make a real stand I dare say we shall be able to prevent their being joined by any in this county had they any inclination to it'.[230]

Hardwicke thought that the moral and propaganda value of the irregular forces was paramount:

> I lay more weight upon the evidence and éclat that will arise from such meetings and associations of their zeal and spirit, and good affections of His Majesty's subjects in support of his Government and against the Pretender, than upon the military utility of their troops, without excluding that. For I think it material to convince Foreign Powers (as I told the King today) that the appearances in England are very different to those in Scotland, and that they will be mistaken if they take their measures from the latter.[231]

Argyll noted the military failings of the Glasgow militia, who joined his regulars at Stirling on 18 September, but also recognized their value, when he wrote that they were:

> so badly armed having no bayonets that I cannot possibly pretend to make any other use of them than to make them serve as garrison to the castle of Stirling. However, I take this step to be so strong a demonstration of the hearty zeal of those honest people, that I should heartily think it would be for His Majesty's Service, if you would write to the provost to thank them in His Majesty's name for this proof of their Duty.[232]

Ray observed, 'Those Troops, tho' they did not enter into immediate service, yet they shew'd the Spirit of the Nation, protected the Kings well meaning Subjects, and kept the Rebels under a manifest Restraint for some Time'.[233]

The Jacobites, too, did not altogether dismiss the psychological value of the militia and volunteers. The author of 'The Duke of Perth's speech' noted that on the Jacobite invasion of England:

> We were entertained with nothing but Associations in all the Parts of England, in Defence of the Elector's Right, and not a Man from that Kingdom, either joined us in Scotland, or made any Interest to promote an Insurrection in your Favour, in their own Country.[234]

Not bad for forces dismissed by their enemies as 'small beer'.

But we should not forget their practical use either. In May 1746, Forbes summed up the use of the Highland militia:

the use they already have been of to the publick is very great, preventing any accession of strength to the rebels before they march'd into England was no small service; the like prevention in some degree, and the destruction of their forces, when the Duke was advancing, was of considerable use, and now are by the Duke employed, under the Earl Loudoun, in Glengarry and might be the leads by which the rebels are to be hunted in their recesses.[235]

Conclusion

During the Jacobite rebellions, irregular forces sprung into being throughout Britain, though more so in Scotland and the north of England, where the danger was more immediate, and where it was more important for local elites to demonstrate their loyalty, than elsewhere. They were variously armed, uniformed, officered and trained and were spread out in penny packets. Yet, considering the myriad difficulties which they faced in coming into being with a semblance of military demeanour, and at relatively short notice, the fact that they were not particularly militarily proficient is no surprise. It was an achievement that so many were in existence.

It is easy to point to the failures of the militia and volunteers at Edinburgh and Carlisle in 1745 and in the Highlands in early 1746. When faced with the full weight of the Jacobite army, they either dispersed in their wake or surrendered after only a matter of days. Nor were regular soldiers always impressed by their actions; certainly not Argyll in 1715. The irregulars failed when they were confronted by such, because it was not something which they were envisaged as carrying out.

The real purpose and achievements of the militia and volunteers lay elsewhere. Their purpose was to assist the regular forces in the field and to prevent their being distracted by Jacobites in their rear. In these tasks, they enjoyed a fair degree of success. The rising at Ormskirk was stopped in its tracks. Vital Jacobite gold was seized in 1746. Jacobite forces were diverted from other tasks in both 1715 and 1746 by irregular opponents, however feeble some of the latter eventually proved to be. Jacobite suspects were rounded up, their properties searched, small parties of Jacobites harassed and potential Jacobite recruits intimidated into inaction. We cannot quantify the exact value of such work, because we do not know how many Jacobite supporters would have otherwise aided the main Jacobite military effort. Inglorious and unheroic work, it is true, but it had to be done by someone, and by doing it they saved the regulars the task. They also served to demonstrate political support in the localities for the government, in both England and Scotland, which may have prompted further support and discouraged Jacobites. In battle and siege they assisted the regulars; especially in scouting and in pursuit, which showed that not all were averse to actual combat if properly supported. It is in this support role that we should view the achievements of the irregular forces, and these were numerous, if not individually spectacular. Without them, the work of the regulars would have been more arduous.

CONCLUSION

The military resources of the British state overcame the challenge posed by the Jacobite rebellions. Success does not invite introspection or criticism, except for, in 1746–7, those individuals who failed to fulfil their obligations: Cope, Oglethorpe, Durand and Major Grant, but not Hawley nor Wade, all of who faced boards of inquiry or courts martial, though all save Grant were acquitted. However, the British method of war was not deemed to be in need of major overhaul. It had proved itself successful in the task allotted to it.

Yet these campaigns were not easy ones and presented numerous challenges to the British state's military resources. Some of these were similar to those faced abroad, but there were additional factors. They faced regular opponents from abroad, but mostly irregular enemies from the British mainland, whose style of campaigning and battlefield tactics were not their own. This meant they had to adapt their orthodox style to combat these enemies, just as British forces were to do in the American colonies and in Canada in the 1750s. Yet their resources included not only the regular established forces, supplemented by foreign auxiliaries, but also the militia and volunteer forces. There were a number of fortresses under their control, too.

Combating domestic rebellion and foreign incursion, both potential and real, necessitated a defensive strategy. The state's goal was to preserve status quo which had been established after the revolution of 1688 and so to retain the Protestant monarchy against the deposed Catholic monarchy of one branch of the Stuarts. The Jacobite armies had to be defeated and dispersed by the state's forces, and any allies from abroad had to be repelled on the field of battle or during a campaign. Those ultimately responsible to the Crown for this were the Secretaries of State, who issued overall instructions to the commanders in the field. The latter then had to employ their forces to the best of their ability in an overall framework as laid out for them, while being given much tactical leeway in how they accomplished these orders. Similarly, militia and volunteer forces, commanded by the county lieutenancy or borough mayoralty were guided by the Secretaries of State.

In order to assist with these sudden emergencies, additional forces had to be raised. This resulted in the expansion of existing units, in the raising of new ones and the summoning of contract troops from abroad. It also led to the calling out of the militia and volunteer forces. Fortresses were hastily repaired.

The opening stages of the campaigns were marked by movement on the part of the Jacobites and it was unclear what their strength and intentions were. The state had to react and could not do so quickly enough, especially under the wartime conditions of 1745. It also resulted in many battalions being tied down in garrison duties, such as in London, Portsmouth, Bristol, Bath and Oxford in 1715, and along the south-eastern coasts in 1745, as well as in and around the capital, because England was the priority, not Scotland. This also resulted in initial Jacobite successes leading to large parts of Scotland being lost to the state's control for several months in 1715 and more so in 1745.

However in the later stages of both the central Scottish theatre in 1715 and the campaign of 1745, the initiative passed to the government, as Mar remained at Perth and the Jacobites made their base at Inverness in February 1746. This allowed both Argyll and Cumberland to be reinforced and then strike at their increasingly weakened foes. Time was on the side of the status quo, who could bring its superior strength into play once the initial surprise was over and their opponents lost their momentum.

Numerically the forces at the state's disposal outnumbered those of the Jacobites. Yet while the Jacobites could concentrate their men in one place at one time, the state could not do so. This was because the state faced two major sources of danger. Firstly, and most apparent, was the army led by the Pretender or his representative, and based from and in Scotland. Secondly there was the danger in 1715 from English Jacobitism, in 1719 from Spain and in 1745 not only from English Jacobites, albeit at a far lower level than in 1715, but also from France. None of these latter produced much actual danger, but this is only obvious in retrospect. The state had to be prepared for them and thus have troops at hand to deal with them. This resulted in the number of troops actually gathered against the Jacobite army or armies in Britain being relatively small in number.

The actual battles were similar in size to those in colonial, but not Continental, warfare. Armies with numbers only in the thousands, and often lacking operational artillery, confronted each other. The results of these battles were usually decisive in either the short or long term or both, excepting perhaps Falkirk. Successful battles were ones in which two or three arms worked together to destroy the Jacobites, such as the infantry and dragoons on Argyll's right at Sherriffmuir, and even more so at Culloden, with artillery bombardment and canister followed up by musketry volleys and bayonet, then the dragoons putting the finishing touches to the victory.

Supporting the regulars were the militia and volunteer forces. They were summoned in some numbers in 1715 and 1745; probably more so in 1745, and more so in Scotland and northern England, where the danger was all the greater. These units were geographically restricted and, individually, relatively small in number. Yet they did free the regulars from performing police roles which often fell to them in peacetime. Some even fought alongside the regulars on the battlefield and during siege warfare, and elsewhere may well have inhibited Jacobite sympathizers from hindering the regulars.

On the whole, the fortresses did not serve as well as expected. Those in Scotland had been built with the express role of nipping another rebellion in the bud. There were too few in 1715, but even in 1745 with the chain of forts in the Highlands, they could neither act proactively and stop the rebellion gathering momentum in 1745 and in 1746 some were very quickly taken by the Jacobites, even though the latter lacked heavy artillery. Yet some, such as Fort William and Stirling and Edinburgh castles held out. Walled cities such as Edinburgh and Carlisle also fell in a short time to the Jacobites. The difficulty was that the garrisons in most of these places were too few in number to operate independently, and in any case, relied on an effective field army operating in their vicinity. Without these they were very vulnerable indeed, as shown in March 1746.

Since the Jacobite rebellions ended in defeat for the Jacobites, we must judge that the British state was militarily successful in a way it was not in the American colonies in 1775–81 or against the Williamite invasion of 1688. Some of the reasons for success in 1715, 1719 and 1745 lie with other factors. There was no successful large-scale foreign intervention and there was no major crisis among the reigning elite as there were in these successful rebellions. However we should not see these campaigns as a simple or inevitable triumph of the 'modern' army over one of 'savages'. The latter routed the former at Prestonpans and fought them to a standstill at Preston 30 years previously, and irregulars had been known to triumph over regular troops outside Europe. To an extent one could point to the deficiencies of the Jacobite armies and their leaders. Few would argue that Mar and Forster missed opportunities in 1715, or that supply and financial deficiencies in 1746 helped doom the later rebellion. The failure of the Spanish or French to land substantial forces in Britain also made a Jacobite victory less likely, as did the lack of any substantial show of English Jacobitism.

Yet we can take this too far. The regular army's campaigns made a significant impact against the Jacobites. In 1715, the regular forces were able to prevent any outbreak of rebellion in most of England by garrisoning towns and cities. The more difficult and dangerous tasks were those of confronting the Jacobite armies in the north of England and in Scotland. Because of the need to garrison centres of supposed disaffection, the strength of the more active forces was reduced, even with the addition of newly raised troops and battalions from Ireland. Contract troops from Holland inevitably took time in arriving. Thus the numbers available to face the Jacobite forces were smaller than those of their opponents. At both Preston and Sherriffmuir mistakes were made; by Wills in underestimating his opponent and so making costly attacks leading to little result, by Argyll in being too involved with the forces under his immediate control that he lost overall control of the battle. Yet the troops fought well and their generals' resolve was undimmed. Both were undefeated at the end of the day's fighting, and by remaining so, the morale of the Jacobite leadership fell, leading to either surrender or retreat. This did not lead to the end of the campaign immediately, but it did mean that reinforcements were able to arrive at Stirling for Argyll while Jacobite strength diminished. The moment of danger had passed, but it had been lengthy one.

In 1745, the regulars faced an uphill struggle, with the need to bring together enough troops to Britain and to recover from initial defeat and setbacks. Furthermore it was impossible to assemble more than one field army against the Jacobites until late November. Faulty intelligence led to the Jacobites being closer to London than either of the two regular armies. However, genuine concerns over a possible French invasion led to most of Cumberland's army being pulled back from pursuit, enabling the Jacobite army to return mostly intact to Scotland. Fortune favoured both sides. As in 1715, much of the regular army was posted in England amid continuing concerns about a French invasion, leaving one field army for Scotland whose numbers were lesser than their opponents. Once again, the full force of the state was unavailable for offensive action. Cumberland's generalship was a crucial part of the eventual victory at Culloden and the men under his command behaved as well as they had on the Continent, which had mostly not been the case at Falkirk three months earlier.

Neither campaign was flawless; financial and supply problems persisted throughout, militia forces did not always perform well and fortresses sometimes fell after the briefest of sieges. These were failings of the system which commanders had to continually work to resolve, as well as dealing with the enemy in the field. A commander had to wield a pen as well as a sword and had to negotiate with civilian allies as well as giving orders to his military subordinates. Most managed to do so reasonably amicably. Yet the main regular armies were resilient, even after serious losses as in 1715 or after defeat as at Falkirk in 1746. Neither was destroyed. There were no significant desertions and the resolve to continue the struggle persisted. The state's war machine had many imperfections indeed, but a handful of talented commanders were able to overcome these, perhaps not brilliantly, but certainly doggedly, and in doing so eventually led their forces to victory.

NOTES

Introduction

1.   B. P. Lenman, *The Jacobite Risings in Britain, 1689–1746* (London: Methuen, 1980), p. 11.

2.   W. A. Speck, *The Butcher: The Duke of Cumberland and the Suppression of the '45* (Welsh Academic Press, 1995); S. Reid, *1745: A Military History of the Last Jacobite Rising* (Spellmount: Staplehurst, 1996); S. Reid, *Culloden* (Barnsley: Pen & Sword Books Ltd, 2005); J. Black, *Culloden and the '45* (Stroud: Sutton, 1990); C. Duffy, *The '45* (London: Cassell, 2003); F. J. McLynn, *France and the Jacobite Rising of 1745* (Edinburgh: Edinburgh University Press, 1981); F. J. McLynn, *The Jacobite Army in England: The Final Campaign* (Edinburgh: John Donald Publishers, Ltd, 1983); F. J. McLynn, *The Jacobites* (London: Routledge and Kegan Paul, Ltd,1985); F. J. McLynn, *Bonnie Prince Charlie* (Oxford: Oxford University Press, 1991).

3.   J. Baynes, *The Jacobite Rising of 1715* (London: Cassell, 1970); D. Szechi, *1715: The Great Jacobite Rising* (New Haven, CT: Yale University Press, 2006); J. D. Oates, *The Last Battle on English Soil* (Lancaster: Centre for North West Regional Studies, forthcoming).

4.   M. Barthorp, *The Jacobite Rebellions, 1689–1745* (London: Osprey Publishing 1982); J. Roberts, *The Jacobite Wars: Scotland and the Military Campaigns of 1715 and 1745* (Edinburgh: Polygon, 2002); J. Sadler; *Culloden and the Last Charge of the Highland Clans* (Stroud: Tempus, 2005).

5.   J. Prebble, *Culloden* (London: Secker & Warburg, 1961); P. Harrington, *Culloden1746: The Highlanders' Last Charge* (Oxford: Osprey Publishing, 1991); S. Reid, *Like Hungry Wolves: Culloden Moor, the 16th April 1746* (London: Windrow & Greene, 1994); Reid, *Culloden*; S. Reid and G. Embleton, *Culloden Moor, 1746* (Oxford: Osprey, 2002); C. P. Sked and H. Horrocks, *Culloden* (Edinburgh: National Trust for Scotland, 1997); A. Pollard (ed.), *Culloden: The History and Archaeology of the Last Clan Battle* (Barnsley: Pen & Sword, 2009).

6.   G. Bailey, *Falkirk or Paradise! The Battle of Falkirk Muir: 17 January 1746* (Edinburgh: John Donald Publishers, 1996).

7.   M. Margulies, *The Battle of Prestonpans, 1745* (Stroud: Tempus, 2007).

8.   K. Tomasson and F. Buist, *Battles of the '45* (London: Batsford, 1962).

9.   Oates, *The Last Battle*.

10. C. Tabraham and D. Grove, *Fortress Scotland and the Jacobites* (London: Batsford, 1995).

11. R. C. Jarvis, *Collected Papers on the Jacobite Risings* (Manchester: Manchester University Press, 1971); J. D. Oates, 'Responses in North East England to the Jacobite Rebellions of 1715 and 1745' (unpublished PhD thesis, Reading University, 2001); J. D. Oates, *The Jacobite Invasion of 1745 in North West England* (Lancaster: Centre for North West Regional Studies, 2006); Oates, *The Last Battle*; J. D. Oates, 'Civil Defence in North East England During the Jacobite Rebellion of 1715', *Journal of the Society for Army Historical Research* (hereafter *JSAHR*) 80:322 (2002), pp. 86–97.

12. J. Brewer, *The Sinews of Power: War, Money and the British State, 1688–1783* (New York: Alfred Knopf, 1988); L. Stone (ed.), *An Imperial State at War* (New Haven, CT: Yale University Press, 1995).

13. J. Houlding, *Fit for Service: The Training of the British Army, 1715–1795* (Oxford: Clarendon Press, 1981); A. J. Guy, *Oeconomy and Discipline: Officership and Administration in the British Army, 1714–1763* (Manchester: Manchester University Press, 1984); A. Hayter, *The Army and the Crowd in Mid-Georgian England* (London: Macmillan, 1978); S. Brumwell, *Redcoats: The British Soldier and the War in the Americas, 1755–1763* (Cambridge: Cambridge University Press, 2002); D. Chandler, *The Art of War in the Age of Marlborough* (London: Batsford, 1975); S. Reid, *Wolfe: The Career of General James Wolfe from Culloden to Quebec* (Spellmount: Staplehurst, 2000).

14. Duffy, *The '45*, p. 25.

15. J. D. Oates, *Sweet William or the Butcher? The Duke of Cumberland and the '45* (Barnsley: Pen and Sword, 2008); Speck, *The Butcher*; Reid, *1745: A Military History*.

16. J. Black, *War and the World, 1450–2000* (New Haven, CT: Yale University Press, 2000), p. 133.

17. Duffy, *The '45*, p. 313; McLynn, *The Jacobite Army*, pp. 130–1.

18. G. Holmes, *The Making of a Great Power, 1660–1722* (London: Longman, 1993), pp. 432–3; and D. Szechi and G. Holmes, *England in the Age of Oligarchy, 1722–1783* (London: Longman, 1993).

19. Holmes, *Great Power*, pp. 432–3, 439.

20. Ibid., p. 439.

21. J. Home, *The History of the Rebellion in the Year 1745* (London: T. Cadell, jun. & W. Davies, 1802), p. 2.

1 Raising the Men

1.   Reid, *Wolfe*, pp. 8–13.

2.   R. Holmes, *Redcoat* (London: Harper Collins, 2001), pp. 157–8.

3.   Ibid., p. 159.

4.   Reid, *Wolfe*, p. 14.

5.   Holmes, *Redcoat*, p. 161.

6.   Ibid., pp. 163, 167–8.

7.   Reid, Wolfe, p. 18.

8.   Ibid., p. 21.

9.   Ibid., pp. 22–3.

10. F. Pottle (ed.), *Boswell's London Journal, 1762–1763* (London: William Heinemann, 1950), p. 137.

11. Anon., *The Case of Lieutenant John Kynaston* (London, *c.*1716), p. 3.

12. H. Fielding, *Tom Jones* (Harmondsworth: Penguin, 2005), p. 330.

13. Irwin to Newcastle, 28 February 1746, British Library Additional Manuscripts (hereafter BL Add. Mss) 32706, f. 231r; Chesterfield to Newcastle, 19 April 1746, National Archives (hereafter TNA), State Papers (hereafter SP) 36/83, f. 109r.

14. Reid, *Wolfe*, pp. 24–6.

15. R. Sedgwick, *Lord Hervey's Memoirs* (Harmondsworth: Penguin Books, 1961), p. 123.

16. Holmes, *Redcoat*, p. 176.

17. Ibid., pp. 176–8; Reid, *Wolfe*, p. 14.

18. Fielding, *Tom Jones*, p. 331.

19. Holmes, *Redcoat*, p. 54.

20. W. J. Hardy (ed.), *Calendar of Middlesex Sessions, 1689–1709*, (London: Sir Richard Nicholson, 1905), p. 269.

21. Ibid., p. 151.

22. Holmes, *Redcoat*, p. 139.

23. J. C. Atkinson (ed.), 'Quarter Session Records', *North Riding Record Society*, 8 (1890) pp. 247, 256–7; W. Le Hardy (ed.), *Hertfordshire Sessions Rolls, 1699–1850* (Hertford, 1905), pp. 48, 61, 98, 99.

24. D. Chandler (ed.), *Oxford History of the British Army* (Oxford: Oxford University Press, 2002), p. 75.

25. Reid, *Wolfe*, p. 83.

26. J. S Arnot and B. Seton, *The Prisoners of the '45* (Edinburgh: Scottish History Society, 1928–9), vol. 1, p. 33.

27. Ibid.

28. Ibid., p. 36.

29. J. Miller, 'Diary of James Miller', *JSAHR*, 1 (1922), pp. 10–11.

30. Irwin to Newcastle, 28 February 1746, BL Add. Mss. 32706, f. 232v.

31. Meeting of county committee, 24 October 1745, Hertfordshire Record Office (hereafter HRO), D/EP, f. 266.

32. Marching orders, 5 October 1745, TNA, SP 36/70, f. 173r; *London Gazette*, 24 September, 1 October 1745.

33. Gower to Congreve, 13 October 1745, William Salt Library (hereafter WSL), S.MS.521.

34. Gower to Congreve, 19 November 1745, WSL, S.MS.522.

35. W. S. Lewis (ed.), *Horace Walpole's Correspondence: Walpole to Mann, 1745–1748* (New Haven, CT: Yale University Press, 1954), vol. 19, pp. 153–4.

36. George II to Congreve, 4 October 1745, WSL, SMS47/18/10/2.

37. Hardy, *Middlesex*, p. 307.

38. Ibid., p. 324

39. Ibid., p. 279

40. Ibid., p. 324.

41. Ibid., p. 128

42. Ibid., p. 268.

43. Ibid., p. 352.

44. A. J. Guy (ed.), *Colonel Samuel Bagshawe and the Army of George II, 1731–1762* (London: Bodley Head, 1990), pp. 210–2.

45. List of enlisted men, 1745, HRO, MIL 4/16; enlisted men to Cooper, 15 May 1746, HRO, MIL 3/91.

46. Hardy, *Middlesex*, p. 324.

47. A. Cormack and A. Jones (eds), *The Journal of Corporal Todd, 1745–1762* (London: Bodley Head, 2001), p. 12.

48. Reid, *Wolfe*, p. 84.
49. Cormack and Jones, *The Journal of Corporal Todd*, p. 6.
50. Holmes, *Redcoat*, p. 141–2.
51. Ibid., p. 144.
52. Ibid., pp. 144–5; Lewis, *Walpole's Correspondence*, vol. 37, p. 125.
53. Holmes, *Redcoat*, p. 145.
54. Ibid., pp. 142–3.
55. Ibid., p. 149.
56. Le Hardy, *Hertfordshire*, pp. 32, 337.
57. Holmes, *Redcoat*, p. 149.
58. Fielding, *Tom Jones*, p. 328.
59. Ibid., p. 329.
60. M. Beresford (ed.), *The Diary of James Woodforde* (Oxford: Oxford University Press, 1986), p. 143.
61. D. Gibson, *A Parson in the Vale of the White Horse, 1753–1761* (Gloucester: Sutton, 1982), p. 68.
62. Route of march, 25 April 1733, TNA, War Office (hereafter WO) 5/30, f. 420.
63. Reid, *Wolfe*, pp. 86–7.
64. Cormack and Jones, *The Journal of Corporal Todd*, pp. 10–11.
65. *Gentleman's Magazine*, 9, p. 83.
66. Reid, *Wolfe*, pp. 87–8.
67. *Articles of War* (London, 1745), p. xxi.
68. Reid, *Wolfe*, pp. 110–15.
69. Jones and Cormack, *The Journal of Corporal Todd*, p. 13.
70. George II to Congreve, 4 October 1745, WSL, SMS47/18/10/2.
71. Gower to Congreve, 19 November 1745, WSL, S.MS. 522.
72. Holmes, *Redcoat*, p. 48.
73. Houlding, *Fit for Service*, p. 87.
74. Arnold to officer in charge of Grove's regiment, 28 September 1733, TNA, WO 5/30, ff. 484–5.
75. Houlding, *Fit for Service*, p. 60.
76. Townshend to Aston, 19 June 1715, TNA, SP 44/116, f. 307.
77. *Gentleman's Magazine*, 8, p. 658.
78. Ibid. 10, pp. 355, 356.
79. *Flying Post*, 3719, 12–14 January 1716.
80. Wyvill to Townshend, 25 June 1715, TNA, SP 35/2, ff. 204r–5r.
81. Forbes to ?, 26 June 1725, TNA, SP 54/15, f. 28.
82. W. Coxe (ed.), *Memoirs of the Life and Administration of Sir Robert Walpole, Earl of Oxford* (London, 1798), vol. 3, p. 349.
83. Houlding, *Fit for Service*, pp. 83, 87.
84. Strickland to officer in charge of Evans' Dragoons, 28 March 1733, TNA, WO 5/30, f. 277.
85. *Gentleman's Magazine*, 15, p. 218.
86. Jones and Cormack, *The Journal of Corporal Todd*, p. 10.
87. *Gentleman's Magazine*, 14, p. 334.
88. Ibid., 5, p. 498.
89. Ibid., 14, p. 276.
90. Ibid., p. 107.

91. Strickland to officers, 15 March 1730, TNA, WO 5/30, f. 1.

92. Strickland to officers, 20 May 1730, TNA, WO 5/30, f. 5; and same to same, 15 May 1730, TNA, WO 5/30, f. 3.

93. Beresford, *The Diary of James Woodforde*, p. 281.

94. Pottle, *Boswell's*, p. 229.

95. M. G. Hobson (ed.), *Oxford Council Acts*, 1701–1752 (Oxford: Oxford University Press, 1954), p. 326.

96. A. Saville (ed.), *Secret Comment: The Diaries of Gertrude Saville, 1722–1757* (Nottingham: Thoroton Society, 1997), pp. 30, 44.

97. Ibid., p. 28.

98. Houlding, *Fit for Service*, p. 19.

2 The Army on Campaign

1. D. Chandler, *Marlborough as Military Commander* (London: Batsford, 1973), p. 63.

2. *Political State of Great Britain* (1717), vol. 13, pp. 606–10.

3. J. Hussey, *Marlborough: Hero of Blenheim* (London: Weidenfeld & Nicholson, 2004), p. 63.

4. List of regiments, 1715, BL Stowe Mss 228, f. 125r.

5. Intelligence, 1 October 1715, TNA, SP 54/9, f. 2D.

6. P. Rae, *History of the Late Rebellion* (London, 1745), p. 171.

7. Royal Commission on Historical Manuscripts, *The Manuscipts of Marquess Townshend* (London: HMSO, 1887), p. 176 (hereafter *HMC Townshend*).

8. Whitman to ?, 16 August 1715, TNA, SP 54/7, f. 46.

9. Whitman to ?, 23 August 1715, TNA, SP 54/7, f. 65.

10. Rae, *History*, p. 65.

11. Argyll to Townshend, 14 September 1715, National Archives of Scotland (hereafter NAS) GD244/624, 11/9.

12. Argyll to Townshend, 13 September 1715, TNA, SP 54/8, f. 49.

13. Same to same, 12 September 1715, TNA, SP 54/8, f. 68.

14. Same to same, 21 September 1715, TNA, SP 54/8, f. 80a.

15. Same to same, 26 September 1715, TNA, SP 54/8, f. 105.

16. Same to same, 28 September 1715, TNA, SP 54/8, f. 111.

17. Same to same, 18 October 1715, TNA, SP 54/9, f. 30.

18. Same to same, 4 November 1715, TNA, SP 54/10, f. 18a.

19. Argyll to Pulteney, November 1715, NAS, GD244/624, 71.

20. Lewis, *Walpole's Correspondence*, vol. 30, p. 94.

21. R. F. Bell (ed.), *Memorials of John Murray of Broughton, Sometime Secretary to Prince Charles Edward 1740–1747* (Edinburgh: Scottish History Society, 1898), p. 180; J. Marchant, *History of the Present Rebellion* (London, 1746), p. 71.

22. G. Wade, C. Cadogan, J. Folliot, C. Lennox and J. Guise, *A Report of the Proceedings and Opinion of the Board of General Officers, on Their Examination into the Conduct, Behaviour and Proceedings of Lieutenant-General Sir John Cope, Knight of the Bath, Colonel Peregrine Lascelles, and Brigadier-General Thomas Fowkes* (Dublin, 1749), pp. 11, 9.

23. Lewis, *Walpole's Correspondence*, vol. 30, pp. 91, 94.

24. T. J. McCann (ed.), *The Correspondence of the Dukes of Richmond and Newcastle, 1724–1750* (Lewes: Sussex Record Society, 1983), p. 174.

25. Newcastle to Cumberland, 26 July 1745, TNA, SP 36/66, ff. 325r–326r; Newcastle to Cumberland, 2 August 1745, TNA, SP 36/67, f. 21r.

26. McCann, The *Correspondence*, p. 172.

27. Ibid., p. 174.

28. J. Fortescue, *The History of the British Army* (London: Macmillan, 1898), vol. 2, pp. 122–3.

29. Cumberland to Newcastle, 6 September 1745, BL Add. Mss 32705, f. 113r.

30. McCann, The *Correspondence*, pp. 176, 178.

31. Ibid., p. 179.

32. Cumberland to Newcastle, 20 September 1745, BL Add. Mss 32705, ff. 155r–156v.

33. Committee, 20 September 1745, BL Add. Mss 33004, f. 85v–r.

34. Ibid., f. 87v.

35. Ibid., ff. 86r–87r.

36. Marchant, *History*, pp. 71, 150, 186.

37. McCann, The *Correspondence*, p. 178.

38. Marchant, *History*, p. 70.

39. Cumberland to Newcastle, 30 November 1745, TNA, SP 36/75, ff. 201r–202v.

40. Return of troops under Wade, October 1745, TNA, SP 36/70, f. 215r.

41. Newcastle to Cholmondeley, 13 November 1745, TNA, SP 36/73, f. 326r; 75; Cumberland to Newcastle, 29 November 1745, TNA, SP 36/73, f. 131r; Cumberland to Newcastle, 30 November 1745, SP36/73, f. 201r; Newcastle to Montagu, 9 November 1745, SP 44/133, f. 2; J. Ray, *A Compleat History of the Rebellion from Its Rise in 1745, to Its Total Suppression in the Glorious Battle of Culloden, in April 1746* (1754), p. 138.

42. Wade et al., *Proceedings*, p. 7.

43. Fortescue, *The History*, vol. 2, p. 139.

44. Bell, *Memorials*, pp. 166, 180.

45. Cumberland to Newcastle, 30 January 1746, TNA, SP 54/27, f. 55A.

46. Argyll to Marlborough, 7 October 1715, BL Add. Mss 61136, f. 195r.

47. Home, *The History*, p. 26.n.

48. Hussey, *Marlborough*, p. 63.

49. R. Hatton, *George I: Elector and King* (Cambridge, MA: Harvard University Press, 1978), pp. 105–6, 124–5, 181.

50. Rae, *History*, p. 207.

51. *Political State of Great Britain* (1715), vol. 10, p. 411.

52. Ibid., p. 412.

53. Argyll to Stanhope, 27 November 1715, TNA, SP 54/10, f. 86A.

54. *Political State of Great Britain* (1717), vol. 13, pp. 702–4.

55. Ibid. (1719), vol. 18, pp. 411–2.

56. Home, *The History*, p. 13.

57. Newcastle to Trevor, 13 August 1745, Buckinghamshire Record Office (hereafter BRO), D/MH TP Bundle 50.

58. J. D. Oates, 'Dutch Forces in Eighteenth Century Britain: A British Perspective', *Journal of the Society for Army Historical Research*, 85:341 (2007), pp. 20–39, at pp. 30–1.

59. Return of forces under Wade, October 1745, TNA, SP 36/70, f. 215r.

60. Malton to Newcastle, 16 September 1745, TNA, SP 36/68, f. 78r.

61. McCann, The *Correspondence*, p. 179.

62. Trevor to Newcastle, 31 December 1745, BRO, D/MH TP Bundle 53.

63. List of troops, BRO, Bundle 54, D/MH January –February 1746.

64. Richmond to Newcastle, 7 December 1745, BL Add. Mss 32705, f. 423r; Rae, *History*, p. 215.
65. List of troops, BRO, Bundle 54, D/MH January –February 1746.
66. Pulteney to Carpenter, 14 October 1715, TNA, SP 44/177, f. 114.
67. Stanhope to Wills, 5 November 1715, TNA, SP 44/117, f. 309.
68. *HMC Townshend*, p. 163.
69. Rae, *History, p.* 328.
70. Newcastle to Wade, 7 November 1745, TNA, SP 36/73, f. 134v.
71. Same to same, 9 November 1745, TNA, SP 36/73, f. 190r.
72. Same to Cumberland, 25 November 1745, TNA, SP 36/75, ff. 10r–11v.
73. Same to same, 4 February 1746, Royal Archives, Cumberland Papers (Microfilm), (here-after RA, CP(M)), 10/162.
74. Townshend to Argyll, 3 January 1716, Townshend Papers, f. 69r, University of Leeds, Brotherton Library (hereafter, ULBL).
75. *HMC Townshend*, p. 176.
76. *Flying Post*, 3708, 8–11 October 1715.
77. Argyll to Stanhope, 1 October 1715, TNA, SP 54/9, f. 2a.
78. Pulteney to Carpenter, 14 October 1715, TNA, SP 44/117, f. 114.
79. ? to Cope, 17 August 1745, TNA, SP 54/25, f. 79a.
80. Townshend to Argyll, December 1715, ULBL, Townshend Papers, f. 60v.
81. Rae, *History*, p. 215.
82. *Flying Post*, 3708, 8–11 October 1715
83. *HMC Townshend*, p. 163.
84. Rae, *History*, p. 170.
85. Stanhope to Argyll, 26 September 1715, ULBL, Townshend Papers, f. 12r.
86. Rae, *History*, p. 170.
87. *St. James Evening Post*, 84, 10–13 December 1715.
88. Rae, *History*, p. 215–6.
89. *Flying Post*, 3708, 8–11 October 1715.
90. Ibid., 3715, 25–27 October 1715; 3717, 29 Oct– 1 November 1715.
91. Rae, *History*, pp. 216–7.
92. *HMC Townshend*, p. 176.
93. Pulteney to colonels, 13 October 1715, TNA, WO 4/17, f. 325.
94. Townshend to Argyll, 4 October 1715, ULBL, Townshend, f. 19v.
95. Stanhope to Argyll, 11 October 1715, ULBL, Townshend, f. 24v.
96. Townshend to Argyll, November 1715, ULBL, Townshend, f. 43r.
97. Argyll to Marlborough, 7 October 1715, BL Add. Mss 61136, f. 195r.
98. S. Cowper (ed.), *The Diary of Lady Cowper* (London: John Murray, 1865), pp. 58–9.
99. Ibid., p. 58.
100. W. E. Matthews (ed.), *Diary of Dudley Ryder, 1715–1716* (London: Methuen & Co., 1939), p. 103.
101. Rae, *History*, p. 328.
102. Ibid., p. 363.
103. *Whitehall Evening Post*, 81, 21–4 March 1719.
104. *Worcester Postman*, 510, 27 March – 3 April 1719.
105. *Weekly Journal*, 14 March 1719.
106. Yonge and Lloyd to officers in charge of regiments, 11 –12 December 1745, TNA, WO 5/37, ff. 220–54.
107. Newcastle to Argyll, 1 August 1745, TNA, SP 54/25, f. 38.

108. Cope to Tweeddale, 3 August 1745, TNA, SP 54/25, f. 44.
109. Wade et al., *Proceedings*, p. 5.
110. *Gentleman's Magazine*, 15, p. 441, 443.
111. McCann, *The Correspondence*, p. 172.
112. Wade et al., Proceedings, p. 5.
113. Tweeddale to Cope, 16 August 1745, TNA, SP 54/27, f. 63a.
114. Tweeddale to Harrington, 16 August 1745, TNA, SP 54 /27, f. 74a.
115. Wade et al., *Proceedings*, pp. 8, 9.
116. *Gentleman's Magazine*, 15, p. 519.
117. Committee, 20 September 1745, BL Add. Mss 33004, ff. 83r–84v.
118. Newcastle to Handasyde, 28 September 1745, TNA, SP 36/69, f. 207v.
119. Same to same, 28 September 1745, TNA, SP 36/69, f. 206r.
120. Wentworth to Newcastle, 4 October 1745, TNA, SP 70, f. 118v; same to same, 5 October 1745, TNA, SP 36/70, f. 201r.
121. Newcastle to Wade, 6 October 1745, TNA, SP 36/70, f. 217r; Wentworth to Newcastle, 6 October 1745, TNA, SP 36/70, f. 224v.
122. Committee, 26 September 1745, BL Add. Mss 33004, ff. 90r–91r.
123. Newcastle to Huske, 24 September 1745, TNA, SP 36/69, ff. 25r–26r.
124. Committee, 24 September 1745, BL Add. Mss 33004, ff. 87r–88v.
125. Committee, 26 September 1745, BL Add. Mss 33004, f. 89v–r.
126. Committee, 26 September 1745, BL Add. Mss 33004, f. 92v.
127. Committee, 30 September 1745, BL Add. Mss 33004, f. 93r.
128. Newcastle to Cumberland, 21 March 1746, BL Add. Mss 32706, f. 325r.
129. Committee, 24 September 1745, BL Add. Mss 33004, f. 87v.
130. McCann, *The Correspondence*, p. 193.
131. Ibid., p. 197; Units for the defence of London, December 1745, RA, CP (M) 7/236.
132. McCann, *The Correspondence*, p. 198.
133. Ibid., p. 198.
134. Ibid., p. 195.
135. Hobson, *Oxford Council Acts*, p. 325.
136. 'Diary of John Lucas', p. 5, Leeds Local Studies Library (hereafter LLSL).
137. W. Brockbank, and F. Kenworthy (eds), *Diary of Dr Richard Kay, 1716–1751 of Baldingstone, Near Bury, a Lancaster Doctor* (Manchester: Chetham Society, 1968), p. 104.
138. Matthews (ed.), *Diary*, p. 80.
139. Newcastle to Wade, 2 November 1745, TNA, SP 36/73, f. 17v.
140. Newcastle to Wade, 11 October 1745, National Library of Scotland (hereafter NLS), ms 302, ff. 36v–37v.
141. Newcastle to Oglethorpe, 19 November 1745, TNA, SP 36/74, ff. 58r–59v; Newcastle to Handasyde, 23 October 1745, TNA, SP 36/72, f. 174v.
142. Carpenter to ?, 21 October 1715, TNA, SP 54/9, f. 63a.
143. *St. James' Evening Post*, 72, 12–15 November 1715.
144. Cope to Newcastle, 24 September 1745, TNA, SP 36/69, f. 5r.; Wade to Cope, 3 November 1745, NLS, Mss 16612, f. 68r.
145. Cope to Newcastle, 28 September 1745, TNA, SP 36/69, f. 163r.
146. J. Maxwell, *Narrative of Charles Prince of Wales' Expedition to Scotland in the Year 1745* (Edinburgh: T. Constable, 1841), p. 71.
147. *Gentleman's Magazine*, 15, p. 443.

148. Yorke, P. C. (ed.), *The Life and Correspondence of Philip Yorke, Earl of Hardwicke, Lord Chancellor of Great Britain Hardwicke* (Cambridge: Cambridge University Press, 1913), vol. 1, p. 519.
149. Postmasters to Newcastle, 25 September 1745, TNA, SP 36/69, ff. 63r, 84r.
150. G. C. Mounsey, *Carlisle in 1745*, (London, 1846), p. 58.
151. Waugh to Newcastle, 14 September 1745, TNA, SP 36/68, f. 47r; same to same, 26 September 1745, TNA, SP 36/69, f. 108r; same to same, 26 September 1745, TNA, SP 36/69, f. 272r; Gilpin to Newcastle, 7 October 1745, TNA, SP 36/70, f. 242r.
152. Waugh to Newcastle, 9 November 1745, TNA, SP 36/73, f. 208r.
153. Cholmondeley to Newcastle, 21 October 1745, TNA, SP 36/72, f. 102r; same to same, 28 October 1745, TNA, SP 36/72, f. 327r.
154. Oates, *The Jacobite Invasion*, p. 72.
155. Craggs to Postmaster General, 31 March 1719, TNA, SP 44/119, f. 270.
156. W. Blaikie (ed.), *Origins of the 'Forty-Five and Other Papers Relating to That Rising* (Edinburgh: Scottish History Society, 1916), p. 400.
157. Bracken to Newcastle, 14 November 1745, TNA, SP 36/76, ff. 157r–158v.
158. J. M. Ellis (ed.), *The Letters of Henry Liddell to William Cotesworth* (Durham: Surtees Society, 1985), p.179.
159. W. D. Dickson (ed.), *Warrender Letters: Correspondence of Sir George Warrender, Bt., Lord Provost of Edinburgh, and Member of Parliament for the City, with Relative Papers, 1715* (Edinburgh: Scottish History Society, 1935), pp. 98–9.
160. Townshend to Cotesworth, 13 October 1715, TNA, SP 44/118, f. 67.
161. *Gentleman's Magazine*, 15, p. 602.
162. Wade et al., *Proceedings*, p. 6.
163. Anon., *History of the Rebellion of the Years 1715 and 1745* (Oxford: Roxburgh Club, 1944), p. 196.
164. Yorke (ed.), *Hardwicke*, vol. 1, p. 500.
165. Cumberland to Newcastle, 25 February 1746, TNA, SP 54/28, f. 43a.
166. Wade to Newcastle, 7 and 12 November 1745, TNA, SP 36/73, ff. 294v, 295r.
167. Cope to Newcastle, 28 September 1745, TNA, SP 36/69, f. 102r.
168. Argyll to Townshend, 21 October 1715, TNA, SP 54/9, f. 69.
169. Waugh to Newcastle, 7 November 1745, TNA, SP 36/73, f. 150r.
170. Argyll to Stanhope, 4 October 1715, TNA, SP 54/9, f. 6A.
171. Townshend to Argyll, September 1715, f1r, Townshend, ULBL.
172. *Calendar of Treasury Books, XXIX, Part 2, 1714–1715*, (London: HMSO, 1957), p. 727.
173. Argyll to Stanhope, 1 October 1715, TNA, SP 54/9, f. 2A.
174. Pulteney to Argyll, 5 January 1716, TNA, WO 4/18, f. 6.
175. Yonge to Wade, 2 October 1745, NLS, ms 302, f. 2r.
176. Yonge to Wade, 19 October 1745, TNA, WO 4/41, f. 25.
177. Wade to Pelham, 17 October 1745, Nottingham University Library (hereafter NUL), NeC1691.
178. Expenditure by Wade, 1745, NUL, NeC 1695; Wade to Pelham, 17 October 1745, NUL, NeC, 1691; Wade's expenditure, 1745, NLS, Ms302, f. 4r.
179. Wentworth to Newcastle, 12 October 1745, NUL, NeC 1673.
180. Wentworth to Newcastle, 17 October 1745, NUL, NeC, 1672.
181. Herdman to Teller, 17 November 1745, HRO, MIL3/68.
182. Hawley to Newcastle, January 1746, TNA, SP 54/27, f. 25.

183. Wade to Newcastle, 1745, TNA, SP 36/71, f. 23r.
184. Cumberland to Newcastle, 10 February 1746, TNA, SP 54/28, f. 20A.
185. Same to same, 5 March 1746, TNA, SP 54/29, f. 3A.
186. Same to same, 5 March 1746, TNA, SP 54/29, f. 3A.
187. Cumberland to Newcastle, 14 February 1746, TNA, SP 54/28, f. 24a.
188. Sawyer to Fawkener, February 1746, TNA, SP 54/29/34H; Newcastle to Cumberland, 22 February 1746, TNA, SP 54/29, f. 38.
189. Cumberland to Newcastle, 3 March 1746, RA, CP (M) 13/269.
190. Wade et al., *Proceedings*, p. 8.
191. Newcastle to Pulteney, 20 December 1745, TNA, SP 44/133, f. 33.
192. Chandler, *Marlborough*, pp. 74–5.
193. *Gentleman's Magazine*, 15, p. 518.
194. Yorke (ed.), *Hardwicke*, vol. 1, p. 447.
195. Wade et al., *Proceedings*, p. 8.
196. Ibid., p. 21.
197. Hawley to Newcastle, 24 January 1746, TNA, SP 54/28, ff. 41, 41F.
198. *Gentleman's Magazine*, 15, p. 519.
199. Yorke (ed.), *Hardwicke*, vol. 1, p. 467.
200. Ibid., p. 496.
201. Cumberland to Newcastle, 5 March 1746, RA, CP (M) 11/236.
202. Wade to Newcastle, 31 October 1745, RA, CP (M) 6/160.
203. Yorke (ed.), *Hardwicke*, vol. 1, p. 510.
204. Anon., *A Journey through Part of England and Scotland. Along with the Army under the Command of His Royal Highness the Duke of Cumberland* (London: J. Stanton, 1746), p. 13.
205. Ibid., p. 51.
206. Ibid., p. 103.
207. Bradshaw to brother, 11 May 1746, RA, CP (M) 14/385.
208. Wade to Newcastle, 20 December 1745, TNA, SP 44/133, f. 33.
209. Cumberland to Newcastle, 14 February 1746, SP 54/28, f. 24a.
210. Wade to same, 20 December 1745, TNA, SP 44/133, f. 33.
211. Newcastle to Pulteney, 4 November 1745, TNA, SP 44/133, f. 1.
212. Newcastle to Pulteney, 15 December 1745, TNA, SP 44/133, f. 26.
213. Yonge to Corbett, 21 October 1745, TNA, WO 4/41, ff. 20, 25; same to Wade, 19 October 1745, TNA, SP 44/133, f. 25; same to same, 7 November 1745, TNA, SP 44/133, f. 50; Yonge to Montagu, 19 November 1745, TNA, SP 44/133, f. 101.
214. Congreve to Congreve, 11 November 1745, Staffordshire Record Office, D1057/M/1/12/2–6; Gower to Chetwynd, 16 November 1745, WSL, S.MS.520.
215. *General Evening Post*, 1896, 19–21 November 1745.
216. Gower to Congreve, 19 November 1745, WSL, S.MS.522.
217. Cadogan to ?, 3 January 1716, TNA, SP 54/11, f. 5.
218. Argyll to Townshend, 10 December 1715, TNA, SP 54/10, f. 119; same to same, 24 December 1715, TNA, SP 54/10, f. 150; same to same, 29 December 1715, TNA, SP 54/10, f. 165.
219. Rae, *History*, p. 362.
220. Argyll to Townshend, 3 January 1716, TNA, SP 54/11, f. 7A.
221. Newcastle to Montagu, 25 September 1745, TNA, SP 44/132, f. 415; same to same, 6 October 1745, TNA, SP 44/132, f. 420.
222. Newcastle to Montagu, 9 November 1745, TNA, SP 44/133, f. 2.

223. Hawley to Montagu, 7 January 1746, TNA, SP 44/133, f. 51; Newcastle to Montagu, 11 January 1746, TNA, SP 44/133, f. 55.
224. Newcastle to Montagu, 26 March 1746, TNA, SP 44/133, f. 112.
225. Yorke (ed.), *Hardwicke*, vol. 1, pp. 467–8.
226. Royal Commission on Historical Manuscripts, *Report on Manuscripts in Various Collections*, vol 8 (London: HMSO, 1913), p. 141 (hereafter *HMC Var. Coll.*).
227. Anon., *A Journey*, p. 14.
228. Magistrates to Cumberland, 11 December 1745, RA, CP (M) 8/4; Fawkener to magistrates, 12 December 1745, RA, CP (M) 8/22; Fawkener to Newcastle, 15 December 1745, RA, CP (M) 8/37a.
229. Magistrates to Cumberland, 18 December 1745, RA, CP (M) 8/63.
230. T. A. Coward, *Picturesque Cheshire* (Sherratt and Hughes, London, 1903), p. 366.
231. Anon., 'Culloden Letter', *Journal of the Society for Army Historical Research*, 35 (1957), pp. 183–5 (p.184).
232. Wade et al., *Proceedings*, p. 8.
233. Yorke (ed.), *Hardwicke*, vol. 1, p. 458.
234. McCann, *The Correspondence, p.* 196.
235. Argyll to Marlborough, 7 October 1715, BL Add. Mss 61136, f. 195r.
236. Cumberland to Newcastle, 2 February 1746, TNA, SP 54/28, f. 4.
237. Newcastle to Cumberland, 8 February 1746, TNA, SP 54/28, f. 13.
238. Committee, 26 September 1745, BL Add. Mss, 33004, f. 92v.
239. *Newcastle Journal*, 341, 19 October 1745.
240. Northumberland Record Office (hereafter, NRO), QSO8, p. 143.
241. *Newcastle Courant*, 2712, 7–14 December 1745.
242. Wade to Newcastle, 4 December 1745, TNA, SP 36/76, f. 228v.
243. Wade to Newcastle, 15 November 1745, TNA, SP 36/ 73, f. 369r.
244. Yorke (ed.), *Hardwicke*, vol. 1, p. 468.
245. Wade et al., *Proceedings*, pp. 17, 19, 22–3.
246. Yorke (ed.), *Hardwicke*, vol. 1, p. 471.
247. Anon., 'Culloden Letter', p. 184.
248. Hawley to Newcastle, 15 January 1746, RA, CP (M) 9/81.
249. Wade et al., *Proceedings*, p. 8.
250. Newcastle to Wade, 23 November 1745, TNA, SP 36/74, f. 210v.
251. P. McNiven (ed.), *Diary of Henry Prescott, LL.B., Deputy Registrar of Chester Diocese* (Record Society of Lancashire and Cheshire, 1994), vol. 3, p. 781.
252. Ibid., p. 785.
253. Wade to Newcastle, 19 December 1745, TNA, SP 36/77, f. 389r.
254. Bland to Richmond, 27 November 1745, RA, CP (M) 8/149.
255. Oglethorpe to Newcastle, 26 October 1745, TNA, SP 36/72, f. 291r.
256. Anon., *A Journey*, p. 10.
257. *General Evening Post*, 1896, 19–21 November 1745.
258. Hawley to Newcastle, 17 January 1746, TNA, SP 54/27, f. 31.
259. Wade to Newcastle, 19 December 1746, TNA, SP 36/77, f. 390r.
260. *Gentleman's Magazine*, 15, p. 518.
261. Yorke (ed.), *Hardwicke*, vol. 1, p. 473.
262. W. H. Anderson (ed.), 'The Battle of Culloden', *Journal of the Society for Army Historical Research*, 1 (1921), p. 24.
263. Yorke (ed.), *Hardwicke*, vol. 1, p. 471.

264. McCann, *The Correspondence*, p. 193.
265. Cumberland to Newcastle, 8 April 1746, RA, CP (M) 13/294.
266. *Gentleman's Magazine*, 16, p. 219.
267. Ibid., p. 23.
268. Ibid., p. 204.
269. Ibid., p. 209.
270. Yorke (ed.), *Hardwicke*, vol. 1, p. 476.
271. *Gentleman's Magazine*, 15, p. 624.
272. McCann, *The Correspondence*, p. 198.
273. Yorke (ed.), *Hardwicke*, vol. 1, p. 468.
274. Ibid., p. 473.
275. Anon., *A Journey*, p. 14.
276. McCann, *The Correspondence*, p. 196.
277. Argyll to Townsend, 4 November 1715, TNA, SP 54/10, f. 18a.
278. Same to same, 19 January 1716, TNA, SP 54/11, f. 41.
279. Same to same, 25 January 1716, TNA, SP 54/11, f. 57.
280. Same to same, 4 February 1716, TNA, SP 54/11, f. 89.
281. Same to same, 30 January 1716, TNA, SP 54/11, f. 68.
282. Yorke (ed.), *Hardwicke*, vol. 1, p. 510.
283. Wade to Newcastle, 28 November 1745, TNA, SP 36/75, f. 97v.
284. Rae, *History*, p. 326.
285. Yorke (ed.), *Hardwicke*, vol. 1, p. 511.
286. Rae, *History*, pp. 327–8.
287. Ibid., p. 232.
288. Ibid., pp. 294–5.
289. Ibid., p. 241.
290. *Gentleman's Magazine*, 16, p. 146.
291. Ibid., pp. 148–9.
292. Ibid., p. 205.
293. Yorke (ed.), *Hardwicke*, vol. 1, p. 515.
294. Lewis, *Walpole's Correspondence*, 37, p. 227–8.
295. Yorke (ed.), *Hardwicke*, vol. 1, p. 475.
296. Anon., 'Culloden Letter', p. 183.
297. Anon., *A Journey*, p. 11.
298. Lewis, *Walpole's Correspondence*, 19, p. 174.
299. Anon., 'Culloden Letter', pp. 183–4.
300. Newcastle to Hawley, 24 January 1746, TNA, SP 54/27, f. 42.
301. Blaikie, *Origins*, p. 159.
302. Cumberland to Newcastle, 30 January 1746, NAS, GD103/2/387.
303. J. H. Findlay, *Wolfe in Scotland* (London: Longmans & Green & Co., 1928), pp. 103–4.
304. Tyrawley to Newcastle, 5 November 1745, NUL, NeC 1707/2.
305. Tyrawley to Newcastle, 1 November 1745, TNA, SP 36/75, f. 1r.
306. Yorke (ed.), *Hardwicke*, vol. 1, p. 473.
307. Wade to Newcastle, 5 December 1745, TNA, SP 36/ 76, f. 167r.
308. Wade to Newcastle, 31 October 1745, RA, CP (M) 6/160.
309. McCann, *The Correspondence*, p. 196.
310. Tyrawley to Newcastle, 5 November 1745, NUL, NeC 1707/2.

311. Cowper, *The Diary of Lady Cowper*, p. 109.

312. Wade to Newcastle, 7 November 1745, TNA, SP 36/73, f. 130r.

313. Wade to Newcastle, 15 November 1745, TNA, SP 36/73, f. 369r.

314. *Gentleman's Magazine*, 15, p. 518.

315. Wade to Newcastle, 10 November 1745, TNA, SP 36/73, f. 294r.

316. Lewis, *Walpole's Correspondence*, vol. 30, pp. 214–5.

317. J. D. Oates, 'Hessian Forces Employed in Scotland in 1746', *JSAHR*, 83:335 (2005), pp. 205–214, at pp. 210–2.

318. Duffy, *The '45*, p. 128.

319. G. F. C. Hepburne Scott (ed.), 'Marchmont Correspondence Relating to the '45', *Miscellany of the Scottish History Society* (Edinburgh: Scottish History Society, 1933), vol. 5, p. 343.

320. *HMC Townshend*, p. 165.

321. Royal Commission on Historical Manuscripts, *Calendar of the Stuart Papers Belonging to His Majesty the King* (London: HMSO, 1902), vol. 1, pp. 438–9 (hereafter *HMC Stuart Papers*).

322. Robert to William Cotesworth, 2 June 1716, Tyne and Wear Archive Service (hereafter TWAS), CP3/22.

323. Maxwell, *Narrative*, p. 16.

324. Ibid., p. 78.

325. Lord Elcho, *Short Account of the Affairs in Scotland, 1744, 1745, 1746* (Edinburgh: John Douglas Publishers Ltd, 1907), p. 302.

326. Rae, *History*, p. 171.

327. Matthews (ed.), *Diary*, pp. 61–2.

328. *Flying Post*, 3660, 18–21 June 1715.

329. Townshend to Pulteney, 30 July 1715, TNA, SP 44/116, f. 346.

330. Pulteney to Kirke, 14 February 1716, TNA, WO 4/17, ff. 334–5.

331. Berkeley to ?, October 1715, BL Add. Mss 40728, f. 97r.

332. *Weekly Journal*, 323, 4 February 1716.

333. *HMC Townshend*, p. 167.

334. Berkeley to ?, 3 September 1715, BL Add. Mss 40728, f. 27v.

335. Ibid., f. 67r; *Political State Great of Britain* (1715), vol. 10, p. 354.

336. *Flying Post*, 3694, 6–8 September 1715.

337. Diary of Tomlinson, 1717, BL Add. Mss 22560, f. 51r.

338. *Weekly Journal*, 21 March 1719.

339. *Worcester Postman*, 513, 17–24 April 1719.

340. Herring to Hardwicke, 3 November 1745, BL Add. Mss 35598, f. 108r.

341. RA, Stuart Mss. (M) 272/16; *General Advertiser*, 3444, 26 October 1745; *York Courant*, 1049, 19 November 1745; *Newcastle Courant*, 2712, 7–14 December 1745.

342. McCann, *The Correspondence*, p. 180n.

343. Elcho, *Short Account*, p. 279.

344. Arnot and Seton, *Prisoners*, vol. 1, p. 37.

345. Rae, *History*, pp. 198–200.

3 The Battle

1. Margulies, *The Battle of Prestonpans*; Bailey, *The Battle of Falkirk*; Prebble, *Culloden*; Harrington, *Culloden 1746*; Reid, *Like Hungry Wolves*; Reid, *Culloden*; Reid and Embleton, *Culloden Moor*; Sked and Horrocks, *Culloden*; Pollard, *Culloden*.
2. Baynes, *The Jacobite Rising*; Szechi, *1715*; Oates, *The Last Battle*.
3. C. Sinclair-Stevenson, *Inglorious Rebellion: The Jacobite Risings of 1708, 1715 and 1719* (London: Hamish Hamilton, 1971).
4. Chandler, *Marlborough*, p. 65.
5. Ibid., pp. 62–3.
6. Cumberland to Newcastle, 28 January 1746, TNA, SP 54/28, f. 47.
7. Cumberland to Newcastle, 30 January 1746, TNA, SP 54/28, f. 55a.
8. Cumberland to Newcastle, 28 November 1746, TNA, SP 36/75, f. 115r.
9. Hawley to Newcastle, 11 January 1746, TNA, SP 54/29, f. 18a.
10. Hawley to Cumberland, 15 January 1746, RA, CP (M) 9/81, Cumberland to Newcastle, 11 January 1746, RA, CP (M) 9/66.
11. Hawley to Cumberland, 23 January 1746, RA, CP (M) 9/134.
12. *Gentleman's Magazine*, 15, pp. 518–9.
13. J. M. Grey (ed.), *The Memoirs of the Life of John Clerk of Penicuik* (Edinburgh: Scottish History Society, 1892), p. 92; *Political State of Great Britain* (1716), vol. 11, p. 167.
14. *Weekly Journal*, 27 June 1719; Return of troops, June 1719, TNA, SP 54/13, f. 78B.
15. Return of troops, 28 October 1715, TNA, SP 54/9, f. 92; return of troops, 2 January 1716, TNA, SP 54/11, f. 2A.
16. Return of troops, 13 January 1716, TNA, SP 54/27, f. 22D.
17. Ray, *A Compleat History*, p. 345.
18. Return of troops, 2 March 1746, TNA, SP 54/29, f. 32D.
19. Hawley to Newcastle, 17 January 1746, TNA, SP 54/27, f. 29B.
20. *Gentleman's Magazine*, 16, pp. 27–8.
21. Ibid., 15, p. 598.
22. Hussey, *Marlborough*, p. 150.
23. Yorke (ed.), *Hardwicke*, vol. 1, p. 522.
24. Marchant, *History*, p. 220.
25. A. Henderson, *The Life of William Augustus, Duke of Cumberland* (London: J. Ridley, 1766), p. 253.
26. M. Hughes, *A Plain Narrative or Journal of the Late Rebellion Begun in 1745* (London, 1746), p. 40.
27. *Gentleman's Magazine*, 15, p. 638.
28. Anon., 'Culloden Letter', p. 184.
29. R. Patten, *History of the Rebellion* (London: J. Baker & T. Warner, 1717), p. 154.
30. Wade et al., *Proceedings*, p. 40.
31. Rae, *History*, p. 302.
32. Ibid., p. 303.
33. *Flying Post*, 3726, 19–22 November 1715.
34. *News Letters of 1715–1716*, p. 69.
35. *Weekly Journal*, 27 June 1719.
36. *Gentleman's Magazine*, 16, p. 210; Yorke (ed.), *Hardwicke*, vol. 1, p. 523.
37. Wade et al., *Proceedings*, p. v.
38. Henderson, *History of the Rebellion* (London, 1748), p. 31.

39. Wade et al., *Proceedings* p. 41.
40. Ibid., p. 56.
41. Ibid., p. 61.
42. Masterton to ?, 21 January 1746, TNA, SP 54/28, f. 55B.
43. T. Constable (ed.), *A Fragment of a Memoir of Field Marshal James Keith* (Edinburgh, 1843), p. 21.
44. *Gentleman's Magazine*, 16, p. 219.
45. Anderson, 'Culloden', p. 24.
46. Bradstreet to brother, 11 May 1746, RA, CP (M) 14/385.
47. *Penny London Post*, 429, 25–7 January 1746.
48. Royal Commission on Historical Manuscripts, *Report on the Manuscripts of the Late Reginald Rawdon Hastings, Esq., of the Manor House, Ashby De La Zouche* (London: HMSO, 1934), vol. 3, p. 54 (hereafter *HMC Hastings*).
49. Bradstreet to brother, 11 May 1746, RA, CP (M) 14/385.
50. Hawley to Cumberland, 23 January 1746, RA, CP (M) 9/134.
51. Cumberland to Hawley, 24 January 1746, RA, CP (M) 9/141.
52. Cumberland to Newcastle, 28 November 1745, TNA, SP 36/75, f. 115r.
53. Argyll to Townshend, 10 November 1715, TNA, SP 54/10, f. 39.
54. Yorke (ed.), *Hardwicke*, vol. 1, p. 521.
55. *Gentleman's Magazine*, 16, pp. 209–10.
56. Wade et al., *Proceedings*, p. 37.
57. Anderson, 'Culloden', p. 22.
58. Anon., 'Culloden', p. 184.
59. Lewis, *Walpole's Correspondence*, vol. 37, p. 239.
60. Rae, *History*, p. 318.
61. Patten, *History*, p. 99.
62. *Penny London Post*, 428, 25–7 January 1746.
63. Patten, *History*, p. 158.
64. Rae, *History*, p. 302.
65. Wade et al., *Proceedings*, p. 39.
66. Rae, *History*, p. 302.
67. *Gentleman's Magazine*, 15, p. 519.
68. B. Rawson (ed.), *The Chevalier de Johnstone: A Memoir of the 45* (London: Folio Society, 1958), p. 35.
69. Wade et al., *Proceedings*, p. 37.
70. Patten, *History*, p. 152.
71. Ibid., p. 160.
72. Yorke (ed.), *Hardwicke*, vol. 1, p. 522.
73. Rae, *History, p.* 304.
74. Constable, *A Fragment*, p. 18.
75. *Gentleman's Magazine*, 15, p. 521.
76. Bradstreet to brother, 11 May 1746, RA, CP (M) 14/385.
77. Patten, *History*, pp. 57, 105.
78. Account, 1715, Blair Castle, Atholl Papers, bundle 45/12/77.
79. Patten, *History*, pp. 104, 108–9.
80. Account, 1715, Atholl Papers, Bundle 45/12/77.
81. A. Carlyle, *Autobiography of the Rev. Alexander Carlyle, Minister of Inverness* (Edinburgh, 1860), p. 141.

82. Lascelles' Narrative, 1745, RA, CP (M) 9/152.
83. Hawley to Newcastle, 19 January 1746, TNA, SP 54/27, f. 32A.
84. Hawley to Newcastle, 17 January 1746, TNA, SP P54/27, f. 29b.
85. Hussey, *Marlborough*, p. 69.
86. *Gentleman's Magazine*, 15, p. 520, Elcho, *Short Account*, p. 267.
87. R. Forbes and J. Chambers (eds), *Jacobite Memoirs* (Edinburgh: William & Robert Chambers, 1834), p. 37.
88. *Gentleman's Magazine*, 15, pp. 520–1.
89. Ibid., p. 598.
90. Anderson, 'Culloden', p. 24.
91. *Gentleman's Magazine*, 15, p. 520.
92. Account of Prestonpans, 26 September 1745, TNA, SP 36/68, f. 238.
93. Wade et al., *Proceedings*, p. 54.
94. Ibid.
95. Ibid., p. 61.
96. Home, *The History*, p. 86n.
97. Wade et al., *Proceedings*, p. 54.
98. Ibid., p. 40.
99. Hawley to Cumberland, 15 January 1746, RA, CP (M) 9/81.
100. Case of Cunningham, 1746, RA, CP (M) 9/102.
101. Case of Cunningham, 1746, RA, CP (M) 9/102.
102. Ray, *A Compleat History*, p. 243; Case of Cunningham, 1746, RA, CP (M) 9/102.
103. *Penny London Post*, 428, 25–7 January 1746.
104. Case of Cunningham, 1746, RA, CP (M) 9/102.
105. Hawley to Cumberland, 15 January 1746, RA, CP (M) 9/115.
106. Anderson, 'Culloden', pp. 22–3; Anon., 'Culloden', p. 184; Yorke (ed.), *Hardwicke*, vol. 1, p. 523.
107. Maxwell, *Narrative*, p. 150.
108. Anderson, 'Culloden', p. 22.
109. Maxwell, *Narrative*, p. 152.
110. Pollard, Culloden, p. 148.
111. Anderson, 'Culloden', p. 22.
112. Rae, *History*, p. 308n.
113. Wade et al., *Proceedings*, p. 87.
114. Home, *The History*, p. 166.
115. Hussey, *Marlborough*, pp. 67–8.
116. Elcho, *Short Account*, p. 460.
117. Tayler and Tayler (eds), *The '45 and After*, p. 151.
118. Cumberland to Newcastle, 30 January 1746, TNA, SP 54/27, f. 55A.
119. Lascelles' Narrative, 1745, RA, CP (M) 9/152.
120. Henderson, *History*, p. 30.
121. Whitney to Lascelles, 11 October 1745, RA, CP (M) 6/111.
122. Anon., *A Journey*, p. 61.
123. *Gentleman's Magazine*, 15, p. 520.
124. Mounsey, *Carlisle*, p. 26.
125. Ibid., p. 27.
126. Anon., *A Journey*, p. 61.
127. Wade et al., *Proceedings*, p. 57.

128. Carlyle, *Autobiography*, pp. 153–4.
129. Maxwell, *Narrative*, p. 41.
130. Rawson (ed.), *Memoir*, pp. 87–8.
131. Grey, *Clerk of Penicuik*, p. 195.
132. Hawley to Cumberland, 17 January 1746, RA, CP (M) 9/99.
133. Cumberland to Hawley, 23 January 1746, RA, CP (M) 9/141.
134. *Gentleman's Magazine*, 16, pp. 41–2.
135. Elcho, *Short Account*, p. 272.
136. Forbes and Chambers, *Jacobite Memoirs*, p. 40.
137. Home, *The History*, p. 87.
138. Ibid.
139. Patten, *History*, pp. 153, 159.
140. Hawley to Newcastle, 17 January 1746, TNA, SP 54/27, f. 29B.
141. Hawley to January 1746, RA, CP (M) 9/99.
142. *Penny London Post*, 428, 25–7 January 1746.
143. Maxwell, *Narrative*, p. 152.
144. *Gentleman's Magazine*, 15, p. 42.
145. Anderson, 'Culloden', p. 22.
146. Anon., 'Culloden', pp. 184.
147. Patten, *History*, p. 108.
148. *Weekly Journal*, 27 June 1719.
149. Yorke (ed.), *Hardwicke*, vol. 1, pp. 523, 524.
150. Ray, *A Compleat History*, p. 346.
151. *Gentleman's Magazine*, 16, p. 220.
152. *Newcastle Courant*, 19–26 April 1746, 2731.
153. Elcho, *Short Account*, pp. 433–4.
154. *HMC Hastings*, p. 55–6.
155. Oman to ?, 23 April 1746, London Metropolitan Archives, WJ/SP/1746/06/15.
156. Blaikie, *Origins*, p. 215.
157. A. Tayler and H. Tayler (eds), *The '45 and After* (London: Thomas Nelson & Sons, 1938), p. 164.
158. Maxwell, *Narrative*, p. 86.
159. Anderson, 'Culloden', p. 23.
160. Hussey, *Marlborough*, p. 68.
161. J. McKnight and D. Laing (eds), *Memoirs of the Insurrection in Scotland in 1715 by John, Master of Sinclair* (Edinburgh, 1858), p. 85.
162. Blaikie, *Origins*, p. 195.
163. Yorke (ed.), *Hardwicke*, vol. 1, p. 446.
164. Lewis, *Walpole's Correspondence*, vol. 37, p. 214.
165. Pollard, *Culloden*, p. 88.
166. Mounsey, *Carlisle*, p. 24.
167. Home, *The History*, pp. 82, 84.
168. Wade et al., *Proceedings*, p. 39.
169. *Gentleman's Magazine*, 16, p. 210.
170. Argyll to Townsend, 14 November 1745, TNA, SP 54/10, f. 48.
171. Patten, *History*, p. 153.
172. Whitney to Lascelles, 11 October 1745, RA, CP (M) 6/111.
173. Wade et al., *Proceedings*, p. 41.

174. Ibid.
175. Whitney to Lascelles, 11 October 1745, RA, CP (M) 6/111.
176. Henderson, *History*, p. 30.
177. Whitney to Lascelles, 11 October 1745, RA, CP (M) 6/111.
178. Deposition of Jack, 21 September 1745, RA, CP (M) 5/163.
179. Whitney to Lascelles, 11 October 1745, RA, CP (M) 6/111.
180. Elcho, *Short Account*, p. 375.
181. Maxwell, *Narrative*, p. 102.
182. Rawson (ed.), *Memoir*, p. 87.
183. E. Dunbar, *Social Life in Former Days* (Edinburgh: Edmonston and Douglas, 1865), p. 352.
184. Hawley to Cumberland, 19 January 1746, RA, CP (M) 9/115, Hawley to Cumberland, 23 January 1746, RA, CP (M) 9/134.
185. Cumberland to Hawley, 23 January 1746, RA, CP (M) 9/141.
186. Ray, *A Compleat History*, p. 36.
187. Maxwell, *Narrative*, p. 103.
188. *Gentleman's Magazine*, 15, p. 625.
189. Rae, *History*, p. 319.
190. Maxwell, *Narrative*, p. 78.
191. Rawson (ed.), *Memoir*, p. 70.
192. *Gentleman's Magazine*, 16, p. 210.
193. *Flying Post*, 3725, 17–19 November 1715.
194. Maxwell, *Narrative*, p. 154.
195. Patten, *History*, p. 159.
196. Rawson (ed.), *Memoir*, p. 125.
197. Rae, *History*, p. 305.
198. Anderson, 'Culloden', p. 23.
199. Ibid.
200. *Weekly Journal*, 27 June 1719.
201. *HMC Townshend*, pp. 170–1.
202. Elcho, *Short Account*, pp. 275–6.
203. Ibid., pp. 378–9.
204. Whitney to Lascelles, 11 October 1745, RA, CP (M) 6/111.
205. Argyll to Townshend, 14 November 1715, TNA, SP 54/10, f. 48.
206. Patten, *History*, pp. 154, 169.
207. Ibid., p. 128.
208. Forrester to ?, 15 November 1715, NAS, 220/5/601.
209. Rae, *History*, p. 346.
210. *Gentleman's Magazine*, 16, p. 235.
211. Bradstreet to brother, 11 May 1746, RA, CP (M) 14/385.
212. Anderson, 'Culloden', p. 22.
213. *Calendar of Treasury Books and Papers, 1716*, p. 18; T. Redington, *Calendar of Treasury Papers, 1714–1719* (London: Longman & Co, 1883), p. 502.
214. *Political State of Great Britain* (1716), vol. 11, p. 166.
215. *HMC Townshend*, p. 170.
216. Ibid., p. 171.
217. *Penny London Post*, 429, 25–7 January 1746.
218. B. Willson, *Life and Letters of Wolfe* (London: Heinemann, 1909), pp. 56–7.

219. Hawley to Cumberland, 17 January 1746, RA, CP (M) 9/99.
220. Fitzgerald's Reflection, RA, CP (M) 9/ 110; Marchant, *History*, p. 224.
221. Constable, *A Fragment*, p. 52.
222. *St. James' Evening Post*, 74, 17–19 November 1715.
223. Rae, *History*, p. 323.
224. *Political State* (1716), vol. 11, p. 166; H. Paton (ed.), 'Journal', *Miscellany of the Scottish History Society* (Edinburgh: Scottish History Society, 1890), vol. 1, pp. 520–1.
225. McNiven (ed.), *Diary of Henry Prescott*, vol. 2, p. 475.
226. J. Oates and K. Navickas (eds), *Jacobites and Jacobins, Two Eighteenth-Century Perspectives* (Record Society of Lancashire and Cheshire, 2006), p. 55.
227. Henderson, *History*, p. 116.
228. Ibid., p. 117.
229. Hughes, *A Plain Narrative*, p. 44.
230. Marchant, *History*, p. 395.
231. Anderson, 'Culloden', p. 23.
232. Marchant, *History*, p. 395.

4 The Siege

1. Hussey, *Marlborough*, pp. 60–1.
2. Cumberland to Newcastle, 28 November 1745, TNA, SP 36/75, f. 116r.
3. Bell, *Memorials*, p. 184.
4. J. Kenyon, *The Civil Wars of England* (London: Weidenfeld & Nicolson, 1988), pp. 85–6.
5. Chandler, *Marlborough*, pp. 81–4.
6. J. Chamberlayne, *Present State of Great Britain* (London, 1726), p. 143.
7. Tabraham and Grove, *Fortress Scotland*, pp. 40–1.
8. J. Gifford, C. Mcwillian, D. Walker, *The Buildings of Scotland:* Edinburgh (Harmondsworth: Penguin Books, 1984), p. 86; J. Gifford and F. A. Walker, *Stirling and Central Scotland* (New Haven, CT: Yale University Press, 2002), p. 667.
9. Gifford, Mcwilliam and Walker, *The Buildings*, p. 86.
10. Gifford and Walker, *Stirling*, pp. 668, 671.
11. Tabraham and Grove, *Fortress Scotland*, p. 50.
12. Ibid., pp. 61–3, 81.
13. E. Burt, *Letters from a Gentleman in the North of Scotland to His Friend in London* (London: R. Fenner, 1818), vol. 2, p. 223.
14. Tabraham and Grove, *Fortress Scotland*, pp. 57–9, 62.
15. Ibid., p. 56.
16. Burt, *Letters*, p. 278.
17. Newcastle to Wade, 5 August 1725, TNA, SP 54/15, f. 61.
18. Tabraham and Grove, *Fortress Scotland*, pp. 223, 282.
19. Wade to Newcastle, 9 August 1726, TNA, SP 54/17, f. 47.
20. Black, *War and the World*, pp. 122–3.
21. Rawson (ed.), *Memoir*, p. 49.
22. Mounsey, *Carlisle*, p. 72.
23. Ibid., p. 81.
24. Cope to Newcastle, 6 September 1745, TNA, SP 36/70, f. 212v; Cope to Pelham, 12 October 1745, NUL, Nec 1666; Cope to Pelham, 12 October 1745, NAS, Ms 302, f. 10.

25. Cope to Newcastle, 26 September 1745, TNA, SP 36/69, f. 102r.

26. Rawson (ed.), *Memoir*, pp. 103–4.

27. Tayler and Tayler (eds), *The '45 and After*, p. 133.

28. Pollock to Townshend, 24 September 1715, TNA, SP 54/8, f. 94.

29. Maxwell, *Narrative*, p. 120.

30. Campbell to Cope, 11 September 1745, TNA, SP 54/25, f. 59b.

31. Maxwell, *Narrative*, p. 120.

32. Russell to ?, 4 March 1746, TNA, SP 54/29, f. 14C.

33. Tayler and Tayler, *The '45 and After*, p. 65.

34. Speck, *The Butcher*, pp. 31–2.

35. Cumberland to Newcastle, 14 March 1746, TNA, SP 54/29, f. 14A.

36. P. Rogers (ed.), *Daniel Defoe's Tour of the Whole Island* (Harmondsworth: Penguin, 1971), pp. 521–2.

37. Jack's statement, September 1745, RA, CP (M) 5/163.

38. Ibid.

39. Wilson to Wentworth, 9 September 1745, TNA, SP 54/25, f. 72B, Wentworth to Grant, 11 September 1745, TNA, SP 54/25, f. 73.

40. Pollock to ?, September 1715, TNA, SP 54/8, f. 69; same to same, 28 September 1745, TNA, SP 54/8, f. 116.

41. Isay to ?, 30 September 1745, TNA, SP 54/8, f. 121.

42. Wade et al., *Proceedings*, p. 62.

43. Mounsey, *Carlisle*, p. 82.

44. Newcastle to Montagu, 21 November 1745, TNA, SP 44/133, f. 6.

45. Newcastle to Montagu, 25 October 1745, TNA, SP 44/132, f. 434.

46. Cholmondeley to Newcastle, 21 November 1745, TNA, SP 44/133, f. 7.

47. Newcastle to Montagu, 9 December 1745, TNA, SP 44/133, f. 22.

48. Islay to ?, 30 September 1745, TNA, SP 54/8, f. 121.

49. Tweeddale to Cope, 2 August 1745, TNA, SP 54/25, f. 42.

50. Erle to Richards, 1 August 1715, TNA, SP 35/4, f. 3r.

51. Erle to Richards, 1 August 1715, TNA, SP 35/4, ff. 3r, 5r.

52. Pollock to ?, 24 and 28 September 1715 TNA, SP 54/8, f. 94; Pollock to ?, 28 September 1715, TNA, SP 54/8, f. 116.

53. Pollock to ?, 5 November 1715, TNA, SP 54/10, f. 23.

54. Patten, *History*, p. 36.

55. *Evening Post*, 11–13 October 1715.

56. Cope to Newcastle, 23 September 1745, TNA, SP 36/68, f. 271r.

57. Cholmondeley to Newcastle, 23 November 1745, TNA, SP 36/74, f. 242r.

58. Campbell to Cope, 11 August 1745, TNA, SP 54/25, f. 59b.

59. ? to ?, August 1745, TNA, SP 54/25, f. 84e.

60. *Gentleman's Magazine*, 16, pp. 205–7.

61. Jack's statement, September 1745, RA, CP (M) 5/163.

62. ? to ?, August 1745, TNA, SP 54/25, f. 84e.

63. Cumberland to Newcastle, 14 March 1746, TNA, SP 54/29, f. 14a.

64. Fletcher to Newcastle 25 September 1745, TNA, SP 54/26, f. 36; Craigie to Tweeddale, 23 September 1745, TNA, SP 54/26, f. 35.

65. Newcastle to Fletcher, 3 October 1745, TNA, SP 54/26, f. 51.

66. Handasyde to Newcastle, 21 November 1745, TNA, SP 54/26, f. 82; same to same, 25 November 1745, TNA, SP 54/26, f. 85; Newcastle to Handasyde, 28 November 1745, TNA, SP 54/26, f. 88; supply estimates, December 1745, TNA, SP 54/26, f. 91B.
67. Home, *The History*, p. 73.
68. Ray, *A Compleat History*, pp. 97–8.
69. Home, *The History*, p. 63.
70. Cholmondeley to Newcastle, 26 November 1745, TNA, SP 36/75, f. 63r.
71. Mounsey, *Carlisle*, pp. 61–2, 73.
72. Berwick Record Office (hereafter BERO), B1/14.
73. Ibid.; *Calendar of Treasury Papers, 1717*, p. 20.
74. Herring to Hardwicke, 19 October 1745, BL Add. Mss 35598, f. 100r.
75. Council for defence of Edinburgh, 14 September 1745, TNA, SP 54/26, f. 21.
76. York City Archives, C37, p. 13a, E41B, 17, 57, 59.
77. Ridley to Newcastle, 25 September 1745, TNA, SP 36/69, f. 75r.
78. Robinson to Newcastle, 27 September 1745, TNA, SP 36/69, f. 146v.
79. Huske to Newcastle, 4 October 1745, TNA, SP 36/70, f. 110r; TWAS, 589/14, 40.
80. Ridley to Newcastle, 20 Set. 1745, TNA, SP 36/68, f. 187r; Huske to Newcastle, 4 October 1745, TNA, SP 36/70, f. 110r.
81. Newcastle proclamation, September 1745, Sheffield Archives (hereafter SA), WWM1/314–315.
82. TWAS, 589/12, 71, 86–7.
83. Huske to Newcastle, 4 October 1745, TNA, SP 36/70, f. 110r.
84. Handasyde to Newcastle, 19 October 1745, TNA, SP 36/72, f. 34r.
85. Newcastle to Handasyde, 23 October 1745, TNA, SP 36/72, f. 174r.
86. Anon., *A Journey*, p. 54.
87. Cope to Pelham, 12 October 1745, NUL, NeC 1666; Cope to Pelham, 25 October 1745, NUL, NeC 1668.
88. Watson to Ridley, 16 October 1745, NRO, ZRI27/4/22.
89. Cholmondeley to Newcastle, 17 November 1745, TNA, SP 36/74, f. 2v.
90. *Gentleman's Magazine*, 16, p. 92.
91. Committee, 30 September 1745, BL Add. Mss 33004, f. 93v.
92. Newcastle to Waugh, 3 October 1745, TNA, SP 36/70, f. 82r.
93. Cope to Newcastle, 10 October 1745, TNA, SP 36/71, f. 49v.
94. *Gentleman's Magazine*, 16, pp. 206–7.
95. Campbell to Cope, August 1745, TNA, SP 54/25, f. 66b.
96. August 1745, Ibid., f. 84e.
97. Handasyde to Newcastle, 17 November 1745, TNA, SP 36/74, f. 2v; same to same, 23 November 1745, TNA, SP 36/74, f. 243v.
98. Eerle to ?, 11 August 1745; TNA, SP 35/4, f. 23r; Pulteney to Dubourgay, 29 September 1745, TNA, WO 5/20, p. 114; same to officer in charge of Guards, 29 September 1745, TNA WO 5/20, f. 115.
99. Grant to Fawkener, 23 February 1746, TNA, SP 54/28, f. 43C.
100. John Campbell to Alex Campbell, 22 February 1746, TNA, SP 54/29, f. 39.
101. Cumberland to Newcastle, 28 February 1746, TNA, SP 54/28, f. 47A.
102. Cope to Tweeddale, 1 October 1745, TNA, SP 36/70, f. 15v.
103. Handasyde to Newcastle, 19 October 1745, TNA, SP 36/72, f. 34r.
104. Huske to Newcastle, 20 October 1745, TNA, SP 36/72, f. 80r.
105. Cholmondeley to Newcastle, 19 October 1745, TNA, SP 36/74, f. 2v.

106. Malton to Newcastle, 23 November 1745, TNA, SP 36/74, f. 231r.

107. Malton to Herring, February 1746, SA, WWM1/375.

108. Cholmondeley to Newcastle, 30 November 1745, TNA, SP 36/75, f. 319v.

109. Handasyde to Newcastle, 1 November 1745, TNA, SP 36/73, f. 6r.

110. Handasyde to Newcastle, 28 October 1745, TNA, SP 54/72, f. 322r.

111. Henderson, *History*, p. 96.

112. Ray, *A Compleat History*, p. 81.

113. Molloy to Cope, 30 August 1745, TNA, SP 54/25, f. 106d.

114. Rawson (ed.), *Memoir*, pp. 49, 51.

115. Ibid., p. 85.

116. Ibid., pp. 96–7.

117. Forbes and Chambers, *Jacobite Memoirs*, pp. 43–4.

118. Ibid., p. 108.

119. Elcho, *Short Account*, p. 392.

120. *Gentleman's Magazine*, 16, p. 206.

121. Maxwell, *Narrative*, p. 118.

122. Tayler and Tayler (eds), *The '45 and After*, pp. 133–4.

123. Maxwell, *Narrative*, p. 119.

124. Rawson (ed.), *Memoir*, p. 84.

125. Ibid., p. 85.

126. Ibid., p. 97.

127. Maxwell, *Narrative*, pp. 133–4.

128. Rawson (ed.), *Memoir*, pp. 98, 97.

129. *Gentleman's Magazine*, 16, p. 206.

130. Ibid., p. 148.

131. Ibid., p. 206.

132. Ibid.

133. John Campbell to Alex. Campbell, 22 February 1746, TNA, SP 54/28, f. 39.

134. Elcho, *Short Account*, p. 412.

135. Maxwell, *Narrative*, p. 133; *Gentleman's Magazine*, p. 207.

136. Maxwell, *Narrative*, p. 134.

137. Ibid., p. 28.

138. Tweeddale to Guest, 25 September 1745, TNA, SP 54/25, f. 37b.

139. Forbes and Chambers, *Jacobite Memoirs*, p. 45.

140. Elcho, *Short Account*, pp. 291–3, 306, 308.

141. Committee, 30 September 1745, BL Add. Mss 33004, f. 93v.

142. Fletcher to Newcastle, 11 October 1745, TNA, SP 54/25, f. 61.

143. Forbes and Chambers, *Jacobite Memoirs*, pp. 44–5.

144. Elcho, *Short Account*, pp. 410–1.

145. Ibid., p. 404.

146. Henderson, *History*, p. 55.

147. Elcho, *Short Account*, pp. 313–4.

148. Henderson, *History*, pp. 56–7.

149. Mounsey, *Carlisle*, p. 77.

150. Ibid., p. 65.

151. Ibid., p. 79.

152. Ibid., pp. 94, 79.

153. Elcho, *Short Account*, p. 392.

154. Henderson, *History*, p. 102.
155. Millross' declaration, 15 March 1746, TNA, SP 54/29, f. 14D.
156. Elcho, *Short Account*, p. 394.
157. *Gentleman's Magazine*, 16, p. 165.
158. Ibid., p. 92.
159. Cumberland to Newcastle, 28 February 1746, TNA, SP 54/28, f. 47A; Newcastle to Cumberland, 6 March 1746, TNA, SP 54/29, f. 4A.
160. Mounsey, *Carlisle*, p. 149.
161. Cumberland to Newcastle, 22 December 1745, TNA, SP 36/78, f. 14r; Ray, *A Compleat History*, p. 230; *St. James' Evening Post*, 5607, 24–6 December 1745.
162. Newcastle to Montagu, December 1745, TNA, SP 36/78, ff. 225r–226r.
163. Cumberland to Newcastle, 22 December 1745, TNA, SP 36/78, f. 15r.
164. Fletcher to ?, 17 November 1745, Cumbria Record Office (hereafter Cumbria Record Office, Carlisle) D/Da8.
165. Yorke (ed.), *Hardwicke*, vol. 1, p. 488.
166. Richmond to Newcastle, 30 December 1745, BL Add. Mss 32705, ff. 458r–459r.
167. R. C. Jarvis, *The Jacobite Risings of 1715 and 1745* (Cumberland County Council, 1954), pp. 319–25.
168. Cumberland to Newcastle, 24 December 1745, TNA, SP 36/78, ff. 220v, 230r; same to same, December 1745, RA, CP (M) 8/120.
169. Merseyside Maritime Museum (hereafter, MMM), DX 594, Memoir of Walter Shairp, ff. 27r–28v.
170. Ibid., f. 29v.
171. Cumberland to Newcastle, 24 December 1745, TNA, SP 36/78, f. 230v.
172. Fletcher to ?, 17 November 1745, CRO D/Da8.
173. Cumberland to Newcastle, 30 December 1745, TNA, SP 36/78, f. 270; Richmond to Newcastle, 30 December 1745, BL Add. Mss 32705, f. 468r.
174. *Gentleman's Magazine*, 16, p. 21.
175. Cumberland to Newcastle, 30 December 1745, TNA, SP 36/78, f. 282r.
176. *Gentleman's Magazine*, 16, p. 21.
177. Cumberland to Newcastle, 30 December 1745, TNA, 36/78, f. 271r.
178. Chesterfield to Newcastle, 11 March 1746, BL Add. Mss 32706, f. 287r.
179. Tayler and Tayler (eds), *The '45 and After*, pp. 133–5.
180. Yorke (ed.), *Hardwicke*, vol. 1, p. 519.
181. Tabraham and Grove, *Fortress Scotland*, p. 131.
182. Cumberland to Newcastle, 30 January 1746, TNA, SP 54/27, f. 55A.

5 The Formation of the Militia and Posse

1.   Ray, *A Compleat History*, foreword.
2.   Speck, *The Butcher*, pp. 55–63; L. Colley, *Britons: Forging the Nation, 1707–1837* (New Haven, CT: Yale University Press, 1992), pp. 80–5.
3.   Colley, *Britons,* pp. 84–5.
4.   Speck, *The Butcher*, p. 59.
5.   Duffy, *The '45*, pp. 133–5; McLynn, *The Jacobite Army*, pp. 4–6.
6.   McLynn, *The Jacobites*, p. 106.
7.   Ibid., *The Jacobite Army*, p. 6.

8. C. Collyer, 'Yorkshire and the '45', *Yorkshire Archaeological Journal*, 38 (1955), pp. 145–57; J. D. Oates, *York and the Jacobite Rebellion of 1745* (Borthwick Texts, 2005); J. D. Oates, 'Independent Volunteer Forces in Yorkshire During the Forty-Five', *Yorkshire Archaeological Journal*, 73 (2001), pp. 205–17; J. D. Oates, 'Yorkshire and the Fifteen', *Yorkshire Archaeological Journal*, 75 (2003), pp. 86–97.

9. Jarvis, *The Collected Papers*, vol. 1; J. D. Oates, 'Responses in the North of England to the Jacobite Rebellion of 1715', *Northern History*, 43:1 (2006), pp. 77–95; Oates, *The Jacobite Invasion*; Oates, *The Last Battle*.

10. R. I. Ritchie, 'The Durham Association Regiment', *Journal of the Society for Army Historical Research*, 34 (1956), pp. 106–19.

11. J. R. Western, *The English Militia in the Eighteenth Century* (London: Routledge and Kegan, 1965), p. 73.

12. Jarvis, *The Collected Papers*, vol. 1, pp. 98–9.

13. *Gentleman's Magazine*, 3, p. 8; 15, p. 25.

14. T. Royle, *Civil Wars: The War of the Three Kingdoms 1638–1660* (London: Abacus , 2005), pp. 107, 85, 73–4.

15. Home, *The History*, p. 67.

16. Jarvis, *The Collected Papers*, vol. 1, p. 147.

17. J. Marshall (ed.), *The Autobiography of William Stout* (Manchester: Chetham Society, 1967), p. 8.

18. Maxwell, *Narrative*, p. 77.

19. E. J. Climenson (ed.), *Elizabeth Montagu: the Queen of the Blue-stockings: Her Correspondence from 1720 to 1761* (London: John Murray, 1906), vol. 1, p. 109.

20. Stanhope to Pringle, 27 August 1715, TNA, SP 54/7, f. 98.

21. Lenman, *The Jacobite Risings*, pp. 250–1.

22. Grey, *Clerk of Penicuik*, p. 161.

23. D. Warrand, *More Culloden Papers* (Inverness: Robert Carruthers & Sons, 1930), vol. 4, p. 26.

24. Fletcher to ?, 5 November 1745, TNA, SP 54/26, f. 33A.

25. *Penny London Post* 376, 22–4 September 1745.

26. Vane to Newcastle, 27 September 1745, TNA, SP 36/69, f. 145r.

27. Chandler to Newcastle, 20 September 1745, TNA, SP 36/68, f. 184r.

28. Royal Commission on Historical Manuscripts, *The Manuscripts of the Earl of Carlisle, Preserved at Castle Howard* (London: HMSO, 1897), p. 15 (hereafter *HMC Carlisle*).

29. Yorke (ed.), *Hardwicke*, vol. 1, p. 479.

30. Blaikie, Origins, pp. 123–4.

31. Oates, *Responses in North East England*, pp. 273–84; Oates, *The Jacobite Invasion*, p. 84.

32. Dickson (ed.), *Warrender Letters,* p. 67.

33. Home, *The History*, p. 67.

34. BERO, 2/4, p. 276.

35. J. D Oates, 'Loyalty and Conspiracy in and around Deptford', *Lewisham Historian*, 8 (2001), pp. 1–11; Militia list, 1715, Berkshire Record Office (BEREO), D/EP4/03.

36. J. D. Oates, 'Responses in the Home Counties to the Jacobite Rebellion of 1745', *Southern History*, 28 (2006), pp. 46–73, on pp. 60–1.

37. Jarvis, *The Jacobite Risings*, p. 230.

38. Royal Commission on Historical Manuscripts, *Report on the Manuscripts of the Earl of Ancaster Preserved at Grimsthorpe* (London: HMSO, 1907), p. 444 (hereafter *HMC Ancaster*).

39. Jarvis, *The Jacobite Risings*, pp. 154–5.
40. Chandler to Newcastle, 20 September 1745, TNA, SP 36/68, f. 184r.
41. Stewart to ?, 11 August 1715, TNA, SP 54/7, f. 33.
42. Yorke (ed.), *Hardwicke*, vol. 1, p. 442.
43. Forbes to ?, 8 August 1745, TNA, SP 54/25, f. 51.
44. Argyll to ?, 11 August 1745, TNA, SP 54/25, f. 61a.
45. Yorke (ed.), *Hardwicke*, vol. 1, p. 445.
46. Home, *The History*, pp. 67–8.
47. Ibid., p. 69.
48. Craigie to Tweeddale, 10 September 1745, TNA, SP 54/26, f. 16A.
49. Lonsdale to Newcastle, 21 September 1745, TNA, SP 36/69, f. 21v.
50. Newcastle to Lonsdale, 21 October 1745, TNA, SP 36/72, ff. 94r, 234v; Jarvis, *The Jacobite Risings*, pp. 247n, 254.
51. Bruce to Newcastle, 22 February 1746, TNA, SP 54/28, f. 38.
52. Warrand, *More Culloden Papers*, vol. 4, p. 128; Forbes to ?, 10 October 1745, TNA, SP 54/26, f. 58.
53. Returns of militia, 1745, TNA, SP 54/34E, f. 34B.
54. Militia list, 1715, BEREO, D/EP4/03.
55. Yorke (ed.), *Hardwicke*, vol. 2, p. 264
56. Crisap to ?, 1716, TNA, SP 35/2, f. 117r.
57. Warrand, *More Culloden Papers*, vol. 4, p. 49.
58. *HMC Carlisle*, p. 17.
59. S. D. Smith (ed.), *Letter Books of Joseph Symson, 1711–1720* (Oxford: Oxford University Press, 2003), p. 342.
60. Lord Justice Clerk to?, 3 August 1715, TNA, SP 54/7, f. 12; Provost of Glasgow University to 3 August 1715, TNA, SP 54/7, f. 13; Stewart to ?, 26 August 1715, TNA, SP 54/7, f. 80.
61. A. W. Anderson (ed.), *The Papers of the Rev. John Anderson* (Dumbarton: Bennett & Thomson, 1914), p. 35.
62. Hepburne Scott, 'Marchmont Correspondence', p. 337.
63. Lenman, *The Jacobite Risings*, p. 210.
64. Fletcher to ?, 16 September 1745, TNA, SP 54/26, f. 25.
65. Elcho, *Short Account*, p. 253.
66. Blaikie, Origins, p. 63.
67. Ibid., p. 139.
68. MacLeod to Loudoun, 26 September 1745, TNA, SP 54/25, f. 92B.
69. BL Add. Mss 37221, f. 39v.
70. T. Picton, *Municipal Records* (Liverpool: Gilbert G. Walmsley, 1886), p. 105.
71. Home, *The History, p.* 67.
72. Lonsdale to Newcastle, 9 September 1745, TNA, SP 36/69, f. 20r.
73. Argyll to Tweeddale, 11 August 1745, TNA, SP 54/25, f. 59a.
74. *Gentlemen's Magazine*, 1745, p. 608.
75. Newcastle to Montagu, 18 October 1745, TNA, SP 44/132, f. 423.
76. Yorke (ed.), *Hardwicke*, vol. 1, p. 438; Home, *The History*, p. 53.
77. Home, *The History*, p. 74.
78. *Gentleman's Magazine,* 15, p. 612.
79. Ibid., p. 619.
80. Rothes to ?, 15 September 1715, TNA, SP 54/8, f. 67.

81. Durham Dean and Chapter Library (hereafter DDCL), Sharp MSS, 150/24, Bowes to Chandler, 27 September 1745.

82. J. Stuart (ed.), *Extracts from the Burgh of Aberdeen* (Edinburgh: Scottish Burgh Record Society, 1872), p. 349

83. *Newcastle Journal*, 359, 5 October 1745.

84. Durham Record Office, D/St/C1/3/186.

85. Stuart (ed.), *Extracts*, p. 350.

86. Crisap to ?, 1716, TNA, SP 35/2, f. 117r.

87. Durham University Library and Special Collections (hereafter, DULASC), Clavering correspondence, 25, Maughan to Clavering, 11 November 1745.

88. West Yorkshire Archive Service (hereafter WYAS): Wakefield, QS10/13, p. 103.

89. Lancashire Record Office (hereafter LRO), PR29456/2/1, PR3360/4/1/1, PR3168/79.

90. *Kentish Post*, 2945, 21–5 December 1745, 2947, 28 December–1 January 1746.

91. Jarvis, *The Jacobite Risings*, pp. 249–58.

92. Argyll to Townshend, 17 December 1715, TNA, SP 54/10, f. 133.

93. Tweeddale to Pringle, 27 October 1715, TNA, SP 54/8, f. 89.

94. G. C. Miller, *Hoghton Tower* (Preston: Guardian Press, 1948), p. 117.

95. Jarvis, *The Collected Papers*, vol. 1, pp. 240–1.

96. Argyll to Townshend, 24 September 1745, TNA, SP 54/8, f. 89.

97. Cotesworth to Liddell, 11 October 1715, HRO, D/EP F195.

98. Lonsdale to ?, 4 November 1715, BL Add. Mss 63093, f. 60r.

99. Rae, *History*, p. 206.

100. Ibid., pp. 183–4, 204.

101. Deputy Lieutenants of Hampshire to Newcastle, 28 September 1745, TNA, SP 36/69, f. 152r.

102. Stirling to ?, 3 August 1715, TNA, SP 54/7, f. 13.

103. *London Evening Post*, 2826, 15–17 December 1745; D'Arcy to Newcastle, 19 November 1745, TNA, SP 36/74, f. 82r.

104. Home, *The History*, p. 53.

105. Stanhope to Roxburgh, 27 August 1715, TNA, SP 54/7, f. 98.

106. Bell, *Memorials*, p. 196.

107. R. Sedgwick, *The Commons, 1715–1754* (London: HMSO, 1970), vol. 1, p. 479.

108. McNiven (ed.), *Diary of Henry Prescott*, vol. 2, p. 472.

109. Lowther to Newcastle, 25 September 1745, TNA, SP 36/69, f. 48.

110. Home, *The History*, p. 73.

111. Rae, *History*, pp. 182–3.

112. Stuart (ed.), *Extracts*, pp. 374–5.

113. Derby to Newcastle, 22 October 1745, TNA, SP 36/72, f. 156r; Newcastle to Derby, 9 November 1745, TNA, SP 36/73, f. 202v.

114. *Glasgow Courant*, 2, November 1715.

115. Rae, *History*, pp. 184–5.

116. C. E. Whiting (ed.), *Two Yorkshire Diaries* (Leeds: Yorkshire Archeaological Society, 1952), p. 105.

117. Fletcher to Newcastle, 2 January 1746, TNA, SP 54/27, f. 1A.

118. Malton to Newcastle, 30 October 1745, TNA, SP 36/72, f. 363r.

119. *St. James Evening Post*, 65, 27–9 October 1715.

120. Ibid.

121. Returns of militia, 20 February 1746, TNA, SP 54/28, f. 34E.

122. Arnot and Seton, *Prisoners*, vol. 1, pp. 276–7; returns of militia, 27 February 1746, TNA, SP 54/27/10.

123. Home to ?, 2 January 1746, TNA, SP 54/27, f. 2A.

124. TNA, Assizes 8/37.

125. West Riding Accounts, 1746, York Minister Library (hereafter YML).

126. Warrand, *More Culloden Papers*, vol. 4, p. 110–1.

127. Robinson to Robinson, 26 November 1715, WYAS: Leeds, Vyner, 6006/13154.

128. Militia list, 1715, BEREO, D/EP4/03.

129. Johnson to Liddell, 15 October 1715, HRO, D/EP F195; Ellis, *Liddell to Cotesworth*, p. 189.

130. Oates, *Responses in North East England*, pp. 273–84; Oates, *The Jacobite Invasion*, p. 84.

131. Jarvis, *The Jacobite Risings*, pp. 149–50.

132. Militia accounts, October 1715, DULSC, Clavering Correspondence, 42.

133. *General Advertiser*, 3402, 1 October 1745.

134. Militia returns, 1715, SA, RA, M16/1.

135. 'Diary of John Lucas', p. 33, LLHL.

136. R. J. Williamson, *Historical Records of the Regiment of Lancashire Militia* (London: Simpkins, Marshal & Co., 1876), p. 11; Matthews (ed.), *Diary*, pp. 174–5, 231, 234.

137. Lucas, p. 33, LLHL; York City Archives, F12, f. 33a (hereafter YCA).

138. Oates, *Responses in North East England*, pp. 690–1, 694.

6 The Formation of the Loyalist Volunteer Forces

1. *HMC Anacaster*, p. 444.

2. Newcastle to Tankerville, 21 September 1745, TNA, SP 36/68, ff. 232r–233v.

3. Lonsdale to Newcastle, 24 September 1745, TNA, SP 36/ 69, f. 20r.

4. Return of militia and volunteers, 6 October 1745, TNA, SP 36/70, f. 221r.

5. Home, *The History*, pp. 156–7; Blaikie, *Origins*, pp. 104–5.

6. Warrand, *More Culloden Papers*, vol. 4, p. 56.

7. Chesterfield to Newcastle, 6 December 1745, TNA, SP 54/26, f. 21.

8. R. Lodge (ed.), *Private Correspondence of Chesterfield and Newcastle 1744–46* (London: Royal Historical Society, 1930), p. 93.

9. Yorke (ed.), *Hardwicke*, vol. 1, p. 477.

10. Rae, *History*, p. 204.

11. Arnot and Seton, *Prisoners*, vol. 1, pp. 269–72.

12. *Gentleman's Magazine*, 15, pp. 499, 554.

13. Lewis, *Walpole's Correspondence*, vol. 19, p. 126.

14. Bowes to Chandler, 27 September 1745, DDCL, Sharp Mss, 150, 15.

15. Derby to Newcastle, 27 September 1745, TNA, SP 36/69, f. 126r.

16. List of subscribers, 1745, Hampshire Record Office, 84M95/1.

17. *York Poll Book*, 1741; *York Journal,* 57–61, 23 December 1746 – 20 January 1747.

18. Ray, *A Compleat History*, p. 106.

19. *HMC Ancaster*, p. 444.

20. Hildeseley to Teller, 17 October 1745, HRO, MIL3/1, 25; Rooke to same, 26 October 1745, HRO, MIL3/26; Allen to same, 31 October 1745, HRO, MIL3/35.

21. *London Evening Post,* 2810, 7–9 November 1745.

22. E. Cruickshanks, *Political Untouchables: The Tories and the '45* (London: Duckworth, 1979), p. 134.

23. *Gentleman's Magazine*, 15 (1745), p. 554; *York Journal,* 57–61, 23 December 1746 – 20 January 1747.
24. *London Evening Post*, 3–5 October 1745.
25. *Westminster Journal,* 202, 12 October 1745.
26. Hardwicke to Herring, 3 October 1745, BL Add. Mss 35598, f. 80v.
27. *York Journal,* 57–61, 23 December 1746 – 20 January 1747.
28. List of subscribers, 1745, Bodleian Library, MS Eng. Hist. c501.
29. Patten to Derby, 15 October 1745, LRO, DDK1741/7.
30. C. H. Cooper, *Annals of Cambridge* (Cambridge: Warwick, 1862), vol. 4, pp. 252–4.
31. Hildeseley to Teller, 23 October 1745, HRO, MIL3/4; Webster to same, 6 November 1745, HRO, MIL3/57.
32. Webster to Teller, 6 November 1745, HRO, MIL3/57; Rooke to same, 26 October 1745, HRO, MIL3/25.
33. W. Cobbett, *Parliamentary History of England* (London: Bagshaw, 1823), vol. 13, pp. 1351–2.
34. Malton-Fitzwilliam, 2 November 1745, Northampton Record Office (hereafter, NORO).
35. YCA, E41B, f. 29; Herring to Hardwicke, 4 October 1745, BL Add. Mss 35598, f. 83r.
36. Picton, *Municipal Records*, p. 110.
37. Williamson, *Historical Records*, p. 39; *Yorkshire List*, 1747.
38. J. D. Oates, *Seditious Words and Loyal Addresses: Jacobitism in Hampshire* (Hampshire County Council, 2007), p. 16.
39. Cooper, *Annals*, IV, pp. 252–4.
40. Quoted in Colley, *Britons*, p. 87.
41. YCA, E130, f. 9; YCA, E41B, ff. 22–3.
42. Malton to Newcastle, 19 September 1745, TNA, SP 36/68, f. 167r.
43. Newcastle to Montagu, 18 October 1745, TNA, SP 44/132, f. 423.
44. Newcastle to Lyttleton, 10 September 1745, TNA, SP 44/132, f. 411.
45. Herring to Hardwicke, 19 October 1745, BL Add. Mss 35598, f. 98r.
46. Malton to Fitzwilliam, 14 October 1745, NORO.
47. Irwin to Newcastle, 26 October 1745, TNA, SP 36/72, f. 275r.
48. Graves to Robinson, 25 November 1745, WYAS: Leeds, NH 2875/8.
49. YCA, E41B, ff. 22–3.
50. Bowes to Chandler, November 1745, DDCL, Sharp MSS, 150/24.
51. Herring to Hardwicke, 4 October 1745, BL Add. Mss 33598, f. 84r; *Gentleman's Magazine*, 16, p. 40.
52. *Evening Post*, 967, 15–18 October 1715.
53. YCA, E41B, ff. 8, 10, 16A–B.
54. Ridge to Newcastle, 10 October 1745, TNA, SP 36/71, f. 243r.
55. *London Evening Post*, 2796, 8–10 October 1745.
56. *St. James Evening Post*, 5599, 5–7 December 1745; *General Advertiser*, 3404, 5 October 1745.
57. Jarvis, *The Collected Papers*, vol. 1, pp. 239–240.
58. MMM, DX 594, ff.3v, 4r.
59. *HMC Var. Coll.*, vol. 8, p. 154; Milnes to Irwin, 19 October 1745, WYAS: Leeds, TN/PO3/3C/52.
60. *Newcastle Courant,* 2703, 5–12 October 1745.
61. *York Courant*, 1044, 15 October 1745.
62. Argyll to Townshend, 24 September 1745, TNA, SP 54/8, f. 89.
63. Committee for defence of Edinburgh, 11–14 September 1745, TNA, SP 54/26, f. 21.

64. Rae, *History*, pp. 183–4, 204.
65. MMM, DX 594, ff. 2v, 3r.
66. Irwin to Newcastle, 24 September 1745, 71, TNA, SP 36/69, ff. 23r–24v; same to same, 10 October 1745, TNA, SP 36/69, f. 33r; Malton to Newcastle, 25 October 1745, TNA, SP 36/72, f. 220r.
67. Accounts, 1745, Borthwick Institute of Historical Research (hereafter, BIHR), XXI/4.
68. Deputy lieutenants of Hampshire to Newcastle, 28 September 1745, TNA, SP 36/69, f. 152r.
69. *London Evening Post*, 2826, 15–17 December 1745; TNA, SP 36/74, f. 82r.
70. Home, *The History*, p. 74.
71. MMM, DX 594, f. 2r.
72. Oates and Navickas, 'Jacobites and Jacobins', pp. 18–33.
73. Oates, *Responses in North East England,* pp. 695–6.
74. Arnot and Seton, *Prisoners*, vol. 1, pp. 279–80.
75. Argyll to ?, 10 January 1746, TNA, SP 54/27, f. 10.
76. Fletcher to Newcastle, 5 November 1745, TNA, SP 54/27, f. 10; 26, f. 73a.
77. Reasons for a speedy regulation of a formidable Militia in the Kingdom of Great Britain, BL Add. Mss 33048, f. 388v.
78. *General Advertiser,* 3414, 17 October 1745.
79. Malton to Newcastle, 30 October 1745, TNA, SP 36/72, f. 363r.
80. *York Poll Book*, 1741; YCA, E41b, ff. 11–4.
81. *Newcastle Courant*, 2703, 5–12 October 1745; *York Courant*, 1044, 15 October 1745.
82. *General Advertiser*, 3463, 5 December 1745.
83. Home, *The History*, p. 71n.
84. Ray, *A Compleat History*, pp. 28–9.
85. Council for defence of Edinburgh, 11–14 September 1745, TNA, SP 54/26, f. 21.
86. Blaikie, *Origins*, p. 139.
87. Hall to ?, 12 October 1745, BIHR, BP C & P, XXI/I.
88. Returns of volunteers, 1745, WYAS: Leeds, TN/PO3/3D/1–7.
89. Malton to Finch, October 1715, SA, WMM/1/312; same to Fitzwilliam, 6 November 1745, SA, WWM/1, 296.
90. *London Evening Post*, 2794, October 1745.
91. Matthews (ed.), *Diary*, p. 231.
92. Cowper to Cowper, 9 September 1716, HRO, D/EP F195, f. 4v; *London Evening Post*, 2802, 19–22 October 1745.
93. Marshall (ed.), *Stout*, pp. 172–3.
94. J. Bate, *A Parochial Letter to the Inhabitants of Deptford* (London: Author, 1745), p. 9.
95. *Newcastle Journal*, 337, 21 September 1745.
96. Johnston to Devonshire, 7 September 1745, Chatsworth House, Devonshire papers, 317.
97. *Manchester Mercury*, 455, 15 October 1745.
98. Herring to Hardwicke, 26 October 1745, BL Add. Mss 35598, f. 102v.
99. Warrand, *More Culloden Papers*, vol. 4, p. 101.
100. Cormack and Jones, *The Journals of Corporal Todd*, p. 1.
101. Home to ?, 2 January 1746, TNA, SP 54/27, f. 2A.
102. A. Ward, *History and Antiquities of York*, I (York: A. Ward, 1785), pp. 352–3.
103. YCA, E41B, f. 8.
104. Minutes lieutenancy minutes, 21 November 1745, North Yorkshire County Record Office, ZPB/1446/1256.
105. Journal of Rockingham, 1745, SA, WWM2/351.

106. Home, *The History*, p. 71n.

107. MMM, DX 594, f. 39r.

108. Irwin to Newcastle, 10 October 1745, TNA, SP 36/71, f. 33r.

109. Cholmondeley to Fawkener, 8 November 1745, RA, CP (M) 7/13.

110. Warrand, *More Culloden Papers*, vol. 4, p. 110–1.

111. Saville, *Secret Comment*, p. 261.

112. Irwin to Newcastle, 18 October 1745, TNA, SP 36/71, f. 241r.

113. Nowell to Irwin, 10 November 1745, WYAS: Leeds, NP1510/35.

114. Brockbank and Kenworthy, *Diary of Dr Richard Kay*, p. 103.

115. Malton to Newcastle, 19 September 1745, TNA, SP 36/68, f. 167r.

116. Irwin to Newcastle, 28 September 1745, TNA, SP 36/69, f. 197r.

117. Malton to Newcastle, 30 September 1745, TNA, SP 36/69, f. 274r.

118. *London Evening Post*, 2795, 3–5 October 1745; *Derby Mercury*, XIV, 33, 1–8 November 1745.

119. Malton to Fitzwilliam, 11 and 16 November 1745, NORO.

120. Oates, *Responses in North East England*, pp. 695–700.

121. Oates, *The Jacobite Invasion*, pp. 36, 58, 102.

7 The Militia and Volunteer Forces in Action

1.   Jarvis, *The Collected Papers*, vol. 1, p. 97.

2.   J. Stevenson, *Popular Disturbances in England* (London: Longman, 1978), p. 35; Barthorp, *The Jacobite Rebellions*, p. 27.

3.   McLynn, *The Jacobites*, p. 106.

4.   Duffy, *The '45*, p. 45.

5.   Szechi, *1715*, p. 195.

6.   Reid, *1745*, p. 133.

7.   J. Black, *War for America* (Stroud: Sutton, 1991), p. 15.

8.   Jarvis, *The Collected Papers*, vol. 1, pp. 81–2; Oates, *Responses in the North of England*; Oates, *The Jacobite Invasion*.

9.   MMM, DX 594, f. 1r.

10. Ibid., f. 4.

11. YCA, E41B, ff. 1–2.

12. Graham to Montrose, 4 August 1715, TNA, SP 54/7, f. 19.

13. McCann, *The Correspondence*, p. 176.

14. Irwin to Newcastle, 20 November 1745, TNA, SP 36/74, f. 111r.

15. Earl of Rothes to ?, 10 October 1745, TNA, SP 54/26, f. 56.

16. Henderson, *History*, p. 75.

17. Miller, *Hoghton Tower*, p. 118; Newcastle to Hoghton, November 1745, TNA, SP 36/73, f. 241r.

18. Herring to Hardwicke, 21 September 1745, BL Add. Mss 35598, ff. 62r–63r; Malton to Fitzwilliam, 11 November 1745, NORO.

19. Wentworth to Malton, 23 November 1745, SA, WWM2/311.

20. Warrand, *More Culloden Papers*, vol. 4, p. 56.

21. Cumberland to Newcastle, 26 January 1746, TNA, SP 54/27, f. 47A.

22. Malton to Fitzwilliam, 11 November 1745, NORO; Malton to Newcastle, 23 November 1745 TNA, SP 36/74, f. 231r.

23. Herring to Hardwicke, 21 September 1745, BL Add. Mss 35598, ff. 62r–63r.

24. Fletcher to Newcastle, 5 November 1746, TNA, SP 54/26, f. 73A.

25. Herring to Hardwicke, 21 September 1745, BL Add. Mss 35598, f. 64v.
26. Lonsdale to Newcastle, 9 September 1745, TNA, SP 36/67, ff. 199v–220v.
27. D'Arcy to Newcastle, 19 November 1745, TNA, SP 36/74, f. 82r.
28. Irwin to Newcastle, 14 September 1745, SP36/68, f. 54r.
29. *Gentleman's Magazine*, 16, pp. 204–5, 149, 25.
30. McLynn, *Bonnie Prince Charlie*, p. 192.
31. MMM, DX 594, f. 13r.
32. Derby to Richmond, 24 November 1745, RA, CP (M), 7/112.
33. William Fletcher to ?, 17 November 1745, CRO, Whitehaven, YD/Da.8.
34. Malton to Newcastle, 23 November 1745, TNA, SP 36/74, f. 231r.
35. Rawson (ed.), *Memoir*, p. 66; *Gentleman's Magazine*, 16, p. 101.
36. Elcho, *Short Account*, p. 350.
37. *Gentleman's Magazine*, 15, p. 611.
38. Gentlemen of Penrith to Lonsdale, 16 November 1745, 23, Resolution of militia, 14 November 1745, CRO, Whitehaven, Y/Pen. Acc.2689/27; Waugh to Newcastle, November 1745, TNA, SP 36/76, f. 16v.
39. *Gentleman's Magazine*, 16, p. 60.
40. Scott, *Memoirs*, p. 39.
41. *Original Weekly Journal*, 355, 19–26 November 1715; S. Hibbert-Ware, *Lancashire Memorials of 1715* (Manchester: Chetham Society, 1845), p. 75.
42. Lonsdale to ?, 4 November 1715, BL Add. Mss 63093, f. 61v.
43. Yorke (ed.), *Hardwicke*, vol. 1, p. 446.
44. Ibid., p. 452.
45. Ibid., p. 458.
46. Herring to Hardwicke, 27 September 1745, BL Add. Mss 35598, f. 70v.
47. Yorke (ed.), *Hardwicke*, vol. 1, p. 517.
48. Argyll to Stanhope, 18 September 1715, TNA, SP 54/8, f. 67.
49. Tweeddale to Pringle, 27 October 1715, TNA, SP 54/8, f. 89.
50. Yorke (ed.), *Hardwicke*, vol. 1, p. 515.
51. Ibid., p. 493.
52. Ibid., p. 519.
53. Irwin to Newcastle, 10 October 1745, TNA, SP 36/71, f. 197r, same to same, 13 December 1745, TNA, SP 36/77, f. 23r.
54. MMM, DX 594 f. 4v–r.
55. Chandler to Bowes, 3 December 1745, DCCL, Sharp 150, 36, same to same, 17 December 1745, DCCL, Sharp, 46.
56. MMM, DX 594, f. 9v.
57. Ibid., f. 16v.
58. Henderson, *History*, pp. 55–6.
59. Ibid., Elcho, *Short Account*, pp. 312–3.
60. Patten, *History*, pp. 82–3.
61. Home, *The History*, p. 198.
62. Derby to Richmond, 23 November 1745, RA, CP (M) 7/112.
63. Derby to Newcastle, 22 November 1745, TNA, SP 36/73, ff. 186r–7v.
64. *Gentleman's Magazine*, 16, p. 69.
65. J. Fergusson, *Argyll in the Forty Five* (London: Faber & Faber, 1952), pp. 132, 137.
66. Returns of militia, 20 March 1746, TNA, SP 54/31, f. 24B.
67. Prince of Hesse to Cumberland, 31 March 1746, TNA, SP 54/30, f. 2b, Fletcher to Newcastle, 5 April 1746, TNA, SP 54/30, f. 3f.

68. Fergusson, *Argyll*, pp. 138, 140.
69. Campbell's journal, 20–5 March 1746, TNA, SP 54/30, f. 3C.
70. Patten, *History*, p. 34.
71. Rae, *History*, pp. 245–9.
72. Patten, *History*, pp. 69, 71.
73. Rae, *History*, p. 277.
74. Lord Macaulay, *History of England* (London: Everyman, 1980), vol. 1, pp. 447–8.
75. MMM, DX 594, ff. 14r–15v.
76. Rae, *History*, p. 283.
77. Islay to ?, 23 October 1715, TNA, SP 54/9, f. 80.
78. Anderson, *The Papers*, pp. 35–6.
79. Rae, *History*, pp. 283–90.
80. A. Steuart (ed.), *News Letters of 1715–6* (Edinburgh: W. and R. Chambers, 1910), p. 101.
81. Anderson, *The Papers*, pp. 36–7.
82. Patten, *History*, p. 180.
83. Rae, *History,* pp. 329–32.
84. Ibid., pp. 332–3.
85. Patten, *History*, p. 214.
86. Argyll to Townshend, 3 November 1715, TNA, SP 54/10, f. 8.
87. Lovat to Pollock, 17 January 1716, TNA, SP 54/11, f. 73e.
88. Patten, *History*, p. 261.
89. Wightman to ?, 29 December 1715, TNA, SP 54/10, f. 162.
90. Tweeddale to Pringle, 27 October 1715, TNA, SP 54/8, f. 89.
91. *Gentleman's Magazine*, 15, p. 619.
92. Elcho, *Short Account*, p. 308.
93. *Gentleman's Magazine,* 16, p. 22.
94. Blaikie, *Origins*, p. 106.
95. Ibid., pp. 142–5.
96. Home, *The History, p.* 159.
97. Blaikie, *Origins*, p. 107.
98. Ibid., p. 142.
99. Maxwell, *Narrative*, p. 129.
100. Ray, *A Compleat History, p.* 61.
101. Elcho, *Short Account*, p. 410; Blaikie, *Origins*, pp. 184–5; *Gentleman's Magazine*, 16, p. 301.
102. Grey, *Clerk of Penicuik*, p. 200.
103. Ray, *A Compleat History*, pp. 348–51.
104. *London Evening Post*, 2823, 7–9 December 1745; Armitage to Lonsdale, 29 November 1745, CRO, Whitehaven, D/Pen.Acc.2698/34.
105. Johnstone, *Memoir*, p. 75.
106. Elcho, *Short Account*, p. 343.
107. Blaikie, *Origins*, pp. 184–5.
108. Saville, *Secret Comment*, p. 263.
109. TNA, Treasury Soldiers, 20/7, f. 2.
110. Tayler and Tayler (eds), *The '45 and After*, p. 104; Blaikie, *Origins*, p. 180.
111. Forbes and Chambers, *Jacobite Memoirs*, pp. 54–5.
112. Fawkener to Lonsdale, 12 December 1745, CRO, Whitehaven, D/Pen.Acc.2689/41.

113. Royle, *Civil War*, pp. 321–2.
114. Dickson (ed.), *Warrender Letters*, p. 92
115. Rae, *History*, p. 300n.
116. Argyll to Townshend, 15 November 1715, TNA, SP 54/10, f. 51.
117. Rae, *History*, p. 232
118. Ibid., p. 241.
119. Miller, *Hoghton Tower*, p. 113.
120. *Daily Courant*, 4391, 19 November 1715.
121. *Flying Post*, 3723, 12–15 November 1715.
122. Forbes and Chambers, *Jacobite Memoirs*, p. 41.
123. Ray, *A Compleat History*, p. 244.
124. Blaikie, *Origins*, p. 433.
125. W. Thornton, *The Counterpoise* (London, 1754), p. 40.
126. *Gentleman's Magazine*, 16, p. 28.
127. Cumberland to Newcastle, 28 February 1746, TNA, SP 54/28, f. 47A.
128. *Gentleman's Magazine*, 16, pp. 209, 212, 241.
129. Fergusson, *Argyll, p.* 174.
130. *Gentleman's Magazine*, 16, p. 93.
131. Ibid., p. 28, 241.
132. Ray, *A Compleat History*, pp. 260–1.
133. Cumberland to Newcastle, 20 February 1746, TNA, SP 54/29, f. 20A.
134. Warrand, *More Culloden Papers*, vol. 4, p. 48.
135. *Gentleman's Magazine*, 16, p. 28.
136. Ray, *A Compleat History*, p. 51.
137. HMC *Stuart Papers,* vol. 1, pp. 476–8.
138. Elcho, *Short Account*, p. 254.
139. Home, *The History*, pp. 81–3.
140. Rae, *History*, p. 262.
141. Home, *The History*, pp. 155–6.
142. MMM, DX594, f. 25v.
143. Ibid., f. 32r.
144. Ibid., f. 33r.
145. *Penny London Post*, 425, 15–17 January 1746.
146. Cumberland to Campbell, 28 February 1746, TNA, SP 54/28, f. 47A.
147. *London Gazette*, 5378, 1–5 November 1715.
148. Lewis, *Walpole's Correspondence*, vol. 19, p. 127.
149. *Caledonian Mercury*, 3923, 3 December 1745; Oglethorpe to Newcastle, 24 November 1745, TNA, SP 36/74, f. 266r.
150. Cuthbert Readshaw to Sykes, December 1745, Hull University Library, DDSY (3) 1/48.
151. Vernon to ?, 29 October 1745, National Maritime Museum, Ver1/3/A.
152. *HMC Var. Coll.*, vol. 8, p. 133–4; Royal Commission on Historical Manuscripts, *Report on the Manuscripts of Lady Du Cane* (London: HMSO, 1905), p. 77 (hereafter *HMC Du Cane*).
153. *Gentleman's Magazine*, 16, p. 209.
154. *Gentleman's Magazine,* 16, pp. 208, 209; Ray, *A Compleat History*, p. 238.
155. Cockburne to Pringle, 25 November 1715, TNA, SP 54/10, f. 81.
156. Ferguson, *Argyll*, p. 174.
157. *Gentleman's Magazine*, 16, pp. 315, 429.

158. Rae, *History*, pp. 278–9.
159. Cumberland to Newcastle, 20 February 1746, TNA, SP 54/28, f. 20A.
160. Cameron of Lochiel's declaration, 20 March 1746, TNA, SP 54/30, f. 4A.
161. Macaulay, *History*, vol. 1, p. 462.
162. Royle, *Civil War*, p. 222; Black, *War for America*, p. 43.
163. Argyll to Townshend, 18 October 1715, TNA, SP 54/9, f. 53.
164. Argyll to Townshend, 4 November 1715, TNA, SP 54/10, f. 18a.
165. Argyll to Townshend, 10 November 1715, TNA, SP 54/10, f. 39.
166. Wentworth to Newcastle, 11 November 1745 NUL, NeC1678; same to same, 22 November 1745, NUL, NeC, 1681.
167. Ray, *A Compleat History*, p. 34.
168. Herdman to Teller, 17 November 1745, HRO, MIL3/68.
169. Wentworth to Newcastle, 21 December 1745, NUL, NeC1685.
170. Home, *The History*, pp. 164–5n.
171. Cumberland to Newcastle, 28 February 1746, TNA, SP 54/28, f. 47A.
172. Blaikie, *Origins*, pp. 158–9.
173. Henderson, *History*, p. 86.
174. Cholmondeley to Newcastle, 24 November 1745, BL Add. Mss 32705, f. 375r.
175. MMM, DX 594, ff. 9v–10v.
176. Ray, *A Compleat History*, p. 60.
177. Macaulay, *History,* vol. 1, pp. 447–8.
178. Yorke (ed.), *Hardwicke*, vol. 1, p. 472.
179. Graves to Robinson, 9 December 1745, WYAS: Leeds NH2875/12, Burton to ?, 9 December 1745, WYAS: Leeds, NP/D3/4/11/13.
180. R. C. Latham and W. E. Matthews (eds), *Diary of Samuel Pepys* (London: G. Bell and Sons, 1972–1983), vol. 5, p. 99, vol. 9, pp. 132, 134, 466; Szechi and Holmes, *England in the Age of Oligarchy*, p. 185.
181. Coxe, *Memoirs*, vol. 3, p. 351.
182. McNiven (ed.), *Diary of Henry Prescott*, vol. 2, p. 472.
183. Robinson to Robinson, 9 June 1716, WYAS:Leeds, Vyner, 6006/13229.
184. *Flying Post*, 3660, 18–21 June 1715.
185. *Penny London Post*, 405, 29 November –2 December 1745.
186. Maxwell, *Narrative*, p. 78.
187. Redington, *Calendar of Treasury Papers*, 1714–1719, pp. 128, 210, 126.
188. Rae, *History*, pp. 170–1, 214–5.
189. J. D. Oates, 'Jacobitism and Popular Disturbances in Northern England, 1714–1719', *Northern History*, 41:1 (2004), pp. 111–28.
190. Williamson to Newcastle, 10 June 1740, TNA, SP 36/51, f. 29v.
191. Chandler to Newcastle, 27 January 1746, TNA, SP 36/80, f. 430r.
192. Oates and Navickas, 'Jacobites and Jacobins', p. 48.
193. Coxe, *Memoirs*, vol. 3, p. 36.
194. Rae, *History*, p. 228.
195. Henderson, *History*, pp. 78–9.
196. D. Forbes, *Culloden Papers*, (London, 1815), p. 247.
197. Ibid., p. 250.
198. Blaikie, *Origins*, p. 206.
199. Militia accounts, October 1715, DULASC, CC 42.
200. Home, *The History*, pp. 104–5.

201. Whiting, *Two Yorkshire Diaries*, p. 119.
202. F. Tyrer (ed.), *Diary of Nicholas Blundell, 1712–1719* (Record Society of Lancashire and Cheshire, 1970), p. 151.
203. *Political State of Great Britain* (1716), pp. 536–7, 541.
204. Matthews (ed.), *Diary*, p. 175.
205. Jarvis, *The Jacobite Risings*, p. 166.
206. Yonge to officer commanding, 5 December 1745, TNA, WO 5/37, f. 212.
207. Stainforth to Mayer, 26 December 1745, NRO, ZAL Box40/4.
208. Ray, *History*, pp. 222–3.
209. Newcastle to Lord Mayor, 13 December 1745, BL Add. Mss 37412, f. 40r.
210. Corporation of London Records Office, Lieutenancy Minutes, 1744–1749, pp. 26, 28, 36, 38, 42, 86, 88.
211. Macaulay, *History*, vol. 1, p. 450.
212. YCA, E41B, ff. 16b, 20; Herring to Hardwicke, 13 December 1745, BL Add.Mss 35598, f. 140r.
213. Ibid., f. 26.
214. Dickson (ed.), *Warrender Letters*, p. 92.
215. Hepburn to ?, 12 October 1715, TNA, SP 54/9, f. 36B.
216. Cockburne to ?, 10 September 1715, TNA, SP 54/8, f. 37c.
217. Fletcher to Tweeddale, 6 September 1745, TNA, SP 54/26, f. 7a.
218. Ibid., f. 17.
219. Oates, *The Jacobite Invasion*, pp. 69, 78; Jarvis, *The Jacobite Risings*, pp. 167–8, 170–2.
220. Malton to Newcastle, 23 November 1745, TNA, SP 36/74, f. 231r; Jarvis, *The Jacobite Risings*, p. 163.
221. McNiven (ed.), *Diary of Henry Prescott*, vol. 2, pp. 473–4.
222. YCA, E41B, f. 20.
223. *General Advertiser*, 15 February 1746; *York Journal*, 11 March 1746.
224. Graves to Robinson, 25 November 1745, WYAS: Leeds, NH2875/8.
225. Lonsdale to ?, 4 November 1715, BL Add. Mss 63093, f. 61v.
226. Cope to Newcastle, 3 October 1745, TNA, SP 36/70, f. 92r; Nealson to Newcastle, 29 September 1745, TNA, SP 36/69, f. 241r.
227. Grey, *Clerk of Penicuik*, p. 90.
228. Ibid., p. 89.
229. Elcho, *Short Account*, p. 338.
230. Malton to Fitzwilliam, 11 November 1745, NORO.
231. Hardwicke to Herring, 21 September 1745, BL Add. Mss 35598, ff. 62r–63v.
232. Argyll to Stanhope, 18 September 1715, TNA, SP 54/8, f. 74A.
233. Ray, *A Compleat History*, pp. 61–2.
234. W. B. Blaikie, *Itinerary of Prince Charles Edward Stuart* (Edinburgh: Scottish History Society, 1897), pp. 86–7.
235. Forbes, *Culloden Papers*, p. 275.

WORKS CITED

Manuscript Sources

Blair Atholl Castle: Atholl Papers 45/12/77.

Bodleian Library: MS Eng. Hist. c501.

Borthwick Institute of Historical Research: BP C & P, XXI/I, 4.

British Library: Additional Manuscripts, 3030; 22560; 32705–6; 33004; 33048; 35598; 37221; 37412; 40728; 61136; 63093; Stowe, 228.

Berkshire Record Office: D/EP4/03.

Berwick Record Office: Archive 2/4.

Chatsworth House: Devonshire papers, 317.

Corporation of London Records Office: Lieutenancy Minutes, 1744–1749.

Cumbria Archive Service, Whitehaven: YD/Da.8; Y/Pen. Acc.2689.

Durham Dean and Chapter Library: Sharp Mss, 109, 150.

Durham Record Office: D/St/C1/3/186.

Durham University Library Archives and Special Collections: Clavering Correspondence, CC 42.

Hampshire Record Office: 84M95/1.

Hertfordshire Record Office: Cowper Mss, D/EP F195; MIL3 and 4.

Hull University Library: Skyes correspondence, DDSY (3) 1/48.

Lancashire Record Office: Derby Correspondence, DDK1741/7.

Lancashire parish accounts: PR29456/2/1; PR3360/4/1/1; PR3168/79.

Leeds Library Local and Family History Library: 'Diary of John Lucas'.

Merseyside Maritime Museum: Journal of Walter Shairp, DX 594.

The National Archives: Assizes 8/37; Privy Council 2/85, 99; State Papers Domestic 35 and 36; State Papers Order Books, 41 and 44; State Papers for Scotland, 54; War Office 4 and 5.

National Maritime Museum: Vernon Papers, Ver1/3/A.

Northampton Record Office: Fitzwalter-Malton Correspondence, 1745.

Northumberland Record Office: ZAL Box40/4.

North Yorkshire County Record Office: Lieutenancy Minutes, ZPB/1446/1256.

Nottingham University Library: Newcastle Papers, NeC, 1678, 1681, 1685.

The Royal Archives: Cumberland Papers (Microfilm), CP 6–14.

Sheffield Archives: Rockingham Mss, WWM/1 and 2; RA, M16/1.

West Yorkshire Archive Service, Leeds Archives: Newby Hall, NH2875; Nostell Priory, NP1510; NP/D3/4/11/13; Vyner Mss, 6006; Temple Newsam, TN/PO3/3C; Wakefield; West Riding Quarter Sessions, QS10/13.

William Salt Library: S.MS.521–522; SMS47/18/10/2.

York City Archives: E130; E41B; F12.

York Minister Library: West Riding Accounts.

Manuscript Collections

Royal Commission on Historical Manuscripts (HMC)

Report on the Manuscripts of the Earl of Ancaster Preserved at Grimsthorpe (London: HMSO, 1907).

The Manuscripts of the Earl of Carlisle, Preserved at Castle Howard (London: HMSO, 1897).

Report on the Manuscripts of Lady Du Cane (London: HMSO, 1905).

Report on the Manuscripts of the Late Reginald Rawdon Hastings, Esq., of the Manor House, Ashby De La Zouche (London: HMSO, 1934), vol. 3 .

Calendar of the Stuart Papers Belonging to His Majesty the King(London: HMSO, 1902), vol. 1.

The Manuscipts of Marquess Townshend (London: HMSO, 1887).

Report on Manuscripts in Various Collections, vol 8 (London: HMSO, 1913).

Newspapers

Daily Courant.

Evening Post.

Flying Post.

General Advertiser.

General Evening Post.

Gentleman's Magazine.

Glasgow Courant.

Kentish Post.

London Evening Post.

London Gazette.

Manchester Mercury.

Newcastle Courant.

Newcastle Journal.

Original Weekly Journal.

The Penny London Post.

St James Evening Post.

The Westminster Journal.

York Courant.

York Journal.

Published Sources

Anderson, W. H. (ed.), *The Papers of the Rev. John Anderson* (Dumbarton: Bennett & Thomson, 1914).

Anderson, W. H. (ed.), 'The Battle of Culloden', *Journal of the Society for Army Historical Research*, 1 (1921), pp. 21–4.

Anon., *The Case of Lieutenant John Kynaston* (London, *c*.1716).

—, *A Journey through Part of England and Scotland. Along with the Army under the Command of His Royal Highness the Duke of Cumberland* (London: J. Stanton, 1746).

—, *History of the Rebellion of the Years 1715 and 1745* (Roxburgh Club: Oxford, 1944).

—, 'The Battle of Culloden', *Journal of the Society for Army Historical Research*, 36 (1957), pp. 183–5.

Arnot, J. S., and B. Seton, *The Prisoners of the '45* (Edinburgh: Scottish History Society, 1928–9), vols 1–3.

Articles of War (1745).

Atkinson, J. C. (ed.), 'Quarter Session Records', *North Riding Record Society*, 8 (1890).

Bailey, G., *Falkirk or Paradise! The Battle of Falkirk Muir: 17 January 1746* (Edinburgh: John Donald Publishers, 1996).

Barthorp, M., *The Jacobite Rebellions, 1689–1745* (London: Osprey Publishing, 1982).

Bate, J., *A Parochial Letter to the Inhabitants of Deptford* (London: Author, 1745).

Baynes, J., *The Jacobite Rising of 1715* (London: Cassell, 1970).

Bell, R. F. (ed.), *Memorials of John Murray of Broughton, Sometime Secretary to Prince Charles Edward 1740–1747* (Edinburgh: Scottish History Society, 1898).

Beresford, M. (ed.), *The Diary of James Woodforde* (Oxford: Oxford University Press, 1986).

Black, J., *War for America* (Stroud: Sutton, 1991).

—, *Culloden and the '45* (Stroud: Sutton, 1990).

—, *War and the World, 1450–2000* (New Haven, CT: Yale University Press, 2000).

Blaikie, W. B., *Itinerary of Prince Charles Edward Stuart* (Edinburgh: Scottish History Society, 1897).

— (ed.), *Origins of the 'Forty-Five and Other Papers Relating to That Rising* (Edinburgh: Scottish History Society, 1916).

Brewer, J., The *Sinews of Power: War, Money and the British State, 1688–1783* (New York: Alfred Knopf, 1988).

Brockbank, W., and F. Kenworthy (eds), *Diary of Dr Richard Kay, 1716–1751 of Baldingstone, Near Bury, a Lancaster Doctor* (Manchester: Chetham Society, 1968).

Brumwell, S., *Redcoats: The British Soldier and War in the Americas, 1755–1763* (Cambridge: Cambridge University Press, 2002).

Burt, E., *Letters from a Gentleman in the North of Scotland to His Friend in London* (London: R. Fenner, 1818).

Carlyle, A., *Autobiography of the Rev. Alexander Carlyle, Minister of Inverness* (Edinburgh, 1860).

Chamberlayne, J., *Present State of Great Britain* (London, 1726).

Chandler, D., *Marlborough as Military Commander* (London: Batsford, 1973).

—, *The Art of War in the Age of Marlborough* (London: Batsford, 1975).

— (ed.), *The Oxford History of the British Army* (Oxford: Oxford University Press, 2002).

Climenson, E. J. (ed.), *Elizabeth Montagu: the Queen of the Blue-stockings: Her Correspondence from 1720 to 1761* (London: John Murray, 1906), vol. 1.

Cobbett, W., *Parliamentary History of England* (London: Bagshaw, 1823), vol. 13.

Colley, C., *Britons: Forging the Nation, 1707–1837* (New Haven, CT: Yale University Press, 1992).

Collyer, C., 'Yorkshire and the '45', *Yorkshire Archaeological Journal* 38, (1955), pp. 145–57.

Constable, T. (ed.), *A Fragment of a Memoir of Field Marshal James Keith* (Edinburgh, 1843).

Cooper, C. H., *Annals of Cambridge* (Cambridge: Warwick, 1862), vol. 4.

Cormack A., and A. Jones (eds), *The Journals of Corporal Todd, 1745–1762* (London: Bodley Head, 2001).

Coward, T. A., *Picturesque Cheshire* (London: Sherratt & Hughes, 1903).

Cowper, S. (ed.), *The Diary of Lady Cowper* (London: John Murray, 1864).

Coxe, W. (ed.), *Memoirs of the Life and Administration of Sir Robert Walpole, Earl of Oxford* (London, 1798), vol. 3.

Cruickshanks, E., *Political Untouchables: The Tories and the '45* (London: Duckworth, 1979).

Dickson, W. D. (ed.), *Warrender Letters: Correspondence of Sir George Warrender, Bt., Lord Provost of Edinburgh, and Member of Parliament for the City, with Relative Papers, 1715* (Edinburgh: Scottish History Society, 1935).

Duffy, C., *The '45* (London: Cassell, 2003).

Dunbar, E., *Social Life in Former Days* (Edinburgh: Edmonston & Douglas, 1865).

Lord Elcho, *A Short Account of the Affairs of Scotland in the Years 1744, 1745, 1746* (Edinburgh: John Douglas Publishers Ltd, 1907).

Ellis, J. M. (ed.), *The Letters of Henry Liddell to William Cotesworth* (Durham: Surtees Society, 1985).

Fergusson, J., *Argyll in the Forty Five* (London: Faber & Faber, 1952).

Fielding, H., *Tom Jones* (Harmondsworth: Penguin, 2005).

Findlay, J. H., *Wolfe in Scotland* (London: Longmans, Green & Co., 1928).

Forbes, D., *Culloden Papers* (London, 1815).

Forbes R., and R. Chambers, *Jacobite Memoirs of the Rebellion of 1745* (Edinburgh: William & Robert Chambers, 1834).

Fortescue, J., *The History of the British Army* (London: Macmillan, 1935), vol. 2.

Gibson, D., *A Parson in the Vale of the White Horse, 1753–1761* (Gloucester: Sutton, 1982).

Gifford, J., C. Mcwillian and D. Walker, *The Buildings of Scotland*: *Edinburgh* (Harmondsworth: Penguin Books, 1984).

Gifford J., and F. A. Walker, *Stirling and Central Scotland* (New Haven, CT: Yale University Press, 2002).

Grey, J. M. (ed.), *The Memoirs of the Life of John Clerk of Penicuik* (Edinburgh: Scottish History Society, 1892).

Guy, A. J., *Oeconomy and Discipline: Officership and Administration in the British Army, 1714–1763* (Manchester: Manchester University Press, 1984).

— (ed.), *Colonel Samuel Bagshawe and the Army of George II, 1731–1762* (London: Bodley Head, 1990).

Hardy, W. J. (ed.), *Calendar of Middlesex Sessions, 1689–1709* (London: Sir Richard Nicholson, 1905).

Harrington, P., *Culloden 1746: The Highlanders' Last Charge* (Oxford: Osprey Publishing, 1991)

Hatton, R., *George I: Elector and King* (Cambridge, MA: Harvard University Press, 1978).

Hayter, A., *The Army and the Crowd in Mid-Georgian England* (London: Macmillan, 1978).

Henderson, A., *History of the Rebellion* (London, 1748).

—, *The Life of William Augustus, Duke of Cumberland* (London: J. Ridley, 1766).

Hepburne Scott, G. F. C. (ed.), 'Marchmont Correspondence Relating to the '45', *Miscellany of the Scottish History Society* (Edinburgh: Scottish History Society, 1890, 1933), vol. 5, pp. 315–51.

Hibbert-Ware, S., *Lancashire Memorials of 1715* (Manchester: Chetham Society, 1845).

Hobson, M. G. (ed.), *Oxford Council Acts, 1701–1752* (Oxford: Oxford University Press, 1954).

Holmes, G., *The Making of a Great Power, 1660–1722* (London: Longman, 1993).

Holmes, R., *Redcoat* (London: Harper Collins, 2001).

Home, J., *The History of the Rebellion in the Year 1745* (London: T. Cadell, jun. and W. Davies, 1802).

Houlding, J. A., *Fit for Service: The Training of the British Army, 1715–1795* (Oxford: Clarendon Press, 1981).

Hughes, M., *A Plain Narrative or Journal of the Late Rebellion Begun in 1745* (London, 1746).

Hussey, J., *Marlborough: Hero of Blenheim* (London: Weidenfeld & Nicolson, 2004).

Latham, R. C., and W. E. Matthews (eds), *Diary of Samuel Pepys* (London: G. Bell & Sons, 1972–83), vols 5 and 9.

Le Hardy, W. (ed.), *Hertfordshire Sessions Rolls, 1699–1850* (Hertford, 1905).

Jarvis, R. C., *The Jacobite Risings of 1715 and 1745* (Cumberland County Council, 1954).

—, *Collected Papers on the Jacobite Risings* (Manchester: Manchester University Press, 1971).

Kenyon, J., *The Civil Wars of England* (London: Weidenfeld & Nicolson, 1988).

Lenman, B. P., *The Jacobite Risings in Britain, 1689–1746* (London: Methuen, 1980).

Lewis, W. S. (ed.), *Horace Walpole's Correspondence: Walpole to Mann* (New Haven, CT: Yale University Press, 1955 and 1974), vols 19 and 37.

Lodge, R. (ed.), *Private Correspondence of Chesterfield and Newcastle 1744–46* (London: Royal Historical Society, 1930).

Lord Macaulay, *History of England* (London: Everyman, 1980).

McCann, T. J. (ed.), *The Correspondence of the Dukes of Richmond and Newcastle, 1724–1750* (Lewes: Sussex Record Society, 1983).

McKnight, J., and D. Laing (eds), *Memoirs of the Insurrection in Scotland in 1715 by John, Master of Sinclair* (Edinburgh, 1858).

McLynn, F. J., *The Jacobites* (London: Routledge and Kegan Paul, Ltd, 1985).

—, *France and the Jacobite Rising of 1745* (Edinburgh: Edinburgh University Press, 1981)

—, *Bonnie Prince Charlie* (Oxford: Oxford University Press, 1991).

—, *The Jacobite Army in England: The Final Campaign* (Edinburgh: John Donald Publishers, Ltd, 1983).

McNiven, P. (ed.), *Diary of Henry Prescott, LL.B., Deputy Registrar of Chester Diocese* (Record Society of Lancashire and Cheshire, 1994).

Marchant, J., *History of the Present Rebellion* (London, 1746).

Margulies, M., *The Battle of Prestonpans, 1745* (Stroud: Tempus, 2007).

Marshall, J. (ed.), *The Autobiography of William Stout* (Manchester: Chetham Society, 1967).

Matthews, W. E. (ed.), *Diary of Dudley Ryder* (London: Methuen & Co., 1939).

Maxwell, J., *Narrative of Charles Prince of Wales' Expedition to Scotland in the Year 1745* (Edinburgh: T. Constable, 1841).

Miller, G. C., *Hoghton Tower* (Preston: Guardian Press, 1948).

Miller, J., 'Diary of James Miller', *Journal of the Society for Army Historical Research*, 1 (1922), pp. 208–26.

Mounsey, G., *Carlisle in 1745* (London, 1846).

Oates, J. D., 'Responses in North East England to the Jacobite Rebellions of 1715 and 1745' (unpublished PhD thesis, Reading University, 2001).

—, 'Loyalty and Conspiracy in and around Deptford', *Lewisham Historian*, 8 (2000), pp. 1–11.

—, 'Independent Volunteer Forces in Yorkshire During the Forty-Five', *Yorkshire Archaeological Journal*, 73 (2001), pp. 205–17.

—, 'Civil Defence in North East England During the Jacobite Rebellion of 1715', *Journal of the Society for Army Historical Research*, 80:322 (2002), pp. 86–97.

—, 'Yorkshire and the Fifteen', *Yorkshire Archaeological Journal*, 75 (2003), pp. 145–57.

—, *York and the Jacobite Rebellion of 1745* (Borthwick Texts, 2005).

—, 'Hessian Forces Employed in Scotland in 1746', *Journal of the Society for Army Historical Research*, 83:335 (2005), pp. 205–14.

—, 'Responses in the Home Counties to the Jacobite Rebellion of 1745', *Southern History,* 28 (2006), pp. 46–73.

—, 'Jacobitism and Popular Disturbances in Northern England, 1714–1719', *Northern History*, 41:1 (2004), pp. 111–28.

—, 'Responses in the North of England to the Jacobite Rebellion of 1715', *Northern History*, 43:1 (2006), pp. 77–95.

—, *The Jacobite Invasion of 1745 in North West England* (Lancaster: Centre for North West Regional Studies, 2006).

—, 'Dutch Forces in Eighteenth Century Britain: A British Perspective', *Journal of the Society for Army Historical Research*, 85:341 (2007), pp. 20–39.

—, *Seditious Words and Loyal Addresses: Jacobitism in Hampshire* (Hampshire County Council, 2007).

—, *Sweet William or the Butcher? The Duke of Cumberland and the '45* (Barnsley: Pen & Sword, 2008).

—, *The Last Battle on English Soil* (Lancaster: Centre for North West Regional Studies, forthcoming).

Oates J., and K. Navickas (eds), *Jacobites and Jacobins, Two Eighteenth-Century Perspectives* (Record Society of Lancashire and Cheshire, 2006).

Patten, R., *History of the Rebellion* (London: J. Baker & T. Warner, 1717).

Picton, T., *Municipal Records of Liverpool* (Liverpool: Gilbert G. Walmsley, 1886).

The Political State of Great Britain (1716, 1717, 1719).

Pollard, A. (ed.), *Culloden: The History and Archaeology of the Last Clan Battle* (Barnsley: Pen & Sword, 2009).

Pottle, F. (ed.), *Boswell's London Journal, 1762–1763* (London: William Heinemann, 1950).

Prebble, J., *Culloden* (London: Secker & Warburg, 1961).

Rae, P., *History of the Late Rebellion* (London, 1745).

Rawson, B. (ed.), *The Chevalier de Johnstone: A Memoir of the 45* (London: Folio Society, 1958).

Ray, J., *A Compleat History of the Rebellion from Its Rise in 1745, to Its Total Suppression in the Glorious Battle of Culloden, in April 1746* (1754).

Redington, T., *Calendar of Treasury Papers, 1714–1719 Preserved in Her Majesty's Public Record Office* (London: Longman and Co, 1883).

Reid, S., *1745: A Military History of the Last Jacobite Rising* (Spellmount: Staplehurst, 1996).

—, *Like Hungry Wolves: Culloden Moor, the 16th April 1746* (London: Windrow & Greene, 1994).

—, *Wolfe: The Career of General James Wolfe from Culloden to Quebec* (Spellmount: Staplehurst, 2000).

—, *Culloden* (Barnsley: Pen & Sword, 2005).

Reid, S., and G. Embleton, *Culloden Moor, 1746* (Oxford: Osprey, 2002).

Ritchie, R. I., 'The Durham Association Regiment', *Journal of the Society for Army Historical Research*, 34 (1956), pp. 106–19.

Roberts, J., *The Jacobite Wars: Scotland and the Military Campaigns of 1715 and 1745* (Edinburgh: Polygon, 2002).

Rogers, P. (ed.), *Daniel Defoe's Tour of the Whole Island* (Harmondsworth: Penguin, 1971).

Royle, T., *Civil War: The War of the Three Kingdoms 1638–1660* (London: Abacus, 2005).

Sadler; J., *Culloden and the Last Charge of the Highland Clans* (Stroud: Tempus, 2005).

Saville, A. (ed.), *Secret Comment: The Diaries of Gertrude Saville, 1722–1757* (Nottingham: Thoroton Society, 1997).

Sedgwick, R., *Lord Hervey's Memoirs* (Harmondsworth: Penguin Books Ltd, 1961).

Sedgwick, R., *The Commons, 1715–1754* (London: HMSO, 1970), vol. 1.

Sinclair-Stevenson, C., *Inglorious Rebellion: The Jacobite Risings of 1708, 1715 and 1719* (London: Hamish Hamilton, 1971).

Sked, C. P., and H. Horrocks, *Culloden* (Edinburgh: National Trust for Scotland, 1997).

Smith, S. D. (ed.), *Letter Books of Joseph Symson, 1711–1720* (Oxford: Oxford University Press, 2003).

Speck, W. A., *The Butcher: The Duke of Cumberland and the Suppression of the '45* (Welsh Academic Press, 1995).

Steuart, A. (ed.), *News Letters of 1715–16* (Edinburgh: W. & R. Chambers, 1910).

Stevenson, J., *Popular Disturbances in England* (London: Longman, 1978).

Stone, L. (ed.), *An Imperial State at War* (New Haven, CT: Yale University Press, 1995).

Stuart, J. (ed.), *Extracts from the Burgh of Aberdeen* (Edinburgh: Scottish Burgh Record Society, 1872).

Szechi, D., *1715: The Great Jacobite Rising* (New Haven, CT: Yale University Press, 2006).

Szechi, D., and Holmes, G., *England in the Age of Oligarchy, 1722–1783* (London: Longman, 1993).

Tabraham, C., and D. Grove, *Fortress Scotland and the Jacobites* (London: Batsford, 1995).

Tayler, A., and H. Tayler (eds), *The '45 and After* (London: Thomas Nelson & Sons, 1938).

Thornton, W., *The Counterpoise* (London, 1754).

Tommasson, K., and F. Buist, *Battles of the '45* (London: Batsford, 1962).

Tyrer, F. (ed.), *Diary of Nicholas Blundell, 1712–1719* (Record Society of Lancashire and Cheshire, 1970).

Wade, G., C. Cadogan, J. Folliot, C. Lennox and J. Guise, *A Report of the Proceedings and Opinion of the Board of General Officers, on Their Examination into the Conduct, Behaviour and Proceedings of Lieutenant-General Sir John Cope, Knight of the Bath, Colonel Peregrine Lascelles, and Brigadier-General Thomas Fowkes* (Dublin, 1749).

Ward, A., *History and Antiquities of York*, I (York: A. Ward, 1785).

Warrand, D., *More Culloden Papers* (Inverness: Robert Carruthers and Sons, 1930), vol. 4.

Western, J. R., *The English Militia in the Eighteenth Century* (London: Routledge and Kegan, 1965).

Whiting, C. E. (ed.), *Two Yorkshire Diaries* (Leeds: Yorkshire Archeaological Society, 1952).

Williamson, R. J., *Historical Records of the Regiment of Lancashire Militia* (London: Simpkins, Marshal & Co., 1876).

Willson, B., *Life and Letters of Wolfe* (London: Heinemann, 1909).

York Poll Book (1741).

Yorke, P. C. (ed.), *The Life and Correspondence of Philip Yorke, Earl of Hardwicke, Lord Chancellor of Great Britain Hardwicke* (Cambridge: Cambridge University Press, 1913), vol. 1.

INDEX

Aberdeen, 14, 42, 48, 50, 56, 58–60, 137–38, 140, 154, 175, 176
Aberdeen, Earl of, 130
Alnwick, 137
American War of Independence, 3, 10, 17, 30, 34, 67, 165
Anderson, Rev. John, 135, 173
Argyll, Duke of, 25, 59, 61, 62, 66, 69, 123, 173, 179, 181, 193, 196
    appointed commander, 25, 33
    concern for manpower, 26, 37, 65, 70
    concern for quality of troops, 30
    criticism of militia, 168, 178, 184, 192, 193
    despatches troops, 58
    Dutch troops, 31
    given orders, 33–4
    lacks artillery, 51
    march to Perth, 57
    money concerns, 46, 51
    protects Edinburgh, 35
    reinforced, 30, 38
    at Sherriffmuir, 34, 72–6, 78, 81, 87, 90, 94, 196, 198
    suggests negotiation, 35
army, 1–2, 195–8
    desertion, 62, 65
    divided loyalties, 62–5
    new regiments, 13, 29, 51
    peacetime roles, 17–21, 24
    intelligence, 23, 42–6
    recruitment, 7–17, 21, 29, 131
    size, 24–33, 69–70
    supply, 46–54
    transport 25, 42, 53–4
    see also artillery, cavalry, infantry, individual regiments, battles

artillery, 5, 7, 10, 17, 29–30, 51–3, 57, 58, 68–9, 70, 72, 74, 78–82, 86, 89, 91, 95, 98, 100, 104–7, 109, 111–16, 118–20, 151, 196
associations, 132, 146, 147
Austrian Succession, War of, 32, 34

Bagshawe, Colonel Samuel, 9, 14
Bath, 35–6, 196
Bedford, Duke of, 9, 13
Belford, Major, 52, 120
Berwick, 21, 41, 50–2, 58, 64, 99–102, 105–6, 108–11, 131, 139, 146, 149, 155, 156, 169, 178, 191
Blackett, Edward, 138
Blakeney, Major General William, 112, 114
Bland, Major General Humphrey, 10, 55, 59, 119
Blenheim, 67–8, 71, 94
Board of Ordnance, 23, 51–2, 119, 137, 149, 150
Bowes, Sir George, 137, 140, 147
Bradshaw, Enoch, 50, 73, 74, 91
Bristol, 36–7, 163, 172, 186, 196
Brodie, Alexander, 129
Burlington, Earl of, 138, 141, 143

Cadogan, Lieutenant General William, 31, 33, 36, 51, 59, 61
Campbell, Major General John, 137, 171, 180, 182–3
Carlisle, 11, 30, 35, 44–6, 49, 52, 61–2, 79, 99, 101–2, 105, 107, 111–2, 117, 119, 121, 123–4, 126, 131, 137, 139, 146, 155–6, 162, 164–6, 169, 177, 181–2, 193, 197
Carlisle, Earl of, 130, 132

Carmarthen, Earl of, 129

Carpenter, Lieutenant General George, 25, 33, 37, 43, 59, 61, 69, 90–1

Catholics, 35–6, 40, 93, 138, 141, 148, 150, 155, 159, 162–3, 186–9, 191

Cavalry, 7, 16, 18–19, 24–7, 29–30, 36, 38, 40–2, 56, 57–8, 70, 74–7, 85–9, 91, 95, 119, 139, 196

Chandler, Bishop Edward, 130, 132, 187

Charles I, 4, 36, 66, 128

Charles II, 4, 132

Charles Edward Stuart, 2, 39, 43, 63, 80, 88, 94, 95, 113–14, 116–117, 125, 162, 169–70, 176, 183

Chester, 21, 35, 40, 55, 74, 97, 99, 101, 105–7, 110–11, 139, 148, 169, 191

Chesterfield, Earl of, 107, 121, 146

Cholmondeley, Earl of, 44, 97, 105, 106–7, 110–11, 157, 169, 185

Civil Wars, 3, 7, 98–9, 104, 178

clergymen, 20, 141, 147–9, 155 (and see individual clergymen)

Clerk, Sir John, 83, 129, 176, 191

Clifton, 67, 68, 71, 76, 78, 85, 88–9, 92

constables, 17, 23, 29, 53, 120, 127, 132, 138

Conway, Colonel Henry, 15, 59, 62, 75, 86, 105, 120

Cope, Sir John, 28, 30, 40, 56, 64, 69, 71, 105, 135, 175, 180, 191, 195
    appointed commander, 33
    concern for troop levels, 27
    defence of Berwick, 102, 106, 109, 110, 111
    gathers intelligence, 43, 45, 46, 188
    given initiative, 134
    given orders, 38, 39
    holds council of war, 39, 62
    lacks gunners, 30
    lack of Scottish support, 135, 167
    march through Highlands, 64
    at Prestonpans, 29, 40, 72–6, 79, 82, 86, 185
    recommends Molloy as officer, 8, 122
    summons officers, 39
    supply concerns, 48–9, 52, 54

Cotesworth, William, 44–5, 139, 171

Craigie, Robert, 132

Crewe, Bishop Nathaniel, 129

Crisap, Joseph, 135, 138

Cromwell, Oliver, 8, 127

Culloden, 1, 2, 5, 13, 61, 65, 67, 69–70, 72–4, 76–8, 80–1, 84–6, 89–95, 122, 125, 176, 179, 182, 196, 198

Cumberland, Duke of, 14, 27, 29, 30, 41, 52, 54, 56–7, 62, 66, 68–9, 71, 82–3, 88, 166, 176
    admired by troops, 50, 59, 60, 61
    appointed commander-in-chief, 33, 41, 59
    concern for fortresses, 56, 97, 103, 110, 119, 122, 123, 124, 182
    criticism of militia, 177, 185
    criticism of new regiments, 29
    at Culloden, 72–4, 76–7, 82–4, 91, 176, 177, 179, 198
    given orders, 26, 34
    Hessian troops, 33, 53, 62
    intelligence reports, 45–6
    marches in England, 42, 74
    praise of militia, 163, 179–180, 185
    resists return to England, 27–9
    sends out detachments, 58, 183
    siege of Carlisle, 119–21, 156, 181
    slowness of marches, 49
    supply concerns, 47–9, 65

Cunningham, Captain Archibald, 79, 80

Daniel, John, 85–6, 188

D'Arcy, Sir Conyers, 152, 164

Dawes, Sir William, 141

Deptford, 131, 155

Derby, 2, 41, 46, 74, 147, 177

Derby, Earl of, 139–40, 165, 169, 177

Dettingen, 30, 71, 82, 152

Devonshire, Duke of, 155, 186

dissenters, 52, 148, 154, 178

Doncaster, 40

Dumfries, 35, 44, 140–41, 172, 175

Durand, Lieutenant Colonel James, 102, 107–8, 111, 118, 122–3, 195

Durham, 129–32, 137–40, 143, 147, 150, 158, 169, 187, 188

Dutch forces, 17, 26, 29–32, 38–41, 55, 58, 62–3, 67, 121, 151, 182

Edinburgh, 4, 19, 21, 28–30, 35, 39, 43–4, 46, 48–9 51, 56, 58, 60, 65, 74, 76, 79, 81, 99–101, 103–8, 110–11, 113, 116–17, 122–3, 128, 131, 133, 137, 140–1, 143, 145–6, 149, 151–2, 154, 156, 158, 164, 167, 175, 179, 181, 184–5, 188, 190

Elcho, Lord, 63, 65, 83, 84, 88, 90, 116–17, 119, 136, 166, 177, 192

Falkirk, 1, 30, 5, 55, 60, 67, 70, 73–80, 83, 86–8, 90, 92–5, 97, 114, 122, 123, 179–80, 190, 196–8

Fawkener, Sir Everard, 44, 48, 177

Finchley, 41, 181

Fitzgerald, Captain George, 92

Fletcher, Andrew, 107, 117, 119, 129, 136, 141, 153, 163

Fontenoy, 30, 69, 71, 74, 82, 94, 97

Forbes, Duncan, 30, 132, 134, 142, 146, 163, 175, 188, 192

Forrester, Colonel, 90, 92

Forster, Thomas, 5

Fort Augustus, 21, 39, 101, 103–4, 113–14, 119, 122–3, 175, 183, 188

Fort George, 101–3, 110–11, 113–14, 118–19, 121–3, 124

Fort William, 21, 39, 44, 99–101, 103–4, 106–7, 110–11, 113–17, 122–3, 171, 176, 182

France, 2, 4, 27–9, 31–3, 35, 38, 41–2, 63, 98–9, 112, 162, 196

Gardiner, Colonel James, 77, 86–8, 93

George I, 20–1, 63, 93, 129, 155

George II, 4, 10, 13, 32, 63, 117, 132, 147–8, 159

Glasgow, 19, 44, 135–7, 139–41, 143, 145, 163, 174, 179, 181, 185, 190, 192

Glenorchy, Lord, 44, 86, 132–3, 146, 167, 168

Glenshiel, 31, 32, 67–8, 70, 72, 76, 81, 84, 90–5

Gomez, Serra, 47, 50

Gordon, Duke of, 130

Gower, Lord, 12–13, 17

Grant, Major, 113, 118, 122, 195

Guest, General Joshua 8, 79, 116–17

Halifax, 61, 153, 159

Halkett, Sir Peter, 83

Hamilton, Duchess of, 146

Handasyde, Lieutenant General Roger, 35, 107, 111, 124

Hardwicke, Earl of, 133, 135, 137, 148, 150, 168, 186, 192

Hastings, Lady Elizabeth, 73

Hawley, Lieutenant General Henry, 30, 42, 47, 49, 42, 52, 54–5, 60, 68–70, 73, 74, 77–8, 80, 81, 83, 88, 92, 124, 179–80, 185, 190, 195

Henderson, Andrew, 73, 82, 87, 93, 118

Herring, Archbishop Thomas, 146, 150, 155, 163–4, 167, 190

Hessian forces, 17, 30–2, 53, 58, 62, 67, 117, 181

Hexham, 49, 58, 138, 188

Hoghton, Sir Henry, 139, 163, 169, 178

Home, John, 5, 79, 83, 133, 154, 188

Hughes, Michael, 72, 93

Hull, 55, 99, 101, 139, 145, 158, 169

Huske, Major General John, 39, 41, 52, 72, 84, 95, 109

infantry, 5, 7, 17, 21, 24–30, 36, 38, 40–2, 56, 69–70, 74, 76–8, 80–5, 88–9, 91, 95, 99, 111, 119, 196

Ireland, 16, 25, 27, 37–8, 40, 107, 155, 197

Irwin, Viscount, 9, 12, 129, 150, 152–6, 157, 164, 169

James II, 21, 36, 42, 62, 66, 70, 94, 99, 127

Johnson, John, 142, 171

Johnstone, James, 75, 102, 112–14, 166, 171, 177

Justices of the Peace, 13, 17–18, 23, 44, 53, 190

Kay, Richard, 43, 157

Kerr, Lord Robert, 84

Lancashire, 18, 40, 44, 128, 134, 138–41, 143, 147–9, 154, 158–9, 164–5, 169–70, 177–8, 187, 191

Lascelles, Colonel Peregrine, 77, 82

Leeds, 19, 42, 143, 154, 158, 186

Ligonier, Sir John, 28–9, 33, 40–1, 50–1, 61, 97, 111, 182

Linn, Private Edward, 56, 73–4, 80, 84–5,
    89, 91, 93
Liverpool, 52, 126, 131, 137, 146–7,
    149–51, 159, 163, 169, 186, 188
Liverpool Blues, 151–3, 156, 159, 162,
    164–5, 169, 181–2, 186
London, 2, 11, 14, 18, 20–1, 23, 26, 27–9,
    32–3, 36, 40–2, 44, 46–8, 52–3, 64,
    66, 99, 129, 132, 133–5, 164, 181, 184,
    186, 189, 196
Lonsdale, Earl of, 130, 132, 134–5, 137,
    139, 145, 164, 167, 191
Lords Lieutenant, 23, 36, 44, 53, 111, 127,
    129, 139–40, 145–6, 149, 153
Loudon, Lord, 87, 134, 137, 164, 167, 170,
    175–6, 179, 180, 185, 188, 193
Lowther, Sir James, 140
Lucas, John, 42, 143

MacKay, Ensign Hugh, 91
Malplaquet, 69
Malton, Earl of, 32, 108, 111, 149–50,
    152–4, 156–8, 163, 165, 185
Manchester, 18–19, 33, 63, 157, 186, 187,
    191
Mar, Earl of, 5, 37, 51, 94, 123, 173–4, 188,
    196, 197
Marlborough, Duke of, 9, 20, 23, 31, 37, 51,
    59, 61, 67–71, 92, 94, 97
Maxwell, James, 63, 80, 84–5, 89, 103,
    113–14, 116, 128, 176, 187
mayors, 44, 52, 102, 108, 110–11, 127, 137,
    142, 145–6, 168, 184, 189, 195
militia, 1, 6, 27, 30, 70, 91, 106, 115,
    125–45, 147, 154, 159, role, 19, 74,
    128, 161–2, 164
    arms, 135–8
    ceremonial role, 191
    effectiveness, 161–2, 197
    leadership, 129–30, 132, 140–1
    legislation, 127–8, 132–4, 136, 144, 145
    limitations, 191–2
    manpower, 141
    oppose Jacobites, 164–85
    organization, 134–5
    policing, 185–90
    training, 35, 41, 127, 135, 139–40
    uniforms, 138–9

Molloy, Sergeant Terrence, 8, 112, 122
Monmouth rebellion, 94, 129, 165, 172,
    184, 187
Montagu, Sir Edward, 128
Morpeth, 41, 137, 182
Murray, John, 27, 30, 98, 136, 140, 151
Murray, Lord George, 5, 83, 85, 113, 177, 192

Nassau, Colonel Maurice, 91
Newcastle, 18, 29–30, 34, 36, 39–42, 44–5,
    48–9, 52–3, 55–6, 62, 64, 79, 99, 101,
    105–6, 108–9, 126, 131, 134–5, 137,
    139, 142–3, 149, 151, 154–5, 162–3,
    171–2, 182, 185
Newcastle, Duke of, 41, 47, 119
    concern for fortress defence, 101, 107,
        109, 117, 119
    issues commissions for volunteer forces,
        134
    letters to, 9, 11, 28, 32, 47–8, 53, 60, 68,
        97, 107, 109–11, 119, 121, 137, 139,
        149, 157, 165, 169, 185
    military billeting, 55
    orders to generals, 34, 38, 53, 60
    orders intelligence gathering, 43
    recall of troops to England, 26–8
    hopes for militia/volunteer action, 145,
        148, 162, 186, 189
newspapers, 36, 53, 64, 128, 137, 155
Nicholson, Sir William, 141
Northumberland, 33, 36, 45, 53, 130–2,
    139, 141–3, 145, 148, 158, 171–2
Nottingham, 126

Oglethorpe, Major General James, 39, 55,
    64, 158, 182, 195
Oman, William, 85
O'Sullivan, Colonel John William, 82, 85,
    102, 103, 112–13, 177
Oudenarde, 38,
Oxford, 20, 36, 42, 99, 196

Patten, Robert, 75, 77, 106, 170–2, 174
Pattinson, Thomas, 137
Pelham, Henry, 8, 25, 48,
Perth, 42, 46–9, 51, 57, 122–3, 133, 152,
    164, 166, 168, 174, 179–80, 196
Perth, Duke of, 5, 177, 192

Pollock, Colonel, 123
Portsmouth, 11, 21, 36, 99, 101, 105, 110, 150, 189, 196
posse, 106, 125, 130, 142, 145, 167, 170, 171, 187
Prescott, Henry, 55, 93, 140, 191
Preston, 1, 4, 36, 38, 42–3, 57, 67, 68, 70, 75–8, 81, 84, 85–6, 88–95, 139, 142, 147, 154, 165, 178, 197, 198
Prestonpans, 1, 5, 28, 30, 40, 44, 64, 67, 70–3, 75–83, 86–8, 90, 93–5, 107, 147, 151, 171, 179–80, 197
Pulteney, William, 26, 33, 55

Rae, Peter, 35, 63, 152, 172–3
Ray, James, 125, 147, 154, 180, 192
Read, Rev. George, 142
regiments:
　Barrell's Foot, 73, 83, 84, 92
　Blakeney's Foot, 40
　Bligh's Foot, 17, 58, 97, 110
　Clayton's Foot, 42
　Cobham's Dragoons, 50, 63, 86, 88, 180
　Dubourgay's Foot, 110
　Echlin's Foot, 30
　Elliott's Foot, 35, 139
　Evans' Dragoons, 35, 178
　Foot Guards, 12, 14, 20, 24, 64, 119
　Forfar's Foot, 24
　Frank's Foot, 35
　Fraser's Foot, 41
　Gardiner's Dragoons, 30, 88, 165
　Gore's Dragoons, 18
　Gower's Foot, 12, 13, 17, 51, 110
　Grant's Foot, 110
　Guise's Foot, 111, 118, 178
　Hamilton's Dragoons, 30, 45, 88, 165, 179
　Handasyde's Foot, 11
　Harrison's Foot, 18
　Honeywood's Dragoons, 64
　Horse Grenadiers, 41
　Horse Guards, 20, 24, 27, 41
　Kingston's Light Horse, 13, 86, 179
　Kirke's Foot, 64
　Lee's Foot, 83
　Ligonier's Dragoons, 45, 88
　Lord John Murray's Foot, 64
　Lowther's Marines, 64

Montagu's Foot, 25
Monro's Foot, 84, 92, 171
Ross' Foot, 110
Royal Fusiliers, 14, 25
Royal Regiment of Dragoons, 24
Royal Scots, 14
St George's Dragoons, 119
Shannon's Foot, 25
Stair's Dragoons, 24
Stanhope's Dragoons, 165
Wade's Horse, 20
Richmond, Duke of, 27–9, 32, 39, 41–2, 53, 56–7, 61, 120, 162
riots, 17–19, 63, 186–7
Robinson, Lieutenant, 49, 54, 57, 167
Rothes, Earl of, 58, 137, 162, 166–7, 178
Roxborough, Earl of, 129
Ruthven Barracks, 8, 21, 98, 100–1, 103, 112, 119, 122–3
Ryder, Dudley, 12, 38, 43, 63

Salton, Lord, 130
Saville, Gertrude, 20, 21, 157
Scarborough, Earl of, 129
Scott, Captain Caroline, 111, 116, 120
Sedgemoor, 5, 70, 165, 181, 184
Shairp, Walter, 151–3, 156, 162, 165, 169, 172, 181–2, 186
Sheriffmuir, 5, 26, 34, 35, 51, 67, 69–70, 72, 75–6, 78, 81, 83, 85, 87, 89, 92–5, 178, 196, 198
Sheriffs, 18, 130, 142, 187, 190–1
Spanish Succession, War of, 3, 24, 34, 38, 50, 97
Stanhope, James, 25–6, 33–4, 36–7, 129, 140
Stewart, David, 132
Stirling, 21, 25–6, 30, 35, 37, 38, 42, 49, 52, 55–8, 68–9, 74, 75, 99–101, 103, 112–14, 119, 122–3, 139, 164, 166, 170, 178, 180, 184, 190, 192, 197–8
Stout, William, 128, 155
Strathbogie, 56, 59
Swiss forces, 31, 32
Symson, Joseph, 135

Talbot, Major, 75
Taylor, Private Alexander, 52, 54, 60, 72, 75

Todd, William, 14, 16–17, 20, 156
Tom Jones (novel), 8–10, 15
Tories, 35–6, 63, 129, 141, 148–9, 154
Tower of London, 19–20, 51, 58, 64, 137, 149, 186
Townshend, Viscount, 18, 26, 33–5, 37, 45, 92, 190, 191
Trained Bands, 128, 172, 181, 189
Tweeddale, Marquis of, 30, 38–9, 105, 129, 138, 139, 168, 175
Tyrawley, Earl of, 61

Vernon, Admiral Edward, 182
Volunteer forces, 1, 6, 9, 27, 30, 70
    arming, 149–50
    ceremonial role of, 191
    effectiveness, 161–2, 197
    funding, 147–9
    limitations, 191–2
    numbers, 158–9
    officers, 153
    oppose Jacobites, 164–85
    other ranks, 153–6
    policing, 185–90
    raising, 145
    role, 161–2, 164, 193–4
    training, 35, 151–3
    uniforms, 150–1

Wade, General (later Field Marshal) George, 27, 29, 33–4, 36, 40–50, 52–5, 57, 61–2, 100–1, 118, 120, 123–4, 165, 182, 185, 195
Walpole, Horace, 13, 15, 27, 60, 147, 182

Walpole, Sir Robert, 10, 37, 126
Warrington, Earl of, 155
Waugh, Dr John, 44, 46, 166
Wentworth, Major General, 40, 47, 163, 184–5
Westmorland, 130–2, 134, 138–9, 142, 164, 166, 182, 189, 191
Whetman, Major General, 25, 33
Whitefoord, Lieutenant Colonel Charles, 74, 79, 87
Whitney, Lieutenant Colonel Shugborough, 82, 87–8, 90, 93
Wightman, Major General Joseph, 69, 72, 83, 89, 174
William III, 4, 62, 94, 99
Wills, Major General Charles, 25, 33, 37, 43, 59, 61, 69, 75, 88, 91, 92, 154, 178, 198
Winn, Sir Rowland, 149, 157
Wolfe, Major James, 8, 10, 19, 61, 92

Yonge, William, 46–7
York, 99, 104, 108, 111, 126, 139, 143, 146–50, 153, 156, 158–9, 162, 165, 186–7, 189–91
Yorke, Lieutenant Colonel Joseph, 45, 49–50, 54–7, 59–61, 72, 76, 80, 120, 122, 130, 168
Yorkshire, 9, 126, 130–1, 143, 145, 147, 149–53, 156, 158–9, 163, 165, 179, 182, 185, 191